ML for the Working Programmer

ML for the Working Programmer

2nd edition

Lawrence C. Paulson
University of Cambridge

CAMBRIDGE
UNIVERSITY PRESS

PUBLISHED BY THE PRESS SYNDICATE OF THE UNIVERSITY OF CAMBRIDGE
The Pitt Building, Trumpington Street, Cambridge, United Kingdom

CAMBRIDGE UNIVERSITY PRESS
The Edinburgh Building, Cambridge CB2 2RU, UK
40 West 20th Street, New York, NY 10011–4211, USA
10 Stamford Road, Oakleigh, VIC 3166, Australia
Ruiz de Alarcón 13, 28014 Madrid, Spain
Dock House, The Waterfront, Cape Town 8001, South Africa

http://www.cambridge.org

First edition published 1991
First published in paperback (with corrections) 1992
Reprinted 1993, 1995
Second edition published 1996
Reprinted (with corrections) 1997
Reprinted 1998, 2000 (twice)

Printed in the United Kingdom at the University Press, Cambridge

A catalogue record for this book is available from the British Library

ISBN 0 521 57050 6 hardback
ISBN 0 521 56543 X paperback

The cover illustration is taken from *Work* by Ford Madox Brown
© Manchester City Art Galleries, and is reproduced with their permission.

Trademarks. Miranda is a trademark of Research Software Limited. Sun and SuperSPARC are trademarks of Sun Microsystems. Unix is a trademark of AT&T Bell Laboratories. Poplog is a trademark of the University of Sussex. MLWorks is a trademark of Harlequin Limited. DEC and PDP are trademarks of Digital Equipment Corporation.

Dedication. For Sue, Nathan and Sarah.

DISCLAIMER OF WARRANTY
The programs listed in this book are provides 'as is' without warranty of any kind. We make no warranties, express or implied, that the programs are free of error, or are consistent with any particular standard of merchantability, or that they will meet your requirements for any particular application. They should not be relied upon for solving a problem whose incorrect solution could result in injury to a person or loss of property. If you do use the programs or procedures in such a manner, it is at your own risk. The author and publisher disclaim all liability for direct, incidental or consequential damages resulting from your use of the programs, modules or functions in this book.

CONTENTS

PREFACE TO THE SECOND EDITION

With each reprinting of this book, a dozen minor errors have silently disappeared. But a reprinting is no occasion for making improvements, however valuable, that would affect the page numbering: we should then have several slightly different, incompatible editions. An accumulation of major changes (and the Editor's urgings) have prompted this second edition.

As luck would have it, changes to ML have come about at the same time. ML has a new standard library and the language itself has been revised. It is worth stressing that the changes do not compromise ML's essential stability. Some obscure technical points have been simplified. Anomalies in the original definition have been corrected. Existing programs will run with few or no changes. The most visible changes are the new character type and a new set of top level library functions.

The new edition brings the book up to date and greatly improves the presentation. Modules are now introduced early — in Chapter 2 instead of Chapter 7 — and used throughout. This effects a change of emphasis, from data structures (say, binary search trees) to abstract types (say, dictionaries). A typical section introduces an abstract type and presents its ML signature. Then it explains the ideas underlying the implementation, and finally presents the code as an ML structure. Though reviewers have been kind to the first edition, many readers have requested such a restructuring.

The programs have not just been moved about, but rewritten. They now reflect modern thoughts on how to use modules. The open declaration, which obscures a program's modular structure, seldom appears. Functors are only used where necessary. Programs are now indented with greater care. This, together with the other changes, should make them much more readable than hitherto. They are also better: there is a faster merge sort and simpler, faster priority queues.

The new standard library would in any case have necessitated an early mention of modules. Although it entails changes to existing code, the new library brings ML firmly into the fold of realistic languages. The library has been designed, through a long process of consultation, to provide comprehensive support without needless complication. Its organization demonstrates the benefits of ML modules. The string processing, input/output and system interface modules provide real gains in power.

The library forced much rewriting. Readers would hardly like to read about the function *foldleft* when the library includes a similar function called *foldl*. But these functions are not identical; the rewriting involved more than a change of name. Many sections that previously described useful functions now survey corresponding library structures.

The updated bibliography shows functional programming and ML used in a wide variety of applications. ML meets the requirements for building reliable systems. Software engineers expect a language to provide type safety, modularity, compile-time consistency checking and fault tolerance (exceptions). Thanks in part to the library, ML programs are portable. Commercially supported compilers offer increasing quality and efficiency. ML can now run as fast as C, especially in applications requiring complicated storage management. The title of this book, which has attracted some jibes, may well prove to be prophetic.

My greatest surprise was to see the first edition in the hands of beginning programmers, when the first page told them to look elsewhere. To help beginners I have added a few especially simple examples, and removed most references from the main text. The rewritten first chapter attempts to introducing basic programming concepts in a manner suitable both to beginners and to experienced C programmers. That is easier than it sounds: C does not attempt to give programmers a problem-solving environment, merely to dress up the underlying hardware. The first chapter still presupposes some basic knowledge of computers. Instructors may still wish to start with Chapter 2, with its simple on-line sessions.

At the end of the book is a list of suggested projects. They are intentionally vague; the first step in a major project is to analyse the requirements precisely. I hope to see ML increasingly adopted for project work. The choice of ML, especially over insecure languages like C, may eventually be recognized as a mark of professionalism.

I should like to thank everyone whose comments, advice or code made an impact on this edition. They include Matthew Arcus, Jon Fairbairn, Andy Gordon, Carl Gunter, Michael Hansen, Andrew Kennedy, David MacQueen, Brian Monahan, Arthur Norman, Chris Okasaki, John Reppy, Hans Rischel, Peter Sestoft, Mark Staples and Mads Tofte. Sestoft also gave me a pre-release of Moscow ML, incorporating library updates. Alison Woollatt of CUP coded the LATEX class file. Franklin Chen and Namhyun Hur reported errors in previous printings.

PREFACE

This book originated in lectures on Standard ML and functional programming. It can still be regarded as a text on functional programming — one with a pragmatic orientation, in contrast to the rather idealistic books that are the norm — but it is primarily a guide to the effective use of ML. It even discusses ML's imperative features.

Some of the material requires an understanding of discrete mathematics: elementary logic and set theory. Readers will find it easier if they already have some programming experience, but this is not essential.

The book is a programming manual, not a reference manual; it covers the major aspects of ML without getting bogged down with every detail. It devotes some time to theoretical principles, but is mainly concerned with efficient algorithms and practical programming.

The organization reflects my experience with teaching. Higher-order functions appear late, in Chapter 5. They are usually introduced at the very beginning with some contrived example that only confuses students. Higher-order functions are conceptually difficult and require thorough preparation. This book begins with basic types, lists and trees. When higher-order functions are reached, a host of motivating examples is at hand.

The exercises vary greatly in difficulty. They are not intended for assessing students, but for providing practice, broadening the material and provoking discussion.

Overview of the book. Most chapters are devoted to aspects of ML. Chapter 1 introduces the ideas behind functional programming and surveys the history of ML. Chapters 2–5 cover the functional part of ML, including an introduction to modules. Basic types, lists, trees and higher-order functions are presented. Broader principles of functional programming are discussed.

Chapter 6 presents formal methods for reasoning about functional programs. If this seems to be a distraction from the main business of programming, consider that a program is worth little unless it is correct. Ease of formal reasoning is a major argument in favour of functional programming.

Chapter 7 covers modules in detail, including functors (modules with parameters). Chapter 8 covers ML's imperative features: references, arrays and input/output. The remainder of the book consists of extended examples. Chapter 9 presents a functional parser and a λ-calculus interpreter. Chapter 10 presents a theorem prover, a traditional ML application.

The book is full of examples. Some of these serve only to demonstrate some aspect of ML, but most are intended to be useful in themselves — sorting, functional arrays, priority queues, search algorithms, pretty printing. Please note: although I have tested these programs, they undoubtedly contain some errors.

Information and warning boxes. Technical asides, descriptions of library functions, and notes for further study appear from place to place. They are highlighted for the benefit of readers who wish to skip over them:

ⓘ *King Henry's claim.* There is no bar to make against your highness' claim to France but this, which they produce from Pharamond, *In terram Salicam mulieres ne succedant*, 'No woman shall succeed in Salique land': which Salique land the French unjustly gloze to be the realm of France, and Pharamond the founder of this law and female bar. But their own authors faithfully affirm that the land Salique is in Germany . . . [1]

ML is not perfect. Certain pitfalls can allow a simple coding error to waste hours of a programmer's time. The new standard library introduces incompatibilities between old and new compilers. Warnings of possible hazards appear throughout the book. They look like this:

☠ *Beware the Duke of Gloucester.* O Buckingham! take heed of yonder dog. Look, when he fawns, he bites; and when he bites, his venom tooth will rankle to the death. Have not to do with him, beware of him; Sin, Death, and Hell have set their marks on him, and all their ministers attend on him.

I hasten to add that nothing in ML can have consequences quite this dire. No fault in a program can corrupt the ML system itself. On the other hand, programmers must remember that even correct programs can do harm in the outside world.

How to get a Standard ML compiler. Because Standard ML is fairly new on the scene, many institutions will not have a compiler. The following is a partial list of existing Standard ML compilers, with contact addresses. The examples in this

---

[1] No technical aside in this book is as long as the Archbishop's speech, which extends to 62 lines.

book were developed under Moscow ML, Poly/ML and Standard ML of New Jersey. I have not tried the other compilers.

To obtain *MLWorks*, contact Harlequin Limited, Barrington Hall, Barrington, Cambridge, CB2 5RG, England. Their email address is web@harlequin.com.

To obtain *Moscow ML*, contact Peter Sestoft, Mathematical Section, Royal Veterinary and Agricultural University, Thorvaldsensvej 40, DK-1871 Frederiksberg C, Denmark. Or get the system from the World Wide Web:

        http:/www.dina.kvl.dk/~sestoft/mosml.html

To obtain *Poly/ML*, contact Abstract Hardware Ltd, 1 Brunel Science Park, Kingston Lane, Uxbridge, Middlesex, UB8 3PQ, England. Their email address is lambda@ahl.co.uk.

To obtain *Poplog Standard ML*, contact Integral Solutions Ltd, Berk House, Basing View, Basingstoke, Hampshire, RG21 4RG, England. Their email address is isl@isl.co.uk.

To obtain *Standard ML of New Jersey*, contact Andrew Appel, Computer Science Department, Princeton University, Princeton NJ 08544-2087, USA. Better still, fetch the files from the World Wide Web:

        http://www.cs.princeton.edu/~appel/smlnj/

The programs in this book and answers to some exercises are available by email; my address is lcp@cl.cam.ac.uk. If possible, please use the World Wide Web; my home page is at

        http://www.cl.cam.ac.uk/users/lcp/

Acknowledgements. The editor, David Tranah, assisted with all stages of the writing and suggested the title. Graham Birtwistle, Glenn Bruns and David Wolfram read the text carefully. Dave Berry, Simon Finn, Mike Fourman, Kent Karlsson, Robin Milner, Richard O'Keefe, Keith van Rijsbergen, Nick Rothwell, Mads Tofte, David N. Turner and the staff of Harlequin also commented on the text. Andrew Appel, Gavin Bierman, Phil Brabbin, Richard Brooksby, Guy Cousineau, Lal George, Mike Gordon, Martin Hansen, Darrell Kindred, Silvio Meira, Andrew Morris, Khalid Mughal, Tobias Nipkow, Kurt Olender, Allen Stoughton, Reuben Thomas, Ray Toal and Helen Wilson found errors in previous printings. Piete Brooks, John Carroll and Graham Titmus helped with the computers. I wish to thank Dave Matthews for developing Poly/ML, which was for many years the only efficient implementation of Standard ML.

Of the many works in the bibliography, Abelson and Sussman (1985), Bird and Wadler (1988) and Burge (1975) have been especially helpful. Reade (1989) contains useful ideas for implementing lazy lists in ML.

The Science and Engineering Research Council has supported LCF and ML in numerous research grants over the past 20 years.

I wrote most of this book while on leave from the University of Cambridge. I am grateful to the Computer Laboratory and Clare College for granting leave, and to the University of Edinburgh for accommodating me for six months.

Finally, I should like to thank Sue for all she did to help, and for tolerating my daily accounts of the progress of every chapter.

1
Standard ML

The first ML compiler was built in 1974. As the user community grew, various dialects began to appear. The ML community then got together to develop and promote a common language, Standard ML — sometimes called SML, or just ML. Good Standard ML compilers are available.

Standard ML has become remarkably popular in a short time. Universities around the world have adopted it as the first programming language to teach to students. Developers of substantial applications have chosen it as their implementation language. One could explain this popularity by saying that ML makes it easy to write clear, reliable programs. For a more satisfying explanation, let us examine how we look at computer systems.

Computers are enormously complex. The hardware and software found in a typical workstation are more than one mind can fully comprehend. Different people understand the workstation on different levels. To the user, the workstation is a word processor or spreadsheet. To the repair crew, it is a box containing a power supply, circuit boards, etc. To the machine language programmer, the workstation provides a large store of bytes, connected to a processor that can perform arithmetic and logical operations. The applications programmer understands the workstation through the medium of the chosen programming language.

Here we take 'spreadsheet', 'power supply' and 'processor' as ideal, abstract concepts. We think of them in terms of their functions and limitations, but not in terms of how they are built. Good abstractions let us use computers effectively, without being overwhelmed by their complexity.

Conventional 'high level' programming languages do not provide a level of abstraction significantly above machine language. They provide convenient notations, but only those that map straightforwardly to machine code. A minor error in the program can make it destroy other data or even itself. The resulting behaviour can be explained only at the level of machine language — if at all!

ML is well above the machine language level. It supports *functional programming*, where programs consist of functions operating on simple data structures. Functional programming is ideal for many aspects of problem solving, as argued

1

briefly below and demonstrated throughout the book. Programming tasks can be approached mathematically, without preoccupation with the computer's internal workings. ML also provides **mutable** variables and arrays. Mutable objects can be updated using an assignment command; using them, any piece of conventional code can be expressed easily. For structuring large systems, ML provides **modules**: parts of the program can be specified and coded separately.

Most importantly of all, ML protects programmers from their own errors. Before a program may run, the compiler checks that all module interfaces agree and that data are used consistently. For example, an integer may not be used as a store address. (It is a myth that real programs must rely on such tricks.) As the program executes, further checking ensures safety: even a faulty ML program continues to behave as an ML program. It might run forever and it might return to the user with an error message. But it cannot crash.

ML supports a level of abstraction that is oriented to the requirements of the programmer, not those of the hardware. The ML system can preserve this abstraction, even if the program is faulty. Few other languages offer such assurances.

Functional Programming

Programming languages come in several varieties. Languages like Fortran, Pascal and C are called **procedural**: their main programming unit is the procedure. A popular refinement of this approach centres on objects that carry their own operations about with them. Such **object-oriented** languages include C++ and Modula-3. Both approaches rely on commands that act upon the machine state; they are both **imperative** approaches.

Just as procedural languages are oriented around commands, functional languages are oriented around expressions. Programming without commands may seem alien to some readers, so let us see what lies behind this idea. We begin with a critique of imperative programming.

1.1   *Expressions versus commands*

Fortran, the first high-level programming language, gave programmers the arithmetic expression. No longer did they have to code sequences of additions, loads and stores on registers: the FORmula TRANslator did this for them. Why are expressions so important? Not because they are familiar: the Fortran syntax for

$$\sqrt{\frac{\sin^2 \theta}{1 + |\cos \phi|}}$$

has but a passing resemblance to that formula. Let us consider the advantages of expressions in detail. Expressions in Fortran can have *side effects*: they can change the state. We shall focus on pure expressions, which merely compute a value.

Expressions have a recursive structure. A typical expression like

$$f(E_1 + E_2) - g(E_3)$$

is built out of other expressions E_1, E_2 and E_3, and may itself form part of a larger expression.

The value of an expression is given recursively in terms of the values of its subexpressions. The subexpressions can be evaluated in any order, or even in parallel.

Expressions can be transformed using mathematical laws. For instance, replacing $E_1 + E_2$ by $E_2 + E_1$ does not affect the value of the expression above, thanks to the commutative law of addition. This ability to substitute equals for equals is called *referential transparency*. In particular, an expression may safely be replaced by its value.

Commands share most of these advantages. In modern languages, commands are built out of other commands. The meaning of a command like

```
while B₁ do (if B₂ then C₁ else C₂)
```

can be given in terms of the meanings of its parts. Commands even enjoy referential transparency: laws like

```
(if B then C₁ else C₂); C ≡ if B then (C₁; C) else (C₂; C)
```

can be proved and applied as substitutions.

However, the meaning of an expression is simply the result of evaluating it, which is why subexpressions can be evaluated independently of each other. The meaning of an expression can be extremely simple, like the number 3. The meaning of a command is a state transformation or something equally complicated. To understand a command, you have to understand its full effect on the machine's state.

1.2   *Expressions in procedural programming languages*

How far have programming languages advanced since Fortran? Consider Euclid's Algorithm, which is defined by recursion, for computing the Greatest Common Divisor (GCD) of two natural numbers:

$$gcd(0, n) = n$$

$$gcd(m, n) = gcd(n \bmod m, m) \qquad \text{for } m > 0$$

In Pascal, a procedural language, most people would code the GCD as an imperative program:

```
function gcd(m,n: integer): integer;
  var prevm: integer;
begin
  while m<>0 do
    begin prevm := m;   m := n mod m;   n := prevm end;
  gcd := n
end;
```

Here it is in Standard ML as a functional program:

```
fun gcd(m,n) =
      if m=0 then n
             else gcd(n mod m, m);
```

The imperative program, though coded in a 'high-level' language, is hardly clearer or shorter than a machine language program. It repeatedly updates three quantities, one of which is just a temporary storage cell. Proving that it correctly implements Euclid's algorithm requires Floyd-Hoare proof rules — a tedious enterprise. In contrast, the functional version obviously implements Euclid's Algorithm.

A recursive program in Pascal would be only a slight improvement. Recursive procedure calls are seldom implemented efficiently. Thirty years after its introduction to programming languages, recursion is still regarded as something to eliminate from programs. Correctness proofs for recursive procedures have a sad history of complexity and errors.

Pascal expressions do not satisfy the usual mathematical laws. An optimizing compiler might transform $f(z) + u/2$ into $u/2 + f(z)$. However, these expressions may not compute the same value if the 'function' f changes the value of u. The meaning of an expression in Pascal involves states as well as values. For all practical purposes, referential transparency has been lost.

In a purely functional language there is no state. Expressions satisfy the usual mathematical laws, up to the limitations of the machine (for example, real arithmetic is approximate). Purely functional programs can also be written in Standard ML. However, ML is not pure because of its assignments and input/output commands. The ML programmer whose style is 'almost' functional had better not be lulled into a false sense of referential transparency.

1.3 Storage management

Expressions in procedural languages have progressed little beyond Fortran; they have not kept up with developments in data structures. Suppose we have employee records consisting of name, address, and other details. We cannot write record-valued expressions, or return an employee record from a function; even if the language permits this, copying such large records is prohibitively slow.

To avoid copying large objects, we can refer to them indirectly. Our record-valued function could allocate storage space for the employee record, and return its address. Instead of copying the record from one place to another, we copy its address instead. When we are finished with the record, we deallocate (release) its storage. (Presumably the employee got sacked.) Addresses used in this way are called *references* or *pointers*.

Deallocation is the bugbear of this approach. The program might release the storage prematurely, when the record is still in use. Once that storage is reallocated, it will be used for different purposes at the same time. Anything could happen, leading (perhaps much later) to a mysterious crash. This is one of the most treacherous programming errors.

If we never deallocate storage, we might run out of it. Should we then avoid using references? But many basic data structures, such as the linked list, require references.

Functional languages, and some others, manage storage automatically. The programmer does not decide when to deallocate a record's storage. At intervals, the run-time system scans the store systematically, marking everything that is accessible and reclaiming everything that is not. This operation is called *garbage collection*, although it is more like recycling. Garbage collection can be slow and may require additional space, but it pays dividends.

Languages with garbage collection typically use references heavily in their internal representation of data. A function that 'returns' an employee record actually returns only a reference to it, but the programmer does not know or care. The language gains in expressive power. The programmer, freed from the chore of storage management, can work more productively.

1.4 Elements of a functional language

Functional programs work with values, not states. Their tools are expressions, not commands. How can assignments, arrays and loops be dispensed with? Does not the outside world have state? These questions pose real challenges. The functional programmer can exploit a wide range of techniques to solve problems.

Lists and trees. Collections of data can processed as lists of the form

$$[a, b, c, d, e, \dots].$$

Lists support sequential access: scanning from left to right. This suffices for most purposes, even sorting and matrix operations. A more flexible way of organizing data is as a tree:

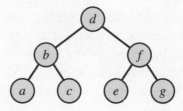

Balanced trees permit random access: any part can be reached quickly. In theory, trees offer the same efficiency as arrays; in practice, arrays are often faster. Trees play key rôles in symbolic computation, representing logical terms and formulæ in theorem provers. Lists and trees are represented using references, so the run-time system must include a garbage collector.

Functions. Expressions consist mainly of function applications. To increase the power of expressions, functions must be freed from arbitrary restrictions. Functions may take any type of arguments and return any type of result. As we shall see, 'any type' includes functions themselves, which can be treated like other data; making this work also requires a garbage collector.

Recursion. Variables in a functional program obtain their values from outside (when a function is called) or by declaration. They cannot be updated, but recursive calls can produce a changing series of argument values. Recursion is easier to understand than iteration — if you do not believe this, recall our two GCD programs. Recursion eliminates the baroque looping constructs of procedural languages.[1]

Pattern-matching. Most functional languages allow a function to analyse its argument using pattern-matching. A function to count the elements of a list looks like this in ML:

---

[1] Recursion does have its critics. Backus (1978) recommends providing iteration primitives to replace most uses of recursion in function definitions. However, his style of functional programming has not caught on.

```
fun length []      = 0
  | length (x::xs) = 1 + length xs;
```

We instantly see that the length of the empty list ([]) is zero, and that the length of a list consisting of the element *x* prefixed to the list *xs* is the length of *xs* plus one. Here is the equivalent definition in Lisp, which lacks pattern-matching:

```
(define (length x)
  (if (null? x)
      0
      (+ 1 (length (cdr x))))))
```

ML function declarations often consider half a dozen cases, with patterns much more complicated than $x::xs$. Expressing such functions without using patterns is terribly cumbersome. The ML compiler does this internally, and can do a better job than the programmer could.

Polymorphic type checking. Programmers, being human, often err. Using a non-existent part of a data structure, supplying a function with too few arguments, or confusing a reference to an object with the object itself are serious errors: they could make the program crash. Fortunately, the compiler can detect them before the program runs, provided the language enforces a type discipline. ***Types*** classify data as integers, reals, lists, etc., and let us ensure that they are used sensibly.

Some programmers resist type checking because it can be too restrictive. In Pascal, a function to compute the length of a list must specify the — completely irrelevant! — type of the list's elements. Our ML length function works for all lists because ML's type system is ***polymorphic***: it ignores the types of irrelevant components. Our Lisp version also works for all lists, because Lisp has no compile-time type checking. Lisp is more flexible than ML; a single list can mix elements of different types. The price of this freedom is hours spent hunting errors that might have been caught automatically.

Higher-order functions. Functions themselves are computational values. Even Fortran lets a function be passed as an argument to another function, but few procedural languages let function values play a full rôle as data structures.

A ***higher-order*** function (or ***functional***) is a function that operates on other functions. The functional *map*, when applied to a function f, returns another function; that function takes

$$[x_1, \ldots, x_n] \quad \text{to} \quad [f(x_1), \ldots, f(x_n)].$$

Another higher-order function, when applied to a function f and value e, returns

$$f(x_1, f(x_2, \ldots, f(x_n, e) \ldots)).$$

If $e = 0$ and $f = +$ (yes, the addition operator is a function) then we get the sum of $x_1, \ldots, x_n$, computed by

$$x_1 + (x_2 + \cdots + (x_n + 0) \cdots).$$

If $e = 1$ and $f = \times$ then we get their product, computed by

$$x_1 \times (x_2 \times \cdots \times (x_n \times 1) \cdots).$$

Other computations are expressed by suitable choices for f and e.

Infinite data structures. Infinite lists like $[1, 2, 3, \ldots]$ can be given a computational meaning. They can be of great help when tackling sophisticated problems. Infinite lists are processed using ***lazy evaluation***, which ensures that no value — or part of a value — is computed until it is actually needed to obtain the final result. An infinite list never exists in full; it is rather a process for computing successive elements upon demand.

The search space in a theorem prover may form an infinite tree, whose success nodes form an infinite list. Different search strategies produce different lists of success nodes. The list can be given to another part of the program, which need not know how it was produced.

Infinite lists can also represent sequences of inputs and outputs. Many of us have encountered this concept in the ***pipes*** of the Unix operating system. A chain of processes linked by pipes forms a single process. Each process consumes its input when available and passes its output along a pipe to the next process. The outputs of intermediate processes are never stored in full. This saves storage, but more importantly it gives us a clear notation for combining processes. Mathematically, every process is a function from inputs to outputs, and the chain of processes is their composition.

Input and output. Communication with the outside world, which has state, is hard to reconcile with functional programming. Infinite lists can handle sequential input and output (as mentioned above), but interactive programming and process communication are thorny issues. Many functional approaches have been investigated; ***monads*** are one of the most promising (Peyton Jones and Wadler, 1993). ML simply provides commands to perform input and output; thus, ML abandons functional programming here.

ⓘ   *Functional languages: a survey.* The mainstream functional languages adopt lazy evaluation, pattern-matching and ML-style polymorphic types. Miranda is an elegant language by David A. Turner (1990a). Lazy ML is a dialect of ML with lazy evaluation; its compiler generates efficient code (Augustsson and Johnsson, 1989). Haskell was designed by a committee of researchers as a common language (Hudak *et al.*, 1992); it has been widely adopted.

John Backus (1978) introduced the language FP in a widely publicized lecture. FP provides many higher-order functions (called 'combining forms'), but the programmer may not define new ones. Backus criticized the close coupling between programming languages and the underlying hardware, coining the phrase *von Neumann bottleneck* for the connection between the processor and the store. Many have argued that functional languages are ideal for parallel hardware. Sisal has been designed for parallel numerical computations; Cann (1992) claims that Sisal sometimes outperforms Fortran.

Many implementation techniques for functional programming, such as garbage collection, originated with Lisp (McCarthy *et al.*, 1962). The language includes low-level features that can be misused to disastrous effect. Later dialects, including Scheme (Abelson and Sussman, 1985) and Common Lisp, provide higher-order functions. Although much Lisp code is imperative, the first functional programs were written in Lisp. Most ML dialects include imperative features, but ML is more disciplined than Lisp. It has compile-time type checking, and allows updates only to mutable objects.

1.5   *The efficiency of functional programming*

A functional program typically carries a large run-time system with a resident compiler. The garbage collector may require a uniform representation of data, making it occupy additional storage. The functional programmer is sometimes deprived of the most efficient data structures, such as arrays, strings and bit vectors. A functional program may therefore be less efficient than the corresponding C program, particularly in its storage demands.

ML is best suited for large, complex applications. Type checking, automatic storage allocation and other advantages of functional programming can make the difference between a program that works and one that doesn't. Efficiency becomes a secondary issue; besides, with a demanding application, the difference will be less pronounced. Most functional programs ought to run nearly as fast as their procedural counterparts — perhaps five times slower in the worst case.

Efficiency is regarded with suspicion by many researchers, doubtless because many programs have been ruined in its pursuit. Functional programmers have sometimes chosen inefficient algorithms for the sake of clarity, or have sought to enrich their languages rather than implement them better. This attitude, more than technical reasons, has given functional programming a reputation for inefficiency.

We must now redress the balance. Functional programs must be efficient, or nobody will use them. Algorithms, after all, are designed to be efficient. The Greatest Common Divisor of two numbers can be found by searching through all possible candidates. This exhaustive search algorithm is clear, but useless. Euclid's Algorithm is fast and simple, having sacrificed clarity.

The exhaustive search algorithm for the GCD is an example of an *executable specification*. One approach to program design might start with this and apply *transformations* to make it more efficient, while preserving its correctness. Eventually it might arrive at Euclid's Algorithm. Program transformations can indeed improve efficiency, but we should regard executable specifications with caution. The Greatest Common Divisor of two integers is, by definition, the largest integer that exactly divides both; the specification does not mention search at all. The exhaustive search algorithm is too complicated to be a good specification.

Functional programming and logic programming are instances of *declarative programming*. The ideal of declarative programming is to free us from writing programs — just state the requirements and the computer will do the rest. Hoare (1989c) has explored this ideal in the case of the Greatest Common Divisor, demonstrating that it is still a dream. A more realistic aim for declarative programming is to make programs easier to understand. Their correctness can be justified by simple mathematical reasoning, without thinking about bytes. Declarative programming is still programming; we still have to code efficiently.

This book gives concrete advice about performance and tries to help you decide where efficiency matters. Most natural functional definitions are also reasonably efficient. Some ML compilers offer *execution profiling*, which measures the time spent by each function. The function that spends the most time (never the one you would expect) becomes a prime candidate for improvement. Such bottom-up optimization can produce dramatic results, although it may not reveal global causes of waste. These considerations hold for programming generally — be it functional, procedural, object-oriented or whatever.

Correctness must come first. Clarity must usually come second, and efficiency third. Any sacrifice of clarity makes the program harder to maintain, and must be justified by a significant efficiency gain. A judicious mixture of realism and principle, with plenty of patience, makes for efficient programs.

ⓘ   *Applications of functional programming.* Functional programming techniques are used in artificial intelligence, formal methods, computer aided design, and other tasks involving symbolic computation. Substantial compilers have been written in (and for) Standard ML (Appel, 1992) and Haskell (Peyton Jones, 1992). Networking software has been written in ML (Biagioni *et al.*, 1994), in a project to demonstrate ML's utility for systems programming. A major natural language processing system, called

LOLITA, has been written in Haskell (Smith *et al.*, 1994); the authors adopted functional programming in order to manage the complexity of their system. Hartel and Plasmeijer (1996) describe six major projects, involving diverse applications. Wadler and Gill (1995) have compiled a list of real world applications; these cover many domains and involve all the main functional languages.

Standard ML

Every successful language was designed for some specific purpose: Lisp for artificial intelligence, Fortran for numerical computation, Prolog for natural language processing. Conversely, languages designed to be general purpose — such as the 'algorithmic languages' Algol 60 and Algol 68 — have succeeded more as sources of ideas than as practical tools.

ML was designed for theorem proving. This is not a broad field, and ML was intended for the programming of one particular theorem prover — a specific purpose indeed! This theorem prover, called Edinburgh LCF (Logic for Computable Functions) spawned a host of successors, all of which were coded in ML. And just as Lisp, Fortran and Prolog have applications far removed from their origins, ML is being used in diverse problem areas.

1.6   *The evolution of Standard ML*

As ML was the Meta Language for the programming of proof strategies, its designers incorporated the necessary features for this application:

- The inference rules and proof methods were to be represented as functions, so ML was given the full power of higher-order functional programming.
- The inference rules were to define an abstract type: the type of theorems. Strong type checking (as in Pascal) would have been too restrictive, so ML was given polymorphic type checking.
- Proof methods could be combined in complex ways. Failure at any point had to be detected so that another method could be tried. So ML was allowed to raise and trap exceptions.
- Since a theorem prover would be useless if there were loopholes, ML was designed to be secure, with no way of corrupting the environment.

The ML system of Edinburgh LCF was slow: programs were translated into Lisp and then interpreted. Luca Cardelli wrote an efficient compiler for his version of ML, which included a rich set of declaration and type structures. At Cambridge University and INRIA, the ML system of LCF was extended and its performance improved. ML also influenced HOPE; this purely functional language adopted polymorphism and added recursive type definitions and pattern-matching.

Robin Milner led a standardization effort to consolidate the dialects into Standard ML. Many people contributed. The module language — the language's most complex and innovative feature — was designed by David MacQueen and refined by Milner and Mads Tofte. In 1987, Milner won the British Computer Society Award for Technical Excellence for his work on Standard ML. The first compilers were developed at the Universities of Cambridge and Edinburgh; the excellent Standard ML of New Jersey appeared shortly thereafter.

Several universities teach Standard ML as the students' first programming language. ML provides a level base for all students, whether they arrive knowing C, Basic, machine language or no language at all. Using ML, students can learn how to analyse problems mathematically, breaking the bad habits learned from low-level languages. Significant computations can be expressed in a few lines. Beginners especially appreciate that the type checker detects common errors, and that nothing can crash the system!

Section 1.5 has mentioned applications of Standard ML to networking, compiler construction, etc. Theorem proving remains ML's most important application area, as we shall see below.

ⓘ *Further reading.* Gordon *et al.* (1979) describe LCF. Landin (1966) discusses the language ISWIM, upon which ML was originally based. The formal definition of Standard ML has been published as a book (Milner *et al.*, 1990), with a separate volume of commentary (Milner and Tofte, 1990).

Standard ML has not displaced all other dialects. The French, typically, have gone their own way. Their language CAML provides broadly similar features with the traditional ISWIM syntax (Cousineau and Huet, 1990). It has proved useful for experiments in language design; extensions over Standard ML include lazy data structures and dynamic types. CAML Light is a simple byte-code interpreter that is ideal for small computers. Lazy dialects of ML also exist, as mentioned previously. HOPE continues to be used and taught (Bailey, 1990).

1.7   *The ML tradition of theorem proving*

Theorem proving and functional programming go hand in hand. One of the first functional programs ever written is a simple theorem prover (McCarthy *et al.*, 1962). Back in the 1970s, when some researchers were wondering what functional programming was good for, Edinburgh LCF was putting it to work.

Fully automatic theorem proving is usually impossible: for most logics, no automatic methods are known. The obvious alternative to automatic theorem proving, proof checking, soon becomes intolerable. Most proofs involve long, repetitive combinations of rules.

Edinburgh LCF represented a new kind of theorem prover, where the level of automation was entirely up to the user. It was basically a programmable proof checker. Users could write proof procedures in ML — the Meta Language — rather than typing repetitive commands. ML programs could operate on expressions of the Object Language, namely Scott's Logic of Computable Functions.

Edinburgh LCF introduced the idea of representing a logic as an abstract type of theorems. Each axiom was a primitive theorem while each inference rule was a function from theorems to theorems. Type checking ensured that theorems could be made only by axioms and rules. Applying inference rules to already known theorems constructed proofs, rule by rule, in the forward direction.

Tactics permitted a more natural style, backward proof. A tactic was a function from goals to subgoals, justified by the existence of an inference rule going the other way. The tactic actually returned this inference rule (as a function) in its result: tactics were higher-order functions.

Tacticals provided control structures for combining simple tactics into complex ones. The resulting tactics could be combined to form still more complex tactics, which in a single step could perform hundreds of primitive inferences. Tacticals were even more 'higher-order' than tactics. New uses for higher-order functions turned up in rewriting and elsewhere.

ⓘ *Further reading.* Automated theorem proving originated as a task for artificial intelligence. Later research applied it to reasoning tasks such as planning (Rich and Knight, 1991). Program verification aims to prove software correct. Hardware verification, although a newer field, has been more successful; Graham (1992) describes the verification of a substantial VLSI chip and surveys other work.

Offshoots of Edinburgh LCF include HOL88, which uses higher-order logic (Gordon and Melham, 1993) and Nuprl, which supports constructive reasoning (Constable *et al.*, 1986).

Other recent systems adopt Standard ML. LAMBDA is a hardware synthesis tool, for designing circuits and simultaneously proving their correctness using higher-order logic. ALF is a proof editor for constructive type theory (Magnusson and Nordström, 1994).

1.8   *The new standard library*

The ML definition specifies a small library of standard declarations, including operations on numbers, strings and lists. Many people have found this library inadequate. For example, it has nothing to convert a character string such as "3.14" into a real number. The library's shortcomings have become more apparent as people have used ML for systems programming and other unforeseen areas. A committee, comprising several compiler writing teams, has drafted a new ML standard library (Gansner and Reppy, 1996). As of this writing it is still under development, but its basic outlines are known.

The library requires some minor changes to ML itself. It introduces a type of characters, distinct from character strings of length one. It allows the coexistence of numeric types that differ in their internal representations, and therefore in their precisions; this changes the treatment of some numerical functions.

The library is organized using ML modules. The numerous functions are components of ML **structures**, whose contents is specified using ML **signatures**. The functions are invoked not by their name alone, but via the name of their structure; for example, the sign function for real numbers is *Real . sign*, not just *sign*. Many function names occur in more than one structure; the library also provides *Int . sign*. When we later discuss modules, the library will help motivate the key concepts. Here is a summary of the library's main components, with the relevant structures:

- Operations on lists and lists of pairs belong to the structures *List* and *ListPair*. Some of these will be described in later chapters.
- Integer operations belong to the structure *Int*. Integers may be available in various precisions. These may include the usual hardware integers (structure *FixedInt*), which are efficient but have limited size. They could include unlimited precision integers (structure *IntInf*), which are essential for some tasks.
- Real number operations belong to the structure *Real*, while functions such as *sqrt*, *sin* and *cos* belong to *Math*. The reals may also be available in various precisions. Structures have names such as *Real*32 or *Real*64, which specify the number of bits used.
- Unsigned integer arithmetic is available. This includes bit-level operations such as logical 'and', which are normally found only in low-level languages. The ML version is safe, as it does not allow the bits to be converted to arbitrary types. Structures have names such as *Word*8.
- Arrays of many forms are provided. They include mutable arrays like those of imperative languages (structure *Array*), and immutable arrays (structure *Vector*). The latter are suitable for functional programming, since they cannot be updated. Their initial value is given by some calculation — one presumably too expensive to perform repeatedly.
- Operations on characters and character strings belong to structures *Char* and *String* among others. The conversion between a type and its textual representation is defined in the type's structure, such as *Int*.
- Input/output is available in several forms. The main ones are text I/O, which transfers lines of text, and binary I/O, which transfers arbitrary streams of bytes. The structures are *TextIO* and *BinIO*.

- Operating system primitives reside in structure *OS*. They are concerned with files, directories and processes. Numerous other operating system and input/output services may be provided.
- Calendar and time operations, including processor time measurements, are provided in structures *Date*, *Time* and *Timer*.
- Declarations needed by disparate parts of the library are collected into structure *General*.

Many other packages and tools, though not part of the library, are widely available. The resulting environment provides ample support for the most demanding projects.

1.9   *ML and the working programmer*

Software is notoriously unreliable. Wiener (1993) describes countless cases where software failures have resulted in loss of life, business crises and other calamities. Software products come not with a warranty, but with a warranty disclaimer. Could we prevent these failures by coding in ML instead of C? Of course not — but it would be a step in the right direction.

Part of the problem is the prevailing disdain for safety. Checks on the correct use of arrays and references are costly, but they can detect errors before they do serious harm. C. A. R. Hoare has said,

> ... it is absurd to make elaborate security checks on debugging runs, when no trust is put in the results, and then remove them in production runs, when an erroneous result could be expensive or disastrous. What would we think of a sailing enthusiast who wears his life-jacket when training on dry land but takes it off as soon as he goes to sea? (Hoare, 1989b, page 198)

This quote, from a lecture first given in 1973, has seldom been heeded. Typical compilers omit checks unless specifically commanded to include them. The C language is particularly unsafe: as its arrays are mere storage addresses, checking their correct usage is impractical. The standard C library includes many procedures that risk corrupting the store; they are given a storage area but not told its size! In consequence, the Unix operating system has many security loopholes. The Internet Worm exploited these, causing widespread network disruption (Spafford, 1989).

ML supports the development of reliable software in many ways. Compilers do not allow checks to be omitted. Appel (1993) cites its safety, automatic storage allocation, and compile-time type checking; these eliminate some major errors altogether, and ensure the early detection of others. Appel shares the view that functional programming is valuable, even in major projects.

Moreover, ML is defined formally. Milner *et al.* (1990) is not the first formal definition of a programming language, but it is the first one that compiler writers can understand.[2] Because the usual ambiguities are absent, compilers agree to a remarkable extent. The new standard library will strengthen this agreement. A program ought to behave identically regardless of which compiler runs it; ML is close to this ideal.

A key advantage of ML is its module system. System components, however large, can be specified and coded independently. Each component can supply its specified services, protected from external tampering. One component can take other components as parameters, and be compiled separately from them. Such components can be combined in many ways, configuring different systems.

Viewed from a software engineering perspective, ML is an excellent language for large systems. Its modules allow programmers to work in teams, and to reuse components. Its types and overall safety contribute to reliability. Its exceptions allow programs to respond to failures. Comparing ML with C, Appel admits that ML programs need a great deal of space, but run acceptably fast. Software developers have a choice of commercially supported compilers.

We cannot soon expect to have ML programs running in our digital watches. With major applications, however, reliability and programmer productivity are basic requirements. Is the age of C drawing to a close?

---

[2] This is possible thanks to recent progress in the theory of programming languages. The ML definition is an example of a structural operational semantics (Hennessy, 1990).

2
Names, Functions and Types

Most functional languages are interactive. If you enter an expression, the computer immediately evaluates it and displays the result. Interaction is fun; it gives immediate feedback; it lets you develop programs in easily managed pieces.

We can enter an expression followed by a semicolon ...

```
2+2;
```

... and ML responds

```
> 4 : int
```

Here we see some conventions that will be followed throughout the book. Most ML systems print a prompt character when waiting for input; here, the input is shown in typewriter characters. The response is shown, in slanted characters,

```
> on a line like this.
```

At its simplest, ML is just a calculator. It has integers, as shown above, and real numbers. ML can do simple arithmetic ...

```
3.2 - 2.3;
> 0.9 : real
```

... and square roots:

```
Math.sqrt 2.0;
> 1.414213562 : real
```

Again, anything typed to ML must end with a semicolon (;). ML has printed the value and type. Note that *real* is the type of real numbers, while *int* is the type of integers.

Interactive program development is more difficult with procedural languages because they are too verbose. A self-contained program is too long to type as a single input.

17

Chapter outline

This chapter introduces Standard ML and functional programming. The basic concepts include declarations, simple data types, record types, recursive functions and polymorphism. Although this material is presented using Standard ML, it illustrates general principles.

The chapter contains the following sections:

Value declarations. Value and function declarations are presented using elementary examples.

Numbers, character strings and truth values. The built-in types *int*, *real*, *char*, *string* and *bool* support arithmetic, textual and logical operations.

Pairs, tuples and records. Ordered pairs and tuples allow functions to have multiple arguments and results.

The evaluation of expressions. The difference between strict evaluation and lazy evaluation is not just a matter of efficiency, but concerns the very meaning of expressions.

Writing recursive functions. Several worked examples illustrate the use of recursion.

Local declarations. Using `let` or `local`, names can be declared with a restricted scope.

Introduction to modules. Signatures and structures are introduced by developing a generic treatment of arithmetic operations.

Polymorphic type checking. The principles of polymorphism are introduced, including type inference and polymorphic functions.

Value declarations

A *declaration* gives something a name. ML has many kinds of things that can be named: values, types, signatures, structures and functors. Most names in a program stand for values, like numbers, strings — and functions. Although functions are values in ML, they have a special declaration syntax.

2.1   *Naming constants*

Any value of importance can be named, whether its importance is universal (like the constant π) or transient (the result of a previous computation). As a trivial example, suppose we want to compute the number of seconds in an hour. We begin by letting the name *seconds* stand for 60.

```
val seconds = 60;
```

The value declaration begins with ML keyword `val` and ends with a semicolon. Names in this book usually appear in *italics*. ML repeats the name, with its value and type:

```
> val seconds = 60 : int
```

Let us declare constants for minutes per hour and hours per day:

```
val minutes = 60;
> val minutes = 60 : int
val hours = 24;
> val hours = 24 : int
```

These names are now valid in expressions:

```
seconds*minutes*hours;
> 86400 : int
```

If you enter an expression at top level like this, ML stores the value under the name *it*. By referring to *it* you can use the value in a further calculation:

```
it div 24;
> 3600 : int
```

The name *it* always has the value of the last expression typed at top level. Any previous value of *it* is lost. To save the value of *it*, declare a permanent name:

```
val secsinhour = it;
> val secsinhour = 3600 : int
```

Incidentally, names may contain underscores to make them easier to read:

```
val secs_in_hour = seconds*minutes;
> val secs_in_hour = 3600 : int
```

To demonstrate real numbers, we compute the area of a circle of radius r by the formula $area = \pi r^2$:

```
val pi = 3.14159;
> val pi = 3.14159 : real
val r = 2.0;
> val r = 2.0 : real
val area = pi * r * r;
> val area = 12.56636 : real
```

2.2   Declaring functions

The formula for the area of a circle can be made into an ML function like this:

```
fun area (r) = pi*r*r;
```

The keyword `fun` starts the function declaration, while *area* is the function name, *r* is the ***formal parameter***, and *pi*r*r* is the ***body***. The body refers to *r* and to the constant *pi* declared above.

Because functions are values in ML, a function declaration is a form of value declaration, and so ML prints the value and type:

```
> val area = fn : real -> real
```

The type, which in standard mathematical notation is *real* → *real*, says that *area* takes a real number as argument and returns another real number. The value of a function is printed as `fn`. In ML, as in most functional languages, functions are abstract values: their internal structure is hidden.

Let us call the function, repeating the area calculation performed above:

```
area(2.0);
> 12.56636 : real
```

Let us try it with a different argument. Observe that the parentheses around the argument are optional:

```
area 1.0;
> 3.14159 : real
```

The parentheses are also optional in function declarations. This definition of *area* is equivalent to the former one.

```
fun area r = pi*r*r;
```

The evaluation of function applications is discussed in more detail below.

Comments. Programmers often imagine that their creations are too transparent to require further description. This logical clarity will not be evident to others unless the program is properly commented. A comment can describe the purpose of a declaration, give a literature reference, or explain an obscure matter. Needless to say, comments must be correct and up-to-date.

A comment in Standard ML begins with (* and ends with *) , and may extend over several lines. Comments can even be nested. They can be inserted almost anywhere:

```
fun area r =      (*area of circle with radius r*)
        pi*r*r;
```

Functional programmers should not feel absolved from writing comments. People once claimed that Pascal was self-documenting.

Redeclaring a name. Value names are called **variables**. Unlike variables in imperative languages, they cannot be updated. But a name can be reused for another purpose. If a name is declared again then the new meaning is adopted afterwards, but does not affect existing uses of the name. Let us redeclare the constant *pi*:

```
val pi = 0.0;
> val pi = 0.0 : real
```

We can see that *area* still takes the original value of *pi*:

```
area(1.0);
> 3.14159 : real
```

At this point in the session, several variables have values. These include *seconds*, *minutes*, *area* and *pi*, as well as the built-in operations provided by the library. The set of bindings visible at any point is called the **environment**. The function *area* refers to an earlier environment in which *pi* denotes 3.14159. Thanks to the permanence of names (called **static binding**), redeclaring a function cannot damage the system, the library or your program.

Correcting your program. Because of static binding, redeclaring a function called by your program may have no visible effect. When modifying a program, be sure to recompile the entire file. Large programs should be divided into modules; Chapter 7 will explain this in detail. After the modified module has been recompiled, the program merely has to be relinked.

2.3   Identifiers in Standard ML

An **alphabetic name** must begin with a letter, which may be followed by any number of letters, digits, underscores (_), or primes ('), usually called single quotes. For instance:

```
x     UB40     Hamlet_Prince_of_Denmark     h''3_H
```

The case of letters matters, so q differs from Q. Prime characters are allowed because ML was designed by mathematicians, who like variables called x, x', x''. When choosing names, be certain to avoid ML's keywords:

```
abstype and andalso as case datatype do
else end eqtype exception fn fun functor
handle if in include infix infixr let local
nonfix of op open orelse raise rec
sharing sig signature struct structure
then type val where while with withtype
```

Watch especially for the short ones: as, fn, if, in, of, op.

ML also permits **symbolic names**. These consist of the characters

```
! % & $ # + - * / : < = > ? @ \ ~ ` ^ |
```

Names made up of these characters can be as long as you like:

```
---->      $^$^$^$      !!?@**??!!      :-|==>->#
```

Certain strings of special characters are reserved for ML's syntax and should not be used as symbolic names:

```
:   |   =   =>   ->   #   :>
```

A symbolic name is allowed wherever an alphabetic name is:

```
val +-+-+ = 1415;
> val +-+-+ = 1415 : int
```

Names are more formally known as *identifiers*. An identifier can simultaneously denote a value, a type, a structure, a signature, a functor and a record field.

Exercise 2.1   On your computer, learn how to start an ML session and how to terminate it. Then learn how to make the ML compiler read declarations from a file — a typical command is *use* `"myfile"`.

Numbers, character strings and truth values

The simplest ML values are integer and real numbers, strings and characters, and the booleans or truth values. This section introduces these types with their constants and principal operations.

2.4   *Arithmetic*

ML distinguishes between integers (type *int*) and real numbers (type *real*). Integer arithmetic is exact (with unlimited precision in some ML systems) while real arithmetic is only as accurate as the computer's floating-point hardware.

Integers.   An integer constant is a sequence of digits, possibly beginning with a minus sign (~). For instance:

```
0     ~23     01234     ~85601435654678
```

Integer operations include addition (+), subtraction (–), multiplication (*), division (*div*) and remainder (*mod*). These are infix operators with conventional precedences: thus in

$$(((m{*}n){*}k) \; - \; (m \; div \; j)) \; + \; j$$

all the parentheses can be omitted without harm.

Real numbers. A real constant contains a decimal point or E notation, or both. For instance:

```
0.01     2.718281828     ~1.2E12     7E~5
```

The ending E*n* means 'times the *n*th power of 10.' A negative exponent begins with the unary minus sign (~). Thus 123.4E~2 denotes 1.234.

Negative real numbers begin with unary minus (~). Infix operators for reals include addition (+), subtraction (-), multiplication (*) and division (/). Function application binds more tightly than infix operators. For instance, *area a + b* is equivalent to (*area a*) + *b*, not *area* (*a + b*).

⚠ *Unary plus and minus.* The unary minus sign is a tilde (~). Do not confuse it with the subtraction sign (-)! ML has no unary plus sign. Neither + nor - may appear in the exponent of a real number.

Type constraints. ML can deduce the types in most expressions from the types of the functions and constants in it. But certain built-in functions are ***overloaded***, having more than one meaning. For example, + and * are defined for both integers and reals. The type of an overloaded function must be determined from the context; occasionally types must be stated explicitly.

For instance, ML cannot tell whether this squaring function is intended for integers or reals, and therefore rejects it.

```
fun square x = x*x;
> Error- Unable to resolve overloading for *
```

Suppose the function is intended for real numbers. We can insert the type *real* in a number of places.

We can specify the type of the argument:

```
fun square (x : real) = x*x;
> val square = fn : real -> real
```

We can specify the type of the result:

```
fun square x : real = x*x;
> val square = fn : real -> real
```

Equivalently, we can specify the type of the body:

```
fun square x = x*x : real;
> val square = fn : real -> real
```

Type constraints can also appear within the body, indeed almost anywhere.

⚠️ *Default overloading.* The standard library introduces the notion of a default overloading; the compiler may resolve the ambiguity in *square* by choosing type *int*. Using a type constraint in such cases is still advisable, for clarity. The motivation for default overloadings is to allow different precisions of numbers to coexist. For example, unless the precision of 1.23 is determined by its context, it will be assumed to have the default precision for real numbers. As of this writing there is no experience of using different precisions, but care is plainly necessary.

ⓘ *Arithmetic and the standard library.* The standard library includes numerous functions for integers and reals, of various precisions. Structure *Int* contains such functions as *abs* (absolute value), *min*, *max* and *sign*. Here are some examples:

```
Int.abs ~4;
> 4 : int
Int.min(7, Int.sign 12);
> 1 : int
```

Structure *Real* contains analogous functions such as *abs* and *sign*, as well as functions to convert between integers and reals. Calling *real*(*i*) converts *i* to the equivalent real number. Calling *round*(*r*) converts *r* to the nearest integer. Other real-to-integer conversions include *floor*, *ceil* and *trunc*. Conversion functions are necessary whenever integers and reals appear in the same expression.

Structure *Math* contains higher mathematical functions on real numbers, such as *sqrt*, *sin*, *cos*, *atan* (inverse tangent), *exp* and *ln* (natural logarithm). Each takes one real argument and returns a real result.

Exercise 2.2   A Lisp hacker says: 'Since the integers are a subset of the real numbers, the distinction between them is wholly artificial — foisted on us by hardware designers. ML should simply provide numbers, as Lisp does, and automatically use integers or reals as appropriate.' Do you agree? What considerations are there?

Exercise 2.3   Which of these function definitions require type constraints?

```
fun double(n) = 2*n;
fun f u = Math.sin(u)/u;
fun g k = ~ k * k;
```

2.5   *Strings and characters*

Messages and other text are strings of characters. They have type *string*. String constants are written in double quotes:

```
"How now! a rat? Dead, for a ducat, dead!";
> "How now! a rat? Dead, for a ducat, dead!" : string
```

The concatenation operator (^) joins two strings end-to-end:

```
"Fair " ^ "Ophelia";
> "Fair Ophelia" : string
```

The built-in function *size* returns the number of characters in a string. Here *it* refers to "Fair Ophelia":

```
size (it);
> 12 : int
```

The space character counts, of course. The empty string contains no characters; *size* (" ") is 0.

Here is a function that makes noble titles:

```
fun title (name) = "The Duke of " ^ name;
> val title = fn : string -> string
title "York";
> "The Duke of York" : string
```

Special characters. **Escape sequences**, which begin with a backslash (\), insert certain special characters into a string. Here are some of them:

- \n inserts a newline character (line break).
- \t inserts a tabulation character.
- \" inserts a double quote.
- \\ inserts a backslash.
- \ followed by a newline and other white-space characters, followed by another \ inserts nothing, but continues a string across the line break.

Here is a string containing newline characters:

```
"This above all:\nto thine own self be true\n";
```

The type char. Just as the number 3 differs from the set {3}, a character differs from a one-character string. Characters have type *char*. The constants have the form #*s*, where *s* is a string constant consisting of a single character. Here is a letter, a space and a special character:

```
#"a"    #" "    #"\n"
```

The functions *ord* and *chr* convert between characters and character codes. Most implementations use the ASCII character set; if k is in the range $0 \leq k \leq 255$ then $chr(k)$ returns the character with code k. Conversely, $ord(c)$ is the integer code of the character c. We can use these to convert a number between 0 and 9 to a character between #"0" and #"9":

```
fun digit i = chr(i + ord #"0");
> val digit = fn : int -> char
```

The functions *str* and *String . sub* convert between characters and strings. If *c* is a character then *str*(*c*) is the corresponding string. Conversely, if *s* is a string then *String . sub*(*s*, *n*) returns the *n*th character in *s*, counting from zero. Let us try these, first expressing the function *digit* differently:

```
fun digit i = String.sub("0123456789", i);
> val digit = fn : int -> char
str (digit 5);
> "5" : string
```

The second definition of *digit* is preferable to the first, as it does not rely on character codes.

> **ℹ** *Strings, characters and the standard library.* Structure *String* contains numerous operations on strings. Structure *Char* provides functions such as *isDigit*, *isAlpha*, etc., to recognize certain classes of character. A **substring** is a contiguous subsequence of characters from a string; structure *Substring* provides operations for extracting and manipulating them.
>
> The ML *Definition* only has type *string* (Milner *et al.*, 1990). The standard library introduces the type *char*. It also modifies the types of built-in functions such as *ord* and *chr*, which previously operated on single-character strings.

Exercise 2.4   For each version of *digit*, what do you expect in response to the calls *digit* ˜1 and *digit* 10? Try to predict the response before experimenting on the computer.

2.6   *Truth values and conditional expressions*

To define a function by cases — where the result depends on the outcome of a test — we employ a conditional expression.[1] The test is an expression *E* of type *bool*, whose values are *true* and *false*. The outcome of the test chooses one of two expressions E_1 or E_2. The value of the conditional expression

if *E* then E_1 else E_2

is that of E_1 if *E* equals *true*, and that of E_2 if *E* equals *false*. The else part is mandatory.

The simplest tests are the relations:

- less than (<)

---

[1]   Because a Standard ML expression can update the state, conditional expressions can also act like the if commands of procedural languages.

- greater than (>)
- less than or equals (<=)
- greater than or equals (>=)

These are defined on integers and reals; they also test alphabetical ordering on strings and characters. Thus the relations are overloaded and may require type constraints. Equality (=) and its negation (<>) can be tested for most types.

For example, the function *sign* computes the sign (1, 0, or −1) of an integer. It has two conditional expressions and a comment.

```
fun sign(n) =
          if n>0 then 1
     else if n=0 then 0
     else (*n<0*)     ~1;
> val sign = fn : int ->int
```

Tests are combined by ML's boolean operations:

- logical or (called `orelse`)
- logical and (called `andalso`)
- logical negation (the function *not*)

Functions that return a boolean value are known as **predicates**. Here is a predicate to test whether its argument, a character, is a lower-case letter:

```
fun isLower c = #"a" <= c andalso c <= #"z";
> val isLower = fn : char -> bool
```

When a conditional expression is evaluated, either the `then` or the `else` expression is evaluated, never both. The boolean operators `andalso` and `orelse` behave differently from ordinary functions: the second operand is evaluated only if necessary. Their names reflect this sequential behaviour.

Exercise 2.5 Let *d* be an integer and *m* a string. Write an ML boolean expression that is true just when *d* and *m* form a valid date: say 25 and "October". Assume it is not a leap year.

Pairs, tuples and records

In mathematics, a collection of values is often viewed as a single value. A vector in two dimensions is an ordered pair of real numbers. A statement about two vectors $\vec{v}_1$ and $\vec{v}_2$ can be taken as a statement about four real numbers, and those real numbers can themselves be broken down into smaller pieces, but thinking at a high level is easier. Writing $\vec{v}_1 + \vec{v}_2$ for their vector sum saves us from writing $(x_1 + x_2, y_1 + y_2)$.

Dates are a more commonplace example. A date like 25 October 1415 consists of three values. Taken as a unit, it is a triple of the form (*day*, *month*, *year*). This elementary concept has taken remarkably long to appear in programming languages, and only a few handle it properly.

Standard ML provides ordered pairs, triples, quadruples and so forth. For $n \geq 2$, the ordered collection of n values is called an n-tuple, or just a ***tuple***. The tuple whose components are $x_1, x_2, \ldots, x_n$ is written $(x_1, x_2, \ldots, x_n)$. Such a value is created by an expression of the form $(E_1, E_2, \ldots, E_n)$. With functions, tuples give the effect of multiple arguments and results.

The components of an ML tuple may themselves be tuples or any other value. For example, a period of time can be represented by a pair of dates, regardless of how dates are represented. It also follows that nested pairs can represent n-tuples. (In Classic ML, the original dialect, $(x_1, \ldots, x_{n-1}, x_n)$ was merely an abbreviation for $(x_1, \ldots, (x_{n-1}, x_n) \ldots)$.)

An ML ***record*** has components identified by name, not by position. A record with 20 components occupies a lot of space on the printed page, but is easier to manage than a 20-tuple.

2.7   *Vectors: an example of pairing*

Let us develop the example of vectors. To try the syntax for pairs, enter the vector $(2.5, -1.2)$:

```
(2.5, ~1.2);
> (2.5, ~1.2) : real * real
```

The vector's type, which in mathematical notation is *real* × *real*, is the type of a pair of real numbers. Vectors are ML values and can be given names. We declare the zero vector and two others, called *a* and *b*.

```
val zerovec = (0.0, 0.0);
> val zerovec = (0.0, 0.0) : real * real
val a = (1.5, 6.8);
> val a = (1.5, 6.8) : real * real
val b = (3.6, 0.9);
> val b = (3.6, 0.9) : real * real
```

Many functions on vectors operate on the components. The length of (x, y) is $\sqrt{x^2 + y^2}$, while the negation of (x, y) is $(-x, -y)$. To code these functions in ML, simply write the argument as a pattern:

```
fun lengthvec (x,y) = Math.sqrt(x*x + y*y);
> val lengthvec = fn : real * real -> real
```

The function *lengthvec* takes the pair of values of *x* and *y*. It has type *real* × *real* → *real*: its argument is a pair of real numbers and its result is another real number.[2] Here, *a* is a pair of real numbers.

```
lengthvec a;
> 6.963476143 : real
lengthvec (1.0, 1.0);
> 1.414213562 : real
```

Function *negvec* negates a vector with respect to the point $(0, 0)$.

```
fun negvec (x,y) : real*real = (~x, ~y);
> val negvec = fn : real * real -> real * real
```

This function has type *real* × *real* → *real* × *real*: given a pair of real numbers it returns another pair. The type constraint *real* × *real* is necessary because minus (~) is overloaded.

We negate some vectors, giving a name to the negation of *b*:

```
negvec (1.0, 1.0);
> (~1.0, ~1.0) : real * real
val bn = negvec(b);
> val bn = (~3.6, ~0.9) : real * real
```

Vectors can be arguments and results of functions and can be given names. In short, they have all the rights of ML's built-in values, like the integers. We can even declare a type of vectors:

```
type vec = real*real;
> type vec
```

Now *vec* abbreviates *real* × *real*. It is only an abbreviation though: every pair of real numbers has type *vec*, regardless of whether it is intended to represent a vector. We shall employ *vec* in type constraints.

2.8 *Functions with multiple arguments and results*

Here is a function that computes the average of a pair of real numbers.

```
fun average(x,y) = (x+y)/2.0;
> val average = fn : (real * real) -> real
```

---

[2] function *Math.sqrt*, which is defined only for real numbers, constrains the overloaded operators to type *real*.

This would be an odd thing to do to a vector, but *average* works for any two numbers:

```
average(3.1,3.3);
> 3.2 : real
```

A function on pairs is, in effect, a function of two arguments: *lengthvec*(x, y) and *average*(x, y) operate on the real numbers x and y. Whether we view (x, y) as a vector is up to us. Similarly *negvec* takes a pair of arguments — and returns a pair of results.

Strictly speaking, every ML function has one argument and one result. With tuples, functions can effectively have any number of arguments and results. Currying, discussed in Chapter 5, also gives the effect of multiple arguments.

Since the components of a tuple can themselves be tuples, two vectors can be paired:

```
((2.0, 3.5), zerovec);
> ((2.0, 3.5), (0.0, 0.0)) : (real*real) * (real*real)
```

The sum of vectors (x_1, y_1) and (x_2, y_2) is (x_1+x_2, y_1+y_2). In ML, this function takes a pair of vectors. Its argument pattern is a pair of pairs:

```
fun addvec ((x1,y1), (x2,y2)) : vec = (x1+x2, y1+y2);
> val addvec = fn : (real*real) * (real*real) -> vec
```

Type *vec* appears for the first time, constraining addition to operate on real numbers. ML gives *addvec* the type

$$((real \times real) \times (real \times real)) \rightarrow vec$$

which is equivalent to the more concise $(vec \times vec) \rightarrow vec$. The ML system may not abbreviate every *real* $\times$ *real* as *vec*.

Look again at the argument pattern of *addvec*. We may equivalently view this function as taking

- one argument: a pair of pairs of real numbers
- two arguments: each a pair of real numbers
- four arguments: all real numbers, oddly grouped

Here we add the vectors (8.9,4.4) and *b*, then add the result to another vector. Note that *vec* is the result type of the function.

```
addvec((8.9, 4.4), b);
> (12.5, 5.3) : vec
addvec(it, (0.1, 0.2));
> (12.6, 5.5) : vec
```

Vector subtraction involves subtraction of the components, but can be expressed by vector operations:

```
fun subvec(v1,v2) = addvec(v1, negvec v2);
> val subvec = fn : (real*real) * (real*real) -> vec
```

The variables *v*1 and *v*2 range over pairs of reals.

```
subvec(a,b);
> (~2.1, 5.9) : vec
```

The distance between two vectors is the length of the difference:

```
fun distance(v1,v2) = lengthvec(subvec(v1,v2));
> val distance = fn : (real*real) * (real*real) -> real
```

Since *distance* never refers separately to *v*1 or *v*2, it can be simplified:

```
fun distance pairv = lengthvec(subvec pairv);
```

The variable *pairv* ranges over pairs of vectors. This version may look odd, but is equivalent to its predecessor. How far is it from *a* to *b*?

```
distance(a,b);
> 6.262587325 : real
```

A final example will show that the components of a pair can have different types: here, a real number and a vector. Scaling a vector means multiplying both components by a constant.

```
fun scalevec (r, (x,y)) : vec = (r*x, r*y);
> val scalevec = fn : real * (real*real) -> vec
```

The type constraint *vec* ensures that the multiplications apply to reals. The function *scalevec* takes a real number and a vector, and returns a vector.

```
scalevec(2.0, a);
> (3.0, 13.6) : vec
scalevec(2.0, it);
> (6.0, 27.2) : vec
```

Selecting the components of a tuple. A function defined on a pattern, say (x,y), refers to the components of its argument through the pattern variables *x* and *y*. A `val` declaration may also match a value against a pattern: each variable in the pattern refers to the corresponding component.

Here we treat *scalevec* as a function returning two results, which we name *xc* and *yc*.

```
val (xc,yc) = scalevec(4.0, a);
> val xc = 6.0 : real
> val yc = 27.2 : real
```

The pattern in a `val` declaration can be as complicated as the argument pattern of a function definition. In this contrived example, a pair of pairs is split into four parts, which are all given names.

```
val ((x1,y1), (x2,y2)) = (addvec(a,b), subvec(a,b));
> val x1 = 5.1 : real
> val y1 = 7.7 : real
> val x2 = ~2.1 : real
> val y2 = 5.9 : real
```

The 0-tuple and the type unit. Previously we have considered *n*-tuples for $n \geq 2$. There is also a 0-tuple, written () and pronounced 'unity,' which has no components. It serves as a placeholder in situations where no data needs to be conveyed. The 0-tuple is the sole value of type *unit*.

Type *unit* is often used with procedural programming in ML. A procedure is typically a 'function' whose result type is *unit*. The procedure is called for its effect — not for its value, which is always (). For instance, some ML systems provide a function *use* of type *string* → *unit*. Calling *use* `"myfile"` has the effect of reading the definitions on the file `"myfile"` into ML.

A function whose argument type is *unit* passes no information to its body when called. Calling the function simply causes its body to be evaluated. In Chapter 5, such functions are used to delay evaluation for programming with infinite lists.

Exercise 2.6   Write a function to determine whether one time of day, in the form (*hours*, *minutes*, AM or PM), comes before another. As an example, (11, 59, `"AM"`) comes before (1, 15, `"PM"`).

Exercise 2.7   Old English money had 12 pence in a shilling and 20 shillings in a pound. Write functions to add and subtract two amounts, working with triples (*pounds*, *shillings*, *pence*).

2.9   *Records*

A record is a tuple whose components — called *fields* — have labels. While each component of an *n*-tuple is identified by its position from 1 to *n*, the fields of a record may appear in any order. Transposing the components of a tuple is a common error. If employees are taken as triples (*name*, *age*, *salary*) then there is a big difference between `("Jones", 25, 15300)` and `("Jones", 15300, 25)`. But the records

> {*name*=`"Jones"`, *age*=25, *salary*=15300}

and

> {*name*=`"Jones"`, *salary*=15300, *age*=25}

are equal. A record is enclosed in braces { ... }; each field has the form *label* = *expression*.

Records are appropriate when there are many components. Let us record five fundamental facts about some Kings of England, and note ML's response:

```
val henryV =
   {name    = "Henry V",
    born    = 1387,
    crowned = 1413,
    died    = 1422,
    quote   = "Bid them achieve me and then sell my bones"};
> val henryV =
>   {born = 1387,
>    died = 1422,
>    name = "Henry V",
>    quote = "Bid them achieve me and then sell my bones",
>    crowned = 1413}
> : {born: int,
>    died: int,
>    name: string,
>    quote: string,
>    crowned: int}
```

ML has rearranged the fields into a standard order, ignoring the order in which they were given. The record type lists each field as *label* : *type*, within braces. Here are two more Kings:

```
val henryVI =
   {name    = "Henry VI",
    born    = 1421,
    crowned = 1422,
    died    = 1471,
    quote   = "Weep, wretched man, \
\ I'll aid thee tear for tear"};

val richardIII =
   {name    = "Richard III",
    born    = 1452,
    crowned = 1483,
```

```
died    = 1485,
quote   = "Plots have I laid...."};
```

The *quote* of *henryVI* extends across two lines, using the backslash, newline, backslash escape sequence.

Record patterns. A record pattern with fields *label = variable* gives each variable the value of the corresponding label. If we do not need all the fields, we can write three dots (. . .) in place of the others. Here we get two fields from Henry V's famous record, calling them *nameV* and *bornV*:

```
val {name=nameV, born=bornV, ...} = henryV;
> val nameV = "Henry V" : string
> val bornV = 1387 : int
```

Often we want to open up a record, making its fields directly visible. We can specify each field in the pattern as *label = label*, making the variable and the label identical. Such a specification can be shortened to simply *label*. We open up Richard III:

```
val {name,born,died,quote,crowned} = richardIII;
> val name = "Richard III" : string
> val born = 1452 : int
> val died = 1485 : int
> val quote = "Plots have I laid..." : string
> val crowned = 1483 : int
```

To omit some fields, write (. . .) as before. Now *quote* stands for the quote of Richard III. Obviously this makes sense for only one King at a time.

Record field selections. The selection #*label* gets the value of the given *label* from a record.

```
#quote richardIII;
> "Plots have I laid..." : string
#died henryV - #born henryV;
> 35 : int
```

Different record types can have labels in common. Both employees and Kings have a *name*, whether "Jones" or "Henry V". The three Kings given above have the same record type because they have the same number of fields with the same labels and types.

Here is another example of different record types with some labels in common: the *n*-tuple $(x_1, x_2, \ldots, x_n)$ is just an abbreviation for a record with numbered fields:

$$\{1 = x_1, 2 = x_2, \ldots, n = x_n\}$$

Yes, a label can be a positive integer! This obscure fact about Standard ML is worth knowing for one reason: the selector #*k* gets the value of component *k* of an *n*-tuple. So #1 selects the first component and #2 selects the second. If there is a third component then #3 selects it, and so forth:

```
#2 ("a","b",3,false);
> "b" : string
```

Partial record specifications. A field selection that omits some of the fields does not completely specify the record type; a function may only be defined over a complete record type. For instance, a function cannot be defined for all records that have fields *born* and *died*, without specifying the full set of field names (typically using a type constraint). This restriction makes ML records efficient but inflexible. It applies equally to record patterns and field selections of the form #*label*. Ohori (1995) has defined and implemented flexible records for a variant of ML.

Declaring a record type. Let us declare the record type of Kings. This abbreviation will be useful for type constraints in functions.

```
type king = {name    : string,
             born     : int,
             crowned  : int,
             died     : int,
             quote    : string};
> type king
```

We now can declare a function on type *king* to return the King's lifetime:

```
fun lifetime(k: king) = #died k - #born k;
> val lifetime = fn : king -> int
```

Using a pattern, *lifetime* can be declared like this:

```
fun lifetime({born,died,...}: king) = died - born;
```

Either way the type constraint is mandatory. Otherwise ML will print a message like 'A fixed record type is needed here.'

```
lifetime henryV;
> 35 : int
lifetime richardIII;
> 33 : int
```

Exercise 2.8   Does the following function definition require a type constraint? What is its type?

> fun *lifetime* ({*name*, *born*, *crowned*, *died*, *quote*}) = *died* − *born*;

Exercise 2.9   Discuss the differences, if any, between the selector #*born* and the function

> fun *born_at* ({*born*}) = *born*;

2.10   *Infix operators*

An ***infix operator*** is a function that is written between its two arguments. We take infix notation for granted in mathematics. Imagine doing without it. Instead of 2+2=4 we should have to write =(+(2,2),4). Most functional languages let programmers declare their own infix operators.

Let us declare an infix operator *xor* for 'exclusive or.' First we issue an ML `infix` directive:

> infix *xor*;

We now must write *p xor q* rather than *xor* (*p*, *q*) :

```
fun (p xor q) = (p orelse q) andalso not (p andalso q);
> val xor = fn : (bool * bool) -> bool
```

The function *xor* takes a pair of booleans and returns a boolean.

```
true xor false xor true;
> false : bool
```

The infix status of a name concerns only its syntax, not its value, if any. Usually a name is made infix before it has any value at all.

Precedence of infixes. Most people take $m \times n + i/j$ to mean $(m \times n) + (i/j)$, giving $\times$ and $/$ higher precedence than $+$. Similarly $i - j - k$ means $(i - j) - k$, since the operator $-$ associates to the left. An ML infix directive may state a precedence from 0 to 9. The default precedence is 0, which is the lowest. The directive `infix` causes association to the left, while `infixr` causes association to the right.

To demonstrate infixes, the following functions construct strings enclosed in parentheses. Operator *plus* has precedence 6 (the precedence of + in ML) and constructs a string containing a + sign.

```
infix 6 plus;
fun (a plus b) = "(" ^ a ^ "+" ^ b ^ ")";
> val plus = fn : string * string -> string
```

Observe that *plus* associates to the left:

```
"1" plus "2" plus "3";
> "((1+2)+3)" : string
```

Similarly, *times* has precedence 7 (like * in ML) and constructs a string containing a * sign.

```
infix 7 times;
fun (a times b) = "(" ^ a ^ "*" ^ b ^ ")";
> val times = fn : string * string -> string
"m" times "n" times "3" plus "i" plus "j" times "k";
> "((((m*n)*3)+i)+(j*k))" : string
```

The operator *pow* has higher precedence than times and associates to the right, which is traditional for raising to a power. It produces a # sign. (ML has no operator for powers.)

```
infixr 8 pow;
fun (a pow b) = "(" ^ a ^ "#" ^ b ^ ")";
> val pow = fn : string * string -> string
"m" times "i" pow "j" pow "2" times "n";
> "((m*(i#(j#2)))*n)" : string
```

Many infix operators have symbolic names. Let ++ be the operator for vector addition:

```
infix ++;
fun ((x1,y1) ++ (x2,y2)) : vec = (x1+x2, y1+y2);
> val ++ = fn : (real*real) * (real*real) -> vec
```

It works exactly like *addvec*, but with infix notation:

```
b ++ (0.1,0.2) ++ (20.0, 30.0);
> (23.7, 31.1) : vec
```

Keep symbolic names separate. Symbolic names can cause confusion if you run them together. Below, ML reads the characters +~ as one symbolic name, then complains that this name has no value:

```
1+~3;
> Unknown name +~
```

Symbolic names must be separated by spaces or other characters:

```
1+ ~3;
> ~2 : int
```

Taking infixes as functions. Occasionally an infix has to be treated like an ordinary function. In ML the keyword op overrides infix status: if ⊕ is an infix operator then op⊕ is the corresponding function, which can be applied to a pair in the usual way.

```
> op++ ((2.5,0.0), (0.1,2.5));
(2.6, 2.5) : real * real
op^ ("Mont","joy");
> "Montjoy" : string
```

Infix status can be revoked. If ⊕ is an infix operator then the directive nonfix⊕ makes it revert to ordinary function notation. A subsequent infix directive can make ⊕ an infix operator again.

Here we deprive ML's multiplication operator of its infix status. The attempt to use it produces an error message, since we may not apply 3 as a function. But * can be applied as a function:

```
nonfix *;
3*2;
> Error: Type conflict...
*(3,2);
> 6 : int
```

The nonfix directive is intended for interactive development of syntax, for trying different precedences and association. Changing the infix status of established operators leads to madness.

The evaluation of expressions

An imperative program specifies commands to update the machine state. During execution, the state changes millions of times per second. Its structure changes too: local variables are created and destroyed. Even if the program has a mathematical meaning independent of hardware details, that meaning is beyond the comprehension of the programmer. Axiomatic and denotational semantic definitions make sense only to a handful of experts. Programmers trying to correct their programs rely on debugging tools and intuition.

Functional programming aims to give each program a straightforward mathematical meaning. It simplifies our mental image of execution, for there are no state changes. Execution is the reduction of an expression to its value, replacing equals by equals. Most function definitions can be understood within elementary mathematics.

When a function is applied, as in $f(E)$, the argument E must be supplied to the body of f. If the expression contains several function calls, one must be chosen according to some evaluation rule. The evaluation rule in ML is ***call-by-value*** (or

strict evaluation), while most purely functional languages adopt ***call-by-need*** (or
lazy evaluation).

Each evaluation rule has its partisans. To compare the rules we shall consider
two trivial functions. The squaring function *sqr* uses its argument twice:

```
fun sqr(x) : int = x*x;
> val sqr = fn : int -> int
```

The constant function *zero* ignores its argument and returns 0:

```
fun zero(x : int) = 0;
> val zero = fn : int -> int
```

When a function is called, the argument is substituted for the function's formal
parameter in the body. The evaluation rules differ over when, and how many
times, the argument is evaluated. The formal parameter indicates where in the
body to substitute the argument. The name of the formal parameter has no other
significance, and no significance outside of the function definition.

2.11   *Evaluation in ML: call-by-value*

Let us assume that expressions consist of constants, variables, function
calls and conditional expressions (if-then-else). Constants have explicit values; variables have bindings in the environment. So evaluation has only to deal
with function calls and conditionals. ML's evaluation rule is based on an obvious
idea.

> To compute the value of $f(E)$, first compute the value of the expression E.

This value is substituted into the body of f, which then can be evaluated. Pattern-
matching is a minor complication. If f is declared by, say

```
fun f (x,y,z) = body
```

then substitute the corresponding parts of E's value for the pattern variables x, y
and z. (A practical implementation performs no substitutions, but instead binds
the formal parameters in the local environment.)

Consider how ML evaluates $sqr(sqr(sqr(2)))$. Of the three function calls, only
the innermost call has a value for the argument. So $sqr(sqr(sqr(2)))$ reduces to
$sqr(sqr(2 \times 2))$. The multiplication must now be evaluated, yielding $sqr(sqr(4))$.
Evaluating the inner call yields $sqr(4 \times 4)$, and so forth. Reductions are written
$sqr(sqr(4)) \Rightarrow sqr(4 \times 4)$. The full evaluation looks like this:

$$sqr(sqr(sqr(2))) \Rightarrow sqr(sqr(2 \times 2))$$
$$\Rightarrow sqr(sqr(4))$$

$$\Rightarrow sqr(4 \times 4)$$
$$\Rightarrow sqr(16)$$
$$\Rightarrow 16 \times 16$$
$$\Rightarrow 256$$

Now consider *zero*(*sqr*(*sqr*(*sqr*(2)))). The argument of *zero* is the expression evaluated above. It is evaluated but the value is ignored:

$$zero(sqr(sqr(sqr(2)))) \Rightarrow zero(sqr(sqr(2 \times 2)))$$

$$\vdots$$

$$\Rightarrow zero(256)$$
$$\Rightarrow 0$$

Such waste! Functions like *zero* are uncommon, but frequently a function's result does not depend on all of its arguments.

ML's evaluation rule is known as ***call-by-value*** because a function is always given its argument's value. It is not hard to see that call-by-value corresponds to the usual way we should perform a calculation on paper. Almost all programming languages adopt it. But perhaps we should look for an evaluation rule that reduces *zero*(*sqr*(*sqr*(*sqr*(2)))) to 0 in one step. Before such issues can be examined, we must have a look at recursion.

2.12   *Recursive functions under call-by-value*

The factorial function is a standard example of recursion. It includes a base case, $n = 0$, where evaluation stops.

```
fun fact n =
        if  n=0  then  1  else  n * fact(n-1);
> val fact = fn : int -> int
fact 7;
> 5040 : int
fact 35;
> 10333147966386144929666651337523200000000 : int
```

ML evaluates *fact*(4) as follows. The argument, 4, is substituted for *n* in the body, yielding

```
if  4 = 0  then  1  else  4 × fact(4 − 1)
```

Since $4 = 0$ is false, the conditional reduces to $4 \times fact(4 - 1)$. Then $4 - 1$ is selected, and the entire expression reduces to $4 \times fact(3)$. Figure 2.1 summarizes

Figure 2.1 *Evaluation of fact*(4)

$$fact(4) \Rightarrow 4 \times fact(4 - 1)$$
$$\Rightarrow 4 \times fact(3)$$
$$\Rightarrow 4 \times (3 \times fact(3 - 1))$$
$$\Rightarrow 4 \times (3 \times fact(2))$$
$$\Rightarrow 4 \times (3 \times (2 \times fact(2 - 1)))$$
$$\Rightarrow 4 \times (3 \times (2 \times fact(1)))$$
$$\Rightarrow 4 \times (3 \times (2 \times (1 \times fact(1 - 1))))$$
$$\Rightarrow 4 \times (3 \times (2 \times (1 \times fact(0))))$$
$$\Rightarrow 4 \times (3 \times (2 \times (1 \times 1)))$$
$$\Rightarrow 4 \times (3 \times (2 \times 1))$$
$$\Rightarrow 4 \times (3 \times 2)$$
$$\Rightarrow 4 \times 6$$
$$\Rightarrow 24$$

Figure 2.2 *Evaluation of facti*(4, 1)

$$facti(4, 1) \Rightarrow facti(4 - 1, 4 \times 1)$$
$$\Rightarrow facti(3, 4)$$
$$\Rightarrow facti(3 - 1, 3 \times 4)$$
$$\Rightarrow facti(2, 12)$$
$$\Rightarrow facti(2 - 1, 2 \times 12)$$
$$\Rightarrow facti(1, 24)$$
$$\Rightarrow facti(1 - 1, 1 \times 24)$$
$$\Rightarrow facti(0, 24)$$
$$\Rightarrow 24$$

---

the evaluation. The conditionals are not shown: they behave similarly apart from $n = 0$, when the conditional returns 1.

The evaluation of *fact*(4) exactly follows the mathematical definition of factorial: $0! = 1$, and $n! = n \times (n-1)!$ if $n > 0$. Could the execution of a recursive procedure be shown as succinctly?

Iterative functions. Something is odd about the computation of *fact*(4). As the recursion progresses, more and more numbers are waiting to be multiplied. The multiplications cannot take place until the recursion terminates with *fact*(0). At that point $4 \times (3 \times (2 \times (1 \times 1)))$ must be evaluated. This paper calculation shows that *fact* is wasting space.

A more efficient version can be found by thinking about how we should compute factorials. By the associative law, each multiplication can be done at once:

$$4 \times (3 \times fact(2)) = (4 \times 3) \times fact(2) = 12 \times fact(2)$$

The computer will not apply such laws unless we force it to. The function *facti* keeps a running product in p, which initially should be 1:

```
fun facti (n,p) =
        if n=0 then p  else   facti(n-1, n*p);
> val facti = fn : int * int -> int
```

Compare the evaluation for *facti*(4, 1), shown in Figure 2.2, with that of *fact*(4). The intermediate expressions stay small; each multiplication can be done at once; storage requirements remain constant. The evaluation is ***iterative*** — also termed ***tail recursive***. In Section 6.3 we shall prove that *facti* gives correct results by establishing the law $facti(n, p) = n! \times p$.

Good compilers detect iterative forms of recursion and execute them efficiently. The result of the recursive call *facti*$(n - 1, n \times p)$ undergoes no further computation, but is immediately returned as the value of *facti*(n, p). Such a ***tail call*** can be executed by assigning the arguments n and p their new values and then jumping back into the function, avoiding the cost of a proper function invocation. The recursive call in *fact* is not a tail call because its value undergoes further computation, namely multiplication by n.

Many functions can be made iterative by adding an argument, like p in *facti*. Sometimes the iterative function runs much faster. Sometimes, making a function iterative is the only way to avoid running out of store. However, adding an extra argument to every recursive function is a bad habit. It leads to ugly, convoluted code that might run slower than it should.

The special rôle of conditional expressions. The conditional expression permits definition by cases. Recall how the factorial function is defined:

$$0! = 1$$

$$n! = n \times (n-1)! \qquad \qquad \text{for } n > 0$$

These equations determine $n!$ for all integers $n \geq 0$. Omitting the condition $n > 0$ from the second equation would lead to absurdity:

$$1 = 0! = 0 \times (-1)! = 0$$

Similarly, in the conditional expression

```
if E then E₁ else E₂,
```

ML evaluates E_1 only if $E = true$, and evaluates E_2 only if $E = false$.

Due to call-by-value, there is no ML function *cond* such that $cond(E, E_1, E_2)$ is evaluated like a conditional expression. Let us try to declare one and use it to code the factorial function:

```
fun cond(p,x,y) : int = if p then x else y;
> val cond = fn : bool * int * int -> int
fun badf n = cond(n=0, 1, n*badf(n-1));
> val badf = fn : int -> int
```

This may look plausible, but every call to *badf* runs forever. Observe the evaluation of *badf*(0):

$$badf(0) \Rightarrow cond(true, 1, 0 \times badf(-1))$$

$$\Rightarrow cond(true, 1, 0 \times cond(false, 1, -1 \times badf(-2)))$$

$$\vdots$$

Although *cond* never requires the values of all three of its arguments, the call-by-value rule evaluates them all. The recursion cannot terminate.

Conditional and/or. ML's boolean infix operators `andalso` and `orelse` are not functions, but stand for conditional expressions.

The expression E_1 `andalso` E_2 abbreviates

```
if E₁ then E₂ else false.
```

The expression E_1 `orelse` E_2 abbreviates

```
if E₁ then true else E₂.
```

These operators compute the boolean and/or, but evaluate E_2 only if necessary. If they were functions, the call-by-value rule would evaluate both arguments. All other ML infixes are really functions.

The sequential evaluation of `andalso` and `orelse` makes them ideal for expressing recursive predicates (boolean-valued functions). The function *powoftwo* tests whether a number is a power of two:

```
fun even n  =   (n mod 2 = 0);
> val even = fn : int -> bool
fun powoftwo n =   (n=1)   orelse
                (even(n)   andalso powoftwo(n div 2));
> val powoftwo = fn : int -> bool
```

You might expect *powoftwo* to be defined by conditional expressions, and so it is, through `orelse` and `andalso`. Evaluation terminates once the outcome is decided:

$$powoftwo(6) \Rightarrow (6 = 1) \ \texttt{orelse} \ (even(6) \ \texttt{andalso} \ \cdots)$$
$$\Rightarrow even(6) \ \texttt{andalso} \ powoftwo(6 \, div \, 2)$$
$$\Rightarrow powoftwo(3)$$
$$\Rightarrow (3 = 1) \ \texttt{orelse} \ (even(3) \ \texttt{andalso} \ \cdots)$$
$$\Rightarrow even(3) \ \texttt{andalso} \ powoftwo(3 \, div \, 2)$$
$$\Rightarrow false$$

Exercise 2.10   Write the reduction steps for *powoftwo*(8).

Exercise 2.11   Is *powoftwo* an iterative function?

2.13   *Call-by-need, or lazy evaluation*

The call-by-value rule has accumulated a catalogue of complaints. It evaluates E superfluously in *zero*(E). And it evaluates $E1$ or $E2$ superfluously in *cond*(E, $E1$, $E2$). Conditional expressions and similar operations cannot be functions. ML provides `andalso` and `orelse`, but we have no means of defining similar things.

Shall we give functions their arguments as expressions, not as values? The general idea is this:

To compute the value of $f(E)$, substitute E immediately into the body of f.
Then compute the value of the resulting expression.

This is the ***call-by-name*** rule. It reduces $zero(sqr(sqr(sqr(2))))$ at once to 0. But it does badly by $sqr(sqr(sqr(2)))$. It duplicates the argument, $sqr(sqr(2))$. The result of this 'reduction' is

$$sqr(sqr(2)) \times sqr(sqr(2)).$$

This happens because $sqr(x) = x \times x$.

Multiplication, like other arithmetic operations, needs special treatment. It must be applied to values, not expressions: it is an example of a ***strict*** function. To evaluate $E_1 \times E_2$, the expressions E_1 and E_2 must be evaluated first.

Let us carry on with the evaluation. As the outermost function is $\times$, which is strict, the rule selects the leftmost call to sqr. Its argument is also duplicated:

$$(sqr(2) \times sqr(2)) \times sqr(sqr(2))$$

A full evaluation goes something like this.

$$
\begin{aligned}
sqr(sqr(sqr(2))) &\Rightarrow sqr(sqr(2)) \times sqr(sqr(2)) \\
&\Rightarrow (sqr(2) \times sqr(2)) \times sqr(sqr(2)) \\
&\Rightarrow ((2 \times 2) \times sqr(2)) \times sqr(sqr(2)) \\
&\Rightarrow (4 \times sqr(2)) \times sqr(sqr(2)) \\
&\Rightarrow (4 \times (2 \times 2)) \times sqr(sqr(2)) \\
&\quad \vdots
\end{aligned}
$$

Does it ever reach the answer? Eventually. But call-by-name cannot be the evaluation rule we want.

The ***call-by-need*** rule (lazy evaluation) is like call-by-name, but ensures that each argument is evaluated at most once. Rather than substituting an expression into the function's body, the occurrences of the argument are linked by pointers. If the argument is ever evaluated, the value will be shared with its other occurrences. The pointer structure forms a directed graph of functions and arguments. As a part of the graph is evaluated, it is updated by the resulting value. This is called ***graph reduction***.

Figure 2.3 presents a graph reduction. Every step replaces an occurrence of $sqr(E)$ by $E \times E$, where the two Es are shared. There is no wasteful duplication: only three multiplications are performed. We seem to have the best of both worlds, for $zero(E)$ reduces immediately to 0. But the graph manipulations are expensive.

Lazy evaluation of $cond(E, E_1, E_2)$ behaves like a conditional expression provided that its argument, the tuple (E, E_1, E_2), is itself evaluated lazily. The de-

Figure 2.3   *Graph reduction of sqr(sqr(sqr(2)))*

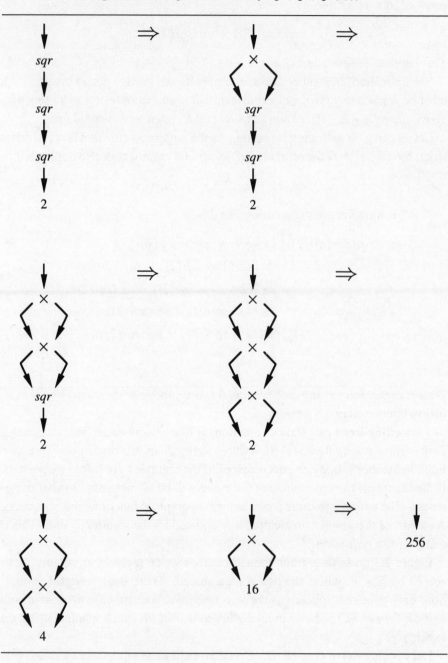

Figure 2.4 *A space leak with lazy evaluation*

$$
\begin{aligned}
facti(4, 1) &\Rightarrow facti(4 - 1, 4 \times 1) \\
&\Rightarrow facti(3 - 1, 3 \times (4 \times 1)) \\
&\Rightarrow facti(2 - 1, 2 \times (3 \times (4 \times 1))) \\
&\Rightarrow facti(1 - 1, 1 \times (2 \times (3 \times (4 \times 1)))) \\
&\Rightarrow 1 \times (2 \times (3 \times (4 \times 1))) \\
&\quad\vdots \\
&\Rightarrow 24
\end{aligned}
$$

---

tails of this are quite subtle: tuple formation must be viewed as a function. The idea that a data structure like (E, E_1, E_2) can be partially evaluated — either E_1 or E_2 but not both — leads to infinite lists.

A comparison of strict and lazy evaluation. Call-by-need does the least possible evaluation. It may seem like the route to efficiency. But it requires much book-keeping. Realistic implementations became possible only after David Turner (1979) applied graph reduction to **combinators**. He exploited obscure facts about the λ-calculus to develop new compilation techniques, which researchers continue to improve. Every new technology has its evangelists: some people are claiming that lazy evaluation is the way, the truth and the light. Why does Standard ML not adopt it?

Lazy evaluation says that $zero(E) = 0$ even if E fails to terminate. This flies in the face of mathematical tradition: an expression is meaningful only if all its parts are. Alonzo Church, the inventor of the λ-calculus, preferred a variant (the λI-calculus) banning constant functions like *zero*.

Infinite data structures complicate mathematical reasoning. To fully understand lazy evaluation, it is necessary to know some domain theory, as well as the theory of the λ-calculus. The output of a program is not simply a value, but a partially evaluated expression. These concepts are not easy to learn, and many of them are mechanistic. If we can only think in terms of the evaluation mechanism, we are no better off than the procedural programmers.

Efficiency is problematical too. Sometimes lazy evaluation saves enormous amounts of space; sometimes it wastes space. Recall that *facti* is more efficient than *fact* under strict evaluation, performing each multiplication at once. Lazy evaluation of *facti*(*n, p*) evaluates *n* immediately (for the test *n* = 0), but not *p*. The multiplications accumulate; we have a space leak (Figure 2.4).

Most lazy programming languages are purely functional. Can lazy evaluation be combined with commands, such as are used in ML to perform input/output? Subexpressions would be evaluated at unpredictable times; it would be impossible to write reliable programs. Much research has been directed at combining functional and imperative programming (Peyton Jones and Wadler, 1993).

Writing recursive functions

Since recursion is so fundamental to functional programming, let us take the time to examine a few recursive functions. There is no magic formula for program design, but perhaps it is possible to learn by example. One recursive function we have already seen implements Euclid's Algorithm:

```
fun gcd(m,n) =
      if m=0 then n
                else gcd(n mod m, m);
> val gcd = fn : int * int -> int
```

The Greatest Common Divisor of two integers is by definition the greatest integer that divides both. Euclid's Algorithm is correct because the divisors of *m* and *n* are the same as those of *m* and *n* − *m*, and, by repeated subtraction, the same as the divisors of *m* and *n* mod *m*. Regarding its efficiency, consider

$$gcd(5499,6812) \Rightarrow gcd(1313, 5499) \Rightarrow gcd(247, 1313)$$
$$\Rightarrow gcd(78, 247) \Rightarrow gcd(13, 78) \Rightarrow gcd(0, 13) \Rightarrow 13.$$

Euclid's Algorithm dates from antiquity. We seldom can draw on 2000 years of expertise, but we should aim for equally elegant and efficient solutions.

Recursion involves reducing a problem to smaller subproblems. The key to efficiency is to select the right subproblems. There must not be too many of them, and the rest of the computation should be reasonably simple.

2.14   *Raising to an integer power*

The obvious way to compute x^k is to multiply repeatedly by *x*. Using recursion, the problem x^k is reduced to the subproblem x^{k-1}. But x^{10} need not involve 10 multiplications. We can compute x^5 and then square it. Since $x^5 = x \times x^4$, we can compute x^4 by squaring also:

$$x^{10} = (x^5)^2 = (x \times x^4)^2 = (x \times (x^2)^2)^2$$

By exploiting the law $x^{2n} = (x^n)^2$ we have improved vastly over repeated multiplication. But the computation is still messy; using instead $x^{2n} = (x^2)^n$ eliminates the nested squaring:

$$2^{10} = 4^5 = 4 \times 16^2 = 4 \times 256^1 = 1024$$

By this approach, *power* computes x^k for real x and integer $k > 0$:

```
fun power(x,k) : real =
      if k=1 then x
      else if k mod 2 = 0 then      power(x*x, k div 2)
                          else x * power(x*x, k div 2);
> val power = fn : real * int -> real
```

Note how *mod* tests whether the exponent is even. Integer division (*div*) truncates its result to an integer if k is odd. The function *power* embodies the equations (for $n > 0$)

$$x^1 = x$$
$$x^{2n} = (x^2)^n$$
$$x^{2n+1} = x \times (x^2)^n.$$

We can test *power* using the built-in exponentiation function *Math.pow*:

```
power(2.0,10);
> 1024.0 : real
power(1.01, 925);
> 9937.353723 : real
Math.pow(1.01, 925.0);
> 9937.353723 : real
```

Reducing x^{2n} to $(x^2)^n$ instead of $(x^n)^2$ makes *power* iterative in its first recursive call. The second call (for odd exponents) can be made iterative only by introducing an argument to hold the result, which is a needless complication.

Exercise 2.12   Write the computation steps for *power*(2.0, 29).

Exercise 2.13   How many multiplications does *power*(x, k) need in the worst case?

Exercise 2.14   Why not take $k = 0$ for the base case instead of $k = 1$?

2.15   *Fibonacci numbers*

The Fibonacci sequence 0, 1, 1, 2, 3, 5, 8, 13, 21, 34, 55, ... , is popular with mathematical hobbyists because it enjoys many fascinating properties. The sequence (F_n) is defined by

$$F_0 = 0$$
$$F_1 = 1$$
$$F_n = F_{n-2} + F_{n-1}. \qquad \text{for } n \geq 2$$

The corresponding recursive function is a standard benchmark for measuring the efficiency of compiled code! It is far too slow for any other use because it computes subproblems repeatedly. For example, since

$$F_8 = F_6 + F_7 = F_6 + (F_5 + F_6),$$

it computes F_6 twice.

Each Fibonacci number is the sum of the previous two:

$$0 + 1 = 1 \quad 1 + 1 = 2 \quad 1 + 2 = 3 \quad 2 + 3 = 5 \quad 3 + 5 = 8 \cdots$$

So we should compute with pairs of numbers. Function *nextfib* takes (F_{n-1}, F_n) and returns the next pair (F_n, F_{n+1}).

```
fun nextfib (prev, curr :int) = (curr, prev+curr);
> val nextfib = fn : int * int -> int * int
```

The special name *it*, by referring to the previous pair, helps us demonstrate the function:

```
nextfib (0,1);
> (1, 1) : int * int
nextfib it;
> (1, 2) : int * int
nextfib it;
> (2, 3) : int * int
nextfib it;
> (3, 5) : int * int
```

Recursion applies *nextfib* the requisite number of times:

```
fun fibpair (n) =
        if n=1 then  (0,1)  else  nextfib (fibpair (n-1));
> val fibpair = fn : int -> int * int
```

It quickly computes (F_{29}, F_{30}), which previously would have required nearly three million function calls:

```
fibpair 30;
> (514229, 832040) : int * int
```

Let us consider in detail why *fibpair* is correct. Clearly $fibpair(1) = (F_0, F_1)$. And if, for $n \geq 1$, we have

$$fibpair(n) = (F_{n-1}, F_n),$$

then

$$fibpair(n + 1) = (F_n, F_{n-1} + F_n) = (F_n, F_{n+1}).$$

We have just seen a proof of the formula $fibpair(n) = (F_{n-1}, F_n)$ by **mathematical induction**. We shall see many more examples of such proofs in Chapter 6. Proving properties of functional programs is often straightforward; this is one of the main advantages of functional languages.

The function *fibpair* uses a correct and fairly efficient algorithm for computing Fibonacci numbers, and it illustrates computing with pairs. But its pattern of recursion wastes space: *fibpair* builds the nest of calls

$$nextfib(nextfib(\cdots nextfib(0, 1) \cdots)).$$

To make the algorithm iterative, let us turn the computation inside out:

```
fun itfib (n, prev, curr) : int =
    if n=1 then curr          (*does not work for n=0*)
    else itfib (n-1, curr, prev+curr);
> val itfib = fn : int * int * int -> int
```

The function *fib* calls *itfib* with correct initial arguments:

```
fun fib (n)  =  itfib(n,0,1);
> val fib = fn : int -> int
fib 30;
> 832040 : int
fib 100;
> 354224848179261915075 : int
```

For Fibonacci numbers, iteration is clearer than recursion:

$$itfib(7, 0, 1) \Rightarrow itfib(6, 1, 1) \Rightarrow \cdots itfib(1, 8, 13) \Rightarrow 13$$

In Section 6.3 we shall show that *itfib* is correct by proving the rather unusual law $itfib(n, F_k, F_{k+1}) = F_{k+n}$.

Exercise 2.15 How is the repeated computation in the recursive definition of F_n related to the call-by-name rule? Could lazy evaluation execute this definition efficiently?

Exercise 2.16   Show that the number of steps needed to compute F_n by its recursive definition is exponential in n. How many steps does *fib* perform? Assume that call-by-value is used.

Exercise 2.17   What is the value of *itfib*(n, F_{k-1}, F_k)?

2.16   *Integer square roots*

The integer square root of n is the integer k such that

$$k^2 \le n < (k+1)^2.$$

To compute this by recursion, we must choose a subproblem: an integer smaller than n. Division by 2 is often helpful, but how can we obtain $\sqrt{2x}$ from $\sqrt{x}$? Observe that $\sqrt{4x} = 2\sqrt{x}$ (for real x); division by 4 may lead to a simple algorithm.

Suppose $n > 0$. Since n may not be exactly divisible by 4, write $n = 4m + r$, where $r = 0, 1, 2,$ or 3. Since $m < n$ we can recursively find the integer square root of m:

$$i^2 \le m < (i+1)^2.$$

Since m and i are integers, $m+1 \le (i+1)^2$. Multiplication by 4 implies $4i^2 \le 4m$ and $4(m+1) \le 4(i+1)^2$. Therefore

$$(2i)^2 \le 4m \le n < 4m + 4 \le (2i+2)^2.$$

The square root of n is $2i$ or $2i + 1$. There is only to test whether $(2i+1)^2 \le n$, determining whether a 1 should be added.

```
fun increase(k,n) = if (k+1)*(k+1) > n then k else k+1;
> val increase = fn : int * int -> int
```

The recursion terminates when $n = 0$. Repeated integer division will reduce any number to 0 eventually:

```
fun introot n =
       if n=0 then 0 else increase(2 * introot(n div 4), n);
> val introot = fn : int -> int
```

There are faster methods of computing square roots, but ours is respectably fast and is a simple demonstration of recursion.

```
introot 123456789;
> 11111 : int
it*it;
> 123454321 : int
introot 20000000000000000000000000000000;
> 141421356237309 : int
it*it;
> 19999999999999998619679798790025 : int
```

Exercise 2.18   Code this integer square root algorithm using iteration in a procedural programming language.

Exercise 2.19   Declare an ML function for computing the Greatest Common Divisor, based on these equations (m and n range over positive integers):

$$GCD(2m, 2n) = 2 \times GCD(m, n)$$
$$GCD(2m, 2n + 1) = GCD(m, 2n + 1)$$
$$GCD(2m + 1, 2n + 1) = GCD(n - m, 2m + 1) \qquad m < n$$
$$GCD(m, m) = m.$$

How does this compare with Euclid's Algorithm?

Local declarations

Reducing the fraction n/d to least terms, where n and d have no common factor, involves dividing both numbers by their GCD.

```
fun fraction (n,d) = (n div gcd(n,d), d div gcd(n,d));
```

The wasteful re-computation of $gcd(n, d)$ can be prevented by first defining an auxiliary function:

```
fun divideboth (n, d, com: int) = (n div com, d div com);
fun fraction (n,d) = divideboth (n, d, gcd(n,d));
```

But this is a contorted way of giving $gcd(n, d)$ the name *com*. ML allows the declaration of names within an expression:

```
fun fraction (n,d) =
    let val com = gcd(n,d)
    in  (n div com, d div com)  end;
> val fraction = fn : int * int -> int * int
```

We have used a `let` expression, which has the general form

```
let D in E end
```

During evaluation, the declaration *D* is evaluated first: expressions within the declaration are evaluated, and their results given names. The environment thus created is visible only inside the `let` expression. Then the expression *E* is evaluated, and its value returned.

Typically *D* is a compound declaration, which consists of a list of declarations:

$$D_1; D_2; \ldots ; D_n$$

The effect of each declaration is visible in subsequent ones. The semicolons are optional and many programmers omit them.

2.17   *Example: real square roots*

The Newton-Raphson method finds roots of a function: in other words, it solves equations of the form $f(x) = 0$. Given a good initial approximation, it converges rapidly. It is highly effective for computing square roots, solving the equation $a - x^2 = 0$. To compute $\sqrt{a}$, choose any positive x_0, say 1, as the first approximation. If x is the current approximation then the next approximation is $(a/x + x)/2$. Stop as soon as the difference becomes small enough.

The function *findroot* performs this computation, where *x* approximates the square root of *a* and *acc* is the desired accuracy (relative to *x*). Since the next approximation is used several times, it is given the name *nextx* using `let`.

```
fun findroot (a, x, acc) =
    let val nextx = (a/x + x) / 2.0
    in  if abs (x-nextx) < acc*x
            then  nextx  else  findroot (a, nextx, acc)
    end;
> val findroot = fn : (real * real * real) -> real
```

The function *sqroot* calls *findroot* with suitable starting values.

```
fun sqroot a = findroot (a, 1.0, 1.0E~10);
> val sqroot = fn : real -> real
sqroot 2.0;
> 1.414213562 : real
it*it;
> 2.0 : real
```

Nested function declarations. Our square root function is still not ideal. The arguments *a* and *acc* are passed unchanged in every recursive call of *findroot*. They can be made global to *findroot* for efficiency and clarity.

A further `let` declaration nests *findroot* within *sqroot*. The accuracy *acc* is declared first, to be visible in *findroot*; the argument *a* is also visible.

```
fun sqroot a =
    let val acc = 1.0E~10
        fun findroot x =
            let val nextx = (a/x + x) / 2.0
            in  if abs (x–nextx) < acc*x
                then  nextx  else  findroot nextx
            end
    in  findroot 1.0  end;
> val sqroot = fn : real -> real
```

As we see from ML's response, *findroot* is not visible outside *sqroot*.

Most kinds of declaration are permitted within `let`. Values, functions, types and exceptions may be declared.

When not to use `let`. Consider taking the minimum of $f(x)$ and $g(x)$. You could name these quantities using `let`:

```
let val a = f x
    val b = g x
in
    if a<b then a else b
end
```

Better, declare a function for the minimum of two real numbers:

```
fun min(a,b) : real =  if a<b then a else b;
```

Now *min* (*f* x, *g* x) is clear because *min* computes something familiar. Take every opportunity to declare meaningful functions, even if they are only needed once.

2.18   *Hiding declarations using* `local`

A `local` declaration resembles a `let` expression:

```
local D₁ in D₂ end
```

This declaration behaves like the list of declarations D_1; D_2 except that D_1 is visible only within D_2, not outside. Since a list of declarations is regarded as one declaration, both D_1 and D_2 can declare any number of names.

While `let` is frequently used, `local` is not. Its sole purpose is to hide a declaration. Recall *itfib* and *fib*, which compute Fibonacci numbers. The function *itfib* should be called only from *fib*:

```
local
    fun itfib (n, prev, curr) : int =
            if n=1 then curr
            else itfib (n-1, curr, prev+curr)
in
    fun fib (n) = itfib(n,0,1)
end;
> val fib = fn : int -> int
```

Here the `local` declaration makes *itfib* private to *fib*.

Exercise 2.20   Above we have used `local` to hide the function *itfib*. Why not simply nest the declaration of *itfib* within *fib*? Compare with the treatment of *findroot* and *sqroot*.

Exercise 2.21   Using `let`, we can eliminate the expensive squaring operation in our integer square root function. Code a variant of *introot* that maps n to its integer square root k, paired with the difference $n - k^2$. Only simple multiplications and divisions are needed; an optimizing compiler could replace them by bit operations.

2.19   *Simultaneous declarations*

A simultaneous declaration defines several names at once. Normally the declarations are independent. But `fun` declarations allow recursion, so a simultaneous declaration can introduce mutually recursive functions.

A `val` declaration of the form

$$\text{val } Id_1 = E_1 \text{ and } \cdots \text{ and } Id_n = E_n$$

evaluates the expressions $E_1, \ldots, E_n$ and then declares the identifiers $Id_1, \ldots, Id_n$ to have the corresponding values. Since the declarations do not take effect until all the expressions are evaluated, their order is immaterial.

Here we declare names for π, e and the logarithm of 2.

```
val pi   = 4.0 * Math.atan 1.0
and e    = Math.exp 1.0
and log2 = Math.ln 2.0;
> pi = 3.141592654 : real
> e = 2.718281828 : real
> log2 = 0.693147806 : real
```

A single input declares three names. The simultaneous declaration emphasizes that they are independent.

Now let us declare the chimes of Big Ben:

```
val one = "BONG ";
> val one = "BONG " : string
val three = one^one^one;
> val three = "BONG BONG BONG " : string
val five = three^one^one;
> val five = "BONG BONG BONG BONG BONG " : string
```

There must be three separate declarations, and in this order.

A simultaneous declaration can also swap the values of names:

```
val one = three and three = one;
> val one = "BONG BONG BONG " : string
> val three = "BONG " : string
```

This is, of course, a silly thing to do! But it illustrates that the declarations occur at the same time. Consecutive declarations would give *one* and *three* identical bindings.

Mutually recursive functions. Several functions are **mutually recursive** if they are declared recursively in terms of each other. A recursive descent parser is a typical case. This sort of parser has one function for each element of the grammar, and most grammars are mutually recursive: an ML declaration can contain expressions, while an expression can contain declarations. Functions to traverse the resulting parse tree will also be mutually recursive.

Parsing and trees are discussed later in this book. For a simpler example, consider summing the series

$$\frac{\pi}{4} = 1 - \frac{1}{3} + \frac{1}{5} - \frac{1}{7} \cdots + \frac{1}{4k+1} - \frac{1}{4k+3} \cdots$$

By mutual recursion, the final term of the summation can be either positive or negative:

```
fun pos d = neg(d-2.0) + 1.0/d
and neg d = if d>0.0 then pos(d-2.0) - 1.0/d
                      else 0.0;
> val pos = fn : real -> real
> val neg = fn : real -> real
```

Two functions are declared. The series converges leisurely:

```
4.0 * pos(201.0);
> 3.151493401
4.0 * neg(8003.0);
> 3.141342779
```

Mutually recursive functions can often be combined into one function with the help of an additional argument:

```
fun sum(d,one) =
    if d>0.0 then sum(d-2.0, ~one) + one/d else 0.0;
```

Now $sum(d, 1.0)$ returns the same value as $pos(d)$, and $sum(d, {\sim}1.0)$ returns the same value as

$neg(d)$.

Emulating goto statements. Functional programming and procedural programming are more alike than you may imagine. Any combination of goto and assignment statements — the worst of procedural code — can be translated into a set of mutually recursive functions. Here is a simple case:

```
var x := 0;  y := 0;  z := 0;
F:  x := x+1; goto G
G:  if y<z then goto F  else  (y := x+y;  goto H)
H:  if z>0 then (z := z-x;  goto F)  else  stop
```

For each of the labels, F, G and H, declare mutually recursive functions. The argument of each function is a tuple holding all of the variables.

```
fun F(x,y,z) = G(x+1,y,z)
and G(x,y,z) = if y<z then F(x,y,z)  else  H(x,x+y,z)
and H(x,y,z) = if z>0 then F(x,y,z-x)  else  (x,y,z);
> val F = fn : int * int * int -> int * int * int
> val G = fn : int * int * int -> int * int * int
> val H = fn : int * int * int -> int * int * int
```

Calling $f(0, 0, 0)$ gives x, y and z their initial values for execution, and returns the result of the procedural code.

```
f(0,0,0);
> (1, 1, 0) : int * int * int
```

Functional programs are referentially transparent, yet can be totally opaque. If your code starts to look like this, beware!

Exercise 2.22   What is the effect of this declaration?

```
val (pi,log2) = (log2,pi);
```

Exercise 2.23   Consider the sequence (P_n) defined for $n \geq 1$ by

$$P_n = 1 + \sum_{k=1}^{n-1} P_k.$$

(In particular, $P_1 = 1$.) Express this computation as an ML function. How efficient is it? Is there a faster way of computing P_n?

Introduction to modules

An engineer understands a device in terms of its component parts, and those, similarly, in terms of their subcomponents. A bicycle has wheels; a wheel has a hub; a hub has bearings, and so forth. It takes several stages before we reach the level of individual pieces of metal and plastic. In this way one can understand the entire bike at an abstract level, or parts of it in detail. The engineer can improve the design by modifying one part, often without thinking about the other parts.

Programs (which are more complicated than bicycles!) should also be seen as consisting of components. Traditionally, a subprogram is a procedure or function, but these are too small — it is like regarding the bicycle as composed of thousands of metal shapes. Many recent languages regard programs as consisting of *modules*, each of which defines its own data structures and associated operations. The interface to each module is specified separately from the module itself. Different modules can therefore be coded by different members of a project team; the compiler can check that each module meets its interface specification.

Consider our vector example. The function *addvec* is useless in isolation; it must be used together with other vector operations, all sharing the same representation of vectors. We can guess that the other operations are related because their names all end with *vec*, but nothing enforces this naming convention. They should be combined together to form a program module.

An ML *structure* combines related types, values and other structures, with a uniform naming discipline. An ML *signature* specifies a class of structures by listing the name and type (or other attributes) of each component.

Standard ML's signatures and structures have analogues in other languages, such as Modula-2's definition and implementation modules (Wirth, 1985). ML also provides *functors* — structures taking other structures as parameters — but we shall defer these until Chapter 7.

2.20   *The complex numbers*

Many types of mathematical object can be added, subtracted, multiplied and divided. Besides the familiar integer and real numbers, there are the rational numbers, matrices, polynomials, etc. Our example below will be the complex numbers, which are important in scientific mathematics. We shall gather up their arithmetic operations using a structure *Complex*, then declare a signature for *Complex* that also matches any structure that defines the same arithmetic operations. This will provide a basis for generic arithmetic.

We start with a quick introduction to the complex numbers. A **complex number** has the form $x + iy$, where x and y are real numbers and i is a constant postulated to satisfy $i^2 = -1$. Thus, x and y determine the complex number.

The complex number zero is $0 + i0$. The sum of two complex numbers consists of the sums of the x and y parts; the difference is similar. The definitions of product and reciprocal look complicated, but are easy to justify using algebraic laws and the axiom $i^2 = -1$:

$$(x + iy) + (x' + iy') = (x + x') + i(y + y')$$
$$(x + iy) - (x' + iy') = (x - x') + i(y - y')$$
$$(x + iy) \times (x' + iy') = (xx' - yy') + i(xy' + x'y)$$
$$1/(x + iy) = (x - iy)/(x^2 + y^2)$$

In the reciprocal above, the y component is $-y/(x^2 + y^2)$. We can now define the complex quotient z/z' as $z \times (1/z')$.

By analogy with our vector example, we could implement the complex numbers by definitions such as

```
type complex = real*real;
val complexzero = (0.0, 0.0);
```
$\vdots$

but it is better to use a structure.

> **ⓘ** *Further reading.* Penrose (1989) explains the complex number system in more detail, with plenty of motivation and examples. He discusses the connections between the complex numbers and fractals, including a definition of the Mandelbrot set. Later in the book, the complex numbers play a central rôle in his discussion of quantum mechanics. Penrose gives the complex numbers a metaphysical significance; that might be taken with a pinch of salt! Feynman *et al.* (1963) give a more technical but marvellously enjoyable description of the complex numbers in Chapter 22.

2.21   *Structures*

Declarations can be grouped to form a structure by enclosing them in the keywords `struct` and `end`. The result can be bound to an ML identifier using a `structure` declaration:

```
structure Complex =
  struct
  type t    = real*real;
  val zero  = (0.0, 0.0);
  fun sum   ((x,y),  (x′,y′))  =  (x+x′,  y+y′)  : t;
  fun diff  ((x,y),  (x′,y′))  =  (x-x′,  y-y′)  : t;
  fun prod  ((x,y),  (x′,y′))  =  (x*x′ - y*y′,  x*y′ + x′*y)  : t;
  fun recip (x,y)             =
                                let val t = x*x + y*y
                                in   (x/t,  ~y/t)   end
  fun quo    (z,z′)           = prod(z,  recip z′);
  end;
```

Where structure *Complex* is visible, its components are known by compound names such as *Complex . zero* and *Complex . sum*. Inside the structure body, the components are known by their ordinary identifiers, such as *zero* and *sum*; note the use of *recip* in the declaration of *quo*. The type of complex numbers is called *Complex . t*. When the purpose of a structure is to define a type, that type is commonly called *t*.

We may safely use short names. They cannot clash with names occurring in other structures. The standard library exploits this heavily, for example to distinguish the absolute value functions *Int . abs* and *Real . abs*.

Let us experiment with our new structure. We declare two ML identifiers, *i* and *a*; a mathematician would normally write their values as *i* and 0.3, respectively.

```
val i = (0.0, 1.0);
> val i = (0.0, 1.0) : real * real
val a = (0.3, 0.0);
> val a = (0.3, 0.0) : real * real
```

In two steps we form the sum $a + i + 0.7$, which equals $1 + i$. Finally we square that number to obtain $2i$:

```
val b = Complex.sum(a,i);
> val b = (0.3, 1.0) : Complex.t
Complex.sum(b, (0.7, 0.0));
> (1.0, 1.0) : Complex.t
Complex.prod(it,it);
> (0.0, 2.0) : Complex.t
```

Observe that *Complex . t* is the same type as *real* × *real*; what is more confusing, it is the same type as *vec* above. Chapter 7 describes how to declare an ***abstract type***, whose internal representation is hidden.

Structures look a bit like records, but there are major differences. A record's components can only be values (including, perhaps, other records). A structure's components may include types and exceptions (as well as other structures). But you cannot compute with structures: they can only be created when the program modules are being linked together. Structures should be seen as encapsulated environments.

2.22   *Signatures*

A signature is a description of each component of a structure. ML responds to our declaration of the structure *Complex* by printing its view of the corresponding signature:

```
structure Complex = ... ;
> structure Complex :
>   sig
>   type t
>   val diff  : (real * real) * (real * real) -> t
>   val prod  : (real * real) * (real * real) -> t
>   val quo   : (real * real) * (real * real) -> t
>   val recip : real * real -> real * real
>   val sum   : (real * real) * (real * real) -> t
>   val zero  : real * real
>   end
```

The keywords `sig` and `end` enclose the signature body. It shows the types of all the components that are values, and mentions the type t. (Some compilers display `eqtype t` instead of `type t`, informing us that t is a so-called equality type.)

The signature inferred by the ML compiler is frequently not the best one for our purposes. The structure may contain definitions that ought to be kept private. By declaring our own signature and omitting the private names, we can hide them from users of the structure. We might, for instance, hide the name *recip*.

The signature printed above expresses the type of complex numbers sometimes as t and sometimes as *real* × *real*. If we use t everywhere, then we obtain a general signature that specifies a type t equipped with operators *sum*, *prod*, etc.:

```
signature ARITH =
   sig
   type t
   val zero : t
   val sum : t * t -> t
   val diff : t * t -> t
   val prod : t * t -> t
   val quo  : t * t -> t
   end;
```

The declaration gives the name *ARITH* to the signature enclosed within the brackets `sig` and `end`. We can declare other structures and make them conform to signature *ARITH*. Here is the skeleton of a structure for the rational numbers:

```
structure Rational : ARITH =
  struct
  type t   = int*int;
  val zero = (0, 1);
    ⋮
  end;
```

A signature specifies the information that ML needs to integrate program units safely. It cannot specify what the components actually do. A well-documented signature includes comments describing the purpose of each component. Comments describing a component's implementation belong in the structure, not in the signature. Signatures can be combined in various ways to form new signatures; structures can similarly be combined.

ML functors can express generic modules: for example, ones that take any structure conforming to signature *ARITH*. The standard library offers extensive possibilities for this. An ML system may provide floating point numbers in various precisions, as structures matching signature *FLOAT*. A numerical algorithm can be coded as a functor. Applying the functor to a floating point structure specializes the algorithm to the desired precision. ML thus has some of the power of object-oriented languages such as C++ — though in a more restrictive form, since structures are not computable values.

Exercise 2.24   Declare a structure *Real*, matching signature *ARITH*, such that *Real . t* is the type *real* and the components *zero*, *sum*, *prod*, etc., denote the corresponding operations on type *real*.

Exercise 2.25   Complete the declaration of structure *Rational* above, basing your definitions on the laws $n/d + n'/d' = (nd' + n'd)/dd'$, $(n/d) \times (n'/d') = nn'/dd'$, and $1/(n/d) = d/n$. Use the function *gcd* to maintain the fractions in lowest terms, and ensure that the denominator is always positive.

Polymorphic type checking

Until recently, the debate on type checking has been deadlocked, with two rigid positions:

- Weakly typed languages like Lisp and Prolog give programmers the freedom they need when writing large programs.

- Strongly typed languages like Pascal give programmers security by restricting their freedom to make mistakes.

Polymorphic type checking offers a new position: the security of strong type checking, as well as great flexibility. Programs are not cluttered with type specifications since most type information is deduced automatically.

A type denotes a collection of values. A function's argument type specifies which values are acceptable as arguments. The result type specifies which values could be returned as results. Thus, *div* demands a pair of integers as argument; its result can only be an integer. If the divisor is zero then there will be no result at all: an error will be signalled instead. Even in this exceptional situation, the function *div* is faithful to its type.

ML can also assign a type to the identity function, which returns its argument unchanged. Because the identity function can be applied to an argument of any type, it is ***polymorphic***. Generally speaking, an object is polymorphic if it can be regarded as having multiple types. ML polymorphism is based on ***type schemes***, which are like patterns or templates for types. For instance, the identity function has the type scheme $\alpha \rightarrow \alpha$.

2.23   *Type inference*

Given little or no explicit type information, ML can infer all the types involved with a function declaration. Type inference follows a natural but rigorous procedure. ML notes the types of any constants, and applies type checking rules for each form of expression. Each variable must have the same type everywhere in the declaration. The type of each overloaded operator (like +) must be determined from the context.

Here is the type checking rule for the conditional expression. If E has type *bool* and E_1 and E_2 have the same type, say τ, then

```
if E then E₁ else E₂
```

also has type τ. Otherwise, the expression is ill-typed.

Let us examine, step by step, the type checking of *facti*:

```
fun facti (n,p) =
        if n=0 then p  else  facti(n-1, n*p);
```

The constants 0 and 1 have type *int*. Therefore $n=0$ and $n-1$ involve integers, so n has type *int*. Now $n*p$ must be integer multiplication, so p has type *int*. Since p is returned as the result of *facti*, its result type is *int* and its argument type is *int* × *int*. This fits with the recursive call. Having made all these checks, ML can respond

```
> val facti = fn : int * int -> int
```

If the types are not consistent, the compiler rejects the declaration.

Exercise 2.26 Describe the steps in the type checking of *itfib*.

Exercise 2.27 Type check the following function declaration:

```
fun f (k,m) = if k=0 then 1 else f(k-1);
```

2.24 *Polymorphic function declarations*

If type inference leaves some types completely unconstrained then the declaration is polymorphic — literally, 'having many forms.' Most polymorphic functions involve pairs, lists and other data structures. They usually do something simple, like pairing a value with itself:

```
fun pairself x = (x,x);
> val pairself = fn : 'a -> 'a * 'a
```

This type is polymorphic because it contains a ***type variable***, namely ′a. In ML, type variables begin with a prime (single quote) character.

```
'b        'c       'we_band_of_brothers        '3
```

Let us write α, β, γ for the ML type variables ′a, ′b, ′c, because type variables are traditionally Greek letters. Write $x : \tau$ to mean 'x has type τ,' for instance *pairself* : $\alpha \rightarrow (\alpha \times \alpha)$. Incidentally, × has higher precedence than →; the type of *pairself* can be written $\alpha \rightarrow \alpha \times \alpha$.

A polymorphic type is a type scheme. Substituting types for type variables forms an ***instance*** of the scheme. A value whose type is polymorphic has infinitely many types. When *pairself* is applied to a real number, it effectively has type *real* → *real* × *real*.

```
pairself 4.0;
> (4.0, 4.0) : real * real
```

Applied to an integer, *pairself* effectively has type *int* → *int* × *int*.

```
pairself 7;
> (7, 7) : int * int
```

Here *pairself* is applied to a pair; the result is called *pp*.

```
val pp = pairself ("Help!",999);
> val pp = (("Help!", 999), ("Help!", 999))
> : (string * int) * (string * int)
```

Projection functions return a component of a pair. The function *fst* returns the first component; *snd* returns the second:

```
fun fst (x,y) = x;
> val fst = fn : 'a * 'b -> 'a
fun snd (x,y) = y;
> val snd = fn : 'a * 'b -> 'b
```

Before considering their polymorphic types, we apply them to *pp*:

```
fst pp;
> ("Help!", 999) : string * int
snd (fst pp);
> 999 : int
```

The type of *fst* is $\alpha \times \beta \to \alpha$, with two type variables. The argument pair may involve any two types τ_1 and τ_2 (not necessarily different); the result has type τ_1.

Polymorphic functions can express other functions. The function that takes $((x, y), w)$ to x could be coded directly, but two applications of *fst* also work:

```
fun fstfst z = fst (fst z);
> val fstfst = fn : ('a * 'b) * 'c -> 'a
fstfst pp;
> "Help!" : string
```

The type $(\alpha \times \beta) \times \gamma \to \alpha$ is what we should expect for *fstfst*. Note that a polymorphic function can have different types within the same expression. The inner *fst* has type $(\alpha \times \beta) \times \gamma \to \alpha \times \beta$; the outer *fst* has type $\alpha \times \beta \to \alpha$.

Now for something obscure: what does this function do?

```
fun silly x = fstfst (pairself (pairself x));
> val silly = fn : 'a -> 'a
```

Not very much:

```
silly "Hold off your hands.";
> "Hold off your hands." : string
```

Its type, $\alpha \to \alpha$, suggests that *silly* is the identity function. This function can be expressed rather more directly:

```
fun I x = x;
> val I = fn : 'a -> 'a
```

> *Further issues.* Milner (1978) gives an algorithm for polymorphic type checking and proves that a type-correct program cannot suffer a run-time type er-

ror. Damas and Milner (1982) prove that the types inferred by this algorithm are ***principal***: they are as polymorphic as possible. Cardelli and Wegner (1985) survey several approaches to polymorphism. For Standard ML, things are quite complicated.

Equality testing is polymorphic in a limited sense: it is defined for most, not all, types. Standard ML provides a class of ***equality type variables*** to range over this restricted collection of types. See Section 3.14.

Recall that certain built-in functions are overloaded: addition (+) is defined for integers and reals, for instance. Overloading sits uneasily with polymorphism. It complicates the type checking algorithm and frequently forces programmers to write type constraints. Fortunately there are only a few overloaded functions. Programmers cannot introduce further overloading.

Summary of main points
- A variable stands for a value; it can be redeclared but not updated.
- Basic values have type *int*, *real*, *char*, *string* or *bool*.
- Values of any types can be combined to form tuples and records.
- Numerical operations can be expressed as recursive functions.
- An iterative function employs recursion in a limited fashion, where recursive calls are essentially jumps.
- Structures and signatures serve to organize large programs.
- A polymorphic type is a scheme containing type variables.

3

Lists

In a public lecture, C. A. R. Hoare (1989a) described his algorithm for finding the ith smallest integer in a collection. This algorithm is subtle, but Hoare described it with admirable clarity as a game of solitaire. Each playing card carried an integer. Moving cards from pile to pile by simple rules, the required integer could quickly be found.

Then Hoare changed the rules of the game. Each card occupied a fixed position, and could only be moved if exchanged with another card. This described the algorithm in terms of arrays. Arrays have great efficiency, but they also have a cost. They probably defeated much of the audience, as they defeat experienced programmers. Mills and Linger (1986) claim that programmers become more productive when arrays are restricted to stacks, queues, etc., without subscripting.

Functional programmers often process collections of items using lists. Like Hoare's stacks of cards, lists allow items to be dealt with one at a time, with great clarity. Lists are easy to understand mathematically, and turn out to be more efficient than commonly thought.

Chapter outline

This chapter describes how to program with lists in Standard ML. It presents several examples that would normally involve arrays, such as matrix operations and sorting.

The chapter contains the following sections:

Introduction to lists. The notion of list is introduced. Standard ML operates on lists using pattern-matching.

Some fundamental list functions. A family of functions is presented. These are instructive examples of list programming, and are indispensable when tackling harder problems.

Applications of lists. Some increasingly complicated examples illustrate the variety of problems that can be solved using lists.

The equality test in polymorphic functions. Equality polymorphism is introduced and demonstrated with many examples. These include a useful collection of functions on finite sets.

Sorting: A case study. Procedural programming and functional programming are compared in efficiency. In one experiment, a procedural program runs only slightly faster than a much clearer functional program.

Polynomial arithmetic. Computers can solve algebraic problems. Lists are used to add, multiply and divide polynomials in symbolic form.

Introduction to lists

A *list* is a finite sequence of elements. Typical lists are [3,5,9] and ["fair","Ophelia"]. The empty list, [], has no elements. The order of elements is significant, and elements may appear more than once. For instance, the following lists are all different:

        [3,4]   [4,3]   [3,4,3]   [3,3,4]

The elements of a list may have any type, including tuples and even other lists. Every element of a list must have the same type. Suppose this type is τ; the type of the list is then τ *list*. Thus

```
    [(1,"One"), (2,"Two"), (3,"Three")] : (int*string) list
    [ [3.1], [], [5.7, ~0.6] ]          : (real list) list
```

The empty list, [], has the polymorphic type α *list*. It can be regarded as having any type of elements.

Observe that the type operator *list* has a postfix syntax. It binds more tightly than $\times$ and $\rightarrow$. So *int* $\times$ *string list* is the same type as *int* $\times$ (*string list*), not (*int* $\times$ *string*)*list*. Also, *int list list* is the same type as (*int list*)*list*.

3.1   *Building a list*

Every list is constructed by just two primitives: the constant *nil* and the infix operator ::, pronounced 'cons' for 'construct.'

- *nil* is a synonym for the empty list, [].
- The operator :: makes a list by putting an element in front of an existing list.

Every list is either *nil*, if empty, or has the form $x :: l$ where x is its **head** and l its **tail**. The tail is itself a list. The list operations are not symmetric: the first element of a list is much more easily reached than the last.

If l is the list $[x_1, \dots, x_n]$ and x is a value of correct type then $x :: l$ is the list $[x, x_1, \dots, x_n]$. Making the new list does not affect the value of l. The list

[3, 5, 9] is constructed as follows:

$$nil = []$$
$$9 :: [] = [9]$$
$$5 :: [9] = [5, 9]$$
$$3 :: [5, 9] = [3, 5, 9]$$

Observe that the elements are taken in reverse order. The list [3, 5, 9] can be written in many ways, such as $3 :: (5 :: (9 :: nil))$, or $3 :: (5 :: [9])$, or $3 :: [5, 9]$. To save writing parentheses, the infix operator 'cons' groups to the right. The notation $[x_1, x_2, \ldots, x_n]$ stands for $x_1 :: x_2 :: \cdots :: x_n :: nil$. The elements may be given by expressions; a list of the values of various real expressions is

```
[ Math.sin 0.5, Math.cos 0.5, Math.exp 0.5 ];
> [0.479425539, 0.877582562, 1.64872127] : real list
```

List notation makes a list with a fixed number of elements. Consider how to build the list of integers from m to n:

$$[m, m + 1, \ldots, n]$$

First compare m and n. If $m > n$ then there are no numbers between m and n; the list is empty. Otherwise the head of the list is m and the tail is $[m + 1, \ldots, n]$. Constructing the tail recursively, the result is obtained by

$$m :: [m + 1, \ldots, n].$$

This process corresponds to a simple ML function:

```
fun upto (m,n) =
    if m>n then []  else  m :: upto(m+1,n);
> val upto = fn : int * int -> int list
upto(2,5);
> [2, 3, 4, 5] : int list
```

ℹ️ *Lists in other languages.* Weakly typed languages like Lisp and Prolog represent lists by pairing, as in (3, (5, (9, "nil"))). Here "nil" is some end marker and the list is [3, 5, 9]. This representation of lists does not work in ML because the type of a 'list' would depend on the number of elements. What type could *upto* have?

ML's syntax for lists differs subtly from Prolog's. In Prolog, [5 | [6]] is the same list as [5, 6]. In ML, [5::[6]] is the same list as [[5,6]].

3.2   Operating on a list

Lists, like tuples, are structured values. In ML, a function on tuples can be written with a pattern for its argument, showing its structure and naming the components. Functions over lists can be written similarly. For example,

```
fun prodof3 [i,j,k] : int = i*j*k;
```

declares a function to take the product of a list of numbers — but only if there are exactly three of them!

List operations are usually defined by recursion, treating several cases. What is the product of a list of integers?

- If the list is empty, the product is 1 (by convention).
- If the list is non-empty, the product is the head times the product of the tail.

It can be expressed in ML like this:

```
fun prod []      = 1
  | prod (n::ns) = n * (prod ns);
> val prod = fn : int list -> int
```

The function consists of two clauses separated by a vertical bar (|). Each clause treats one argument pattern. There may be several clauses and complex patterns, provided the types agree. Since the patterns involve lists, and the result can be the integer 1, ML infers that *prod* maps a list of integers to an integer.

```
prod[2,3,5];
> 30 : int
```

Empty versus non-empty is the commonest sort of case analysis for lists. Finding the maximum of a list of integers requires something different, for the empty list has no maximum. The two cases are

- The maximum of the one-element list [m] is m.
- To find the maximum of a list with two or more elements [m, n, ...], remove the smaller of m or n and find the maximum of the remaining numbers.

This gives the ML function

```
fun maxl [m] : int   = m
  | maxl (m::n::ns) = if m>n then maxl(m::ns)
                             else maxl(n::ns);
> ***Warning:  Patterns not exhaustive
> val maxl = fn : int list -> int
```

Note the warning message: ML detects that *maxl* is undefined for the empty list.
Also, observe how the pattern *m* :: *n* :: *ns* describes a list of the form [*m, n, . . .*].
The smaller element is dropped in the recursive call.

The function works — except for the empty list.

```
maxl [ ~4, 0, ~12];
> 0 : int
maxl [];
> Exception: Match
```

An **exception**, for the time being, can be regarded as a run-time error. The function *maxl* has been applied to an argument for which it is undefined. Normally
exceptions abort execution. They can be trapped, as we shall see in the next chapter.

Intermediate lists. Lists are sometimes generated and consumed within a computation. For instance, the factorial function has a clever definition using *prod*
and *upto*:

```
fun factl (n) = prod (upto (1,n));
> val factl = fn : int -> int
factl 7;
> 5040 : int
```

This declaration is concise and clear, avoiding explicit recursion. The cost of
building the list [1, 2, . . . , *n*] may not matter. However, functional programming
should facilitate reasoning about programs. This does not happen here. The trivial law

$$factl(m + 1) = (m + 1) \times factl(m)$$

has no obvious proof. Opening up its definition, we get

$$factl(m + 1) = prod(upto(1, m + 1)) = ?$$

The next step is unclear because the recursion in *upto* follows its first argument,
not the second. The honest recursive definition of factorial seems better.

Strings and lists. Lists are important in string processing. Most functional languages provide a type of single characters, regarding strings as lists of characters.
With the new standard library, ML has acquired a character type — but it does not
regard strings as lists. The built-in function *explode* converts a string to a list of
characters. The function *implode* performs the inverse operation, joining a list
of characters to form a string.

```
explode "Banquo";
> [#"B", #"a", #"n", #"q", #"u", #"o"] : char list
implode it;
> "Banquo" : string
```

Similarly, the function *concat* joins a list of strings to form a string.

Some fundamental list functions

Given a list we can find its length, select the *n*th element, take a prefix or suffix, or reverse the order of its elements. Given two lists we can append one to the other, or, if they have equal length, pair corresponding elements. The functions declared in this section are indispensable, and will be taken for granted in the rest of the book. All of these functions are polymorphic.

Efficiency becomes a central concern here. For some functions, a naïve recursive definition is less efficient than an iterative version. For others, an iterative style impairs both readability and efficiency.

3.3   *Testing lists and taking them apart*

The three basic functions on lists are *null*, *hd* and *tl*.

The function null. This function tests whether a list is empty:

```
fun null    []   = true
  | null (_::_) = false;
> val null = fn : 'a list -> bool
```

The function is polymorphic: testing whether a list is empty does not examine its elements. The underscores (_) in the second pattern take the place of components whose values are not needed in the clause. These underscores, called **wildcard** patterns, save us from inventing names for such components.

The function hd. This function returns the head (the first element) of a non-empty list:

```
fun hd (x::_) = x;
> ***Warning:  Patterns not exhaustive
> val hd = fn : 'a list -> 'a
```

This pattern has a wildcard for the tail, while the head is called *x*. Since there is no pattern for the empty list, ML prints a warning. It is a partial function like *maxl*.

Here we have a list of lists. Its head is a list and the head of that is an integer. Each use of *hd* removes one level of brackets.

```
hd[[[1,2], [3]], [[4]]];
> [[1, 2], [3]] : (int list) list
hd it;
> [1, 2] : int list
hd it;
> 1 : int
```

What if we type *hd it;* once more?

The function tl. This returns the tail of a non-empty list. The tail, remember, is the list consisting of the all elements but the first.

```
fun tl (_::xs) = xs;
> ***Warning:  Patterns not exhaustive
> val tl = fn : 'a list -> 'a list
```

Like *hd*, this is a partial function. Its result is always another list:

```
tl ["Out","damned","spot!"];
> ["damned", "spot!"] : string list
tl it;
> ["spot!"] : string list
tl it;
> [] : string list
tl it;
> Exception: Match
```

Attempting to take the tail of the empty list is an error.

Through *null*, *hd* and *tl*, all other list functions can be written without pattern-matching. The product of a list of integers can be computed like this:

```
fun prod ns = if null ns then 1
                         else (hd ns) * (prod (tl ns));
```

If you prefer this version of *prod*, you might as well give up ML for Lisp. For added clarity, Lisp primitives have names like CAR and CDR. Normal people find pattern-matching more readable than *hd* and *tl*. A good ML compiler analyses the set of patterns to generate the best code for the function. More importantly, the compiler prints a warning if the patterns do not cover all possible arguments of the function.

Exercise 3.1 Write a version of *maxl* using *null*, *hd* and *tl*, instead of pattern-matching.

Exercise 3.2 Write a function to return the last element of a list.

3.4   *List processing by numbers*

We now declare the functions *length*, *take* and *drop*, which behave as follows:

$$l = [\underbrace{x_0, \dots, x_{i-1}}_{take(l,\,i)}, \underbrace{x_i, \dots, x_{n-1}}_{drop(l,\,i)}] \qquad length(l) = n$$

The function length. The length of a list can be computed by a naïve recursion:

```
fun nlength []        = 0
  | nlength (x::xs) = 1 + nlength xs;
> val nlength = fn : 'a list -> int
```

Its type, α *list* $\rightarrow$ *int*, permits *nlength* to be applied to a list regardless of the type of its elements. Let us try it on a list of lists:

```
nlength[[1,2,3], [4,5,6]];
> 2 : int
```

Did you think the answer would be 6?

Although correct, *nlength* is intolerably wasteful for long lists:

$$nlength[1, 2, 3, \dots, 10000] \Rightarrow 1 + nlength[2, 3, \dots, 10000]$$
$$\Rightarrow 1 + (1 + nlength[3, \dots, 10000])$$
$$\vdots$$
$$\Rightarrow 1 + (1 + 9998)$$
$$\Rightarrow 1 + 9999 \Rightarrow 10000$$

The ones pile up, wasting space proportional to the length of the list, and could easily cause execution to abort. Much better is an iterative version of the function that accumulates the count in another argument:

```
local
      fun addlen (n, [])   = n
        | addlen (n, x::l) = addlen (n+1, l)
in
      fun length l = addlen (0,l)
end;
> val length = fn : 'a list -> int
length (explode"Throw physic to the dogs!");
> 25 : int
```

The function *addlen* adds the length of a list to another number, initially 0. Since *addlen* has no other purpose, it is declared `local` to *length*. It executes as follows:

$$addlen(0, [1, 2, 3, \ldots , 10000]) \Rightarrow addlen(1, [2, 3, \ldots , 10000])$$
$$\Rightarrow addlen(2, [3, \ldots , 10000])$$
$$\vdots$$
$$\Rightarrow addlen(10000, []) \Rightarrow 10000$$

The greatly improved efficiency compensates for the loss of readability.

The function take. Calling *take* (l, i) returns the list of the first i elements of l:

```
fun take ([], i)   = []
  | take (x::xs, i) = if i>0 then x::take(xs, i-1)
                             else [];
> val take = fn : 'a list * int -> 'a list
take (explode"Throw physic to the dogs!", 5);
> [#"T", #"h", #"r", #"o", #"w"] : char list
```

Here is a sample computation:

$$take([9, 8, 7, 6], 3) \Rightarrow 9 :: take([8, 7, 6], 2)$$
$$\Rightarrow 9 :: (8 :: take([7, 6], 1))$$
$$\Rightarrow 9 :: (8 :: (7 :: take([6], 0)))$$
$$\Rightarrow 9 :: (8 :: (7 :: []))$$
$$\Rightarrow 9 :: (8 :: [7])$$
$$\Rightarrow 9 :: [8, 7]$$
$$\Rightarrow [9, 8, 7]$$

Observe that 9 :: (8 :: (7 :: [])) above is an expression, not a value. Evaluating it constructs the list [9, 8, 7]. Allocating the necessary storage takes time, particularly if we consider its contribution to the cost of later garbage collections. Indeed, *take* probably spends most of its time building its result.

The recursive calls to *take* get deeper and deeper, like *nlength*, which we have recently deplored. Let us try to make an iterative version of *take* by accumulating the result in an argument:

```
fun rtake ([], _, taken)   = taken
  | rtake (x::xs, i, taken) =
          if i>0  then  rtake(xs, i-1, x::taken)
                  else  taken;
> val rtake = fn : 'a list * int * 'a list -> 'a list
```

The recursion is nice and shallow ...

$$rtake([9, 8, 7, 6], 3, []) \Rightarrow rtake([8, 7, 6], 2, [9])$$
$$\Rightarrow rtake([7, 6], 1, [8, 9])$$
$$\Rightarrow rtake([6], 0, [7, 8, 9])$$
$$\Rightarrow [7, 8, 9]$$

... but the output is reversed!

If a reversed output is acceptable, *rtake* is worth considering. However, the size of the recursion in *take* is tolerable compared with the size of the result. While *nlength* returns an integer, *take* returns a list. Building a list is slow, which is usually more important than the space temporarily consumed by deep recursion. Efficiency is a matter of getting the costs into proportion.

The function drop. The list *drop* (l, i) contains all but the first i elements of l:

```
fun drop ([], _)   = []
  | drop (x::xs, i) = if i>0 then drop (xs, i-1)
                              else x::xs;
> val drop = fn : 'a list * int -> 'a list
```

Luckily, the obvious recursion is iterative.

```
take (["Never","shall","sun","that","morrow","see!"], 3);
> ["Never", "shall", "sun"] : string list
drop (["Never","shall","sun","that","morrow","see!"], 3);
> ["that", "morrow", "see!"] : string list
```

Exercise 3.3 What do *take* (l, i) and *drop* (l, i) return when $i > length(l)$, and when $i < 0$? (The library versions of *take* and *drop* would raise exceptions.)

Exercise 3.4 Write a function *nth* (l, n) to return the *n*th element of l (where the head is element 0).

3.5   *Append and reverse*

The infix operator @, which appends one list to another, and *rev*, which reverses a list, are built-in functions. Their definitions deserve close attention.

The append operation. Append puts the elements of one list after those of another list:

$$[x_1, \dots, x_m] \, @ \, [y_1, \dots y_n] = [x_1, \dots, x_m, y_1, \dots y_n]$$

What sort of recursion accomplishes this? The traditional name **append** suggests that the action takes place at the end of a list, but lists are always built from the front. The following definition, in its essentials, dates to the early days of Lisp:

```
infixr 5 @;
fun ([]      @ ys) = ys
  | ((x::xs) @ ys) = x :: (xs@ys);
> val @ = fn : 'a list * 'a list -> 'a list
```

Its type, $\alpha\ list \times \alpha\ list \to \alpha\ list$, accepts any two lists with the same element type — say, lists of strings and lists of lists:

```
["Why", "sinks"] @ ["that", "cauldron?"];
> ["Why", "sinks", "that", "cauldron?"] : string list
[[2,4,6,8], [3,9]] @ [[5], [7]];
> [[2, 4, 6, 8], [3, 9], [5], [7]] : int list list
```

The computation of [2, 4, 6] @ [8, 10] goes like this:

$$
\begin{aligned}
[2, 4, 6] \text{ @ } [8, 10] &\Rightarrow 2 :: ([4, 6] \text{ @ } [8, 10]) \\
&\Rightarrow 2 :: (4 :: ([6] \text{ @ } [8, 10])) \\
&\Rightarrow 2 :: (4 :: (6 :: ([] \text{ @ } [8, 10]))) \\
&\Rightarrow 2 :: (4 :: (6 :: [8, 10])) \\
&\Rightarrow 2 :: (4 :: [6, 8, 10]) \\
&\Rightarrow 2 :: [4, 6, 8, 10] \\
&\Rightarrow [2, 4, 6, 8, 10]
\end{aligned}
$$

The last three steps put the elements from the first list on to the second. As with *take*, the cost of building the result exceeds that of the deep recursion; an iterative version is not needed. The cost of evaluating *xs* @ *ys* is proportional to the length of *xs* and is completely independent of *ys*. Even *xs* @ [] makes a copy of *xs*.

In Pascal and C you can implement lists using pointer types, and join them by updating the last pointer of one list to point towards another. Destructive updating is faster than copying, but if you are careless your lists could end up in knots. What happens if the two lists happen to be the same pointer? ML lists involve internal pointers used safely. If you like living dangerously, ML has explicit pointer types — see Chapter 8.

The function rev. List reversal can be defined using append. The head of the list becomes the last element of the reversed list:

```
fun nrev []     = []
  | nrev (x::xs) = (nrev xs) @ [x];
> val nrev = fn : 'a list -> 'a list
```

This is grossly inefficient. If *nrev* is given a list of length $n > 0$, then append calls cons (::) exactly $n-1$ times to copy the reversed tail. Constructing the list $[x]$ calls cons again, for a total of n calls. Reversing the tail requires $n-1$ more conses, and so forth. The total number of conses is

$$0 + 1 + 2 + \cdots + n = \frac{n(n+1)}{2}.$$

This cost is quadratic: proportional to n^2.

We have already seen, in *rtake*, another way of reversing a list: repeatedly move elements from one list to another.

```
fun revAppend ([],    ys) = ys
  | revAppend (x::xs, ys) = revAppend (xs, x::ys);
> val revAppend = fn : 'a list * 'a list -> 'a list
```

Append is never called. The number of steps is proportional to the length of the list being reversed. The function resembles append but reverses its first argument:

```
revAppend (["Macbeth","and","Banquo"], ["all", "hail!"]);
> ["Banquo", "and", "Macbeth", "all", "hail!"] : string list
```

The efficient reversal function calls *revAppend* with an empty list:

```
fun rev xs = revAppend(xs,[]);
> val rev = fn : 'a list -> 'a list
```

Here a slightly longer definition pays dramatically. Reversing a 1000-element list, *rev* calls :: exactly 1000 times, *nrev* 500,500 times. Furthermore, the recursion in *revAppend* is iterative. Its key idea — of accumulating list elements in an extra argument rather than appending — applies to many other functions.

Exercise 3.5 Modify the append function to handle *xs* @ [] efficiently.

Exercise 3.6 What would happen if we changed $[x]$ to x in the definition of *nrev*?

Exercise 3.7 Show the computation steps to reverse the list $[1, 2, 3, 4]$ using *nrev* and then *rev*.

3.6 *Lists of lists, lists of pairs*

Pattern-matching and polymorphism cope nicely with combinations of data structures. Observe the types of these functions.

The function concat. This function makes a list consisting of all the elements of a list of lists:

```
fun concat []     = []
  | concat(l::ls) = l @ concat ls;
> val concat = fn : 'a list list -> 'a list
concat [["When","shall"], ["we","three"], ["meet","again"]];
> ["When", "shall", "we", "three", "meet", "again"]
> : string list
```

The copying in *l* @ *concat ls* is reasonably fast, for *l* is usually much shorter than *concat ls*.

The function zip. This function pairs corresponding members of two lists:

$$zip([x_1, \ldots , x_n], [y_1, \ldots , y_n]) = [(x_1, y_1), \ldots , (x_n, y_n)]$$

If the two lists differ in length, let us ignore surplus elements. The declaration requires complex patterns:

```
fun zip(x::xs,y::ys)  =  (x,y)  ::  zip(xs,ys)
  | zip _             =  [];
> val zip = fn : 'a list * 'b list -> ('a*'b) list
```

The second pattern in the definition of *zip*, with its wildcard, matches all possibilities. But it is only considered if the first pattern fails to match. ML considers a function's patterns in the order given.

The function unzip. The inverse of *zip*, called *unzip*, takes a list of pairs to a pair of lists:

$$unzip[(x_1, y_1), \ldots , (x_n, y_n)] = ([x_1, \ldots , x_n], [y_1, \ldots , y_n])$$

Building two lists simultaneously can be tricky in functional languages. One approach uses an extra function:

```
fun conspair ((x,y),  (xs,ys))  =  (x::xs,  y::ys);

fun unzip []             = ([],[])
  | unzip(pair::pairs) = conspair(pair,  unzip pairs);
```

A let declaration, where pattern-matching takes apart the result of the recursive call, eliminates the function *conspair*:

```
fun unzip []              = ([],[])
  | unzip((x,y)::pairs) =
        let val (xs,ys) = unzip pairs
        in  (x::xs, y::ys)  end;
> val unzip = fn : ('a*'b) list -> 'a list * 'b list
```

An iterative function can construct several results in its arguments. This is the simplest way to unzip a list, but the resulting lists are reversed.

```
fun rev_unzip([], xs, ys)              = (xs,ys)
  | rev_unzip((x,y)::pairs, xs, ys) =
        rev_unzip(pairs, x::xs, y::ys);
```

ⓘ *Lists and the standard library.* The standard library provides most of the functions described above. Append (the infix @), reverse (*rev*), *null*, *hd*, *tl* and *length* are available at top level. *List* provides *take*, *drop* and *concat*, among others. *ListPair* provides *zip* and *unzip*.

Please use the library versions of these functions. Those given here omit error handling. The library versions respond to erroneous inputs by raising exceptions such as *List*. *Empty* (if you request the head of the empty list) and *Subscript* (if you attempt to *take* more elements than exist). Library versions will also be tuned for efficiency.

Exercise 3.8   Compare the following function with *concat*, considering its effect and efficiency:

```
fun f []              = []
  | f([]::ls)       = f(ls)
  | f((x::l)::ls) = x :: f(l::ls);
```

Exercise 3.9   Give an equivalent definition of *zip* that does not depend upon the order in which patterns are considered.

Exercise 3.10   Is $rev(rtake(l,i,[]))$ more efficient than $take(l,i)$? Consider all the costs involved.

Applications of lists

This section demonstrates how lists can perform sophisticated tasks, like binary arithmetic and matrix operations. Feel free to skip the harder ones if you like.

Two examples from the classic book *A Discipline of Programming* (Dijkstra, 1976) are also solved. Dijkstra presents programs in all their 'compelling and deep logical beauty.' His programs use arrays; do lists possess greater beauty?

3.7   *Making change*

Let us start with something simple: making change. The task is to express some amount of money in terms of coins drawn from a list of coin values. Naturally, we expect to receive change using the largest coins possible. This is easy if coin values are supplied in decreasing order:

```
fun change (coinvals, 0)        = []
  | change (c::coinvals, amount) =
        if amount<c then change(coinvals, amount)
                    else c :: change(c::coinvals, amount-c);
> ***Warning:  Patterns not exhaustive
> val change = fn : int list * int -> int list
```

The function definition could hardly be more intuitive. If the target amount is zero, no coins are required; if the largest coin value c is too large, discard it; otherwise use it and make change for the amount less c.

Let us declare ML identifiers for British and U.S. coin values:

```
val gb_coins = [50,20,10,5,2,1]
and us_coins = [25,10,5,1];
```

Thus, 43 pence is expressed differently from 43 cents:

```
change(gb_coins, 43);
> [20, 20, 2, 1] : int list
change(us_coins, 43);
> [25, 10, 5, 1, 1, 1] : int list
```

Making change is less trivial than it first appears. Suppose the only coin values we have are 5 and 2?

```
change([5,2], 16);
> Exception: Match
```

The compiler warned us of this possibility when we declared *change*. But 16 is easily expressed using fives and twos! Our algorithm is greedy: it always chooses the largest coin value, trying to express 16 as $5 + 5 + 5 + c$, only now $c = 1$ is not possible.

Can we design a better algorithm? **Backtracking** means responding to failure by undoing the most recent choice and trying again. One way of implementing backtracking involves exceptions, as shown below in Section 4.8. An alternative approach is to compute the list of all solutions. Observe the use of *coins* to hold the list of coins chosen so far.

```
fun allChange (coins, coinvals, 0)          = [coins]
  | allChange (coins, [],         amount)   = []
  | allChange (coins, c::coinvals, amount) =
        if amount<0 then []
        else allChange(c::coins, c::coinvals, amount-c) @
             allChange(coins, coinvals, amount);
> val allChange = fn
> : int list * int list * int -> int list list
```

The 'patterns not exhaustive' warning has disappeared; the function considers all cases. Given an impossible problem, it returns the empty list instead of raising an exception:

```
allChange([], [10,2], 27);
> [] : int list list
```

Let us try some more interesting examples:

```
allChange([], [5,2], 16);
> [[2, 2, 2, 5, 5], [2, 2, 2, 2, 2, 2, 2, 2]]
> : int list list
allChange([], gb_coins, 16);
> [[1, 5, 10], [2, 2, 2, 10], [1, 1, 2, 2, 10], ...]
> : int list list
```

There are 25 ways of making change for 16 pence! At first sight, this approach looks untenable. To control the exponential growth in solutions we can use lazy evaluation, generating only the solutions required (see Section 5.14).

ℹ *Further reading.* Making change is much harder than it first appears, in the general case. It is closely related to the ***subset-sum*** problem, which is NP-complete. This means it is highly unlikely that there exists an efficient algorithm to decide whether or not a given set of coins can be used to express a given sum. Cormen *et al.* (1990) discuss algorithms for finding approximate solutions.

Exercise 3.11   Write a function to express integers as Roman numerals. Supplied with suitable arguments, your function should be able to express 1984 as either MDCCCCLXXXIIII or MCMLXXXIV.

Exercise 3.12   The change functions expect *coinvals* to consist of strictly decreasing positive integers. What happens if this precondition is violated?

Exercise 3.13   We are seldom fortunate enough to have an infinite supply of coins. Modify *allChange* to make change from a finite purse.

Exercise 3.14 Modify *allChange* to accumulate its result in an extra argument, eliminating the call to append. Compare its efficiency with the original version by making change for 99 pence.

3.8 Binary arithmetic

Functional programming may seem far removed from hardware, but lists are good for simulating digital circuits. Binary addition and multiplication are defined here for lists of zeros and ones.

Addition. If you have forgotten the rules for binary sums, have a look at the binary version of $11 + 30 = 41$:

$$
\begin{array}{r}
11110 \\
+ \quad 1011 \\
\hline
101001
\end{array}
$$

Addition works from right to left. The two bits plus any carry (from the right) give a sum bit for this position and a carry to the left. Right to left is the wrong direction for lists; the head of a list is its leftmost element. So the bits will be kept in reverse order.

The two binary numerals may have unequal lengths. If one bit list terminates then the carry must be propagated along the other bit list.

```
fun bincarry (0, ps)     = ps
  | bincarry (1, [])     = [1]
  | bincarry (1, p::ps) = (1-p) :: bincarry(p, ps);
> ***Warning:  Patterns not exhaustive
> val bincarry = fn : int * int list -> int list
```

Yes, patterns may contain constants: integers, reals, booleans and strings. Function *bincarry* can propagate a carry of 0 or 1, the only sensible values. It is undefined for others.

The binary sum is defined for two bit lists and a carry. When either list terminates, *bincarry* deals with the other. If there are two bits to add, their sum and carry are computed:

```
fun binsum (c, [], qs)        = bincarry (c,qs)
  | binsum (c, ps, [])        = bincarry (c,ps)
  | binsum (c, p::ps, q::qs) =
        ((c+p+q) mod 2) :: binsum((c+p+q) div 2, ps, qs);
> val binsum = fn
> : int * int list * int list -> int list
```

Let us try $11 + 30 = 41$, remembering that the bits are kept in reverse order:

```
binsum(0, [1,1,0,1], [0,1,1,1,1]);
> [1, 0, 0, 1, 0, 1] : int list
```

Multiplication. The binary product is computed by shifting and adding. For instance, $11 \times 30 = 330$:

$$
\begin{array}{r}
11110 \\
\times \qquad 1011 \\
\hline
11110 \\
11110 \\
+ \quad 11110 \\
\hline
101001010
\end{array}
$$

Here, shifting is performed by inserting a 0:

```
fun binprod ([], _)      = []
  | binprod (0::ps, qs) = 0::binprod(ps,qs)
  | binprod (1::ps, qs) = binsum(0, qs, 0::binprod(ps,qs));
> ***Warning:  Patterns not exhaustive
> val binprod = fn : int list * int list -> int list
```

Let us evaluate $11 \times 30 = 330$:

```
binprod([1,1,0,1], [0,1,1,1,1]);
> [0, 1, 0, 1, 0, 0, 1, 0, 1] : int list
```

A structure for binary arithmetic. In a large program, it is poor style to associate related functions merely by a naming convention such as the prefix *bin*. The binary arithmetic functions should be grouped into a structure, say *Bin*. Shorter names can be used inside the structure, making the code more readable. Outside, the structure's components have uniform compound names. The function declarations above can easily be packaged into a structure:

```
structure Bin =
  struct
  fun carry (0, ps)    = ...
  fun sum (c, [], qs) = ...
  fun prod ([], _)     = ...
  end;
```

With a little more effort, structure *Bin* can be made to match signature *ARITH* of Section 2.22. This would give the operators for binary numerals precisely the same interface as those for complex numbers. It would include binary arithmetic in our collection of structures that can be used in generic arithmetic packages. But binary arithmetic is quite different from complex arithmetic; division is not exact, for example. Noting which properties are needed in a particular case is our responsibility.

Exercise 3.15 Write functions to compute the binary sum and product of a list of boolean values, using no built-in arithmetic.

Exercise 3.16 Write a function to divide one binary numeral by another.

Exercise 3.17 Using the results of the previous exercise, or by writing dummy functions, extend structure *Bin* so that it matches signature *ARITH*.

Exercise 3.18 Decimal numerals can be held as lists of integers from 0 to 9. Write functions to convert between binary and decimal: both directions. Compute the factorial of 100.

3.9   *Matrix transpose*

A matrix can be viewed as a list of rows, each row a list of matrix elements. The matrix $\left(\begin{smallmatrix} a & b & c \\ d & e & f \end{smallmatrix}\right)$, for instance, can be declared in ML by

```
val matrix = [ ["a","b","c"],
               ["d","e","f"] ];
> val matrix = [["a", "b", "c"], ["d", "e", "f"]]
> : string list list
```

Matrix transpose works well with this list representation because it goes sequentially along rows and columns, with no jumping. The transpose function changes the list of rows

$$A = \begin{matrix} [[x_{11}, & x_{12}, & \ldots, & x_{1m}], \\ \vdots & \vdots & & \vdots \\ [x_{n1}, & x_{n2}, & \ldots, & x_{nm}]] \end{matrix}$$

to the list of the columns of A:

$$A^T = \begin{matrix} [[x_{11}, & \ldots, & x_{n1}], \\ [x_{12}, & \ldots, & x_{n2}], \\ \vdots & & \vdots \\ [x_{1m}, & \ldots, & x_{nm}]] \end{matrix}$$

One way to transpose a matrix is by repeatedly taking columns from it. The heads of the rows form the first column of the matrix:

```
fun headcol []                        = []
   | headcol ((x::_) :: rows) = x :: headcol rows;
> ***Warning:   Patterns not exhaustive
> val headcol = fn : 'a list list -> 'a list
```

The tails of the rows form a matrix of the remaining columns:

```
fun tailcols []                       = []
   | tailcols ((_::xs) :: rows) = xs :: tailcols rows;
> ***Warning:   Patterns not exhaustive
> val tailcols = fn : 'a list list -> 'a list list
```

Consider their effect on our small matrix:

```
headcol matrix;
> ["a", "d"] : string list
tailcols matrix;
> [["b", "c"], ["e", "f"]] : string list list
```

Calling *headcol* and *tailcols* chops the matrix like this:

$$\begin{pmatrix} a & b & c \\ d & e & f \end{pmatrix}$$

These functions lead to an unusual recursion: *tailcols* takes a list of n lists and returns a list of n shorter lists. This terminates with n empty lists.

```
fun transp ([]::rows) = []
   | transp rows          = headcol rows :: transp (tailcols rows);
> val transp = fn : 'a list list -> 'a list list
transp matrix;
> [["a", "d"], ["b", "e"], ["c", "f"]] : string list list
```

The transposed matrix is

$$\begin{pmatrix} a & d \\ b & e \\ c & f \end{pmatrix}.$$

ⓘ   *A neater way.* Many of the programs presented here can be expressed more concisely using higher-order functions such as *map*, which applies a function to every element of a list. Higher-order functions are discussed later on. You may want to peek at Section 5.7, where matrix transpose is reconsidered.

Exercise 3.19   What input pattern do *headcol* and *tailcols* not handle? What does *transp* return if the rows of the 'matrix' do not have the same length?

Exercise 3.20   What does *transp* do given the empty list? Explain.

Exercise 3.21   Write an alternative transpose function. Instead of turning columns into rows, it should turn rows into columns.

3.10   Matrix multiplication

We begin with a quick review of matrix multiplication. The **dot product** (or inner product) of two vectors is

$$(a_1, \ldots, a_k) \cdot (b_1, \ldots, b_k) = a_1 b_1 + \cdots + a_k b_k.$$

If A is an $m \times k$ matrix and B is a $k \times n$ matrix then their **product** $A \times B$ is an $m \times n$ matrix. For each i and j, the (i, j) element of $A \times B$ is the dot product of row i of A with column j of B. Example:

$$\begin{pmatrix} 2 & 0 \\ 3 & -1 \\ 0 & 1 \\ 1 & 1 \end{pmatrix} \times \begin{pmatrix} 1 & 0 & 2 \\ 4 & -1 & 0 \end{pmatrix} = \begin{pmatrix} 2 & 0 & 4 \\ -1 & 1 & 6 \\ 4 & -1 & 0 \\ 5 & -1 & 2 \end{pmatrix}$$

The $(1,1)$ element of the product above is computed by

$$(2, 0) \cdot (1, 4) = 2 \times 1 + 0 \times 4 = 2.$$

In the dot product function, the two vectors must have the same length; ML prints a warning that some cases are not covered. Henceforth these warnings will usually be omitted.

```
fun dotprod([], [])     = 0.0
  | dotprod(x::xs,y::ys) = x*y + dotprod(xs,ys);
> ***Warning:  Patterns not exhaustive
> val dotprod = fn : real list * real list -> real
```

If A has just one row, so does $A \times B$. Function *rowprod* computes the product of a row with B. The matrix B must be given as its transpose: a list of columns, not a list of rows.

```
fun rowprod(row, [])      = []
  | rowprod(row, col::cols) =
         dotprod(row,col) :: rowprod(row,cols);
> val rowprod = fn
> : real list * real list list -> real list
```

Each row of $A \times B$ is obtained by multiplying a row of A by the columns of B:

```
fun rowlistprod([], cols)       = []
  | rowlistprod(row::rows, cols) =
         rowprod(row,cols) :: rowlistprod(rows,cols);
> val rowlistprod = fn
> : real list list * real list list -> real list list
```

The matrix product function makes *transp* construct a list of the columns of *B*:

```
fun matprod(rowsA, rowsB) = rowlistprod(rowsA, transp rowsB);
> val matprod = fn
> : real list list * real list list -> real list list
```

Here are the declarations of the sample matrices, omitting ML's response:

```
val rowsA = [ [2.0,   0.0],
              [3.0, ~1.0],
              [0.0,   1.0],
              [1.0,   1.0] ]
and rowsB = [ [1.0,   0.0,   2.0],
              [4.0, ~1.0,   0.0] ];
```

Here is their product:

```
matprod(rowsA, rowsB);
> [[2.0,   0.0, 4.0],
>  [~1.0, 1.0, 6.0],
>  [4.0, ~1.0, 0.0],
>  [5.0, ~1.0, 2.0]] : real list list
```

Exercise 3.22   A matrix is negated by negating each of its components; thus $-\left(\begin{smallmatrix} a & b \\ c & d \end{smallmatrix}\right) = \left(\begin{smallmatrix} -a & -b \\ -c & -d \end{smallmatrix}\right)$. Write a function to negate a matrix.

Exercise 3.23   Two matrices of the same dimensions are added by adding corresponding components; thus $\left(\begin{smallmatrix} a & b \\ c & d \end{smallmatrix}\right) + \left(\begin{smallmatrix} a' & b' \\ c' & d' \end{smallmatrix}\right) = \left(\begin{smallmatrix} a+a' & b+b' \\ c+c' & d+d' \end{smallmatrix}\right)$. Write a function to add two matrices.

3.11   *Gaussian elimination*

One of the classic matrix algorithms, Gaussian elimination may seem an unlikely candidate for functional programming. This algorithm (Sedgewick, 1988) can compute the determinant or inverse of a matrix, or solve systems of independent linear equations such as the following:

$$
\begin{aligned}
x + 2y + 7z &= 7 \\
-4w \quad\quad + 3y - 5z &= -2 \\
4w - x - 2y - 3z &= 9 \\
-2w + x + 2y + 8z &= 2
\end{aligned}
\qquad (*)
$$

Gaussian elimination works by isolating each of the variables in turn. Equation (*), properly scaled and added to another equation, eliminates *w* from it.

Repeating this operation, which is called **pivoting**, eventually reduces the system to a triangular form:

$$-4w \quad + 3y - 5z = -2$$
$$x + 2y + 7z = 7$$
$$3y - \quad z = 14$$
$$3z = 3$$

Now the solutions come out, beginning with $z = 1$.

Equation $(*)$ is a good choice for eliminating w because the absolute value (4) of its coefficient is maximal. Scaling divides the equation by this value; a small divisor (not to mention zero!) could cause numerical errors. Function *pivotrow*, given a list of rows, returns one whose head is greatest in absolute value.

```
fun pivotrow [row]                    = row : real list
  | pivotrow (row1::row2::rows) =
      if abs(hd row1) >= abs(hd row2)
      then pivotrow(row1::rows)
      else pivotrow(row2::rows);
> val pivotrow = fn : real list list -> real list
```

If the selected row has head p, then *delrow*$(p, rows)$ removes it from the list of rows.

```
fun delrow (p, [])          = []
  | delrow (p, row::rows) = if p = hd row   then rows
                            else row :: delrow(p, rows);
> val delrow = fn : ''a * ''a list list -> ''a list list
```

Function *scalarprod* multiplies a row or vector by a constant k:

```
fun scalarprod(k, [])    = [] : real list
  | scalarprod(k, x::xs) = k*x :: scalarprod(k,xs);
> val scalarprod = fn : real * real list -> real list
```

Function *vectorsum* adds two rows or vectors:

```
fun vectorsum ([], [])     = [] : real list
  | vectorsum (x::xs,y::ys) = x+y :: vectorsum(xs,ys);
> val vectorsum = fn : real list * real list -> real list
```

Function *elimcol*, declared inside *gausselim*, refers to the current pivot row by its head p (the leading coefficient) and tail *prow*. Given a list of rows, *elimcol* replaces each by its sum with *prow*, properly scaled. The first element of each sum is zero, but these zeros are never computed; the first column simply disappears.

```
fun gausselim [row] = [row]
  | gausselim rows   =
      let val p::prow = pivotrow rows
          fun elimcol []              = []
            | elimcol ((x::xs)::rows) =
                  vectorsum(xs, scalarprod(~x/p, prow))
                  :: elimcol rows
      in  (p::prow) :: gausselim(elimcol(delrow(p,rows)))
      end;
> val gausselim = fn : real list list -> real list list
```

Function *gausselim* removes the pivot row, eliminates a column, and calls itself recursively on the reduced matrix. It returns a list of pivot rows, decreasing in length, forming an upper triangular matrix.

A system of n equations is solved by Gaussian elimination on an $n \times (n + 1)$ matrix, where the extra column contains the right-side values. The solutions are generated recursively from the triangular matrix. Known solutions are multiplied by their coefficients and added — this is a vector dot product — and divided by the leading coefficient. To subtract the right-side value we employ a trick: a spurious solution of -1.

```
fun solutions []                = [~1.0]
  | solutions ((x::xs)::rows) =
      let val solns = solutions rows
      in ~(dotprod(solns,xs)/x) :: solns  end;
> val solutions = fn : real list list -> real list
```

One way of understanding this definition is by applying it to the example above. We compute the triangular matrix:

```
gausselim [[ 0.0,   1.0,   2.0,   7.0,   7.0],
           [~4.0,   0.0,   3.0,  ~5.0,  ~2.0],
           [ 4.0,  ~1.0,  ~2.0,  ~3.0,   9.0],
           [~2.0,   1.0,   2.0,   8.0,   2.0]];
> [[~4.0,   0.0,   3.0,  ~5.0,  ~2.0],
>  [ 1.0,   2.0,   7.0,   7.0],
>  [ 3.0,  ~1.0,  14.0],
>  [ 3.0,   3.0]] : real list list
```

Ignoring the final -1, the solutions are $w = 3$, $x = -10$, $y = 5$ and $z = 1$.

```
solutions it;
> [3.0, ~10.0, 5.0, 1.0, ~1.0] : real list%
```

ⓘ   *Further reading.* Researchers at the University of Wales have applied the language Haskell to computational fluid dynamics problems. The aim is to investigate the practical utility of functional programming. One paper compares different representations of matrices (Grant *et al.*, 1996). Another considers the possibility of exploiting parallelism, using a simulated parallel processor (Grant *et al.*, 1995). Compared with conventional Fortran implementations, the Haskell ones are much slower and need more space; the authors list some developments that could improve the efficiency.

Exercise 3.24 Show that if the input equations are linearly independent, then division by zero cannot occur within *gausselim*.

Exercise 3.25 Do *pivotrow* and *delrow* work correctly if the heads of several rows have the same absolute value?

Exercise 3.26 Write a function to compute the determinant of a matrix.

Exercise 3.27 Write a function to invert a matrix.

Exercise 3.28 Write a structure *Matrix* that matches signature *ARITH*. You can either use the previous exercise and those of Section 3.10, or write dummy functions. This adds matrices to our collection of arithmetic structures.[1]

3.12 *Writing a number as the sum of two squares*

Dijkstra (1976) presents a program that, given an integer r, finds all integer solutions of $x^2 + y^2 = r$. (Assume $x \geq y \geq 0$ to suppress symmetries.) For instance, $25 = 4^2 + 3^2 = 5^2 + 0^2$, while 48,612,265 has 32 solutions.

Brute force search over all (x, y) pairs is impractical for large numbers, but fortunately the solutions have some structure: if $x^2 + y^2 = r = u^2 + v^2$ and $x > u$ then $y < v$. If x sweeps downwards from $\sqrt{r}$ as y sweeps upwards from 0, then all solutions can be found in a single pass.

Let $Bet(x, y)$ stand for the set of all solutions between x and y:

$$Bet(x, y) = \{(u, v) \mid u^2 + v^2 = r \wedge x \geq u \geq v \geq y\}$$

The search for suitable x and y is guided by four observations:

1 If $x^2 + y^2 < r$ then $Bet(x, y) = Bet(x, y + 1)$. There are plainly no solutions of the form (u, y) for $u < x$.
2 If $x^2 + y^2 = r$ then $Bet(x, y) = \{(x, y)\} \cup Bet(x - 1, y + 1)$. A solution! There can be no other for the same x or y.
3 If $x^2 + y^2 > r > x^2 + (y - 1)^2$ then $Bet(x, y) = Bet(x - 1, y)$. There can be no solutions of the form (x, v).

---

[1] There is a serious problem: what is the component *zero*? The obvious choice is [], but the matrix operations will require careful modification in order to treat this correctly as the zero matrix.

4 Finally, $Bet(x, y) = \emptyset$ if $x < y$.

These suggest a recursive — indeed iterative — search method. Case 3 requires special care if it is to be used efficiently. At the start, make sure $x^2 + y^2 < r$ holds. Increase y until $x^2 + y^2 \geq r$. If $x^2 + y^2 > r$ then y must be the least such, and so Case 3 applies. Decreasing x by one re-establishes $x^2 + y^2 < r$.

Initially $y = 0$ and $x = \sqrt{r}$ (the integer square root of r), so the starting condition holds. Since $x > y$, we know that y will be increased several times when x is decreased. As a further concession to efficiency, therefore, the program takes the computation of x^2 outside the inner recursion:

```
fun squares r =
  let fun between (x,y) =   (*all pairs between x and y*)
          let val diff = r - x*x
              fun above y =   (*all pairs above y*)
                  if y>x then []
                  else if y*y<diff then above (y+1)
                  else if y*y=diff then (x,y)::between(x-1,y+1)
                  else (* y*y>diff *) between(x-1,y)
          in above y   end;
      val firstx = floor(Math.sqrt(real r))
  in between (firstx, 0) end;
> val squares = fn : int -> (int*int) list
```

Execution is fast, even for large r:

```
squares 50;
> [(7, 1), (5, 5)] : (int*int) list
squares 1105;
> [(33, 4), (32, 9), (31, 12), (24, 23)] : (int*int) list
squares 48612265;
> [(6972, 59), (6971, 132), (6952, 531), (6948, 581),
>   (6944, 627), (6917, 876), (6899, 1008), (6853, 1284),
>   (6789, 1588), (6772, 1659), ...] : (int*int) list
```

Dijkstra's program has a different search method: x and y start with equal values, then sweep apart. Our method could well be the one he rejected because 'the demonstration that no solutions had been omitted always required a drawing.'

ⓘ *A smarter way?* A number is the sum of two squares precisely if, in its prime factorization, every factor of the form $4k + 3$ appears with an even exponent. For example, $48, 612, 265 = 5 \times 13 \times 17 \times 29 \times 37 \times 41$ and none of these primes has the form $4k + 3$. The criterion itself merely tells us whether solutions exist, but the theory also provides a means of enumerating the solutions (Davenport, 1952, Chapter V). A program exploiting this theory would pay off only for huge numbers.

3.13   *The problem of the next permutation*

Given a list of integers, we are asked to rearrange the elements to produce the permutation that is next greater under lexicographic ordering. The new permutation should be greater than the one given, with no other permutation in between.

Let us modify the problem slightly. Lexicographic order means the head of the list has the most significance. The next greater permutation will probably differ in the least significant elements. Since the head of a list is the easiest element to reach, let us make it least significant. Fighting the natural order of lists would be foolish. We therefore compute the next permutation under reverse lexicographic ordering.

The problem is hard to visualize — even Dijkstra gives an example. Here are the next eight permutations after 4 3 2 1 (the initial permutation):

$$3\,4\,2\,1$$
$$4\,2\,3\,1$$
$$2\,4\,3\,1$$
$$3\,2\,4\,1$$
$$2\,3\,4\,1$$
$$4\,3\,1\,2$$
$$3\,4\,1\,2$$
$$4\,1\,3\,2$$

The affected part of each is underlined. The sequence of permutations terminates at 1 2 3 4, which has no successor.

To make a greater permutation, some element of the list must be replaced by a larger element to its left. To make the very next permutation, this replacement must happen as far to the left — the least significant position — as possible. The replacement value must be as small as possible, and the elements to the left of the replacement must be arranged in descending order. All this can be done in two steps:

1 Find the leftmost element y that has a greater element to its left. The elements to its left will therefore be an increasing sequence $x_1 \leq \cdots \leq x_n$. (We are really speaking of positions rather than elements, but this only matters if the elements are not distinct.)

2 Replace y by the smallest x_i, with $1 \leq i \leq n$, such that $y < x_i$, and arrange $x_1, \ldots, x_{i-1}, y, x_{i+1}, \ldots, x_n$ in descending order. This can be accomplished by scanning $x_n, x_{n-1}, \ldots, x_1$ until the correct value is found for x_i, placing larger elements in front of the final result.

Calling *next*(*xlist*, *ys*) finds the *y* in *ys* to replace, while *xlist* accumulates the elements passed over. When *xlist* holds the reversed list [x_n, ... , x_1], the function *swap* performs the replacement and rearrangement. The list manipulations are delicate.

```
fun next(xlist, y::ys) : int list =
    if hd xlist <= y then   next(y::xlist, ys)
    else   (*swap y with greatest xk such that x>=xk>y*)
        let fun swap [x]          = y::x::ys
            |   swap (x::xk::xs) = (*x >= xk*)
                if xk>y then x::swap(xk::xs)
                        else (y::xk::xs)@(x::ys)
                        (*x > y >= xk >= xs*)
        in swap(xlist) end;
> val next = fn : int list * int list -> int list
```

Function *nextperm* starts the scan.

```
fun nextperm (y::ys) = next([y], ys);
> val nextperm = fn : int list -> int list
nextperm [1,2,4,3];
> [3, 2, 1, 4] : int list
nextperm it;
> [2, 3, 1, 4] : int list
nextperm it;
> [3, 1, 2, 4] : int list
```

It also works when the elements are not distinct:

```
nextperm [3,2,2,1];
> [2, 3, 2, 1] : int list
nextperm it;
> [2, 2, 3, 1] : int list
nextperm it;
> [3, 2, 1, 2] : int list
```

Exercise 3.29   Write the steps to compute *nextperm*[2, 3, 1, 4].

Exercise 3.30   Does *next* still work if the ≤ comparison is replaced by < in its second line? Justify your answer in terms of the two steps described above.

Exercise 3.31   What does *nextperm*(*ys*) return if there is no next permutation of *ys*? Modify the program so that it returns the initial permutation in that case.

The equality test in polymorphic functions

Polymorphic functions like *length* and *rev* accept lists having elements of any type because they do not perform any operations on those elements. Now consider a function to test whether a value *e* is a member of a list *l*. Is this function polymorphic? Each member of *l* must be tested for equality with *e*. Equality testing is polymorphic, but in a restricted sense.

3.14   *Equality types*

An **equality type** is a type whose values admit equality testing. Equality testing is forbidden on function types and abstract types:

- The equality test on functions is not computable because *f* and *g* are equal just when $f(x)$ equals $g(x)$ for every possible argument *x*. There are other ways of defining equality of functions, but there is no escaping the problem.
- An abstract type provides only those operations specified in its definition. ML hides the representation's equality test, for it seldom coincides with the desired abstract equality.[2]

Equality is defined for the basic types: integers, reals, characters, strings, booleans. For structured values, the equality test compares corresponding components; equality is thus defined for tuples, records, lists and datatypes (introduced in the next chapter) built over the basic types. It is not defined for values containing functions or elements of abstract types.

Standard ML provides **equality type variables** $\alpha^=$, $\beta^=$, $\gamma^=$, ... ranging over the equality types. Equality types contain no type variables other than equality type variables. For example, *int*, *bool* × *string* and (*int list*) × $\beta^=$ are equality types, while *int* → *bool* and *bool* × β are not.

Here is the type of the equality test itself, the infix operator (=):

```
op= ;
> fn : (''a * ''a) -> bool
```

In mathematical notation this type is $\alpha^= \times \alpha^= \to bool$. In ML, an equality type variable begins with two ' characters.

Now let us declare the membership testing function:

```
infix mem;
fun (x mem [])    = false
  | (x mem (y::l)) = (x=y) orelse (x mem l);
> val mem = fn : ''a * ''a list -> bool
```

The type $\alpha^= \times (\alpha^= list) \to bool$ means that *mem* may be applied to any list whose elements permit equality testing.

---

[2] Chapter 7 describes abstract types in detail.

```
"Sally" mem ["Regan","Goneril","Cordelia"];
> false : bool
```

3.15   *Polymorphic set operations*

A function's type contains equality type variables if it performs poly-morphic equality testing, even indirectly, for instance via *mem*. The function *newmem* adds a new element to a list, provided it is really new:

```
fun newmem(x,xs) = if x mem xs then   xs    else   x::xs;
> val newmem = fn : ''a * ''a list -> ''a list
```

Lists constructed by *newmem* can be regarded as finite sets.[3] Let us declare some set operations and note their types. If equality type variables appear, then equal-ity tests are involved.

The function *setof* converts a list to a 'set' by eliminating repeated elements:

```
fun setof []    = []
  | setof(x::xs) = newmem(x, setof xs);
> val setof = fn : ''a list -> ''a list
setof [true,false,false,true,false];
> [true, false] : bool list
```

Observe that *setof* may perform many equality tests. To minimize the use of *setof*, the following functions can be applied to 'sets' — lists of distinct elements — to ensure that their result is a 'set.'

Union. The list *union*(*xs*, *ys*) includes all elements of *xs* not already in *ys*, which is assumed to consist of distinct elements:

```
fun union([],ys)    = ys
  | union(x::xs, ys) = newmem(x, union(xs, ys));
> val union = fn : ''a list * ''a list -> ''a list
```

The type variable ''a indicates equality testing, here via *newmem*.

```
union([1,2,3], [0,2,4]);
> [1, 3, 0, 2, 4] : int list
```

Intersection. Similarly, *inter*(*xs*, *ys*) includes all elements of *xs* that also belong to *ys*:

---

[3] Section 3.22 below considers more deeply the question of representing one data structure using another.

```
fun inter([],ys)      = []
  | inter(x::xs, ys) = if x mem ys then x::inter(xs, ys)
                                   else     inter(xs, ys);
> val inter = fn : ''a list * ''a list -> ''a list
```

A baby's name can be chosen by intersecting the preferences of both parents . . .

```
inter(["John","James","Mark"], ["Nebuchadnezzar","Bede"]);
> [] : string list
```

. . . although this seldom works.

The subset relation. Set T is a ***subset*** of S if all elements of T are also elements of S:

```
infix subs;
fun ([]       subs ys) = true
  | ((x::xs) subs ys) = (x mem ys) andalso (xs subs ys);
> val subs = fn : ''a list * ''a list -> bool
```

Recall that equality types may involve tuples, lists and so forth:

```
[("May",5), ("June",6)] subs [("July",7)];
> false : bool
```

Equality of sets. The built-in list equality test is not valid for sets. The lists $[3, 4]$ and $[4, 3]$ are not equal, yet they denote the same set, $\{3, 4\}$. Set equality ignores order. It can be defined in terms of subsets:

```
infix seq;
fun (xs seq ys) = (xs subs ys) andalso (ys subs xs);
> val seq = fn : ''a list * ''a list -> bool
[3,1,3,5,3,4] seq [1,3,4,5];
> true : bool
```

Sets ought to be declared as an abstract type, hiding the equality test on lists.

Powerset. The ***powerset*** of a set S is the set consisting of all the subsets of S, including the empty set and S itself. It can be computed by removing some element x from S and recursively computing the powerset of $S - \{x\}$. If T is a subset of $S - \{x\}$ then both T and $T \cup \{x\}$ are subsets of S and elements of the powerset. The argument *base* accumulates items (like x) that must be included in each element of the result. In the initial call, *base* should be empty.

```
fun powset ([], base)    = [base]
  | powset (x::xs, base) =
        powset(xs, base) @ powset(xs, x::base);
> val powset = fn : 'a list * 'a list -> 'a list list
```

The ordinary type variables indicate that *powset* does not perform equality tests.

```
powset (rev ["the","weird","sisters"], []);
> [[], ["the"], ["weird"], ["the", "weird"], ["sisters"],
>   ["the", "sisters"], ["weird", "sisters"],
>   ["the", "weird", "sisters"]]  :  string list list
```

Using set notation, the result of *powset* can be described as follows, ignoring the order of list elements:

$$powset(S, B) = \{T \cup B \mid T \subseteq S\}$$

Cartesian product. The **Cartesian product** of S and T is the set of all pairs (x, y) with $x \in S$ and $y \in T$. In set notation,

$$S \times T = \{(x, y) \mid x \in S, \, y \in T\}.$$

Several functional languages support some set notation, following David Turner; see Bird and Wadler (1988) for examples. Since ML does not, we must use recursion over lists. The function to compute Cartesian products is surprisingly complex.

```
fun cartprod ([],    ys) = []
  | cartprod (x::xs, ys) =
        let val xsprod = cartprod(xs,ys)
            fun pairx []        = xsprod
              | pairx (y::ytail) = (x,y) :: (pairx ytail)
        in  pairx ys  end;
> val cartprod = fn : 'a list * 'b list -> ('a * 'b) list
```

The function *cartprod* does not perform equality tests.

```
cartprod([2,5], ["moons","stars","planets"]);
> [(2, "moons"), (2, "stars"), (2, "planets"),
>  (5, "moons"), (5, "stars"), (5, "planets")]
> : (int * string) list
```

Section 5.10 will demonstrate how higher-order functions can express this function. For now, let us continue with simple methods.

Exercise 3.32   How many equality tests does ML perform when evaluating the following expressions?

```
1 mem upto(1,500)
setof(upto(1,500))
```

Exercise 3.33   Compare *union* with the function *itunion* declared below. Which function is more efficient?

```
fun  itunion([],ys)        = ys
  |  itunion(x::xs, ys) = itunion(xs, newmem(x, ys));
```

Exercise 3.34   Write a function *choose* such that *choose*(*k*, *xs*) generates the set of all *k*-element subsets of *xs*. For instance, *choose*(29, *upto*(1, 30)) should return a list containing 30 subsets.

Exercise 3.35   The following function is simpler than *cartprod*. Is it better for computing Cartesian products?

```
fun  cprod ([],    ys) = []
  |  cprod (x::xs, ys) =
         let fun pairx  []        = cprod(xs,ys)
               |  pairx(y::ytail) = (x,y) :: (pairx ytail)
         in  pairx ys  end;
```

3.16   Association lists

A dictionary or table can be represented by a list of pairs. Functions to search such tables involve equality polymorphism. To store the dates of history's greatest battles we could write

```
val battles =
   [("Crecy",1346), ("Poitiers",1356), ("Agincourt",1415),
    ("Trafalgar",1805), ("Waterloo",1815)];
```

A list of (key, value) pairs is called an **association list**. The function *assoc* finds the value associated with a key by sequential search:

```
fun  assoc ([], a)          = []
  |  assoc ((x,y)::pairs, a) = if a=x then [y]
                                    else assoc(pairs, a);
> val assoc = fn : (''a * 'b) list * ''a -> 'b list
```

Its type, $(\alpha^= \times \beta)list \times \alpha^= \to \beta\ list$, indicates that keys must have some equality type $\alpha^=$, while values may have any type β at all. Calling *assoc* (*pairs*, *x*) returns [] if the key *x* is not found, and returns [*y*] if *y* is found paired with *x*. Returning a list of results is a simple method of distinguishing success from failure.

```
assoc(battles, "Agincourt");
> [1415] : int list
assoc(battles, "Austerlitz");
> [] : int list
```

Searching can be slow, but updating is trivial: put a new pair in front. Since *assoc* returns the first value it finds, existing associations can be overridden. Pairing names with types in a block-structured language is a typical application. A name will be paired with several types in the association list if it is declared in nested blocks.

> **ⓘ**   *Equality types: good or bad?* Appel (1993) criticises ML's equality polymorphism on several grounds. They complicate the language definition. They complicate the implementation; data must have run-time tags to support equality testing, or else an equality test must be passed implicitly to functions. Sometimes the standard equality test is inappropriate, as in the case of a set of sets. The polymorphic equality test can be slow.

Part of the justification for equality polymorphism is historical. ML is related to Lisp, where functions like *mem* and *assoc* are among the most basic primitives. But even Lisp has to provide different versions of these functions, performing different sorts of equality tests. If ML did not have equality polymorphism, those functions could still be expressed by taking the testing function as an extra argument.

Equality is really overloaded: its meaning depends upon its type. Other overloaded functions are the arithmetic operators and functions to express values as strings. ML's treatment of overloading seems unsatisfactory, especially compared with Haskell's elegant **type classes** (Hudak *et al.*, 1992). But type classes also complicate the language. More seriously, a program cannot be executed — even in principle — without a full type checking. Odersky *et al.* (1995) discuss an alternative setup; more research is needed.

3.17   *Graph algorithms*

A list of pairs can also represent a directed graph. Each pair (x, y) stands for the edge $x \longrightarrow y$. Thus the list

```
val graph1 = [("a","b"), ("a","c"), ("a","d"),
              ("b","e"), ("c","f"), ("d","e"),
              ("e","f"), ("e","g")];
```

represents the graph shown in Figure 3.1(a).

The function *nexts* finds all successors of a node a — the destinations of all edges leading from a — in the graph:

```
fun nexts (a, [])           = []
  | nexts (a, (x,y)::pairs) =
        if a=x then  y :: nexts(a,pairs)
               else       nexts(a,pairs);
> val nexts = fn : ''a * (''a * 'b) list -> 'b list
```

This function differs from *assoc* by returning all values that are paired with a, not just the first:

Figure 3.1 *A directed graph, and a depth-first traversal*

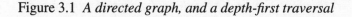

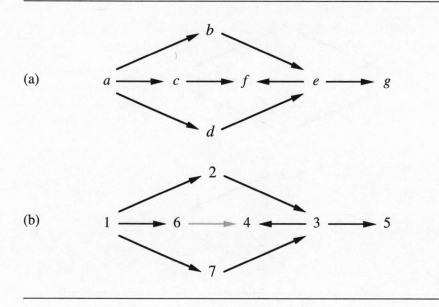

```
nexts("e", graph1);
> ["f", "g"] : string list
```

Depth-first search. Many graph algorithms work by following edges, keeping track of nodes visited so that a node is not visited more than once. In ***depth-first search***, the subgraph reachable from the current node is fully explored before other nodes are visited. The function *depthf* implements this search strategy, using the argument *visited* to accumulate the nodes in reverse order:

```
fun depthf ([],    graph, visited) = rev visited
  | depthf (x::xs, graph, visited) =
        if x mem visited then depthf (xs, graph, visited)
        else depthf (nexts(x,graph) @ xs, graph, x::visited);
> val depthf = fn
> : ''a list * (''a * ''a) list * ''a list -> ''a list
```

The nodes of a graph may have any equality type.

Depth-first search of *graph*1 starting at *a* visits nodes in the order shown in Figure 3.1(b). One of the edges is never traversed. Let us check the traversal by calling our function:

Figure 3.2 *A cyclic graph, and a depth-first traversal*

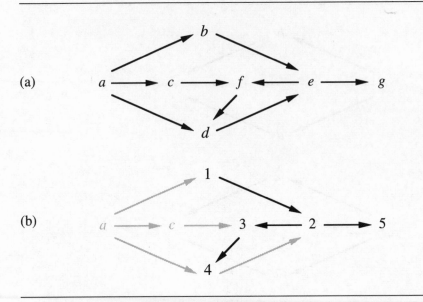

```
depthf(["a"], graph1, []);
> ["a", "b", "e", "f", "g", "c", "d"] : string list
```

Adding an edge from *f* to *d* makes the graph cyclic. If that graph is searched starting at *b*, one of the edges in the cycle is ignored. Also, part of the graph is not accessible from *b* at all; see Figure 3.2.

```
depthf(["b"], ("f","d")::graph1, []);
> ["b", "e", "f", "d", "g"] : string list
```

After visiting a node *x* that has not been visited before, depth-first search recursively visits each successor of *x*. In the list computed by *nexts* (*x*, *graph*) @ *xs*, the successors of *x* precede the other nodes *xs* that are awaiting visits. This list behaves as a stack. **Breadth-first search** results if the list of nodes to visit behaves as a queue.

Depth-first search can also be coded as follows:

```
fun depth ([],     graph, visited) = rev visited
  | depth (x::xs, graph, visited) =
        depth (xs, graph,
                  if x mem visited then   visited
                  else depth (nexts(x,graph), graph, x::visited));
```

A nested recursive call visits the successors of *x*, then another call visits the other nodes, *xs*. The functions *depthf* and *depth* are equivalent, although the proof is subtle. By omitting a call to append (@), *depth* is a bit faster. More importantly, since one call is devoted to visiting *x*, it is easily modified to detect cycles in graphs and perform topological sorting.

Topological sorting. Constraints on the order of events form a directed graph. Each edge $x \longrightarrow y$ means '*x* must happen before *y*.' The graph

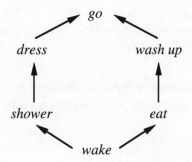

says everything about getting to work. Here it is as a list:

```
val grwork = [("wake","shower"),   ("shower","dress"),
              ("dress","go"),      ("wake", "eat"),
              ("eat","washup"),    ("washup","go")];
```

Finding a linear sequence of events from such a graph is called **topological sorting**. Sedgewick (1988) points out that depth-first search can do this if the visit to node *x* is recorded after its successors have been searched. Thus *x* comes after every node reachable from *x*: a topological sort in reverse.

This means a simple change to *depth*: put *x* on the result of the recursive call instead of the argument. The list forms in reverse so no other reversal is necessary.

```
fun topsort graph =
   let fun sort ([],    visited) = visited
         | sort (x::xs, visited) =
              sort(xs, if x mem visited  then   visited
                       else x :: sort(nexts(x,graph), visited))
       val (starts,_) = ListPair.unzip graph
   in
      sort(starts, [])
   end;
> val topsort = fn : (''a * ''a) list -> ''a list
```

The `let` declaration of *sort* allows this function to refer to *graph*. It also declares *starts*, the list of all starting nodes of edges, to ensure that every node in the graph is reached.

So how do we get to work?

```
topsort grwork;
> ["wake", "eat", "washup", "shower", "dress", "go"]
> : string list
```

Reversing the list of edges gives a different answer for the graph:

```
topsort(rev grwork);
> ["wake", "shower", "dress", "eat", "washup", "go"]
> : string list
```

Cycle detection. Now consider a further constraint: we must go before we eat. The resulting graph contains a cycle and admits no solution. The function call runs forever:

```
topsort(("go","eat")::grwork);
```

Looping is not acceptable; the function should somehow report that no solution exists. Cycles can be detected by maintaining a list of all nodes being searched. This list of nodes, called *path*, traces the edges from the start of the search.

```
fun pathsort graph =
  let fun sort ([],    path, visited) = visited
        | sort (x::xs, path, visited) =
              if x mem path then hd[]    (*abort!!*)
              else sort(xs, path,
                          if x mem visited  then  visited else
                          x :: sort(nexts(x,graph),x::path,visited))
        val (starts,_) = ListPair.unzip graph
  in sort(starts, [], []) end;
> val pathsort = fn : (''a * ''a) list -> ''a list
```

It works on our original graph. Given a cycle it causes an error:

```
pathsort graph1;
> ["a", "d", "c", "b", "e", "g", "f"] : string list
pathsort(("go","eat")::grwork);
> Exception: Match
```

An error message is better than looping, but *pathsort* aborts by making an erroneous function call (namely *hd* [ ]), an ugly trick. The next chapter explains how to declare an ***exception*** for such errors.

Exceptions are not the only way to report cycles. The following function returns two results: a list of visits, as before, and a list of nodes found in cycles. Maintaining two results, let us declare a function to add a visit:

```
fun newvisit (x, (visited, cys)) = (x::visited,  cys);
> val newvisit = fn : 'a * ('a list * 'b) -> 'a list * 'b
```

With the help of this function, topological sorting is easily expressed:

```
fun cyclesort graph =
  let fun sort ([],    path, (visited, cys)) = (visited,  cys)
       | sort (x::xs, path, (visited, cys)) =
            sort (xs, path,
                     if x mem path           then (visited, x::cys)
                     else if x mem visited then (visited,  cys)
                     else newvisit (x,  sort (nexts (x, graph),
                                              x::path,  (visited, cys))))
        val (starts,_) = ListPair.unzip graph
   in sort (starts, [], ([],[])) end;
> val cyclesort = fn
> : (''a *''a) list -> ''a list * ''a list
```

If there is a cycle, then *cyclesort* says where it is:

```
cyclesort (("go","eat")::grwork);
> (["wake", "shower", "dress", "go", "eat", "washup"],
>  ["go"])  :  string list * string list
```

And if not, then *cyclesort* sorts the graph:

```
cyclesort (rev graph1);
> (["a", "b", "c", "d", "e", "f", "g"], [])
> : string list * string list
```

These polymorphic graph functions are too slow for large graphs because of the list searches. Restricting the nodes to integers, more efficient functions can be written using the functional arrays of the next chapter.

Exercise 3.36 Modify *pathsort* to return [] if the graph has a cycle and the singleton list [*visited*] otherwise.

Exercise 3.37 Let (*visited, cys*) be the result of *cyclesort*. If the graph contains many cycles, will *cys* contain a node belonging to each? What can be said about *visited* if the graph contains cycles?

Sorting: A case study

Sorting is one of the most studied topics in the theory of computing. Several sorting algorithms are widely known. To sort n items, ***insertion sort*** takes order n^2 time; ***merge sort*** takes order $n \log n$ time; ***quick sort*** takes order $n \log n$ on average, n^2 in the worst case.

These algorithms usually sort an array. Apart from ***heap sort***, where the array encodes a binary tree, they are easily coded as functions on lists. Their time complexity remains unchanged: not that a list sort will win a race against an array sort! A complexity estimate such as 'order n^2 time' means the execution time is proportional to n^2. The list sort will have a higher constant of proportionality.

This section compares several sorting functions, giving the time taken to sort a list of 10,000 random numbers. These timings are informal but illustrate the practical performance of each algorithm.

The Pascal version of quick sort by Sedgewick (1988) can sort the numbers in 110 msec. This roughly equals the best time for functional sorting. Pascal beats ML if checking is disabled, but we give up the clarity and simplicity of functional programming (never mind safety). The overheads of lists would matter less for sorting, say, a bibliography, where the cost of comparisons would dominate.

ℹ *How timings were measured.* Timings were conducted on a Sun SuperSPARC Model 61 computer running Standard ML of New Jersey, version 108. The measurements were made using standard library facilities (structure *Timer*), and include garbage collection time. Thanks to improvements in hardware and software, ML programs run 20–40 times faster than they did in the first edition of this book.

The Pascal program was compiled using the Pascal 3.0 compiler. With array subscript checking disabled, the run-time drops to 75 msec. With full optimization the program runs in just 34 msec, but afterwards prints a warning that it 'may have produced nonstandard floating-point results.' What risks are worth taking in our quest for speed?

3.18   *Random numbers*

First, we must produce 10,000 random numbers. Park and Miller (1988), complaining that good random number generators are hard to find, recommend the following.

```
local val a = 16807.0  and  m = 2147483647.0
in   fun nextrand seed =
           let val t = a*seed
           in  t - m * real(floor(t/m))   end
end;
> val nextrand = fn : real -> real
```

Calling *nextrand* with any *seed* between 1 and $m - 1$ yields another number in this range, performing the integer calculation

$$(a \times seed) \bmod m.$$

Real arithmetic is used to avoid integer overflow. The function works provided mantissæ are accurate to 46 bits. When trying this on your machine, check that the random numbers are exact integers.

Calling *randlist* $(n, seed, [\,])$ generates a random list of length n starting from *seed*. Because the list accumulates in *tail*, its order is reversed:

```
fun randlist (n,seed,tail) =
    if n=0 then (seed,tail)
    else   randlist(n-1, nextrand seed, seed::tail);
> val randlist = fn
> : int * real * real list -> real * real list
```

The list of 10,000 random numbers is called *rs*. Here are the first 15.

```
val (seed,rs) = randlist(10000, 1.0, []);
> val seed = 1043618065.0 : real
> val rs =
> [1484786315.0, 925166085.0, 1614852353.0, 721631166.0,
>   173942219.0, 1229443779.0, 789328014.0, 570809709.0,
>   1760109362.0, 270600523.0, 2108528931.0, 16480421.0,
>   519782231.0, 162430624.0, 372212905.0, ...] : real list
```

3.19 *Insertion sort*

Insertion sort works by inserting the items, one at a time, into a sorted list. It is slow but simple. Here is the insertion function:

```
fun ins (x, []): real list = [x]
  | ins (x, y::ys)         =
        if x<=y then x::y::ys      (*it belongs here*)
                else y::ins(x,ys);
> val ins = fn : real * real list -> real list
```

The type constraint *real list* resolves overloading of the comparison operator. All the sorting functions have a type constraint.

We insert some numbers into [6.0], which is trivially sorted:

```
ins(4.0, [6.0]);
> [4.0, 6.0] : real list
ins(8.0,it);
> [4.0, 6.0, 8.0] : real list
ins(5.0,it);
> [4.0, 5.0, 6.0, 8.0] : real list
```

Insertion sort calls *ins* on every element of the input:

```
fun insort []     = []
  | insort (x::xs) = ins(x, insort xs);
> val insort = fn : real list -> real list
```

These functions require deep recursion. But this inefficiency is insignificant. Insertion, functional or imperative, does a lot of copying. The execution time of the sort is order n^2. For our 10,000 integers it takes over 32 seconds, nearly 300 times slower than quick sort. Insertion sort can be considered only for short lists or those that are nearly sorted. The algorithm is worth noting because it is simple and because better sorting algorithms (merge sort and heap sort) are refinements of it.

3.20   *Quick sort*

Quick sort, invented by C. A. R. Hoare, was among the first efficient sorting algorithms. It works by divide and conquer:

- Choose some value *a*, called the **pivot**, from the input.
- Partition the remaining items into two parts: the items less than or equal to *a*, and the items greater than *a*.
- Sort each part recursively, then put the smaller part before the greater.

Quick sort is ideal for arrays — the partition step is extremely fast, moving few items. For lists, it copies all the items; *partition* is a good example of an iterative function that builds two results.

```
fun quick []     = []
  | quick [x]    = [x]
  | quick (a::bs) = (*the head "a" is the pivot*)
      let fun partition (left,right,[]) : real list =
                (quick left) @ (a :: quick right)
            | partition (left,right, x::xs)      =
                  if x<=a then partition (x::left,  right, xs)
                          else partition (left, x::right, xs)
      in  partition([],[],bs)  end;
> val quick = fn : real list -> real list
```

This function sorts our 10,000 numbers in about 160 msec:

```
quick rs;
> [1.0, 8383.0, 13456.0, 16807.0, 84083.0, 86383.0,
>   198011.0, 198864.0, 456291.0, 466696.0, 524209.0,
>   591308.0, 838913.0, 866720.0, ...] : real list
```

The append (@) can be eliminated by accumulating the sorted result in a second argument. This version of quick sort, which is left as an exercise, takes only about 110 msec.

Like its procedural counterpart, *quick* takes order $n \log n$ time in the average case. If the input is already in increasing or decreasing order, then quick sort takes order n^2 time.

Exercise 3.38 Express quick sort such that *quicker*(*xs*, *sorted*) accumulates the result in *sorted*, with no use of append.

Exercise 3.39 Write a function *find* such that *find*(*xs*, *i*) returns the *i*th smallest item in the list *xs*. This is called **selection**. Hoare's algorithm for selection is related to quick sort, and is much faster than sorting the list and returning the *i*th element.

Exercise 3.40 Generalize *find* above to *findrange*(*xs*, *i*, *j*), returning the list of the *i*th to *j*th smallest items in the list *xs*.

3.21 *Merge sort*

Several algorithms work by merging sorted lists. The merging function repeatedly takes the smaller of the heads of two lists:

```
fun merge([],ys)           = ys : real list
  | merge(xs,[])           = xs
  | merge(x::xs, y::ys) =
        if x<=y then x::merge(xs,   y::ys)
                else y::merge(x::xs,   ys);
> val merge = fn : real list * real list -> real list
```

When sorting 10,000 items, the recursion in *merge* may be too deep for some ML systems. The fault lies with those ML systems, not with *merge*. As with *take* and *append*, the dominant cost is that of constructing the resulting list. An iterative merging function, although avoiding the deep recursion, would probably have to perform costly list reversals.

Merge sort can be **top-down** or **bottom-up**. Either way, merging is efficient only if the two lists have similar lengths. If a list has only one element, merging degenerates to insertion.

Top-down merge sort. In the top-down approach, the input list is divided into two roughly equal parts using *take* and *drop*. These are sorted recursively and the results merged.

```
fun tmergesort []  =  []
  | tmergesort [x]  =  [x]
  | tmergesort xs   =
      let val k = length xs div 2
      in  merge (tmergesort (List.take(xs,k)),
                 tmergesort (List.drop(xs,k)))
      end;
> val tmergesort = fn : real list -> real list
```

Unlike quick sort, the worst case execution time is order $n \log n$. But it is slower on average, taking about 290 msec to sort the 10,000 numbers. Its calls to *length*, *take* and *drop* scan the input list repeatedly. Here is one way to eliminate them:

```
fun tmergesort' xs =
  let fun sort (0,  xs)    = ([], xs)
        | sort (1, x::xs)  = ([x], xs)
        | sort (n,  xs)    =
            let val (l1, xs1) = sort ((n+1) div 2, xs)
                val (l2, xs2) = sort (n div 2, xs1)
            in (merge (l1,l2), xs2)
            end
      val (l, _) = sort (length xs, xs)
  in l end;
```

Calling *sort* (n, xs) sorts the first n elements of xs and returns the remaining elements. One might expect this to be slow, since it builds so many pairs. But it needs only 200 msec to sort the random numbers. It is still slower than quick sort, but can be recommended as a simple and acceptably fast method.

Bottom-up merge sort. The basic bottom-up approach divides the input into lists of length 1. Adjacent pairs of lists are then merged, obtaining sorted lists of length 2, then 4, then 8 and so on. Finally one sorted list remains. This approach is easy to code but wasteful. Why should the 10,000 numbers be copied into a list of 10,000 singleton lists?

O'Keefe (1982) describes a beautiful way to merge the lists of various lengths simultaneously, never storing these lists in full.

$$A\ B\ C\ D\ E\ F\ G\ H\ I\ J\ K$$

The underlining shows how adjacent lists are merged. First A with B, then C with D, and now AB and CD have equal length and can be merged. O'Keefe accumulates the merges at all levels in one list. Rather than comparing the sizes of lists, he lets the count k of members determine how to add the next member.

If *k* is even then there are two members of equal size *s* to merge. The resulting list is treated as member $k/2$ of size $2s$, which may cause further merging.

```
fun mergepairs([l],      k) = [l]
  | mergepairs(l1::l2::ls, k) =
        if k mod 2 = 1 then l1::l2::ls
        else mergepairs(merge(l1,l2)::ls, k div 2);
> val mergepairs = fn
> : real list list * int -> real list list
```

If $k = 0$ then *mergepairs* merges the entire list of lists into one list. Calling *sorting* (*xs*, [[]], 0) sorts the list *xs*. It takes 270 msec to sort the 10,000 numbers.

```
fun sorting([],     ls, k) = hd(mergepairs(ls,0))
  | sorting(x::xs, ls, k) =
        sorting(xs, mergepairs([x]::ls, k+1), k+1);
> val sorting = fn
> : real list * real list list * int -> real list
```

A *smooth* sort has a linear execution time (order *n*) if its input is nearly sorted, degenerating to $n \log n$ in the worst case. O'Keefe presents a 'smooth applicative merge sort' that exploits order in the input. Rather than dividing it into singleton lists, he divides the input into increasing runs. If the number of runs is independent of *n* (and so 'nearly sorted') then the execution time is linear.

The function *nextrun* returns the next increasing run from a list, paired with the list of unread items. (An imperative program would delete items as they were processed.) The run grows in reverse order, hence the call to *rev*.

```
fun nextrun(run, [])   = (rev run, []: real list)
  | nextrun(run, x::xs) =
            if x < hd run then (rev run, x::xs)
                          else nextrun(x::run, xs);
> val nextrun = fn
> : real list * real list -> real list * real list
```

Runs are repeatedly taken and merged.

```
fun samsorting([],     ls, k) = hd(mergepairs(ls,0))
  | samsorting(x::xs, ls, k) =
        let val (run, tail) = nextrun([x], xs)
        in  samsorting(tail, mergepairs(run::ls,k+1), k+1)
        end;
> val samsorting = fn
> : real list * real list list * int -> real list
```

The main sorting function is

```
fun samsort xs = samsorting(xs, [[]], 0);
> val samsort = fn : real list -> real list
```

The algorithm is both elegant and efficient. Even for our random data, with its short runs, the execution time is 250 msec.

ⓘ   *Historical notes.* Sorting with lists is similar to sorting on tape. Random access is inefficient; data must be scanned in order, either forward or reverse. The fascinating but largely obsolete literature on tape sorting may contain useful ideas. The technique used in *mergepairs* bears a strong resemblance to the oscillating sort developed during the 1960s (Knuth, 1973, 5.4.5).

Merge sorting is seldom done using arrays because it cannot be done in-place: it requires two arrays. Even so, its use was proposed as early as 1945; the idea of exploiting runs in the input is also quite old (Knuth, 1973, 5.2.4).

Exercise 3.41   Use the following function to code a new version of top-down merge sort, and measure its speed. Explain your findings, taking account of garbage collection time if you can measure it.

```
fun alts  ([],xs,ys)       = (xs,ys)
  | alts  ([x],xs,ys)      = (x::xs,  ys)
  | alts  (x::y::l,  xs,  ys) = alts(l,  x::xs,  y::ys);
```

Exercise 3.42   This is the same as the previous exercise, except that you should base the new sorting function on the following:

```
fun takedrop ([],  n,  xs)   = (xs,  [])
  | takedrop (x::l,  n,  xs) =
        if n>0 then takedrop(l,  n-1,  x::xs)
               else (xs,  x::l);
```

Exercise 3.43   Why call *sorting* (*xs*, [[]], 0) and not *sorting* (*xs*, [], 0)?

Exercise 3.44   Write a version of *samsort* that uses both increasing and decreasing runs.

Polynomial arithmetic

Computers were invented to perform numerical arithmetic. They excel at portraying data graphically. But sometimes nothing conveys more information than a symbolic formula. A graph of $E = mc^2$ is simply a straight line!

Computer algebra is concerned with automating symbolic mathematics, as used by scientists and engineers. Systems such as MACSYMA and REDUCE can do stupendous tasks involving differentiation, integration, power series expansions, etc. The most basic symbolic operations perform polynomial arithmetic.

Even this is hard to do efficiently. We shall restrict ourselves to the simplest case of all, **univariate** polynomials. These are polynomials in one variable, say x; they can be added and multiplied straightforwardly:

$$(x + 1) + (x^2 - 2) = x^2 + x - 1$$
$$(x + 1) \times (x^2 - 2) = x^3 + x^2 - 2x - 2$$

In developing a package for arithmetic on univariate polynomials, we touch upon the general problem of data representation. We implement addition and multiplication, using sorting ideas from the previous section. We arrive at another structure matching signature *ARITH* of Section 2.22. Finally we consider how to find greatest common divisors, a challenge even in the univariate case.

Our code will be fast enough to compute $(x^3 + 1)^{1000}$ in under two seconds. This demonstrates what can be accomplished with such simple tools as lists.

3.22 *Representing abstract data*

In Section 3.15 above we considered operations such as *union* and *subset* for finite sets. ML does not provide finite sets as a data structure; instead, we represent them by lists without repetitions. It is worth examining what this really involves. Although finite sets may seem trivial, they exhibit most of the issues involved in data representation.

A collection of abstract objects, here finite sets, is represented using a set of concrete objects, here certain lists. Every abstract object can be represented by at least one concrete object. There may be more than one: recall that $\{3, 4\}$ can be represented by [3, 4] or [4, 3]. Some concrete objects, such as [3, 3], represent no abstract object at all.

Operations on the abstract data are defined in terms of the representations. For example, the ML function *union* implements the abstract function $\cup$ provided *union*(l, l') represents $A \cup A'$ for all lists l and l' that represent the sets A and A', respectively. The ML predicate *subs* (which is an infix operator) implements the abstract relation $\subseteq$ provided l *subs* l' equals *true* whenever $A \subseteq A'$ holds, for all l and l' that represent the sets A and A'. The equality relation is treated similarly; we do not expect equal sets to have equal representations.

These issues come up every time we use a computer, which ultimately represents all data in terms of zeros and ones. Some deeper issues can only be mentioned here. For example, the computer represents real numbers by floating point numbers, but most real numbers cannot be represented, and real arithmetic is implemented only approximately.

3.23   *Representing polynomials*

Now let us consider how to represent univariate polynomials of the form

$$a_n x^n + \cdots + a_0 x^0.$$

Since we only allow one variable, its name does not have to be stored. The *co-efficients* $a_n, \ldots, a_0$ in an abstract polynomial might be real numbers. But real arithmetic on a computer is approximate. We ought to represent coefficients by rational numbers, pairs of integers with no common factor.[4] But this would be a digression, and it really requires arbitrary-precision integers, which some ML systems lack. Therefore, strictly as an expedient, let us represent coefficients by the ML type *real*.

We could represent polynomials by the list of their coefficients, $[a_n, \ldots, a_0]$. To see that this is unacceptable, consider the polynomial $x^{100} + 1$, and then consider squaring it! In a typical polynomial, most of the coefficients are zero. We need a *sparse* representation, in contrast to the *dense* representation that we used earlier for matrices.

Let us represent a polynomial by a list of pairs of the form (k, a_k) for every k such that a_k is non-zero. The pairs should appear in decreasing order in k; this will help us collect terms having the same exponent. For example, `[(2,1.0), (0,~2.0)]` represents $x^2 - 2$.

Our representation is better behaved than that of finite sets because every abstract polynomial has a unique representation. Two polynomials are equal just if their underlying lists are equal. But not every list of (integer, real) pairs represents a polynomial.

We ought to declare polynomials as an abstract type, hiding the underlying lists. For now, let us package the polynomial operations into a structure, following signature *ARITH*.

```
structure Poly =
  struct
  type t  =  (int*real)  list;
  val zero = [];
  fun sum   ...
  fun diff  ...
  fun prod  ...
  fun quo   ...
  end;
```

Here *t* is the type that represents polynomials, and *zero* is the empty list, which represents the zero polynomial. The other components are described below.

---

[4] See Exercise 2.25 on page 63.

3.24 *Polynomial addition and multiplication*

Computing the sum of two polynomials is like merging the corresponding lists; consider $(x^3 - x) + (2x^2 + 1) = x^3 + 2x^2 - x + 1$. But like terms must be combined, and zero terms cancelled; consider $(x^4 - x + 3) + (x - 5) = x^4 - 2$. The ML definition follows the method we should use on paper:

```
fun sum ([], us)              = us : t
  | sum (ts, [])              = ts
  | sum ((m,a)::ts, (n,b)::us) =
          if m>n then (m,a) :: sum (ts, (n,b)::us)
      else if n>m then (n,b) :: sum (us, (m,a)::ts)
      else (* m=n *)
          if a+b=0.0 then sum (ts, us)
                else (m, a+b) :: sum (ts, us);
```

The product of two polynomials is computed using the distributive law. Terms of one polynomial are multiplied against the other polynomial, and the results added:

$$(x^2 + 2x - 3) \times (2x - 1) = x^2(2x - 1) + 2x(2x - 1) - 3(2x - 1)$$
$$= (2x^3 - x^2) + (4x^2 - 2x) + (-6x + 3)$$
$$= 2x^3 + 3x^2 - 8x + 3$$

To implement this method, we first need a function to multiply a term by a polynomial:

```
fun termprod ((m,a), [])       = [] : t
  | termprod ((m,a), (n,b)::ts) =
        (m+n, a*b) :: termprod ((m,a), ts);
```

The naïve multiplication algorithm closely follows the example above:

```
fun nprod ([], us)        = []
  | nprod ((m,a)::ts, us) = sum (termprod ((m,a), us),
                                 nprod (ts, us));
```

Faster multiplication. Experiments show that *nprod* is too slow for large polynomials. It requires over two seconds and numerous garbage collections to compute the square of $(x^3 + 1)^{400}$. (Such large computations are typical of computer algebra.) The reason is that *sum* merges lists of greatly differing length. If *ts* and *us* have 100 terms each, then *termprod*((m,a) , *us*) has only 100 terms, while *nprod*(*ts*,*us*) could have as many as 10,000 terms. Their sum will have at most 10,100 terms, a growth of only 1%.

Merge sort inspires a faster algorithm. Divide one of the polynomials into equal halves, compute two products recursively, and add them. We form as many sums as before, but they are balanced: we compute $(p_1 + p_2) + (p_3 + p_4)$ instead of $p_1 + (p_2 + (p_3 + p_4))$. On average the summands are smaller, and each addition doubles the size of the result.

```
fun prod ([], us)          = []
  | prod ([(m,a)], us) = termprod ((m,a), us)
  | prod (ts, us)          =
      let val k = length ts div 2
      in  sum (prod (List.take(ts,k), us),
               prod (List.drop(ts,k), us))
      end;
```

This is three times as fast as *nprod* for computing the square of $(x^3 + 1)^{400}$. The speedup appears to increase with larger polynomials.

Running some examples. Although we have not fully defined the structure *Poly* yet, suppose we have done so — including a function *show*, to display polynomials as strings. We compute the sum and product of $x + 1$ and $x^2 - 2$, which were shown at the start of this section:

```
val p1 = [(1,1.0),(0,1.0)]
and p2 = [(2,1.0),(0,~2.0)];

Poly.show (Poly.sum (p1, p2));
> "x^2 + x - 1.0" : string
Poly.show (Poly.prod (p1, p2));
> "x^3 + x^2 - 2.0x - 2.0" : string
```

Structure *Poly* also provides exponentiation. The function *power* is defined as in Section 2.14. For a larger example, let us compute $(x - 1)^{10}$:

```
val xminus1 = [(1,1.0), (0,~1.0)];

Poly.show (Poly.power (xminus1, 10));
> "x^10 - 10.0x^9 + 45.0x^8 - 120.0x^7 + 210.0x^6
>   - 252.0x^5+ 210.0x^4 - 120.0x^3 + 45.0x^2
>   - 10.0x + 1.0" : string
```

Here are the first few terms of $(x^2 - 2)^{150}$:

```
Poly.show (Poly.power (p2, 150));
> "x^300 - 300.0x^298 + 44700.0x^296
>   - 4410400.0x^294 + 324164400.0x^292..." : string
```

Exercise 3.45   Code *diff*, a function that computes the difference between two polynomials. Using *termprod* it can be coded in one line, but not efficiently.

Exercise 3.46 Code *show*, the function that produces the output shown in the text. (Functions *Real . toString* and *Int . toString* convert numbers to strings.)

Exercise 3.47 Give a convincing argument that *sum* and *prod* respect the representation of polynomials.

Exercise 3.48 What does it mean to say that *sum* correctly computes the sum of two polynomials? How might you prove it?

3.25 *The greatest common divisor*

Many applications involve **rational functions**: fractions over polynomials. Efficiency demands that a fraction's numerator and denominator should have no common factor. Therefore, we need a function to compute the greatest common divisor (GCD) of two polynomials. This requires functions to compute polynomial quotients and remainders.

Polynomial division. The algorithm for polynomial division resembles ordinary long division. It is actually easier, for it requires no guessing. Each step removes the leading term of the dividend by dividing the leading term of the divisor into it. Each such step yields a term of the quotient. Let us divide $2x^2 + x - 3$ by $x - 1$:

$$
\begin{array}{r}
2x + 3 \\
x - 1 \overline{\smash{)}2x^2 + x - 3} \\
\underline{2x^2 - 2x} \\
3x - 3 \\
\underline{3x - 3} \\
0
\end{array}
$$

Here the remainder is zero. In the general case, the remainder is a polynomial whose leading exponent (called its **degree**) is less than that of the divisor. Let us divide $x^3 + 2x^2 - 3x + 1$ by $x^2 + x - 2$, obtaining a remainder of $-2x + 3$:

$$
\begin{array}{r}
x + 1 \\
x^2 + x - 2 \overline{\smash{)}x^3 + 2x^2 - 3x + 1} \\
\underline{x^3 + x^2 - 2x} \\
x^2 - x + 1 \\
\underline{x^2 + x - 2} \\
-2x + 3
\end{array}
$$

If the divisor's leading coefficient is not unity then fractions will probably appear. This can make the computation much slower, but it does not complicate the basic algorithm. The function *quorem* directly implements the method sketched above, returning the pair (quotient, remainder). The quotient forms in reverse.

```
fun quorem (ts, (n,b)::us) =
  let fun dividing ([],          qs) = (rev qs, [])
        | dividing ((m,a)::ts, qs) =
            if m<n then (rev qs, (m,a)::ts)
            else dividing (sum (ts, termprod ((m-n, ~a/b), us)),
                           (m-n, a/b) :: qs)
  in  dividing (ts, []) end;
```

Dividing $x^2 - 2$ by $x - 1$ yields a quotient of $x + 1$ and a remainder of -1, since $(x-1) \times (x+1) = x^2 - 1$. Assume that *Poly* includes *quorem*, and also a function *showpair* for displaying a pair of polynomials:

```
Poly.quorem (p2, xminus1);
> ([(1, 1.0), (0, 1.0)], [(0, ~1.0)])
> : (int * real) list * (int * real) list
Poly.showpair it;
> "x + 1.0,    - 1.0" : string
```

Let us run the second example of division shown above.

```
Poly.showpair
    (Poly.quorem ([(3,1.0),(2,2.0),(1,~3.0),(0,1.0)],
                  [(2,1.0),(1,1.0),(0,~2.0)]));
> "x + 1.0,    - 2.0x + 3.0" : string
```

We can trivially define the quotient function *quo* in terms of *quorem*. Including the *diff* function of Exercise 3.45 gives structure *Poly* all the components it needs to match signature *ARITH*. Our collection of arithmetic structures now includes the complex numbers, binary numerals, matrices and polynomials! But note, again, that there are important differences among these structures; for each there are additional components that would not make sense for the others. Although *Poly* can match signature *ARITH* when we need it to, normally we take full advantage of its other components.

Euclid's Algorithm for polynomials. We can now compute GCDs using Euclid's Algorithm. Recall that #2 extracts the second component of a pair, here the remainder after polynomial division.

```
fun gcd ([], us) = us
  | gcd (ts, us) = gcd (#2(quorem (us,ts)), ts);
```

Assuming that *Poly* contains *gcd* as a component, we can try it out on some examples. The GCD of $x^8 - 1$ and $x^3 - 1$ is $x - 1$:

```
Poly.show (Poly.gcd ([(8,1.0),(0,~1.0)],
                     [(3,1.0),(0,~1.0)]));
> "x - 1.0" : string
```

The GCD of $x^2 + 2x + 1$ and $x^2 - 1$ is ... $-2x - 2$?

```
Poly.show (Poly.gcd ([(2,1.0),(1,2.0),(0,1.0)],
                     [(2,1.0), (0,~1.0)]));
> " - 2.0x - 2.0" : string
```

The GCD ought to be $x + 1$. This particular difficulty can be solved by dividing through by the leading coefficient, but there are other problems. We must use rational arithmetic: see the warning below. Then computing the GCD often requires operating on enormous integers, even if the initial polynomials have only single-digit coefficients. Many further refinements, typically using modular arithmetic, are essential.

Beware rounding errors. The use of floating point arithmetic (type *real*) is especially bad in *gcd*, because its first line tests for a remainder of zero. Rounding errors during division could give the remainder a small but non-zero coefficient; a common divisor would be missed. For other applications, polynomial arithmetic is fairly well-behaved, because the effects of rounding errors are predictable. (I am grateful to James Davenport for these observations.)

Further reading. Davenport *et al.* (1993) is an excellent introduction to computer algebra. Chapter 2 covers data representation. We learn, for example, that multivariate polynomials can be represented as univariate polynomials whose coefficients are themselves univariate polynomials in some other variable. Thus $y^2 + xy$ is a univariate polynomial in y whose coefficients are 1 and the polynomial x; we could exchange the rôles of x and y. Chapter 4 covers the horrendous complications involved in computing GCDs efficiently.

Summary of main points

- Lists are constructed from the empty list (*nil* or []), using :: ('cons') to attach elements to the front.
- Important library functions include *length*, *take*, *drop*, the infix operator @ (concatenation) and *rev* (reverse).
- A recursive function, by accumulating its results in an extra argument, may avoid inefficient list concatenation.
- Equality polymorphism allows functions to perform equality testing on their arguments. Examples include *mem*, which tests membership in a list, and *assoc*, which searches in a list of pairs.

- The usual sorting algorithms can be implemented using lists, with surprising efficiency.
- Lists can represent binary numerals, matrices, graphs, polynomials, etc., allowing operations to be expressed concisely.

4
Trees and Concrete Data

Concrete data consists of constructions that can be inspected, taken apart, or joined to form larger constructions. Lists are an example of concrete data. We can test whether or not a list is empty, and divide a non-empty list into its head and tail. New elements can be joined to a list. This chapter introduces several other forms of concrete data, including trees and logical propositions.

The ML `datatype` declaration defines a new type along with its *constructors*. In an expression, constructors create values of a datatype; in patterns, constructions describe how to take such values apart. A datatype can represent a class consisting of distinct subclasses — like Pascal's variant records, but without their complications and insecurities. A recursive datatype typically represents a tree. Functions on datatypes are declared by pattern-matching.

The special datatype *exn* is the type of *exceptions*, which stand for error conditions. Errors can be signalled and trapped. An exception handler tests for particular errors by pattern-matching.

Chapter outline

This chapter describes datatypes, pattern-matching, exception handling and trees. It contains the following sections:

The `datatype` declaration. Datatypes, constructors and pattern-matching are illustrated through examples. To represent the King and his subjects, a single type *person* comprises four classes of individual and associates appropriate information with each.

Exceptions. These represent a class of error values. Exceptions can be declared for each possible error. Raising an exception signals an error; handling the exception allows an alternative computation to be performed.

Trees. A tree is a branching structure. Binary trees are a generalization of lists and have many applications.

Tree-based data structures. Dictionaries, flexible arrays and priority queues are implemented easily using binary trees. The update operation creates a new data structure, with minimal copying.

123

A tautology checker. This is an example of elementary theorem proving. A datatype of propositions (boolean expressions) is declared. Functions convert propositions to conjunctive normal form and test for tautologies.

The **datatype** declaration

A heterogeneous class consists of several distinct subclasses. A circle, a triangle and a square are all shapes, but of different kinds. A triangle might be represented by three points, a square by four points and a circle by its radius and centre.

For a harder problem, consider cataloguing all the inhabitants of the Kingdom by their class. These comprise the King, the Peers (or nobility), the Knights and the Peasants. For each we record appropriate information:

- The King is simply himself. There is nothing more to say.
- A Peer has a degree, territory and number in succession (as in 'the 7th Earl of Carlisle.')
- A Knight or Peasant has a name.

In weakly typed languages, these subclasses can be represented directly. We need only take care to distinguish Knights from Peasants; the others will differ naturally. In ML we could try

```
"King"
("Earl","Carlisle",7)          ("Duke","Norfolk",9)
("Knight","Gawain")            ("Knight","Galahad")
("Peasant","Jack Cade")        ("Peasant","Wat Tyler")
```

Unfortunately, these do not all have the same type! No ML function could handle both Kings and Peasants with this representation.

4.1   *The King and his subjects*

An ML type consisting of King, Peers, Knights and Peasants is created by a datatype declaration:

```
datatype person = King
                | Peer of string*string*int
                | Knight of string
                | Peasant of string;
> datatype person
>    con King    : person
>    con Peer    : string * string * int -> person
>    con Knight  : string -> person
>    con Peasant : string -> person
```

Five things are declared, namely the type *person* and its four **constructors** *King*, *Peer*, *Knight* and *Peasant*.

The type *person* consists precisely of the values built by its constructors. Note that *King* has type *person*, while the other constructors are functions that return something of that type. Thus the following have type *person*:

```
King
Peer("Earl","Carlisle",7)    Peer("Duke","Norfolk",9)
Knight "Gawain"              Knight "Galahad"
Peasant "Jack Cade"         Peasant "Wat Tyler"
```

Furthermore, these values are distinct. No *person* can be both a *Knight* and a *Peasant*; no *Peer* can have two different degrees.

Values of type *person*, like other ML values, may be arguments and results of functions and may belong to data structures such as lists:

```
val persons = [King, Peasant "Jack Cade", Knight "Gawain"];
> val persons = [King, Peasant "Jack Cade",
>               Knight "Gawain"] : person list
```

Since each *person* is a unique construction, it can be taken apart. A function over a datatype can be declared through patterns involving the constructors. As with lists, there may be several cases. A person's title depends upon his class and is constructed using string concatenation (^):

```
fun title King              = "His Majesty the King"
  | title (Peer(deg,terr,_)) = "The " ^ deg ^ " of " ^ terr
  | title (Knight name)      = "Sir " ^ name
  | title (Peasant name)     = name;
> val title = fn : person -> string
```

Each case is governed by a pattern with its own set of pattern variables. The *Knight* and *Peasant* cases each involve a variable called *name*, but these variables have separate scopes.

```
title(Peer("Earl", "Carlisle", 7));
> "The Earl of Carlisle" : string
title(Knight "Galahad");
> "Sir Galahad" : string
```

Patterns may be as complicated as necessary, combining tuples and the list constructors with datatype constructors. The function *sirs* returns the names of all the Knights in a list of persons:

```
fun sirs []                    = []
  | sirs ((Knight s) :: ps) = s :: (sirs ps)
  | sirs (p :: ps)            = sirs ps;
> val sirs = fn : person list -> string list
sirs persons;
> ["Gawain"] : string list
```

The cases in a function are considered in order. The third case (with pattern *p*::*ps*) is not considered if *p* is a *Knight*, and therefore must not be taken out of context. Some people prefer that the cases should be disjoint in order to assist mathematical reasoning. But replacing the case for *p*::*ps* with separate cases for *King*, *Peer* and *Peasant* would make the function longer, slower and less readable. The third case of *sirs* makes perfect sense as a conditional equation, holding for all *p* not of the form *Knight*(*s*).

The ordering of cases is even more important when one *person* is compared with another. Rather than testing 16 cases, we test for each *true* case and take all the others for *false*, a total of 7 cases. Note the heavy use of wildcards in patterns.

```
fun superior (King,  Peer _)         = true
  | superior (King,  Knight _)       = true
  | superior (King,  Peasant _)      = true
  | superior (Peer _,  Knight _)     = true
  | superior (Peer _,  Peasant _)    = true
  | superior (Knight _,  Peasant _)  = true
  | superior _                       = false;
> val superior = fn : person * person -> bool
```

Exercise 4.1 Write an ML function to map persons to integers, mapping Kings to 4, Peers to 3, Knights to 2 and Peasants to 1. Write a function equivalent to *superior* that works by comparing the results of this mapping.

Exercise 4.2 Modify type *person* to add the constructor *Esquire*, whose arguments are a name and a village (both represented by strings). What is the type of this constructor? Modify function *title* to generate, for instance,

```
"John Smith, Esq., of Bottisham"
```

Modify *superior* to rank *Esquire* above *Peasant* and below *Knight*.

Exercise 4.3 Declare a datatype of geometric figures such as triangles, rectangles, lines and circles. Declare a function to compute the area of a figure.

4.2   *Enumeration types*

Letting strings denote degrees of nobility may be inadvisable. It does not prevent spurious degrees like `"butcher"` and `"madman"`. There are only five valid degrees; let them be the constructors of a new datatype:

```
datatype degree = Duke | Marquis | Earl | Viscount | Baron;
```

Now type *person* should be redeclared, giving *Peer* the type

$$degree \times string \times int \to person.$$

Functions on type *degree* are defined by case analysis. What is the title of a lady of quality?

```
fun lady Duke     = "Duchess"
  | lady Marquis  = "Marchioness"
  | lady Earl     = "Countess"
  | lady Viscount = "Viscountess"
  | lady Baron    = "Baroness";
> val lady = fn : degree -> string
```

Accuracy being paramount in the Court and Social column, we cannot overestimate the importance of this example for electronic publishing.

A type like *degree*, consisting of a finite number of constants, is an ***enumeration type***. Another example is the built-in type *bool*, which is declared by

```
datatype bool = false | true;
```

The function *not* is declared by cases:

```
fun not true = false
  | not false = true;
```

The standard library declares the enumeration type *order* as follows:

```
datatype order = LESS | EQUAL | GREATER;
```

This captures the three possible outcomes of a comparison. The library structures for strings, integers, reals, times, dates, etc., each include a function *compare* that returns one of these three outcomes:

```
String.compare ("York", "Lancaster");
> GREATER : order
```

Relations that return a boolean value are more familiar. But we need two calls of < to get as much information as we can get from one call to *String.compare*. The first version of Fortran provided three-way comparisons! The more things change, the more they stay the same ...

⚠️ *Beware of redeclaring a datatype.* Each `datatype` declaration creates a new type distinct from all others. Suppose we have declared the type *degree* and the function *lady*. Now, repeat the declaration of *degree*. This declares a new type with new constructors. Asking for the value of *lady(Duke)* will elicit the type error 'expected type *degree*, found type *degree*.' Two different types are now called *degree*. This exasperating situation can happen while a program is being modified interactively. The surest remedy is to terminate the ML session, start a new one, and load the program afresh.

Exercise 4.4   Declare an enumeration type consisting of the names of six different countries. Write a function to return the capital city of each country as a string.

Exercise 4.5   Write functions of type *bool* × *bool* → *bool* for boolean conjunction and disjunction. Use pattern-matching rather than `andalso`, `orelse` or `if`. How many cases have to be tested explicitly?

4.3   *Polymorphic datatypes*

Recall that *list* is a type operator taking one argument.[1] Thus *list* is not a type, while *(int)list* and *((string* × *real)list)list* are. A `datatype` declaration can introduce type operators.

The 'optional' type.   The standard library declares the type operator *option*:

```
datatype 'a option = NONE | SOME of 'a;
> datatype   'a option
>    con NONE : 'a option
>    con SOME : 'a -> 'a option
```

The type operator *option* takes one argument. Type τ *option* contains a copy of type τ, augmented with the extra value *NONE*. It can be used to supply optional data to a function, but its most obvious use is to indicate errors. For example, the library function *Real.fromString* interprets its string argument as a real number, but it does not accept every way of expressing 60,000:

```
Real.fromString "6.0E5";
> SOME 60000.0 : real option
Real.fromString "full three score thousand";
> NONE : real option
```

You can use a `case` expression to consider the alternatives separately; see Section 4.4 below.

---

[1]   The correct term is **type constructor** (Milner *et al.*, 1990). I avoid it here to prevent confusion with a constructor of a datatype.

The disjoint sum type. A fundamental operator forms the ***disjoint sum*** or ***union*** of two types:

```
datatype ('a,'b) sum = In1 of 'a | In2 of 'b;
```

The type operator *sum* takes two arguments. Its constructors are

$$In1 : \alpha \rightarrow (\alpha, \beta) sum$$
$$In2 : \beta \rightarrow (\alpha, \beta) sum$$

The type $(\sigma, \tau) sum$ is the disjoint sum of the types σ and τ. Its values have the form $In1(x)$ for x of type σ, or $In2(y)$ for y of type τ. The type contains a copy of σ and a copy of τ. Observe that $In1$ and $In2$ can be viewed as labels that distinguish σ from τ.

The disjoint sum allows values of several types to be present where normally only a single type is allowed. A list's elements must all have the same type. If this type is *(string, person)sum* then an element could contain a string or a person, while type *(string, int)sum* comprises strings and integers.

$$[In2(King), In1(\texttt{"Scotland"})] : ((string, person)sum)list$$
$$[In1(\texttt{"tyrant"}), In2(1040)] \quad : ((string, int)sum)list$$

Pattern-matching for the disjoint sum tests whether $In1$ or $In2$ is present. The function *concat1* concatenates all the strings included by $In1$ in a list:

```
fun concat1 []          = ""
  | concat1 ((In1 s)::l) = s ^ concat1 l
  | concat1 ((In2 _)::l) =     concat1 l;
> val concat1 = fn : (string, 'a) sum list -> string
concat1 [ In1 "O!", In2 (1040,1057), In1 "Scotland" ];
> "O!Scotland" : string
```

The expression $In1$ `"Scotland"` has appeared with two different types, namely *(string, int × int)sum* and *(string, person)sum*. This is possible because its type is polymorphic:

```
In1 "Scotland";
> In1 "Scotland" : (string, 'a) sum
```

Representing other datatypes. The disjoint sum can express all other datatypes that are not recursive. The type *person* can be represented by

$$((unit, string \times string \times int)sum, (string, string)sum)sum$$

with constructors

$$King = In1(In1())$$
$$Peer(d, t, n) = In1(In2(d, t, n))$$
$$Knight(s) = In2(In1(s))$$
$$Peasant(s) = In2(In2(s))$$

These are valid as both expressions and patterns. Needless to say, type *person* is pleasanter. Observe how *unit*, the type whose sole element is (), represents the one King.

ⓘ   *Storage requirements*. Datatypes require a surprising amount of space, at least with current compilers. A typical value takes four bytes for the tag (which identifies the constructor) and four bytes for each component of the associated tuple. The garbage collector requires a header consisting of a further four bytes. The total comes to twelve bytes for a *Knight* or *Peasant* and twenty bytes for a *Peer*. This would include the integer in a *Peer*, but the strings would be stored as separate objects.

The internal values of an enumeration type require no more space than integers, especially on those ML systems where integers have unlimited precision. List cells typically occupy eight to twelve bytes. With a generational garbage collector, the amount of space taken by an object can vary with its age!

Optimizations are possible. If the datatype has only one constructor, no tag needs to be stored. If all but one of the constructors are constants then sometimes the non-constant constructor does not require a tag; this holds for *list* but not for *option*, since the operand of *SOME* can be anything at all. Compared with Lisp, not having types at run-time saves storage. Appel (1992) discusses such issues. With advances in run-time systems, we can expect storage requirements to decrease.

Exercise 4.6 What are the types of *King*, *Peer*, *Knight* and *Peasant* as declared above?

Exercise 4.7 Exhibit a correspondence between values of type $(\sigma, \tau)sum$ and certain values of type $(\sigma\ list) \times (\tau\ list)$ — those of the form $([x], [])$ or $([], [y])$.

4.4   *Pattern-matching with* `val`, `as`, `case`

A *pattern* is an expression consisting solely of variables, constructors and wildcards. The *constructors* comprise

- numeric, character and string constants
- pairing, tupling and record formation
- list and datatype constructors

In a pattern, all names except constructors are variables. Any meaning they may have outside the pattern is insignificant. The variables in a pattern must be distinct. These conditions ensure that values can be matched efficiently against the pattern and analysed uniquely to bind the variables.

Constructors absolutely must be distinguished from variables. In this book, constructors begin with a capital letter while most variables begin with a small letter.[2] However, the standard constructors *nil*, *true* and *false* are also in lower case. A constructor name may be symbolic or infix, such as :: for lists. The standard library prefers constructor names consisting of all capitals, such as *NONE*.

Mistakes in pattern-matching. Typographical errors in patterns can be hard to locate. The following version of the function *title* contains several errors. Try to spot them before reading on:

```
fun title  Kong              = "His Majesty the King"
  | title  (Peer(deg,terr,_)) = "The " ^ deg ^ " of " ^ terr
  | title  (Knightname)       = "Sir "^ name
  | title  Peasant name       = name;
```

The first error is the misspelling of the constructor *King* as *Kong*. This is a variable and matches all values, preventing further cases from being considered. ML compilers warn if a function has a redundant case; this warning must be heeded!

The second error is *Knightname*: the omission of a space again reduces a pattern to a variable. Since the error leaves the variable *name* undefined, the compiler should complain.

The third error is the omission of parentheses around *Peasant name*. The resulting error messages could be incomprehensible.

Misspelled constructor functions are quickly detected, for

```
fun f (g x) = ...
```

is allowed only if *g* is a constructor. Other misspellings may not provoke any warning. Omitted spaces before a wildcard, as in *Peer_*, are particularly obscure.

Exercise 4.8 Which simple mistake in *superior* would alter the function's behaviour without making any case redundant?

Patterns in value declarations. The declaration

```
val P = E
```

defines the variables in the pattern *P* to have the corresponding values of expression *E*. We have used this in Chapter 2 to select components from tuples:

---

[2] The language Haskell enforces this convention.

```
val (xc,yc) = scalevec(4.0, a);
> val xc = 6.0 : real
> val yc = 27.2 : real
```

We may also write

```
val [x,y,z] = upto(1,3);
> val x = 1 : int
> val y = 2 : int
> val z = 3 : int
```

The declaration fails (raising an exception) if the value of the expression does not match the pattern. When the pattern is a tuple, type checking eliminates this danger.

The following declarations are valid: the values of their expressions match their patterns. They declare no variables.

```
val King = King;
val [1,2,3] = upto(1,3);
```

Constructor names cannot be declared for another purpose using val. In the scope of type *person*, the names *King*, *Peer*, *Knight* and *Peasant* are reserved as constructors. Declarations like these, regarded as attempts at pattern-matching, will be rejected with a type error message:

```
val King = "Henry V";
val Peer = 925;
```

Layered patterns. A variable in a pattern may have the form

```
Id as P
```

If the entire pattern (which includes the pattern *P* as a part) matches, then the value that matches *P* is also bound to the identifier *Id*. This value is viewed both through the pattern and as a whole. The function *nextrun* (from Section 3.21) can be coded

```
fun nextrun(run, [])            = ...
  | nextrun(run as r::_, x::xs) =
          if  x < r then (rev run, x::xs)
                    else nextrun(x::run, xs);
```

Here *run* and *r*::_ are the same list. We now may refer to its head as *r* instead of *hd run*. Whether it is more readable than the previous version is a matter for debate.

The `case` *expression.* This is another vehicle for pattern-matching and has the form

$$\texttt{case } E \texttt{ of } P_1 \texttt{ => } E_1 \texttt{ | } \cdots \texttt{ | } P_n \texttt{ => } E_n$$

The value of E is matched successively against the patterns $P_1, \ldots, P_n$; if P_i is the first pattern to match then the result is the value of E_i. Thus `case` is equivalent to an expression that declares a function by cases and applies it to E. A typical `case` expression tests for a few explicit values, concluding with a catchall case:

```
case p-q of
     0 => "zero"
   | 1 => "one"
   | 2 => "two"
   | n => if n < 10 then "lots"  else  "lots and lots"
```

The function *merge* (also from Section 3.21) can be recoded using `case` to test the first argument before the second:

```
fun merge (xlist, ylist)  :  real list =
   case xlist of
        []     => ylist
      | x::xs => (case ylist of
                      [] => xlist
                    | y::ys  => if x<=y then x::merge (xs,  ylist)
                                        else y::merge (xlist,  ys));
```

In the recursive call, *xlist* and $x::xs$ denote the same list — an effect also obtainable through the pattern *xlist* `as` $x::xs$.as keyword@`as` keyword

⚠ *The scope of* `case`. No symbol terminates the `case` expression, so enclose it in parentheses unless you are certain there is no ambiguity. Below, the second line is part of the inner `case` expression, although the programmer may have intended it to belong to the outer:

```
case x of 1 => case y of 0 => true | 1 => false
        | 2 => true;
```

The following declaration is not syntactically ambiguous, but many ML compilers parse it incorrectly. The `case` expression should be enclosed in parentheses:

```
fun f [x] = case g x of 0 => true | 1 => false
  | f xs   = true;
```

Exercise 4.9 Express the function *title* using a `case` expression to distinguish the four constructors of type *person*.

Exercise 4.10   Describe a simple method for removing all `case` expressions from a program. Explain why your method does not affect the meaning of the program.

Exceptions

A hard problem may be tackled by various methods, each of which succeeds in a fraction of the cases. There may be no better way of choosing a method than to try one and see if it succeeds. If the computation reaches a dead end, then the method fails — or perhaps determines that the problem is impossible. A proof method may make no progress or may reduce its goal to $0 = 1$. A numerical algorithm may suffer overflow or division by zero.

These outcomes can be represented by a datatype whose values are *Success(s)*, where *s* is a solution, *Failure* and *Impossible*. Dealing with multiple outcomes is complicated, as we saw with the topological sorting functions of Section 3.17. The function *cyclesort*, which returns information about success or failure, is more complex than *pathsort*, which expresses failure by (horribly!) calling *hd*[].

ML deals with failure through ***exceptions***. An exception is ***raised*** where the failure is discovered and ***handled*** elsewhere — possibly far away.

4.5   *Introduction to exceptions*

Exceptions are a datatype of error values that are treated specially in order to minimize explicit testing. When an exception is raised, it is transmitted by all ML functions until it is detected by an ***exception handler***. Essentially a `case` expression, the exception handler specifies what to return for each kind of exception.

Suppose that functions *methodA* and *methodB* realize different methods for solving a problem, and that *show* displays a solution as a string. Using a datatype with constructors *Success*, *Failure* and *Impossible*, we can display the outcome of an attempted solution by nested case expressions. If *methodA* fails then *methodB* is tried, while if either reports that the problem is impossible then it is abandoned. In all cases, the result has the same type: *string*.

```
case methodA (problem) of
    Success s => show s
  | Failure   => (case methodB (problem) of
                      Success s => show s
                    | Failure   => "Both methods failed"
                    | Impossible => "No solution exists")
  | Impossible => "No solution exists"
```

Now try exception handling. Instead of a datatype of possible outcomes, declare exceptions *Failure* and *Impossible*:

```
exception Failure;
exception Impossible;
```

Functions *methodA* and *methodB* — and any functions they call within the scope of these exception declarations — can signal errors by code such as

```
if      ...  then raise Impossible
else if ...  then raise Failure
else (*compute successful result*)
```

The attempts to apply *methodA* and *methodB* involve two exception handlers:

```
show  (methodA (problem)
       handle Failure => methodB (problem))
    handle Failure    => "Both methods failed"
         | Impossible => "No solution exists"
```

The first handler traps *Failure* from *methodA*, and tries *methodB*. The second handler traps *Failure* from *methodB* and *Impossible* from either method. Function *show* is given the result of *methodA*, if successful, or else *methodB*.

Even in this simple example, exceptions give a shorter, clearer and faster program. Error propagation does not clutter our code.

4.6   *Declaring exceptions*

An exception name in Standard ML is a constructor of the built-in type *exn*. This is a datatype with a unique property: its set of constructors can be extended. The exception declaration

```
exception Failure;
```

makes *Failure* a new constructor of type *exn*.

While *Failure* and *Impossible* are constants, constructors can also be functions:

```
exception Failedbecause of string;
exception Badvalue of int;
```

Constructor *Failedbecause* has the type *string* → *exn* while *Badvalue* has type *int* → *exn*. They create exceptions *Failedbecause*(*msg*), where *msg* is a message to be displayed, and *Badvalue*(*k*), where *k* may determine the method to be tried next.

Exceptions can be declared locally using `let`, even inside a recursive function. This can result in different exceptions having the same name and other complications. Whenever possible, declare exceptions at top level. The type of a top level exception must be monomorphic.[3]

Values of type *exn* can be stored in lists, returned by functions, etc., like values of other types. In addition, they have a special rôle in the operations `raise` and `handle`.

ⓘ *Dynamic types and exn.* Because type *exn* can be extended with new constructors, it potentially includes the values of any type. We obtain a weak form of dynamic typing. This is an accidental feature of ML; CAML treats dynamics in a more sophisticated manner (Leroy and Mauny, 1993).

For example, suppose we wish to provide a uniform interface for expressing arbitrary data as strings. All the conversion functions can have type *exn → string*. To extend the system with a new type, say *Complex.t*, we declare a new exception for that type, and write a new conversion function of type *exn → string*:

```
exception ComplexToString of Complex.t;
fun convert_complex (ComplexToString z) = ...
```

This function only works when it is applied to constructor *ComplexToString*. A collection of similar functions might be stored in a dictionary, identified by uniform keys such as strings. We obtain a basic form of object-oriented programming.

4.7   *Raising exceptions*

Raising an exception creates an ***exception packet*** containing a value of type *exn*. If *Ex* is an expression of type *exn* and *Ex* evaluates to *e*, then

```
raise Ex
```

evaluates to an exception packet containing *e*. Packets are not ML values; the only operations that recognize them are `raise` and `handle`. Type *exn* mediates between packets and ML values.

During evaluation, exception packets propagate under the call-by-value rule. If expression *E* returns an exception packet then that is the result of the application $f(E)$, for any function *f*. Thus *f* (`raise` *Ex*) is equivalent to `raise` *Ex*. Incidentally, `raise` itself propagates exceptions, and so

```
raise (Badvalue (raise Failure))
```

raises exception *Failure*.

Expressions in ML are evaluated from left to right. If E_1 returns a packet then that is the result of the pair (E_1, E_2); expression E_2 is not evaluated at all. If E_1

---

[3] This restriction relates to imperative polymorphism; see Section 8.3.

returns a normal value and E_2 returns a packet, then that packet is the result of the pair. The evaluation order matters when E_1 and E_2 raise different exceptions.

The evaluation order is also visible in conditional expressions:

```
if E then E₁ else E₂
```

If E evaluates to *true* then only E_1 is evaluated. Its result, whether normal or not, becomes that of the conditional. Similarly, if E evaluates to *false* then only E_2 is evaluated. There is a third possibility. If the test E raises an exception then that is the result of the conditional.

Finally, consider the `let` expression

```
let val P = E₁ in E₂ end
```

If E_1 evaluates to an exception packet then so does the entire `let` expression.

Exception packets are not propagated by testing. The ML system efficiently jumps to the correct exception handler if there is one, otherwise terminating execution.

Standard exceptions. Failure of pattern-matching may raise the built-in exceptions *Match* or *Bind*. A function raises exception *Match* when applied to an argument matching none of its patterns. If a `case` expression has no pattern that matches, it also raises exception *Match*. The ML compiler warns in advance of this possibility when it encounters non-exhaustive patterns (not covering all values of the type).

Because many functions can raise *Match*, this exception conveys little information. When coding a function, have it reject incorrect arguments by raising a suitable exception explicitly; a final case can catch any values that fail to match the other patterns. Some programmers declare a new exception for every function, but having too many exceptions leads to clutter. The standard library follows a middle course, declaring exceptions for whole classes of errors. Here are some examples.

- *Overflow* is raised for arithmetic operations whose result is out of range.
- *Div* is raised for division by zero.
- *Domain* is raised for errors involving the functions of structure *Math*, such as the square root or logarithm of a negative number.
- *Chr* is raised by $chr(k)$ if k is an invalid character code.
- *Subscript* is raised if an index is out of range. Array, string and list operations can raise *Subscript*.

- *Size* is raised upon an attempt to create an array, string or list of negative or grossly excessive size.
- *Fail* is raised for miscellaneous errors; it carries an error message as a string.

The library structure *List* declares the exception *Empty*. Functions *hd* and *tl* raise this exception if they are applied to the empty list:

```
exception Empty;
fun hd (x::_) = x
  | hd []     = raise Empty;
fun tl (_::xs) = xs
  | tl []      = raise Empty;
```

Less trivial is the library function to return the *n*th element in a list, counting from 0:

```
exception Subscript;
fun nth(x::_,   0) = x
  | nth(x::xs,  n)  = if n>0 then nth(xs,n-1)
                            else raise Subscript
  | nth _           = raise Subscript;
```

Evaluating *nth*(*l*, *n*) raises exception *Subscript* if $n < 0$ or if the list *l* has no *n*th element. In the latter case, the exception propagates up the recursive calls to *nth*.

```
nth(explode "At the pit of Acheron", 5);
> #"e" : char
nth([1,2], 2);
> Exception: Subscript
```

The declaration val *P* = *E* raises exception *Bind* if the value of *E* does not match pattern *P*. This is usually poor style (but see Figure 8.4 on page 342). If there is any possibility that the value will not match the pattern, consider the alternatives explicitly using a case expression:

```
case E of P => ··· | P₂ => ···
```

4.8   *Handling exceptions*

An exception handler tests whether the result of an expression is an exception packet. If so, the packet's contents — a value of type *exn* — may be examined by cases. An expression that has an exception handler resembles the case construct:

$$E \text{ handle } P_1 \Rightarrow E_1 \mid \cdots \mid P_n \Rightarrow E_n$$

If E returns a normal value, then the handler simply passes this value on. On the other hand, if E returns a packet then its contents are matched against the patterns. If P_i is the first pattern to match then the result is the value of E_i, for $i = 1, \ldots, n$.

There is one major difference from `case`. If no pattern matches, then the handler propagates the exception packet rather than raising exception *Match*. A typical handler does not consider every possible exception.

In Section 3.7 we considered the problem of making change. The greedy algorithm presented there (function *change*) could not express 16 using 5 and 2 because it always took the largest coin. Another function, *allChange*, treated such cases by returning the list of all possible results.

Using exceptions, we can easily code a backtracking algorithm. We declare the exception *Change* and raise it in two situations: if we run out of coins with a non-zero *amount* or if we cause *amount* to become negative. We always try the largest coin, undoing the choice if it goes wrong. The exception handler always undoes the most recent choice; recursion makes sure of that.

```
exception Change;
fun backChange (coinvals, 0)        = []
  | backChange ([],    amount)      = raise Change
  | backChange (c::coinvals, amount) =
        if amount<0 then raise Change
        else c :: backChange(c::coinvals, amount-c)
              handle Change => backChange(coinvals, amount);
> val change = fn : int list * int -> int list
```

Unlike *allChange*, this function returns at most one solution. Let us compare the two functions by redoing the examples from Section 3.7:

```
backChange([], [10,2], 27);
> Exception: Change
backChange([5,2], 16);
> [5, 5, 2, 2, 2] : int list
backChange(gb_coins, 16);
> [10, 5, 1] : int list
```

There are none, two and 25 solutions; we get at most one of them. Similar examples of exception handling occur later in the book, as we tackle problems like parsing and unification. Lazy lists (Section 5.19) are an alternative to exception handling. Multiple solutions can be computed on demand.

Pitfalls in exception handling. An exception handler must be written with care, as with other forms of pattern matching. Never misspell an exception name; it will be taken as a variable and match all exceptions.

Be careful to give exception handlers the correct scope. In the expression

```
if E then E₁ else E₂ handle ···
```

the handler will only detect exceptions raised by E_2. Enclosing the conditional expression in parentheses brings it entirely within the scope of the handler. Similarly, in

```
case E of P₁ => E₁ | ··· | Pₙ => Eₙ handle ···
```

the handler will only detect exceptions raised by E_n.

Exception handlers in `case` expressions can be syntactically ambiguous. Omitting the parentheses here would make the second line of the `case` expression become part of the handler:

```
case f u of [x] => (g x   handle _ => x)
          | xs  => g u
```

4.9   *Objections to exceptions*

Exceptions can be a clumsy alternative to pattern-matching, as in this function for computing the length of a list:

```
fun len l =  1 + len(tl l) handle _ => 0;
> val len = fn : 'a list -> int
```

Writing ▲ for the exception packet, the evaluation of $len[1]$ goes like this:

$$len[1] \Rightarrow 1 + len(tl[1]) \text{ handle } _ => 0$$
$$\Rightarrow 1 + len[] \text{ handle } _ => 0$$
$$\Rightarrow 1 + (1 + len(tl[]) \text{ handle } _ => 0) \text{ handle } _ => 0$$
$$\Rightarrow 1 + (1 + len▲ \text{ handle } _ => 0) \text{ handle } _ => 0$$
$$\Rightarrow 1 + (1 + ▲ \text{ handle } _ => 0) \text{ handle } _ => 0$$
$$\Rightarrow 1 + (▲ \text{ handle } _ => 0) \text{ handle } _ => 0$$
$$\Rightarrow 1 + 0 \text{ handle } _ => 0$$
$$\Rightarrow 1$$

This evaluation is more complicated than one for the obvious length function defined by pattern-matching. Test for different cases in advance, if possible, rather than trying them willy-nilly by exception handling.

Most proponents of lazy evaluation object to exception handling. Exceptions complicate the theory and can be abused, as we have just seen. The conflict is deeper. Exceptions are propagated under the call-by-value rule, while lazy evaluation follows call-by-need.

ML includes assignments and other commands, and exceptions can be hazardous in imperative programming. It is difficult to write correct programs when execution can be interrupted in arbitrary places. Restricted to the functional parts of a program, exceptions can be understood as dividing the value space into ordinary values and exception packets. They are not strictly necessary in a programming language and could be abused, but they can also promote clarity and efficiency.

Exercise 4.11   Type *exn* does not admit the ML equality operator. Is this restriction justified?

Exercise 4.12   Describe a computational problem from your experience where exception handling would be appropriate. Write the skeleton of an ML program to solve this problem. Include the exception declarations and describe where exceptions would be raised and handled.

Trees

A *tree* is a branching structure consisting of *nodes* with *branches* leading to subtrees. Nodes may carry values, called *labels*. Despite the arboreal terminology, trees are usually drawn upside down:

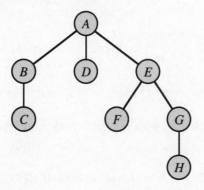

The node labelled *A* is the *root* of the tree, while nodes *C*, *D*, *F* and *H* (which have no subtrees) are its *leaves*.

The type of a node determines the type of its label and how many subtrees it may have. The type of a tree determines the types of its nodes. Two types of tree are especially important. The first has labelled nodes, each with one branch, terminated by an unlabelled leaf. Such trees are simply lists. The second type of tree differs from lists in that each labelled node has two branches instead of one. These are called *binary trees*.

When functional programmers work with lists, they can draw on a body of techniques and a library of functions. When they work with trees, they usually make all their own arrangements. This is a pity, for binary trees are ideal for many applications. The following sections apply them to efficient table lookup, arrays and priority queues. We develop a library of polymorphic functions for binary trees.

4.10   *A type for binary trees*

A binary tree has branch nodes, each with a label and two subtrees. Its leaves are unlabelled. To define binary trees in ML requires a recursive data-type declaration:

```
datatype 'a tree = Lf
                 | Br of 'a * 'a tree * 'a tree;
```

Recursive datatypes are understood exactly like non-recursive ones. Type τ *tree* consists of all the values that can be made by *Lf* and *Br*. There is at least one τ *tree*, namely *Lf*; and given two trees and a label of type τ, we can make another tree. Thus *Lf* is the base case of the recursion.

Here is a tree labelled with strings:

```
val birnam =
  Br("The", Br("wood", Lf,
                       Br("of", Br("Birnam", Lf, Lf),
                               Lf)),
          Lf);
> val birnam = Br ("The", ... , Lf) : string tree
```

Here are some trees labelled with integers. Note how trees can be combined to form bigger ones.

```
val tree2 = Br(2, Br(1,Lf,Lf), Br(3,Lf,Lf));
> val tree2 = Br (2, Br (1, Lf, Lf),
>                    Br (3, Lf, Lf)) : int tree
val tree5 = Br(5, Br(6,Lf,Lf), Br(7,Lf,Lf));
> val tree5 = Br (5, Br (6, Lf, Lf),
>                    Br (7, Lf, Lf)) : int tree
val tree4 = Br(4, tree2, tree5);
> val tree4 =
> Br (4, Br (2, Br (1, Lf, Lf),
>               Br (3, Lf, Lf)),
>        Br (5, Br (6, Lf, Lf),
>               Br (7, Lf, Lf))) : int tree
```

Trees *birnam* and *tree*4 can be pictured as follows:

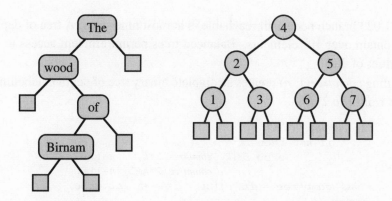

Leaves are shown as squares above, but will henceforth be omitted.

Tree operations are expressed by recursive functions with pattern-matching. The polymorphic function *size* returns the number of labels in a tree:

```
fun size Lf         = 0
  | size (Br(v,t1,t2)) = 1 + size t1 + size t2;
> val size = fn : 'a tree -> int
size birnam;
> 4 : int
size tree4;
> 7 : int
```

Another measure of the size of a tree is its *depth*: the length of the longest path from the root to a leaf.

```
fun depth Lf         = 0
  | depth (Br(v,t1,t2)) = 1 + Int.max(depth t1, depth t2);
> val depth = fn : 'a tree -> int
depth birnam;
> 4 : int
depth tree4;
> 3 : int
```

Observe that *birnam* is rather deep for its size while *tree4* is as shallow as possible. If t is a binary tree then

$$size(t) \leq 2^{depth(t)} - 1$$

If t satisfies $size(t) = 2^{depth(t)} - 1$ then it is a ***complete binary tree***. For instance, *tree4* is a complete binary tree of depth 3.

Informally speaking, a binary tree is ***balanced*** if at each node, both subtrees are of similar size. This concept can be made precise in various ways. The cost of reaching a node in a tree is proportional to its depth — for a balanced tree, to the logarithm of the number of elements. A complete binary tree of depth 10 contains 1,023 branch nodes, all reachable in at most nine steps. A tree of depth 20 can contain over 10^6 elements. Balanced trees permit efficient access to large quantities of data.

Calling *comptree*$(1, n)$ creates a complete binary tree of depth n, labelling the nodes from 1 to 2^n:

```
fun comptree (k,n) =
        if n=0 then Lf
            else Br(k, comptree(2*k,    n-1),
                        comptree(2*k+1, n-1));
> val comptree = fn : int * int -> int tree
comptree (1,3);
> Br (1, Br (2, Br (4, Lf, Lf),
>               Br (5, Lf, Lf)),
>       Br (3, Br (6, Lf, Lf),
>               Br (7, Lf, Lf))) : int tree
```

A function over trees, *reflect* forms the mirror image of a tree by exchanging left and right subtrees all the way down:

```
fun reflect Lf          = Lf
  | reflect (Br(v,t1,t2)) = Br(v, reflect t2, reflect t1);
> val reflect = fn : 'a tree -> 'a tree
reflect tree4;
> Br (4, Br (5, Br (7, Lf, Lf),
>               Br (6, Lf, Lf)),
>       Br (2, Br (3, Lf, Lf),
>               Br (1, Lf, Lf))) : int tree
```

Exercise 4.13 Write a function *compsame*(x, n) to construct a complete binary tree of depth n, labelling all nodes with x. How efficient is your function?

Exercise 4.14 A binary tree is **balanced** (by size) if each node $Br(x, t_1, t_2)$ satisfies $|size(t_1) - size(t_2)| \leq 1$. The obvious recursive function to test whether a tree is balanced applies *size* at every subtree, performing much redundant computation. Write an efficient function to test whether a tree is balanced.

Exercise 4.15 Write a function that determines whether two arbitrary trees t and u satisfy $t = reflect(u)$. The function should not build any new trees, so it should not call *reflect* or *Br*, although it may use *Br* in patterns.

Exercise 4.16 Lists need not have been built into ML. Give a datatype declaration of a type equivalent to α *list*.

Exercise 4.17   Declare a datatype (α, β)*ltree* of labelled binary trees, where branch nodes carry a label of type α and leaves carry a label of type β.

Exercise 4.18   Declare a datatype of trees where each branch node may have any finite number of branches. (Hint: use *list*.)

4.11   *Enumerating the contents of a tree*

Consider the problem of making a list of a tree's labels. The labels must be arranged in some order. Three well-known orders, **preorder**, **inorder** and **postorder**, can be described by a recursive function over trees. Given a branch node, each puts the labels of the left subtree before those of the right; the orders differ only in the position of the label.

A preorder list places the label first:

```
fun preorder Lf          = []
  | preorder (Br(v,t1,t2)) = [v] @ preorder t1 @ preorder t2;
> val preorder = fn : 'a tree -> 'a list
preorder birnam;
> ["The", "wood", "of", "Birnam"] : string list
preorder tree4;
> [4, 2, 1, 3, 5, 6, 7] : int list
```

An inorder list places the label between the labels from the left and right subtrees, giving a strict left-to-right traversal:

```
fun inorder Lf           = []
  | inorder (Br(v,t1,t2)) = inorder t1 @ [v] @ inorder t2;
> val inorder = fn : 'a tree -> 'a list
inorder birnam;
> ["wood", "Birnam", "of", "The"] : string list
inorder tree4;
> [1, 2, 3, 4, 6, 5, 7] : int list
```

A postorder list places the label last:

```
fun postorder Lf          = []
  | postorder (Br(v,t1,t2)) = postorder t1 @ postorder t2 @ [v];
> val postorder = fn : 'a tree -> 'a list
postorder birnam;
> ["Birnam", "of", "wood", "The"] : string list
postorder tree4;
> [1, 3, 2, 6, 7, 5, 4] : int list
```

Although these functions are clear, they take quadratic time on badly unbalanced trees. The culprit is the appending (@) of long lists. It can be eliminated using an extra argument *vs* to accumulate the labels.The following versions perform exactly one cons (::) operation per branch node:

```
fun preord  (Lf,  vs)            = vs
  | preord  (Br(v,t1,t2),  vs)  = v :: preord(t1,  preord(t2,vs));

fun inord  (Lf,  vs)            = vs
  | inord  (Br(v,t1,t2),  vs)   = inord(t1,  v::inord(t2,vs));

fun postord  (Lf,  vs)          = vs
  | postord  (Br(v,t1,t2),  vs) = postord(t1,  postord(t2,v::vs));
```

These definitions are worth study; many functions are declared similarly. For instance, logical terms are essentially trees. The list of all the constants in a term can be built as above.

Exercise 4.19   Describe how *inorder*(*birnam*) and *inord*(*birnam*, []) are evaluated, reporting how many cons operations are performed.

Exercise 4.20   Complete the following equations and explain why they are correct.

$$preorder(reflect(t)) =?$$
$$inorder(reflect(t)) =?$$
$$postorder(reflect(t)) =?$$

4.12   *Building a tree from a list*

Now consider converting a list of labels to a tree. The concepts of preorder, inorder and postorder apply as well to this inverse operation. Even within a fixed order, one list can be converted to many different trees. The equation

$$preorder(t) = [1, 2, 3]$$

has five solutions in *t*:

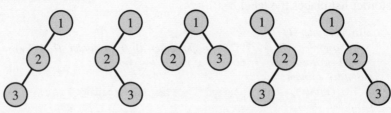

Only one of these trees is balanced. To construct balanced trees, divide the list of labels roughly in half. The subtrees may differ in size (number of nodes) by at most 1.

To make a balanced tree from a preorder list of labels, the first label is attached to the root of the tree:

```
fun balpre  []    = Lf
  | balpre (x::xs) =
      let val k = length xs div 2
      in Br(x, balpre (List.take (xs,k)), balpre (List.drop (xs,k)))
      end;
> val balpre = fn : 'a list -> 'a tree
```

This function is an inverse of *preorder*.

```
balpre (explode "Macbeth");
> Br (#"M", Br (#"a", Br (#"c", Lf, Lf),
>                     Br (#"b", Lf, Lf)),
>             Br (#"e", Br (#"t", Lf, Lf),
>                     Br (#"h", Lf, Lf))) : char tree
implode (preorder it);
> "Macbeth" : string
```

To make a balanced tree from an inorder list, the label is taken from the middle. This resembles the top-down merge sort of Section 3.21:

```
fun balin  []  = Lf
  | balin  xs  =
      let val k      = length xs div 2
          val y::ys = List.drop (xs,k)
      in  Br(y, balin (List.take (xs,k)), balin ys)
      end;
> val balin = fn : 'a list -> 'a tree
```

This function is an inverse of *inorder*.

```
balin (explode "Macbeth");
> Br (#"b", Br (#"a", Br (#"M", Lf, Lf),
>                     Br (#"c", Lf, Lf)),
>             Br (#"t", Br (#"e", Lf, Lf),
>                     Br (#"h", Lf, Lf))) : char tree
implode (inorder it);
> "Macbeth" : string
```

Exercise 4.21 Write a function to convert a postorder list of labels to a balanced tree.

Exercise 4.22 The function *balpre* constructs one tree from a preorder list of labels. Write a function that, given a list of labels, constructs the list of all trees that have those labels in preorder.

4.13   *A structure for binary trees*

As usual in this book, we have been following an imaginary ML session in which we typed in the tree functions one at a time. Now we ought to collect the most important of those functions into a structure, called *Tree*. We really must do so, because one of our functions (*size*) clashes with a built-in function. One reason for using structures is to prevent such name clashes.

We shall, however, leave the `datatype` declaration of *tree* outside the structure. If it were inside, we should be forced to refer to the constructors by *Tree*. *Lf* and *Tree*. *Br*, which would make our patterns unreadable.[4] Thus, in the sequel, imagine that we have made the following declarations:

```
datatype 'a tree = Lf
                 | Br of 'a * 'a tree * 'a tree;

structure Tree =
  struct
  fun size Lf            = 0
    | size (Br(v,t1,t2)) = 1 + size t1 + size t2;

  fun depth   ...
  fun reflect ...
  fun preord  ...
  fun inord   ...
  fun postord ...
  fun balpre  ...
  fun balin   ...
  fun balpost ...
  end;
```

Exercise 4.23   Let us put the `datatype` declaration inside the structure, then make the constructors available outside using these declarations:

```
val Lf = Tree.Lf;
val Br = Tree.Br;
```

What is wrong with this idea?

Tree-based data structures

Computer programming consists of implementing a desired set of high level operations in terms of a given set of primitive operations. Those high level

---

[4] There is a means — the `open` declaration — of making a structure's components available directly by names such as *Lf* and *Br*. Opening the whole of *Tree* would defeat the purpose of declaring the structure in the first place. Section 7.14 will discuss various ways of dealing with compound names.

operations become the primitive operations for coding the next level. Layered network protocols are a striking example of this principle, which can be seen in any modular system design.

Consider the simpler setting of data structure design. The task is to implement the desired data structure in terms of the programming language's primitive data structures. Here a data structure is described not by its internal representation, but by the operations it supports. To implement a new data structure, we must know the precise set of operations desired.

ML gives us two great advantages. Its primitive features easily describe trees; we do not have to worry about references or storage allocation. And we can describe the desired set of operations by a signature.

Typical operations on collections of data include inserting an item, looking up an item, removing an item or merging two collections. We shall consider three data structures that can be represented by trees:

- Dictionaries, where items are identified by name.
- Arrays, where items are identified by an integer.
- Priority queues, where items are identified by priority: only the highest priority item can be removed.

Unlike the data structures described in most texts, ours will be purely functional. Inserting or removing an item will not alter the collection, but create a new collection. It may come as a surprise to hear that this can be done efficiently.

4.14   *Dictionaries*

A ***dictionary*** is a collection of items, each identified by a unique key (typically a string). It supports the following operations:

- ***Lookup*** a key and return the item associated with it.
- ***Insert*** a new key (not already present) and an associated item.
- ***Update*** the item associated with an existing key (insert it if the key is not already present).

We can make this description more precise by writing an ML signature:

```
signature DICTIONARY =
  sig
  type key
  type 'a t
  exception E of key
  val empty  : 'a t
  val lookup : 'a t * key -> 'a
```

```
val insert  : 'a t * key * 'a -> 'a t
val update  : 'a t * key * 'a -> 'a t
end;
```

The signature has more than the three operations described above. What are the other things for?

- *key* is the type of search keys.[5]
- $\alpha\,t$ is the type of dictionaries whose stored items have type α.
- *E* is the exception raised when errors occur. Lookup fails if the key is not found, while insert fails if the key is already there. The exception carries the rejected key.
- *empty* is the empty dictionary.

A structure matching this signature must declare the dictionary operations with appropriate types. For instance, the function *lookup* takes a dictionary and a key, and returns an item. Nothing in signature *DICTIONARY* indicates that trees are involved. We may adopt any representation.

A binary search tree can implement a dictionary. A reasonably balanced tree (Figure 4.1) is considerably more efficient than an association list of (*key, item*) pairs. The time required to search for a key among n items is order n for lists and order $\log n$ for binary search trees. The time required to update the tree is also of order $\log n$. An association list can be updated in constant time, but this does not compensate for the long search time.

In the worst case, binary search trees are actually slower than association lists. A series of updates can create a highly unbalanced tree. Search and update can take up to n steps for a tree of n items.

The keys in an association list may have any type that admits equality, but the keys in a binary search tree must come with a linear ordering. Strings, with alphabetic ordering, are an obvious choice. Each branch node of the tree carries a (*string, item*) pair; its left subtree holds only lesser strings; the right subtree holds only greater strings. The inorder list of labels puts the strings in alphabetic order.

Unlike tree operations that might be coded in Pascal, the **update** and **insert** operations do not modify the current tree. Instead, they create a new tree. This is less wasteful than it sounds: the new tree shares most of its storage with the existing tree.

---

[5] Here it is *string*; Section 7.10 will generalize binary search trees to take the type of search keys as a parameter.

Figure 4.1 *A balanced binary search tree*

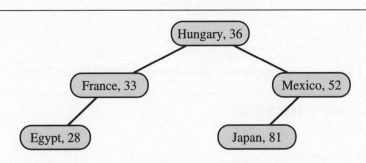

Figure 4.2 presents the structure *Dict*, which is an instance of signature *DIC-TIONARY*. It starts by declaring types *key* and α *t*, and exception *E*. The type declarations are only abbreviations, but they must be present in order to satisfy the signature.

Lookup in a binary search tree is simple. At a branch node, look left if the item being sought is lesser than the current label, and right if it is greater. If the item is not found, the function raises exception *E*. Observe the use of the datatype *order*.

Insertion of a (*string*, *item*) pair involves locating the correct position for the *string*, then inserting the *item*. As with *lookup*, comparing the string with the current label determines whether to look left or right. Here the result is a new branch node; one subtree is updated and the other borrowed from the original tree. If the string is found in the tree, an exception results.

In effect, *insert* copies the path from the root of the tree to the new node. Function *update* is identical apart from its result if the string is found in the tree.

The exception in *lookup* is easily eliminated because that function is iterative. It could return a result of type α *option*, namely *SOME x* if the key is found and *NONE* otherwise. The exception in *insert* is another matter: since the recursive calls construct a new tree, returning *SOME t* or *NONE* would be cumbersome. Function *insert* could call *lookup* and *update*, eliminating the exception but doubling the number of comparisons.

Binary search trees are built from the empty tree (*Lf*) by repeated updates or inserts. We construct a tree *ctree*1 containing France and Egypt:

```
Dict.insert(Lf, "France", 33);
> Br (("France", 33), Lf, Lf) : int Dict.t
```

Figure 4.2 *A structure for dictionaries as binary search trees*

```
structure Dict : DICTIONARY =
  struct

  type key  = string;
  type 'a t  = (key * 'a) tree;

  exception E of key;

  val empty = Lf;

  fun lookup (Lf, b)                = raise E b
    | lookup (Br ((a,x),t1,t2), b) =
        (case String.compare(a,b) of
              GREATER => lookup(t1, b)
            | EQUAL   => x
            | LESS    => lookup(t2, b));

  fun insert (Lf, b, y)            = Br((b,y), Lf, Lf)
    | insert (Br((a,x),t1,t2), b, y) =
        (case String.compare(a,b) of
              GREATER => Br ((a,x),   insert(t1,b,y),  t2)
            | EQUAL   => raise E b
            | LESS    => Br ((a,x),   t1,   insert(t2,b,y)));

  fun update (Lf, b, y)            = Br((b,y), Lf, Lf)
    | update (Br((a,x),t1,t2), b, y) =
        (case String.compare(a,b) of
              GREATER => Br ((a,x),  update(t1,b,y),   t2)
            | EQUAL   => Br ((a,y),  t1,   t2)
            | LESS    => Br ((a,x),  t1,   update(t2,b,y)));

  end;
```

```
val ctree1 = Dict.insert(it, "Egypt", 20);
> val ctree1 = Br (("France", 33),
>                   Br (("Egypt", 20), Lf, Lf),
>                   Lf) : int Dict.t
```

We insert Hungary and Mexico:

```
Dict.insert(ctree1, "Hungary", 36);
> Br (("France", 33), Br (("Egypt", 20), Lf, Lf),
>     Br (("Hungary", 36), Lf, Lf)) : int Dict.t
Dict.insert(it, "Mexico", 52);
> Br (("France", 33), Br (("Egypt", 20), Lf, Lf),
>     Br (("Hungary", 36), Lf,
>         Br (("Mexico", 52), Lf, Lf))) : int Dict.t
```

By inserting Japan, we create the tree *ctree2* consisting of 5 items.

```
val ctree2 = Dict.update(it, "Japan", 81);
> val ctree2 =
> Br (("France", 33), Br (("Egypt", 20), Lf, Lf),
>     Br (("Hungary", 36), Lf,
>         Br (("Mexico", 52),
>             Br (("Japan", 81), Lf, Lf),
>             Lf))) : int Dict.t
```

Note that *ctree1* still exists, even though *ctree2* has been constructed from it.

```
Dict.lookup(ctree1, "France");
> 33 : int
Dict.lookup(ctree2, "Mexico");
> 52 : int
Dict.lookup(ctree1, "Mexico");
> Exception: E
```

Inserting items at random can create unbalanced trees. If most of the insertions occur first, followed by many lookups, then it pays to balance the tree before the lookups. Since a binary search tree corresponds to a sorted inorder list, it can be balanced by converting it to inorder, then constructing a new tree:

```
Tree.inord (ctree2, []);
> [("Egypt", 20), ("France", 33), ("Hungary", 36),
>  ("Japan", 81), ("Mexico", 52)] : (Dict.key * int) list
val baltree = Tree.balin it;
> val baltree =
> Br (("Hungary", 36),
>     Br (("France", 33), Br (("Egypt", 20), Lf, Lf), Lf),
>     Br (("Mexico", 52), Br (("Japan", 81), Lf, Lf), Lf))
> : (Dict.key * int) tree
```

This is the tree illustrated in Figure 4.1.

ⓘ   *Balanced tree algorithms.* The balancing approach outlined above is limited. Using *inord* and *balin* relies on the internal representation of dictionaries as trees; the result type is now *tree* instead of *Dict.t*. Worse, the user must decide when to perform balancing.

There exist several forms of search trees that maintain balance automatically, typically by rearranging elements during updates or lookups. Adams (1993) presents ML code for self-balancing binary search trees. Reade (1992) presents a functional treatment of 2-3 trees, where each branch node may have two or three children.

Exercise 4.24   Give four examples of a binary search tree whose depth equals 5 and that contains only the 5 labels of *ctree2*. For each tree, show a sequence of insertions that creates it.

Exercise 4.25   Write a new version of structure *Dict* where a dictionary is represented by a list of (*key*, *item*) pairs ordered by the keys.

4.15   *Functional and flexible arrays*

What is an array? To most programmers, an array is a block of storage cells, indexed by integers, that can be updated. Conventional programming skill mainly involves using arrays effectively. Since most arrays are scanned sequentially, the functional programmer can use lists instead. But many applications — hash tables and histograms are perhaps the simplest — require random access.

In essence, an array is a mapping defined on a finite range of the integers. The element associated with the integer k is written $A[k]$. Conventionally, an array is modified by the assignment command

$$A[k] := x,$$

changing the machine state such that $A[k] = x$. The previous contents of $A[k]$ are lost. Updating in place is highly efficient, both in time and space, but it is hard to reconcile with functional programming.

A functional array provides a mapping from integers to elements, with an update operation that creates a new array

$$B = update(A, k, x)$$

such that $B[k] = x$ and $B[i] = A[i]$ for all $i \neq k$. The array A continues to exist and additional arrays can be created from it. Functional arrays can be implemented by binary trees. The position of subscript k in the tree is determined by starting at the root and repeatedly dividing k by 2 until it is reduced to 1. Each time the remainder equals 0, move to the left subtree; if the remainder equals 1, move to the right. For instance, subscript 12 is reached by left, left, right:

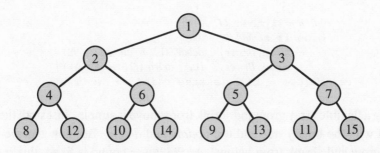

A *flexible* array augments the usual lookup and update with operations to insert or delete elements from either end of the array. A program starts with an empty array and inserts elements as required. Gaps are forbidden: element $n+1$ must be defined after element n, for $n > 0$. Let us examine the underlying tree operations, which have been credited to W. Braun.

The lookup function, *sub*, divides the subscript by 2 until 1 is reached. If the remainder is 0 then the function follows the left subtree, otherwise the right. If it reaches a leaf, it signals error by raising a standard exception.

```
fun sub (Lf, _)            = raise Subscript
  | sub (Br(v,t1,t2), k) =
      if k = 1 then v
      else if k mod 2 = 0
          then sub (t1, k div 2)
          else sub (t2, k div 2);
> val sub = fn : 'a tree * int -> 'a
```

The update function, *update*, also divides the subscript repeatedly by 2. When it reaches 1 it replaces the branch node by another branch with the new label. A leaf may be replaced by a branch, extending the array, provided no intervening nodes have to be generated. This suffices for arrays without gaps.

```
fun update (Lf, k, w) =
      if k = 1 then Br (w, Lf, Lf)
      else raise Subscript
  | update (Br(v,t1,t2), k, w) =
      if k = 1 then Br (w, t1, t2)
      else if k mod 2 = 0
          then Br (v, update(t1, k div 2, w), t2)
          else Br (v, t1, update(t2, k div 2, w));
> val update = fn : 'a tree * int * 'a -> 'a tree
```

Calling *delete*(*ta*, *n*) replaces the subtree rooted at position *n* (if it exists) by a leaf. It resembles *sub*, but builds a new tree.

```
fun delete (Lf, n)            = raise Subscript
  | delete (Br(v,t1,t2), n) =
```

```
        if n = 1 then Lf
        else if n mod 2 = 0
              then Br (v,   delete(t1, n div 2),   t2)
              else Br (v,   t1,   delete(t2, n div 2));
> val delete = fn : 'a tree * int -> 'a tree
```

Letting a flexible array grow and shrink from above is simple. Just store the upper bound with the binary tree and use *update* and *delete*. But how can we let the array grow and shrink from below? As the lower bound is fixed, this seems to imply shifting all the elements.

Consider extending a tree from below with the element *w*. The result has *w* at position 1, replacing the previous element *v*. Its right subtree (positions 3, 5, ...) is simply the old left subtree (positions 2, 4, ...). By a recursive call, its left subtree has *v* at position 2 and takes the rest (positions 4, 6, ...) from the old right subtree (positions 3, 5, ...).

```
fun loext (Lf, w)            = Br(w, Lf, Lf)
  | loext (Br(v,t1,t2), w) = Br(w, loext(t2,v), t1);
> val loext = fn : 'a tree * 'a -> 'a tree
```

So we can extend a flexible array from below, in logarithmic time. To shorten the array, simply reverse the steps. Attempted deletion from the empty array raises the standard exception *Size*. Trees of the form $Br(\_, Lf, Br\_)$ need not be considered: at every node we have $L - 1 \le R \le L$, where L is the size of the left subtree and R is the size of the right subtree.

```
fun lorem Lf                              = raise Size
  | lorem (Br(_,Lf,Lf))                 = Lf
  | lorem (Br(_, t1 as Br(v,_,_), t2)) = Br(v, t2, lorem t1);
> val lorem = fn : 'a tree -> 'a tree
```

It is time for a demonstration. By repeatedly applying *loext* to a leaf, we build an array of the letters A to E in reverse order.

```
loext(Lf,"A");
> Br ("A", Lf, Lf) : string tree
loext(it,"B");
> Br ("B", Br ("A", Lf, Lf), Lf) : string tree
loext(it,"C");
> Br ("C", Br ("B", Lf, Lf), Br ("A", Lf, Lf))
>  : string tree
loext(it,"D");
> Br ("D", Br ("C", Br ("A", Lf, Lf), Lf),
>          Br ("B", Lf, Lf)) : string tree
```

```
val tlet = loext(it,"E");
> val tlet = Br ("E", Br ("D", Br ("B", Lf, Lf), Lf),
>                     Br ("C", Br ("A", Lf, Lf), Lf))
> : string tree
```

The tree *tlet* looks like this:

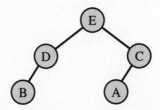

Updating elements of *tlet* does not affect that array, but creates a new array:

```
val tdag = update(update (tlet, 5, "Amen"),
                  2, "dagger");
> val tdag =
> Br ("E", Br ("dagger", Br ("B", Lf, Lf), Lf),
>                        Br ("C", Br ("Amen", Lf, Lf), Lf))
> : string tree
sub(tdag,5);
> "Amen" : string
sub(tlet,5);
> "A" : string
```

The binary tree remains balanced after each operation. Lookup and update with subscript *k* take order log *k* steps, the best possible time complexity for any data structure of unbounded size. Access to a million-element array will be twice as slow as access to a thousand-element array.

The standard library structure *Array* provides imperative arrays. They will be used in Chapter 8 to implement functional (but not flexible) arrays. That implementation gives fast, constant access time — if the array is used in an imperative style. Imperative arrays are so prevalent that functional applications require some imagination.

Here is a signature for flexible arrays. It is based on the structure *Array*, but includes extension and removal from below (*loext, lorem*) and from above (*hiext, hirem*).

```
signature FLEXARRAY =
  sig
  type 'a array
  val empty : 'a array
  val length : 'a array -> int
  val sub   : 'a array * int -> 'a
```

Figure 4.3 *Structures for Braun trees and flexible arrays*

```
structure Braun =
  struct
  fun sub    ...
  fun update ...
  fun delete ...
  fun loext  ...
  fun lorem  ...
  end;


structure Flex : FLEXARRAY =
  struct
  datatype 'a array = Array of 'a tree * int;

  val empty = Array(Lf,0);

  fun length (Array(_,n)) = n;

  fun sub (Array(t,n), k) =
      if 0<=k andalso k<n then Braun.sub(t,k+1)
      else raise Subscript;

  fun update (Array(t,n), k, w) =
      if 0<=k andalso k<n then Array(Braun.update(t,k+1,w), n)
      else raise Subscript;

  fun loext (Array(t,n), w) = Array(Braun.loext(t,w), n+1);

  fun lorem (Array(t,n)) =
      if n>0 then Array(Braun.lorem t, n-1)
      else raise Size;

  fun hiext (Array(t,n), w) = Array(Braun.update(t,n+1,w), n+1);

  fun hirem (Array(t,n)) =
      if n>0 then Array(Braun.delete(t,n) , n-1)
      else raise Size;

  end;
```

```
val update :  'a array * int * 'a -> 'a array
val loext  :  'a array * 'a -> 'a array
val lorem  :  'a array -> 'a array
val hiext  :  'a array * 'a -> 'a array
val hirem  :  'a array -> 'a array
end;
```

Figure 4.3 presents the implementation. The basic tree manipulation functions are packaged as the structure *Braun*, to prevent name clashes with the analogous functions in structure *Flex*. Incidentally, *Braun* subscripts range from 1 to n while *Flex* subscripts range from 0 to $n - 1$. The former arises from the representation, the latter from ML convention.

Structure *Flex* represents a flexible array by a binary tree paired with an integer, its size. It might have declared type *array* as a type abbreviation:

```
type 'a array = 'a tree * int;
```

Instead, it declares *array* as a datatype with one constructor. Such a datatype costs nothing at run-time: the constructor occupies no space. The new type distinguishes flexible arrays from accidental pairs of a tree with an integer, as in the call to *Braun.sub*. The constructor is hidden outside the structure, preventing users from taking apart the flexible array.

ℹ *Further reading.* Dijkstra (1976), a classic work on imperative programming, introduces flexible arrays and many other concepts. Hoogerwoord (1992) describes flexible arrays in detail, including the operation to extend an array from below. Okasaki (1995) introduces **random access lists**, which provide logarithmic time array access as well as constant time list operations (cons, head, tail). A random access list is represented by a list of complete binary trees. The code is presented in ML and is easy to understand.

Exercise 4.26   Write a function to create an array consisting of the element x in subscript positions 1 to n. Do not use *Braun.update*: build the tree directly.

Exercise 4.27   Write a function to convert the array consisting of the elements $x_1, x_2, \ldots, x_n$ (in subscript positions 1 to n) to a list. Operate directly on the tree, without repeated subscripting.

Exercise 4.28   Implement sparse arrays, which may have large gaps between elements, by allowing empty labels in the tree.

4.16   *Priority queues*

A *priority queue* is an ordered collection of items. Items may be inserted in any order, but only the highest priority item may be seen or deleted. Higher priorities traditionally mean lower numerical values, so the basic operations are called *insert*, *min* and *delmin*.

In simulations, a priority queue selects the next event according to its scheduled time. In Artificial Intelligence, priority queues implement **best-first search**: attempted solutions to a problem are stored with priorities (assigned by a rating function) and the best attempt is chosen for further search.

If a priority queue is kept as a sorted list, *insert* takes up to *n* steps for a queue of *n* items. This is unacceptably slow. With a binary tree, *insert* and *delmin* take order log *n* steps. Such a tree, called a **heap**, underlies the well-known sorting algorithm **heap sort**. The labels are arranged such that no label is less than a label above it in the tree. This **heap condition** puts the labels in no strict order, but does put the least label at the root.

Conventionally, the tree is embedded in an array with the labels indexed as follows:

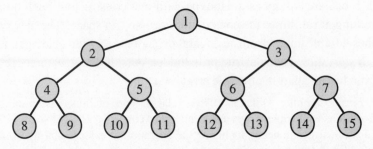

An *n*-item heap consists of nodes 1 to *n*. This indexing scheme always creates a tree of minimum depth. But our functional priority queues are based on the indexing scheme for flexible arrays; it seems more amenable to functional programming, and also assures minimum depth. The resulting program is a hybrid of old and new ideas.

If the heap contains $n-1$ items, then an insertion fills position *n*. However, the new item may be too small to go into that position without violating the heap condition. It may end up higher in the tree, forcing larger items downwards. Function *insert* works on the same principle as *loext*, but maintains the heap condition while inserting the item. Unless the new item *w* exceeds the current label *v*, it becomes the new label and *v* is inserted further down; because *v* does not exceed any item in the subtrees, neither does *w*.

```
fun insert(w: real, Lf)        = Br(w, Lf, Lf)
  | insert(w, Br(v, t1, t2)) =
        if w <= v then Br(w, insert(v, t2), t1)
                  else Br(v, insert(w, t2), t1);
> val insert = fn : real * real tree -> real tree
```

There seems to be no simple way of reversing the *insert* operation. Deletion must remove the item at the root, as that is the smallest. But deletion from an *n*-item heap must vacate position *n*. Item *n* may be too large to go into the root without violating the heap condition. We need two functions: one to remove item *n* and one to re-insert its label in a suitable place.

Function *leftrem* works on the same principle as *lorem*, but does not move labels up or down in the heap. It always removes the leftmost item, exchanging subtrees to give the new heap the correct form. It returns the removed item, paired with the new heap:

```
fun leftrem  (Br(v,Lf,Lf))  =  (v,  Lf)
  | leftrem  (Br(v,t1,t2))  =
        let val (w,  t)  = leftrem t1
        in  (w,  Br(v,t2,t))   end;
> val leftrem = fn : 'a tree -> 'a * 'a tree
```

Function *siftdown* makes a heap from the displaced item and the two subtrees of the old heap. The item moves down the tree. At each branch node, it follows the smaller of the subtrees' labels. It stops when no subtree has a smaller label. Thanks to the indexing scheme, the cases considered below are the only ones possible. If the left subtree is empty then so is the right; if the right subtree is empty then the left subtree can have only one label.

```
fun siftdown (w:real, Lf,  Lf)          = Br(w,Lf,Lf)
  | siftdown (w,  t as Br(v,Lf,Lf),  Lf) =
        if w <= v then Br(w,  t,  Lf)
                  else Br(v,  Br(w,Lf,Lf),  Lf)
  | siftdown (w,  t1 as Br(v1,p1,q1),  t2 as Br(v2,p2,q2)) =
        if w <= v1 andalso w <= v2 then Br(w,t1,t2)
        else if v1 <= v2 then Br(v1,  siftdown(w,p1,q1),  t2)
            (*v2 < v1*)   else Br(v2,  t1,  siftdown(w,p2,q2));
> val siftdown = fn
> : real * real tree * real tree -> real tree
```

Now we can perform deletions. Function *delmin* calls *leftrem* to delete and return an item, then *siftdown* to put the item back in some suitable place. Deletion from the empty heap is an error, and the one-element heap is treated separately.

```
fun delmin Lf                = raise Size
  | delmin (Br(v,Lf,_))  = Lf
  | delmin (Br(v,t1,t2))  =
        let val (w,t) = leftrem t1
        in  siftdown (w,t2,t)   end;
> val delmin = fn : real tree -> real tree
```

Our signature for priority queues specifies the primitives discussed above. It also specifies operations to convert between heaps and lists, and the corresponding sorting function. It specifies *item* as the type of items in the queue; for now this is *real*, but a functor can take any ordered type as a parameter (see Section 7.10).

```
signature PRIORITY_QUEUE =
  sig
  type item
  type t
  val empty    : t
  val null     : t -> bool
  val insert   : item * t -> t
  val min      : t -> item
  val delmin   : t -> t
  val fromList : item list -> t
  val toList   : t -> item list
  val sort     : item list -> item list
  end;
```

Figure 4.4 displays the structure for heaps. It uses the obvious definitions of *empty* and the predicate *null*. The function *min* merely returns the root.

Priority queues easily implement heap sort. We sort a list by converting it to a heap and back again. Function *heapify* converts a list into a heap in a manner reminiscent of top-down merge sort (Section 3.21). This approach, using *siftdown*, builds the heap in linear time; repeated insertions would require order $n \log n$ time. Heap sort's time complexity is optimal: it takes order $n \log n$ time to sort n items in the worst case. In practice, heap sort tends to be slower than other $n \log n$ algorithms. Recall our timing experiments of Chapter 3. Quick sort and merge sort can process 10,000 random numbers in 200 msec or less, but *Heap.sort* takes 500 msec.

Although there are better ways of sorting, heaps make ideal priority queues. To see how heaps work, let us build one and remove some items from it.

```
Heap.fromList [4.0, 2.0, 6.0, 1.0, 5.0, 8.0, 5.0];
> Br (1.0, Br (2.0, Br (6.0, Lf, Lf),
>                   Br (4.0, Lf, Lf)),
>          Br (5.0, Br (8.0, Lf, Lf),
>                   Br (5.0, Lf, Lf))) : Heap.t
Heap.delmin it;
> Br (2.0, Br (5.0, Br (8.0, Lf, Lf),
>                   Br (5.0, Lf, Lf)),
>          Br (4.0, Br (6.0, Lf, Lf), Lf)) : Heap.t
Heap.delmin it;
> Br (4.0, Br (6.0, Br (8.0, Lf, Lf), Lf),
>          Br (5.0, Br (5.0, Lf, Lf), Lf)) : Heap.t
```

Observe that the smallest item is removed first. Let us apply *delmin* twice more:

Figure 4.4 *A structure for priority queues using heaps*

```
structure Heap : PRIORITY_QUEUE =
  struct
  type item = real;
  type t    = item tree;

  val empty = Lf;

  fun null Lf     = true
    | null (Br _) = false;

  fun min (Br(v,_,_)) = v;

  fun insert  ...

  fun leftrem  ...

  fun siftdown ...

  fun delmin  ...

  fun heapify (0, vs)     = (Lf, vs)
    | heapify (n, v::vs) =
        let val (t1, vs1) = heapify (n div 2, vs)
            val (t2, vs2) = heapify ((n-1) div 2, vs1)
        in   (siftdown (v,t1,t2), vs2)  end;

  fun fromList vs = #1 (heapify (length vs, vs));

  fun toList (t as Br(v,_,_)) = v :: toList(delmin t)
    | toList Lf               = [];

  fun sort vs = toList (fromList vs);

  end;
```

```
Heap.delmin it;
> Br (5.0, Br (5.0, Br (8.0, Lf, Lf), Lf),
>                    Br (6.0, Lf, Lf)) : Heap.t
Heap.delmin it;
> Br (5.0, Br (6.0, Lf, Lf), Br (8.0, Lf, Lf)) : Heap.t
```

ML's response has been indented to emphasize the structure of the binary trees.

ⓘ   *Other forms of priority queues.* The heaps presented here are sometimes called **binary** or **implicit** heaps. Algorithms textbooks such as Sedgewick (1988) describe them in detail. Other traditional representations of priority queues can be coded in a functional style. Leftist heaps (Knuth, 1973, page 151) and binomial heaps (Cormen *et al.*, 1990, page 400) are more complicated than binary heaps. However, they allow heaps to be merged in logarithmic time. The merge operation for binomial heaps works by a sort of binary addition. Chris Okasaki, who supplied most of the code for this section, has implemented many other forms of priority queues. Binary heaps appear to be the simplest and the fastest, provided we do not require merge.

Exercise 4.29   Draw diagrams of the heaps created by starting with the empty heap and inserting 4, 2, 6, 1, 5, 8 and 5 (as in the call to *heapoflist* above).

Exercise 4.30   Describe the functional array indexing scheme in terms of the binary notation for subscripts. Do the same for the conventional indexing scheme of heap sort.

Exercise 4.31   Write ML functions for lookup and update on functional arrays, represented by the conventional indexing scheme of heap sort. How do they compare with *Braun . sub* and *Braun . update*?

A tautology checker

This section introduces elementary theorem proving. We define propositions and functions to convert them into various normal forms, obtaining a tautology checker for Propositional Logic. Rather than using binary trees, we declare a datatype of propositions.

4.17   *Propositional Logic*

Propositional Logic deals with **propositions** constructed from atoms a, $b, c, \ldots$, by the connectives $\wedge$, $\vee$, $\neg$. A proposition may be

$$\neg p \quad \text{a negation, 'not } p\text{'}$$

$$p \wedge q \quad \text{a conjunction, '} p \text{ and } q\text{'}$$

$$p \vee q \quad \text{a disjunction, '} p \text{ or } q\text{'}$$

Propositions resemble boolean expressions and are represented by the datatype *prop*:

```
datatype prop = Atom of string
              | Neg  of prop
              | Conj of prop * prop
              | Disj of prop * prop;
```

The implication $p \rightarrow q$ is equivalent to $(\neg p) \lor q$. Here is a function to construct implications:

```
fun implies(p,q) = Disj(Neg p, q);
> val implies = fn : prop * prop -> prop
```

Our example is based on some important attributes — being rich, landed and saintly:

```
val rich   = Atom "rich"
and landed = Atom "landed"
and saintly = Atom "saintly";
```

Here are two assumptions about the rich, the landed and the saintly.

- Assumption 1 is *landed* → *rich*: the landed are rich.
- Assumption 2 is ¬(*saintly* ∧ *rich*): one cannot be both saintly and rich.

A plausible conclusion is *landed* → ¬*saintly*: the landed are not saintly.

Let us give these assumptions and desired conclusion to ML:

```
val assumption1 = implies(landed, rich)
and assumption2 = Neg(Conj(saintly,rich));
> val assumption1 = Disj (Neg (Atom "landed"),
>                         Atom "rich")  : prop
> val assumption2 = Neg (Conj (Atom "saintly",
>                         Atom "rich"))  : prop
val concl = implies(landed, Neg saintly);
> val concl = Disj (Neg (Atom "landed"),
>                   Neg (Atom "saintly"))  : prop
```

If the conclusion follows from the assumptions, then the following proposition is a propositional theorem — a **tautology**. Let us declare it as a goal to be proved:

```
val goal = implies(Conj(assumption1,assumption2), concl);
> val goal =
> Disj (Neg (Conj (Disj (Neg (Atom "landed"),
>                        Atom "rich"),
>                 Neg (Conj (Atom "saintly",
>                            Atom "rich")))),
>      Disj (Neg (Atom "landed"), Neg (Atom "saintly")))
> : prop
```

In mathematical notation this is

$$((landed \rightarrow rich) \land \neg(saintly \land rich)) \rightarrow (landed \rightarrow \neg saintly)$$

For a more readable display, let us declare a function for converting a proposition to a string.

```
fun show  (Atom a)     = a
  | show  (Neg p)      = "(~" ^ show p ^ ")"
  | show  (Conj(p,q))  = "(" ^ show p ^ " & " ^ show q ^ ")"
  | show  (Disj(p,q))  = "(" ^ show p ^ " | " ^ show q ^ ")";
> val show = fn : prop -> string
```

Here is our goal:

```
show goal;
> "((~((((~landed) | rich) & (~(saintly & rich))))
>      | (((~landed) | (~saintly)))"    : string
```

Spaces and line breaks have been inserted in the output above to make it more legible, as elsewhere in this book.

Exercise 4.32 Write a version of *show* that suppresses needless parentheses. If $\neg$ has highest precedence and $\lor$ the lowest then all the parentheses in $((\neg a) \land b) \lor c$ are redundant. Since $\land$ and $\lor$ are associative, suppress parentheses in $(a \land b) \land (c \land d)$.

Exercise 4.33 Write a function to evaluate a proposition using the standard truth tables. One argument should be a list of the true atoms, all others to be assumed false.

4.18   *Negation normal form*

Any proposition can be converted into **negation normal form** (NNF), where $\neg$ is only applied to atoms, by pushing negations into conjunctions and disjunctions. Repeatedly replace

$$\neg\neg p \text{ by } p$$
$$\neg(p \land q) \text{ by } (\neg p) \lor (\neg q)$$
$$\neg(p \lor q) \text{ by } (\neg p) \land (\neg q)$$

Such replacements are sometimes called **rewrite rules**. First, consider whether they make sense. Are they unambiguous? Yes, because the left sides of the rules cover distinct cases. Will the replacements eventually stop? Yes; although they can create additional negations, the negated parts shrink. How do we know when to stop? Here a single sweep through the proposition suffices.

Function *nnf* applies these rules literally. Where no rule applies, it simply makes recursive calls.

```
fun nnf  (Atom a)            = Atom a
  | nnf  (Neg  (Atom a))     = Neg  (Atom a)
  | nnf  (Neg  (Neg p))      = nnf p
  | nnf  (Neg  (Conj(p,q)))  = nnf(Disj(Neg p,  Neg q))
  | nnf  (Neg  (Disj(p,q)))  = nnf(Conj(Neg p,  Neg q))
  | nnf  (Conj(p,q))         = Conj(nnf p,  nnf q)
  | nnf  (Disj(p,q))         = Disj(nnf p,  nnf q);
> val nnf = fn : prop -> prop
```

Assumption 2, $\neg(saintly \wedge rich)$, is converted to $\neg saintly \vee \neg rich$. Function *show* displays the result.

```
nnf assumption2;
> Disj (Neg (Atom "saintly"), Neg (Atom "rich")) : prop
show it;
> "((~saintly) | (~rich))" : string
```

The function *nnf* can be improved. Given $\neg(p \wedge q)$ it evaluates

$$nnf(Disj(Neg\,p, Neg\,q))$$

The recursive call then computes

$$Disj(nnf(Neg\,p), nnf(Neg\,q))$$

Making the function evaluate this expression directly saves a recursive call — similarly for $\neg(p \vee q)$.

It can be faster still. A separate function to compute $nnf(Neg\,p)$ avoids the needless construction of negations. In mutual recursion, function *nnfpos p* computes the normal form of *p* while *nnfneg p* computes the normal form of *Neg p*.

```
fun nnfpos (Atom a)     = Atom a
  | nnfpos (Neg p)      = nnfneg p
  | nnfpos (Conj(p,q))  = Conj(nnfpos p,  nnfpos q)
  | nnfpos (Disj(p,q))  = Disj(nnfpos p,  nnfpos q)
and nnfneg (Atom a)     = Neg  (Atom a)
  | nnfneg (Neg p)      = nnfpos p
  | nnfneg (Conj(p,q))  = Disj(nnfneg p,  nnfneg q)
  | nnfneg (Disj(p,q))  = Conj(nnfneg p,  nnfneg q);
```

4.19 Conjunctive normal form

Conjunctive normal form is the basis of our tautology checker, and also of the resolution method of theorem proving. Hardware designers know it as the maxterm representation of a boolean expression.

A *literal* is an atom or its negation. A proposition is in ***conjunctive normal form*** (CNF) if it has the form $p_1 \wedge \cdots \wedge p_m$, where each p_i is a disjunction of literals.

To check whether p is a tautology, reduce it to an equivalent proposition in CNF. Now if $p_1 \wedge \cdots \wedge p_m$ is a tautology then so is p_i for $i = 1, \ldots, m$. Suppose p_i is $q_1 \vee \cdots \vee q_n$, where $q_1, \ldots, q_n$ are literals. If the literals include an atom and its negation then p_i is a tautology. Otherwise the atoms can be given truth values to falsify each literal in p_i, and therefore p is not a tautology.

To obtain CNF, start with a proposition in negation normal form. Using the distributive law, push in disjunctions until they apply only to literals. Replace

$$p \vee (q \wedge r) \text{ by } (p \vee q) \wedge (p \vee r)$$
$$(q \wedge r) \vee p \text{ by } (q \vee p) \wedge (r \vee p)$$

These replacements are less straightforward than those that yield negation normal form. They are ambiguous — both of them apply to $(a \wedge b) \vee (c \wedge d)$ — but the resulting normal forms are logically equivalent. Termination is assured; although each replacement makes the proposition bigger, it replaces a disjunction by smaller disjunctions, and this cannot go on forever.

A disjunction may contain buried conjunctions; take for instance $a \vee (b \vee (c \wedge d))$. Our replacement strategy, given $p \vee q$, first puts p and q into CNF. This brings any conjunctions to the top. Then applying the replacements distributes the disjunctions into the conjunctions.

Calling *distrib*(p, q) computes the disjunction $p \vee q$ in CNF, given p and q in CNF. If neither is a conjunction then the result is $p \vee q$, the only case where *distrib* makes a disjunction. Otherwise it distributes into a conjunction.

```
fun distrib (p,  Conj(q,r)) = Conj(distrib(p,q), distrib(p,r))
  | distrib (Conj(q,r),  p) = Conj(distrib(q,p), distrib(r,p))
  | distrib (p,  q)         = Disj(p,q)   (*no conjunctions*);
> val distrib = fn : prop * prop -> prop
```

The first two cases overlap: if both p and q are conjunctions then *distrib*(p, q) takes the first case, because ML matches patterns in order. This is a natural way to express the function. As we can see, *distrib* makes every possible disjunction from the parts available:

```
distrib (Conj(rich,saintly), Conj(landed, Neg rich));
> Conj (Conj (Disj (Atom "rich", Atom "landed"),
>              Disj (Atom "saintly", Atom "landed")),
>        Conj (Disj (Atom "rich", Neg (Atom "rich")),
>              Disj (Atom "saintly", Neg (Atom "rich"))))
> : prop
```

```
show it;
> "(((rich | landed) & (saintly | landed)) &
>     ((rich | (~rich)) & (saintly | (~rich))))" : string
```

The conjunctive normal form of $p \wedge q$ is simply the conjunction of those of p and q. Function *cnf* is simple because *distrib* does most of the work. The third case catches both *Atom* and *Neg*.

```
fun cnf (Conj(p,q)) = Conj (cnf p, cnf q)
  | cnf (Disj(p,q)) = distrib (cnf p, cnf q)
  | cnf p           = p      (*a literal*) ;
> val cnf = fn : prop -> prop
```

Finally, we convert the desired goal into CNF using *cnf* and *nnf*:

```
val cgoal = cnf (nnf goal);
> val cgoal = Conj ( ... , ... ) : prop
show cgoal;
> "((((landed | saintly) | ((~landed) | (~saintly))) &
>      (((~rich) | saintly) | ((~landed) | (~saintly)))) &
>     (((landed | rich) | ((~landed) | (~saintly))) &
>      (((~rich) | rich) | ((~landed) | (~saintly)))))"
> : string
```

This is indeed a tautology. Each of the four disjunctions contains some *Atom* and its negation: *landed*, *saintly*, *landed* and *rich*, respectively. To detect this, function *positives* returns a list of the positive atoms in a disjunction, while *negatives* returns a list of the negative atoms. Unanticipated cases indicate that the proposition is not in CNF; an exception results.

```
exception NonCNF;
fun positives (Atom a)        = [a]
  | positives (Neg(Atom _))   = []
  | positives (Disj(p,q))     = positives p @ positives q
  | positives _               = raise NonCNF;
> val positives = fn : prop -> string list
fun negatives (Atom _)        = []
  | negatives (Neg(Atom a))   = [a]
  | negatives (Disj(p,q))     = negatives p @ negatives q
  | negatives _               = raise NonCNF;
> val negatives = fn : prop -> string list
```

Function *taut* performs the tautology check on any CNF proposition, using *inter* (see Section 3.15) to form the intersection of the positive and negative atoms. The final outcome is perhaps an anticlimax.

```
fun taut (Conj(p,q)) = taut p andalso taut q
  | taut p           = not (null (inter (positives p, negatives p)));
> val taut = fn : prop -> bool
```

```
taut cgoal;
> true : bool
```

ⓘ   *Advanced tautology checkers.* The tautology checker described above is not practical. Ordered binary decision diagrams (OBDDs) can solve serious problems in hardware design. They employ directed graphs, where each node represents an 'if-then-else' decision. Moore (1994) explains the ideas and the key optimizations, involving hashing and caching.

The Davis-Putnam procedure makes use of CNF. It can solve hard constraint satisfaction problems and has settled open questions in combinatorial mathematics. Zhang and Stickel (1994) describe an algorithm that could be coded in ML. Uribe and Stickel (1994) describe experimental comparisons between the procedure and OBDDs.

Exercise 4.34   A proposition in conjunctive normal form can be represented as a list of lists of literals. The outer list is a conjunction; each inner list is a disjunction. Write functions to convert a proposition into CNF using this representation.

Exercise 4.35   Modify the definition of *distrib* so that no two cases overlap.

Exercise 4.36   A proposition is in *disjunctive normal form* (DNF) if it has the form $p_1 \vee \cdots \vee p_m$, where each p_i is a conjunction of literals. A proposition is *inconsistent* if its negation is a tautology. Describe a method of testing whether a proposition is inconsistent that involves DNF. Code this method in ML.

Summary of main points
- A `datatype` declaration creates a new type by combining several existing types.
- A pattern consists of constructors and variables.
- Exceptions are a general mechanism for responding to run-time errors.
- A recursive `datatype` declaration can define trees.
- Binary trees may represent many data structures, including dictionaries, functional arrays and priority queues.
- Pattern-matching can express transformations on logical formulæ.

5

Functions and Infinite Data

The most powerful techniques of functional programming are those that treat functions as data. Most functional languages give function values full rights, free of arbitrary restrictions. Like other values, functions may be arguments and results of other functions and may belong to pairs, lists and trees.

Procedural languages like Fortran and Pascal accept this idea as far as is convenient for the compiler writer. Functions may be arguments: say, the comparison to be used in sorting or a numerical function to be integrated. Even this restricted case is important.

A function is **higher-order** (or a *functional*) if it operates on other functions. For instance, the functional *map* applies a function to every element of a list, creating a new list. A sufficiently rich collection of functionals can express all functions without using variables. Functionals can be designed to construct parsers (see Chapter 9) and theorem proving strategies (see Chapter 10).

Infinite lists, whose elements are evaluated upon demand, can be implemented using functions as data. The tail of a lazy list is a function that, if called, produces another lazy list. A lazy list can be infinitely long and any finite number of its elements can be evaluated.

Chapter outline

The first half presents the essential programming techniques involving functions as data. The second half serves as an extended, practical example. Lazy lists can be represented in ML (despite its strict evaluation rule) by means of function values.

The chapter contains the following sections:

Functions as values. The fn notation can express a function without giving it a name. Any function of two arguments can be expressed as a 'curried' function of one argument, whose result is another function. Simple examples of higher-order functions include polymorphic sorting functions and numerical operators.

General-purpose functionals. Higher-order functional programming largely

171

consists of using certain well-known functionals, which operate on lists or other recursive datatypes.

Sequences, or infinite lists. The basic mechanism for obtaining laziness in ML is demonstrated using standard examples. A harder problem is to combine a list of lists of integers into a single list of integers — if the input lists are infinite, they must be combined fairly such that no integers are lost.

Search strategies and infinite lists. The possibly infinite set of solutions to a search problem can be generated as a lazy list. The consumer of the solutions can be designed independently of the producer, which may employ any suitable search strategy.

Functions as values

Functions in ML are abstract values: they can be created; they can be applied to an argument; they can belong to other data structures. Nothing else is allowed. A function is given by patterns and expressions but taken as a 'black box' that transforms arguments to results.

5.1   *Anonymous functions with* fn *notation*

An ML function need not have a name. If x is a variable (of type σ) and E is an expression (of type τ) then the expression

    fn x => E

denotes a function of type $\sigma \to \tau$. Its argument is x and its body is E. Pattern-matching is allowed: the expression

    fn P_1 => E_1 | $\cdots$ | P_n => E_n

denotes the function defined by the patterns $P_1, \ldots, P_n$. It has the same meaning as the let expression

    let fun $f(P_1)$ = E_1 | $\cdots$ | $f(P_n)$ = E_n in f end

provided f does not appear in the expressions $E_1, \ldots, E_n$. The fn syntax cannot express recursion.

For example, fn n=>n*2 is a function that doubles an integer. It can be applied to an argument; it can be given a name by a val declaration.

```
(fn n=>n*2)(9);
> 18 : int
val double = fn n=>n*2;
> val double = fn : int -> int
```

Many ML constructs are defined in terms of the fn notation. The conditional expression

> if E then E_1 else E_2

abbreviates the function application

> (fn *true* => E_1 | *false* => E_2) (E)

The case expression is translated similarly.

Exercise 5.1 Express these functions using fn notation.

```
fun square (x) : real = x*x;
fun cons  (x,y) = x::y;
fun null    []    = true
  | null  (_::_) = false;
```

Exercise 5.2 Modify these function declarations to use val instead of fun:

```
fun area  (r) = pi*r*r;
fun title (name)  =  "The Duke of " ^ name;
fun lengthvec  (x,y)  =  Math.sqrt(x*x + y*y);
```

5.2   Curried functions

A function can have only one argument. Hitherto, functions with multiple arguments have taken them as a tuple. Multiple arguments can also be realized by a function that returns another function as its result. This device is called *currying* after the logician H. B. Curry.[1] Consider the function

```
fun prefix pre =
    let fun cat post = pre^post
    in   cat   end;
> val prefix = fn : string -> (string -> string)
```

Using fn notation, *prefix* is the function

> fn *pre* => (fn *post* => *pre* ^ *post*)

Given a string *pre*, the result of *prefix* is a function that concatenates *pre* to the front of its argument. For instance, *prefix* " Sir " is the function

> fn *post* => "Sir " ^ *post*

---

[1] It has been credited to Schönfinkel, but *Schönfinkeling* has never caught on.

It may be applied to a string:

```
prefix "Sir ";
> fn : string -> string
it "James Tyrrell";
> "Sir James Tyrrell" : string
```

Dispensing with *it*, both function applications may be done at once:

```
(prefix "Sir ") "James Tyrrell";
> "Sir James Tyrrell" : string
```

This is a function call where the function is computed by an expression, namely *prefix* `"Sir "`.

Note that *prefix* behaves like a function of two arguments. It is a ***curried function***. We now have two ways of declaring a function with arguments of types σ_1 and σ_2 and result of type τ. A function over pairs has type $(\sigma_1 \times \sigma_2) \to \tau$. A curried function has type $\sigma_1 \to (\sigma_2 \to \tau)$.

A curried function permits ***partial application***. Applied to its first argument (of type σ_1) its result is a function of type $\sigma_2 \to \tau$. This function may have a general use: say, for addressing Knights.

```
val knightify = prefix "Sir ";
> val knightify = fn : string -> string
knightify "William Catesby";
> "Sir William Catesby" : string
knightify "Richard Ratcliff";
> "Sir Richard Ratcliff" : string
```

Other illustrious personages can be addressed similarly:

```
val dukify = prefix "The Duke of ";
> val dukify = fn : string -> string
dukify "Clarence";
> "The Duke of Clarence" : string
val lordify = prefix "Lord ";
> val lordify = fn : string -> string
lordify "Stanley";
> "Lord Stanley" : string
```

Syntax for curried functions. The functions above are declared by `val`, not `fun`. A `fun` declaration must have explicit arguments. There may be several arguments, separated by spaces, for a curried function. Here is an equivalent declaration of *prefix*:

```
fun prefix pre post = pre^post;
> val prefix = fn : string -> (string -> string)
```

A function call has the form $E\,E_1$, where E is an expression that denotes a function. Since

$$E\,E_1\,E_2\,\cdots\,E_n \text{ abbreviates } (\cdots((E\,E_1)\,E_2)\,\cdots)E_n$$

we may write *prefix* `"Sir "` `"James Tyrrell"` without parentheses. The expressions are evaluated from left to right.

The type of *prefix*, namely *string* → (*string* → *string*), may be written without parentheses: the symbol → associates to the right.

Recursion. Curried functions may be recursive. Calling *replist n x* makes the list consisting of *n* copies of *x*:

```
fun replist n x = if n=0 then [] else x :: replist (n-1) x;
> val replist = fn : int -> 'a -> 'a list
replist 3 true;
> [true, true, true] : bool list
```

Recursion works by the usual evaluation rules, even with currying. The result of *replist* 3 is the function

$$\text{fn } x \Rightarrow \text{ if } 3 = 0 \text{ then } [] \text{ else } x :: replist\,(3-1)\,x$$

Applying this to *true* produces the expression

$$true :: replist\,2\,true$$

As evaluation continues, two further recursive calls yield

$$true :: true :: true :: replist\,0\,true$$

The final call returns *nil* and the overall result is [*true, true, true*].

 An analogy with arrays. The choice between pairing and currying is analogous to the choice, in Pascal, between a 2-dimensional array and nested arrays.

```
A: array [1..20, 1..30] of integer
B: array [1..20] of array [1..30] of integer
```

The former array is subscripted $A[i,j]$, the latter as $B[i][j]$. Nested arrays permit partial subscripting: $B[i]$ is a 1-dimensional array.

Exercise 5.3   What functions result from partial application of the following curried functions? (Do not try them at the machine.)

```
fun plus i j : int = i+j;
fun lesser a b : real = if a<b then a else b;
fun pair x y = (x,y);
fun equals x y = (x=y);
```

Exercise 5.4   Is there any practical difference between the following two declarations of the function *f*? Assume that the function *g* and the curried function *h* are given.

```
fun f x y = h (g x) y;
fun f x   = h (g x);
```

5.3   *Functions in data structures*

Functions and concrete datatypes play complementary rôles in a data structure. Lists and trees provide the outer framework and organize the information, while functions hold potential computations. Although functions are represented by finite programs in the computer, we can often treat them as infinite objects.

Pairs and lists may contain functions as their components:[2]

```
(concat, Math.sin);
> (fn, fn) : (string list -> string) * (real -> real)
[op+, op-, op*, op div, op mod, Int.max, Int.min];
> [fn, fn, fn, fn, fn] : (int * int -> int) list
```

Functions stored in a data structure can be extracted and applied.

```
val titlefns = [dukify, lordify, knightify];
> val titlefns = [fn, fn, fn] : (string -> string) list
hd titlefns "Gloucester";
> "The Duke of Gloucester" : string
```

This is a curried function call: *hd titlefns* returns the function *dukify*. The polymorphic function *hd* has, in this example, the type

$$(string \rightarrow string)list \rightarrow (string \rightarrow string).$$

A binary search tree containing functions might be useful in a desk calculator program. The functions are addressed by name.

```
val funtree = Dict.insert(Dict.insert(Dict.insert(Lf, "sin", Math.sin),
                          "cos", Math.cos),
                 "atan", Math.atan);
> val funtree =
> Br (("sin", fn),
>     Br (("cos", fn), Br (("atan", fn), Lf, Lf), Lf),
>     Lf)     : (real -> real) Dict.t
Dict.lookup (funtree, "cos") 0.0;
> 1.0 : real
```

---

[2] Recall that the keyword op yields the value of an infix operator, as a function.

The functions stored in the tree must have the same type, here *real* → *real*. Although different types can be combined into one datatype, this can be inconvenient. As mentioned at the end of Section 4.6, type *exn* can be regarded as including all types. A more flexible type for the functions is *exn list* → *exn*.

Exercise 5.5 What type does the polymorphic function *Dict*.*lookup* have in the example above?

5.4 *Functions as arguments and results*

The sorting functions of Chapter 3 are coded to sort real numbers. They can be generalized to an arbitrary ordered type by passing the ordering predicate (≤) as an argument. Here is a polymorphic function for insertion sort:

```
fun insort lessequal =
    let fun ins (x, [])     = [x]
          | ins (x, y::ys) =
                    if lessequal(x,y) then x::y::ys
                                      else y :: ins (x,ys)
        fun sort []        = []
          | sort (x::xs) = ins (x, sort xs)
    in  sort  end;
> val insort = fn
> : ('a * 'a -> bool) -> 'a list -> 'a list
```

Functions *ins* and *sort* are declared locally, referring to *lessequal*. Though it may not be obvious, *insort* is a curried function. Given an argument of type $\tau \times \tau \rightarrow$ *bool* it returns the function *sort*, which has type τ *list* → τ *list*. The types of the ordering and the list elements must agree.

Integers can now be sorted. (Although the operator <= is overloaded, its type is constrained by the list of integers.)

```
insort (op<=)  [5,3,7,5,9,8];
> [3, 5, 5, 7, 8, 9] : int list
```

Passing the relation ≥ for *lessequal* gives a decreasing sort:

```
insort (op>=)  [5,3,7,5,9,8];
> [9, 8, 7, 5, 5, 3] : int list
```

Pairs of strings can be sorted using lexicographic ordering:

```
fun leq_stringpair ((a,b), (c,d): string*string)  =
        a<c  orelse  (a=c andalso b<=d);
> val leq_stringpair = fn
> : (string * string) * (string * string) -> bool
```

We sort a list of (family name, forename) pairs:

```
insert leq_stringpair
  [("Herbert","Walter"),          ("Plantagenet","Richard"),
   ("Plantagenet","Edward"),      ("Brandon","William"),
   ("Tyrrell","James"),           ("Herbert","John") ];
> [("Brandon",  "William"), ("Herbert",  "John"),
>  ("Herbert",  "Walter"), ("Plantagenet",  "Edward"),
>  ("Plantagenet",  "Richard"), ("Tyrrell",  "James")]
>  : (string * string) list
```

Functions are frequently passed as arguments in numerical computing. The following functional computes the summation $\sum_{i=0}^{m-1} f(i)$. For efficiency, it uses an iterative function that refers to the arguments f and m:

```
fun summation f m =
    let fun sum (i,z) : real =
                if i=m then z else sum (i+1, z+(f i))
    in  sum(0, 0.0)  end;
> val summation = fn : (int -> real) -> int -> real
```

The fn notation works well with functionals. Here it eliminates the need to declare a squaring function prior to computing the sum $\sum_{k=0}^{9} k^2$:

```
summation (fn k => real(k*k)) 10;
> 285.0 : real
```

The double sum $\sum_{i=0}^{m-1} \sum_{j=0}^{n-1} g(i,j)$ is computed by

```
summation (fn i => summation (fn j => g(i,j)) n) m;
```

This serves as a translation of the $\sum$-notation into ML; the index variables i and j are bound by fn. The inner summation, $\sum_{j=0}^{n-1} g(i,j)$, is a function of i. The function over j is the partial application of g to i.

The partial application can be simplified by summing over a curried function h instead of g. The double sum $\sum_{i=0}^{m-1} \sum_{j=0}^{n-1} h\,i\,j$ is computed by

```
summation (fn i => summation (h i) n) m;
```

Observe that *summation f* has the same type as f, namely $int \rightarrow real$, and that $\sum_{i=0}^{m-1} \sum_{j=0}^{i-1} f(j)$ may be computed by *summation (summation f) m*.

Polymorphic val *declarations.* Because a function can be the result of a computation, you might expect declarations such as the following to be legal:

```
val list5 = replist 5;
> val list5 = fn : 'a -> 'a list
val f = hd [hd];
> val f = fn : 'a list -> 'a
```

They were indeed legal in earlier versions of ML, but now trigger a message such as 'Non-value in polymorphic declaration.' This restriction has to do with references; Section 8.3 explains the details. Changing the function declaration val f = E to

> fun f x = E x

renders it acceptable. The change is harmless unless computing E has side-effects, or is expensive.

The restriction affects all polymorphic val declarations, not just those of functions. Recall that typing E at top level abbreviates typing val *it* = E. For instance, we may not type *hd* [[ ]].

Exercise 5.6 Write a polymorphic function for top-down merge sort, passing the ordering predicate ($\leq$) as an argument.

Exercise 5.7 Write a functional to compute the minimum value $\min_{i=0}^{m-1} f(i)$ of a function f, where m is any given positive integer. Use the functional to express the two-dimensional minimum $\min_{i=0}^{m-1} \min_{j=0}^{n-1} g(i,j)$, for positive integers m and n.

General-purpose functionals

Functional programmers often use higher-order functions to express programs clearly and concisely. Functionals to process lists have been popular since the early days of Lisp, appearing in infinite variety and under many names. They express operations that otherwise would require separate recursive function declarations. Similar recursive functionals can be defined for trees.

A comprehensive set of functionals provides an abstract language for expressing other functions. After reading this section, you may find it instructive to review previous chapters and simplify the function definitions using functionals.

5.5   *Sections*

Imagine applying an infix operator to only one operand, either left or right, leaving the other operand unspecified. This defines a function of one argument, called a *section*. Here are some examples in the notation of Bird and Wadler (1988):

- ("Sir "^) is the function *knightify*
- (/2.0) is the function 'divide by 2'

Sections can be added to ML (rather crudely) by the functionals *secl* and *secr*:

```
fun secl x f y = f(x,y);
> val secl = fn : 'a -> ('a * 'b -> 'c) -> 'b -> 'c
fun secr f y x = f(x,y);
> val secr = fn : ('a * 'b -> 'c) -> 'b -> 'a -> 'c
```

These functionals are typically used with infix functions and op, but may be applied to any function of suitable type. Here are some left sections:

```
val knightify = (secl "Sir " op^);
> val knightify = fn : string -> string
knightify "Geoffrey";
> "Sir Geoffrey" : string
val recip = (secl 1.0 op/);
> val recip = fn : real -> real
recip 5.0;
> 0.2 : real
```

Here is a right section for division by 2:

```
val halve = (secr op/ 2.0);
> val halve = fn : real -> real
halve 7.0;
> 3.5 : real
```

Exercise 5.8   Is there any similarity between sections and curried functions?

Exercise 5.9   What functions do the following sections yield? Recall that *take* removes elements from the head of a list (Section 3.4) while *inter* forms the intersection of two lists (Section 3.15).

```
secr op@ ["Richard"]
secl ["heed", "of", "yonder", "dog!"] List.take
secr List.take 3
secl ["his", "venom", "tooth"] inter
```

5.6   *Combinators*

The theory of the λ-calculus is in part concerned with expressions known as **combinators**. Many combinators can be coded in ML as higher-order functions, and have practical applications.

Composition.   The infix *o* (yes, the letter 'o') denotes function composition. The standard library declares it as follows:

```
infix o;
fun (f o g) x = f (g x);
> val o = fn : ('b -> 'c) * ('a -> 'b) -> 'a -> 'c
```

Composition is familiar to mathematicians; $f \circ g$ is the function that applies g, then f, to its argument. Composition can express many functions, especially using sections. For instance, the functions

```
fn x => ~(Math.sqrt x)
fn a => "beginning" ^ a ^ "end"
fn x => 2.0 / (x-1.0)
```

can be expressed without mentioning their argument:

```
~ o Math.sqrt
(secl "beginning" op^)  o  (secr op^ "end")
(secl 2.0 op/)  o  (secr op- 1.0)
```

To compute the sum $\sum_{k=0}^{9} \sqrt{k}$, the functions *Math.sqrt* and *real* (which converts integers to reals) are composed. Composition is more readable than `fn` notation:

```
summation (Math.sqrt o real) 10;
```

The combinators S, K and I. The identity combinator, *I*, simply returns its argument:

```
fun I x = x;
> val I = fn : 'a -> 'a
```

Composition of a function with *I* has no effect:

```
knightify o I o (prefix "William ") o I;
> fn : string -> string
it "Catesby";
> "Sir William Catesby" : string
```

The combinator *K* makes constant functions. Given x it makes the function that always returns x:

```
fun K x y = x;
> val K = fn : 'a -> 'b -> 'a
```

For a contrived demonstration of constant functions, let us compute the product $m \times z$ by the repeated addition $\sum_{i=0}^{m-1} z$:

```
summation (K 7.0) 5;
> 35.0 : real
```

The combinator *S* is a general form of composition:

```
fun S x y z = x z (y z);
> val S = fn : ('a -> 'b -> 'c) -> ('a -> 'b) -> 'a -> 'c
```

Every function in the λ-calculus can be expressed using just S and K — with no variables! David Turner (1979) has exploited this celebrated fact to obtain lazy evaluation: since no variables are involved, no mechanism is required for binding their values. Virtually all lazy functional compilers employ some refinement of this technique.

Here is a remarkable example of the expressiveness of S and K. The identity function I can be defined as $S\,K\,K$:

```
S  K  K  17;
> 17 : int
```

Exercise 5.10   Write the computation steps of $S\,K\,K\,17$.

Exercise 5.11   Suppose we are given an expression E consisting of infix operators, constants and variables, with one occurrence of the variable x. Describe a method for expressing the function fn x=>E using I, sections and composition instead of fn.

5.7   *The list functionals* map *and* filter

The functional *map* applies a function to every element of a list, returning a list of the function's results:

$$map\,f\,[x_1, \ldots , x_n] = [f\,x_1, \ldots , f\,x_n]$$

The ML library declares *map* as follows:

```
fun map f []      = []
  | map f (x::xs) = (f x) :: map f xs;
> val map = fn : ('a -> 'b) -> 'a list -> 'b list
map recip [0.1, 1.0, 5.0, 10.0];
> [10.0, 1.0, 0.2, 0.1] : real list
map size ["York","Clarence","Gloucester"];
> [4, 8, 10] : int list
```

The functional *filter* applies a predicate — a boolean-valued function — to a list. It returns a list of all elements satisfying the predicate, in their original order.

```
fun filter pred []      = []
  | filter pred (x::xs) =
        if pred x then x :: filter pred xs
                  else      filter pred xs;
> val filter = fn : ('a -> bool) -> 'a list -> 'a list
filter (fn a => size a = 4)
      ["Hie","thee","to","Hell","thou","cacodemon"];
> ["thee", "Hell", "thou"] : string list
```

Pattern-matching in curried functions works exactly as if the arguments were given as a tuple. Both functionals are curried: *map* takes a function of type $\sigma \rightarrow \tau$ to one of type σ *list* $\rightarrow \tau$ *list*, while *filter* takes a function of type $\tau \rightarrow$ *bool* to one of type τ *list* $\rightarrow \tau$ *list*.

Thanks to currying, these functionals work together for lists of lists. Observe that $map(map f)[l_1, l_2, \ldots, l_n]$ applies *map f* to each list $l_1, l_2, \ldots$.

```
map (map double) [[1], [2,3], [4,5,6]];
> [[2], [4, 6], [8, 10, 12]] : int list list
map (map (implode o rev o explode))
    [["When","he","shall","split"],
     ["thy","very","heart","with","sorrow"]];
> [["nehW", "eh", "llahs", "tilps"],
>  ["yht", "yrev", "traeh", "htiw", "worros"]]
> : string list list
```

Similarly, $map(filter\ pred)[l_1, l_2, \ldots, l_n]$ applies *filter pred* to each of the lists l_1, $l_2, \ldots$. It returns a list of lists of elements satisfying the predicate *pred*.

```
map (filter (secr op< "m"))
    [["my","hair","doth","stand","on","end"],
     ["to","hear","her","curses"]];
> [["hair", "doth", "end"], ["hear", "her", "curses"]]
> : string list list
```

Many list functions can be coded trivially using *map* and *filter*. Our matrix transpose function (Section 3.9) becomes

```
fun transp ([]::_) = []
  | transp rows    = map hd rows :: transp (map tl rows);
> val transp = fn : 'a list list -> 'a list list
transp [["have","done","thy","charm"],
        ["thou","hateful","withered","hag!"]];
> [["have", "thou"], ["done", "hateful"],
>  ["thy", "withered"], ["charm", "hag!"]]
> : string list list
```

Recall how we defined the intersection of two 'sets' in terms of the membership relation, in Section 3.15. That declaration can be reduced to a single line:

```
fun inter(xs,ys) = filter (secr (op mem) ys) xs;
> val inter = fn : ''a list * ''a list -> ''a list
```

Exercise 5.12   Show how to replace any expression of the form

$$map f (map g xs),$$

by an equivalent expression that calls *map* only once.

Exercise 5.13   Declare the infix operator *andf* such that

$$\textit{filter}\,(\textit{pred}1\,\textit{andf}\,\textit{pred}2)\,\textit{xs}$$

returns the same value as *filter pred*1 (*filter pred*2 *xs*).

5.8   *The list functionals* takewhile *and* dropwhile
These functionals chop an initial segment from a list using a predicate:

$$[x_0, \ldots, x_{i-1}, \underbrace{x_i, \ldots, x_{n-1}]}$$

$$\underbrace{}_{\textit{takewhile}}\quad\underbrace{}_{\textit{dropwhile}}$$

The initial segment, which consists of elements satisfying the predicate, is returned by *takewhile*:

```
fun takewhile pred []      = []
  | takewhile pred (x::xs) =
          if  pred x then x :: takewhile pred xs
                     else [];
> val takewhile = fn : ('a -> bool) -> 'a list -> 'a list
```

The remaining elements (if any) begin with the first one to falsify the predicate. This list is returned by *dropwhile*:

```
fun dropwhile pred []      = []
  | dropwhile pred (x::xs) =
          if  pred x then dropwhile pred xs
                     else x::xs;
> val dropwhile = fn : ('a -> bool) -> 'a list -> 'a list
```

These two functionals can process text in the form of character lists. The predicate *Char.isAlpha* recognizes letters. Given this predicate, *takewhile* returns the first word from a sentence and *dropwhile* returns the remaining characters.

```
takewhile Char.isAlpha (explode "that deadly eye of thine");
> [#"t", #"h", #"a", #"t"] : char list
dropwhile Char.isAlpha (explode "that deadly eye of thine");
> [#" ", #"d", #"e", #"a", #"d", #"l", ...] : char list
```

Since they are curried, *takewhile* and *dropwhile* combine with other functionals. For instance, *map*(*takewhile pred*) returns a list of initial segments.

5.9   *The list functionals* exists *and* all
These functionals report whether some (or every) element of a list satisfies some predicate. They can be viewed as quantifiers over lists:

```
fun exists pred []      = false
  | exists pred (x::xs) = (pred x)   orelse   exists pred xs;
> val exists = fn : ('a -> bool) -> 'a list -> bool

fun all pred []      = true
  | all pred (x::xs) = (pred x)   andalso   all pred xs;
> val all = fn : ('a -> bool) -> 'a list -> bool
```

By currying, these functionals convert a predicate over type τ to a predicate over type τ *list*. The membership test *x mem xs* can be expressed in one line:

```
fun x mem xs = exists (secr op= x) xs;
> val mem = fn : ''a * ''a list -> bool
```

The function *disjoint* tests whether two lists have no elements in common:

```
fun disjoint(xs,ys) = all (fn x => all (fn y => x<>y) ys) xs;
> val disjoint = fn : ''a list * ''a list -> bool
```

Because of their argument order, *exists* and *all* are hard to read as quantifiers when nested; it is hard to see that *disjoint* tests 'for all *x* in *xs* and all *y* in *ys*, $x \neq y$.' However, *exists* and *all* combine well with the other functionals. Useful combinations for lists of lists include

$$exists(exists\,pred)$$
$$filter(exists\,pred)$$
$$takewhile(all\,pred)$$

5.10   *The list functionals* foldl *and* foldr

These functionals are unusually general. They apply a 2-argument function over the elements of a list:

$$foldl\,f\,e\,[x_1, \ldots, x_n] = f(x_n, \ldots, f(x_1, e) \ldots)$$
$$foldr\,f\,e\,[x_1, \ldots, x_n] = f(x_1, \ldots, f(x_n, e) \ldots)$$

Since expressions are evaluated from the inside out, the *foldl* call applies *f* to the list elements from left to right, while the *foldr* call applies it to them from right to left. The functionals are declared by

```
fun foldl f e []      = e
  | foldl f e (x::xs) = foldl f (f(x, e)) xs;
> val foldl = fn : ('a * 'b -> 'b) -> 'b -> 'a list -> 'b

fun foldr f e []      = e
  | foldr f e (x::xs) = f(x, foldr f e xs);
> val foldr = fn : ('a * 'b -> 'b) -> 'b -> 'a list -> 'b
```

Numerous functions can be expressed using *foldl* and *foldr*. The sum of a list of numbers is computed by repeated addition starting from 0:

```
val sum = foldl op+ 0;
> val sum = fn : int list -> int
sum [1,2,3,4];
> 10 : int
```

The product is computed by repeated multiplication from 1. Binding the function to an identifier is not necessary:

```
foldl op* 1 [1,2,3,4];
> 24 : int
```

These definitions work because 0 and 1 are the **identity elements** of + and ×, respectively; in other words, $0+k = k$ and $1 \times k = k$ for all k. Many applications of *foldl* and *foldr* are of this sort.

Both functionals take as their first argument a function of type $\sigma \times \tau \to \tau$. This function may itself be expressed using functionals. A nested application of *foldl* adds a list of lists:

```
foldl (fn (ns,n) => foldl op+ n ns) 0 [[1], [2,3], [4,5,6]];
> 21 : int
```

This is more direct than *sum*(*map sum* [[1], [2, 3], [4, 5, 6]]), which forms the intermediate list of sums [1, 5, 15].

List construction (the operator ::) has a type of the required form. Supplying it to *foldl* yields an efficient reverse function:

```
foldl op:: [] (explode "Richard");
> [#"d", #"r", #"a", #"h", #"c", #"i", #"R"] : char list
```

An iterative length computation is equally simple:

```
foldl (fn (_,n) => n+1) 0 (explode "Margaret");
> 8 : int
```

To append *xs* and *ys*, apply :: through *foldr* to each element of *xs*, starting with *ys*:

```
foldr op:: ["out", "thee?"] ["And", "leave"];
> ["And", "leave", "out", "thee?"] : string list
```

Applying append through *foldr* joins a list of lists, like the function *List . concat*; note that [] is the identity element of append:

```
foldr op@ [] [[1], [2,3], [4,5,6]];
> [1, 2, 3, 4, 5, 6] : int list
```

Recall that *newmem* adds a member, if not already present, to a list (Section 3.15). Applying that function through *foldr* builds a 'set' of distinct elements:

```
foldr  newmem  []  (explode "Margaret");
> [#"M", #"g", #"a", #"r", #"e", #"t"] : char list
```

To express *map f*, apply a function based on :: and *f*:

```
fun map f = foldr (fn(x,l)=> f x :: l) [];
> val map = fn : ('a -> 'b) -> 'a list -> 'b list
```

Two calls to *foldr* compute the Cartesian product of two lists:

```
fun cartprod (xs, ys) =
    foldr (fn (x, pairs) =>
              foldr (fn (y,l) => (x,y)::l) pairs ys)
          [] xs;
> val cartprod = fn : 'a list * 'b list -> ('a * 'b) list
```

Cartesian products can be computed more clearly using *map* and *List.concat*, at the expense of creating an intermediate list. Declare a curried pairing function:

```
fun pair x y = (x,y);
> val pair = fn : 'a -> 'b -> 'a * 'b
```

A list of lists of pairs is created ...

```
map (fn a => map (pair a) ["Hastings","Stanley"])
    ["Lord","Lady"];
> [[("Lord", "Hastings"), ("Lord", "Stanley")],
>  [("Lady", "Hastings"), ("Lady", "Stanley")]]
> : (string * string) list list
```

... then concatenated to form the Cartesian product:

```
List.concat it;
> [("Lord", "Hastings"), ("Lord", "Stanley"),
>  ("Lady", "Hastings"), ("Lady", "Stanley")]
> : (string * string) list
```

Both algorithms for Cartesian products can be generalized, replacing (x, y) by other functions of x and y, to express sets of the form $\{f(x, y) \mid x \in xs, \ y \in ys\}$.

ⓘ *Functionals and the standard library.* The infix *o*, for function composition, is available at top level. Also at top level are the list functionals *map*, *foldl* and *foldr*; they are separately available as components of structure *List*, as are *filter*, *exists* and *all*. Structure *ListPair* provides variants of *map*, *exists* and *all* that take a 2-argument function and operate on a pair of lists. For example, *ListPair.map* applies a function to pairs of corresponding elements of two lists:

$$ListPair.map f ([x_1, \dots , x_n], [y_1, \dots , y_n]) = [f(x_1, y_1), \dots , f(x_n, y_n)]$$

If the lists have unequal lengths, the unmatched elements are ignored. The same result can be obtained using *List . map* and *ListPair . zip*, but this builds an intermediate list.

Exercise 5.14   Express the function *union* (Section 3.15) using functionals.

Exercise 5.15   Simplify matrix multiplication (Section 3.10) using functionals.

Exercise 5.16   Express *exists* using *foldl* or *foldr*.

Exercise 5.17   Using functionals, express the conditional set expression

$$\{x - y \mid x \in xs, \ y \in ys, \ y < x\}.$$

5.11   *More examples of recursive functionals*

Binary trees and similar recursive types can be processed using recursive functionals. Even the natural numbers 0, 1, 2, ... can be viewed as a recursive type: their constructors are 0 and the successor function.

Powers of a function. If *f* is a function and $n \geq 0$ then f^n is the function such that

$$f^n(x) = \underbrace{f(\cdots f(f(x))\cdots)}_{n \text{ times}}$$

This is the function *repeat f n*:

```
fun repeat f n x =
    if n>0  then   repeat f (n-1) (f x)
                else  x;
> val repeat = fn : ('a -> 'a) -> int -> 'a -> 'a
```

Surprisingly many functions have this form. Examples include *drop* and *replist* (declared in Sections 3.4 and 5.2, respectively):

```
repeat tl 5 (explode "I'll drown you in the malmsey-butt...");
> [#"d", #"r", #"o", #"w", #"n", #" ", ...] : char list
repeat (secl "Ha!" op::) 5 [];
> ["Ha!", "Ha!", "Ha!", "Ha!", "Ha!"] : string list
```

Complete binary trees with a constant label are created by

```
repeat (fn t=>Br("No",t,t)) 3 Lf;
> Br ("No", Br ("No", Br ("No", Lf, Lf),
>                          Br ("No", Lf, Lf)),
>            Br ("No", Br ("No", Lf, Lf),
>                          Br ("No", Lf, Lf)))
> : string tree
```

A suitable function on pairs, when repeated, computes factorials:

```
fun factaux (k,p) = (k+1, k*p);
> val factaux = fn : int * int -> int * int
repeat factaux 5 (1,1);
> (6, 120) : int * int
```

Tree recursion. The functional *treerec*, for binary trees, is analogous to *foldr*. Calling *foldr f e xs*, figuratively speaking, replaces :: by *f* and *nil* by *e* in a list. Given a tree, *treefold* replaces each leaf by some value *e* and each branch by the application of a 3-argument function *f*.

```
fun  treefold f e Lf              = e
  |  treefold f e (Br(u,t1,t2))  = f(u, treefold f e t1, treefold f e t2);
> val treefold = fn
> : ('a * 'b * 'b -> 'b) -> 'b -> 'a tree -> 'b
```

This functional can express many of the tree functions of the last chapter. The function *size* replaces each leaf by 0 and each branch by a function to add 1 to the sizes of the subtrees:

```
treefold (fn(_,c1,c2) => 1+c1+c2) 0
```

The function *depth* computes a maximum at each branch:

```
treefold (fn(_,d1,d2) => 1 + Int.max(d1,d2)) 0
```

Tree recursion over a reversed version of *Br* defines *reflect*:

```
treefold (fn(u,t1,t2) => Br(u,t2,t1)) Lf
```

To compute a preorder list, each branch joins its label to the lists for the subtrees:

```
treefold (fn(u,l1,l2) => [u] @ l1 @ l2) []
```

Operations on terms. The set of terms $x, f(x), g(x, f(x)), \dots$, which is generated by variables and function applications, corresponds to the ML datatype

```
datatype term = Var of string
              | Fun of string * term list;
```

The term $(x + u) - (y \times x)$ could be declared by

```
val tm = Fun("-", [Fun("+", [Var "x", Var "u"]),
                   Fun("*", [Var "y", Var "x"])]);
```

Though it is natural to represent a function's arguments as an ML list, the types *term* and *term list* must be regarded as mutually recursive. A typical function on terms will make use of a companion function on term lists. Fortunately, the companion function need not be declared separately; in most instances it can be expressed using list functionals.

If the ML function *f* : *string* → *term* defines a substitution from variables to terms, then *subst f* extends this over terms. Observe how *map* applies the substitution to term lists.

```
fun subst f  (Var a)        = f a
  | subst f  (Fun(a,args)) = Fun(a,  map  (subst f)  args);
> val subst = fn :  (string -> term) -> term -> term
```

The list of variables in a term could also be computed using *map*:

```
fun vars  (Var a)        = [a]
  | vars  (Fun(_,args)) = List.concat (map vars args);
> val vars = fn : term -> string list
vars tm;
> ["x",  "u",  "y",  "x"] : string list
```

This is wasteful because *List.concat* copies lists repeatedly. Instead, declare a function *accumVars* with an argument to accumulate a list of variables. It can be extended to term lists using *foldr*:

```
fun accumVars  (Var a,  bs)          = a::bs
  | accumVars  (Fun(_,args),  bs) = foldr accumVars bs args;
> val accumVars = fn :  term * string list -> string list
accumVars  (tm,[]);
> ["x",  "u",  "y",  "x"] : string list
```

Here is a demonstration. A trivial substitution, *replace t a* replaces the variable *a* by *t* while leaving other variables unchanged:

```
fun replace t a b = if a=b then t else Var b;
> val replace = fn : term -> string -> string -> term
```

Thus, *subst* (*replace t a*) *u* replaces *a* by *t* throughout the term *u*. Substituting −*z* for *x* in *tm* yields the term $(-z + u) - (y \times -z)$:

```
subst  (replace  (Fun("-",[Var "z"]))  "x")  tm;
> Fun  ("-",
>         [Fun  ("+",  [Fun  ("-",  [Var "z"]),  Var "u"]),
>          Fun  ("*",  [Var "y",  Fun  ("-",  [Var "z"])])])
> : term
```

Now the list of variables contains *z* in place of *x*:

```
accumVars  (it,[]);
> ["z",  "u",  "y",  "z"] : string list
```

Exercise 5.18   Declare the functional *prefold* such that *prefold f e t* is equivalent to *foldr f e* (*preorder t*).

Exercise 5.19   Write a function *nf* such that *repeat nf* computes Fibonacci numbers.

Exercise 5.20   What is this function good for?

```
fun funny f 0 = I
  | funny f n = if n mod 2 = 0
                then funny (f o f) (n div 2)
                else funny (f o f) (n div 2) o f;
```

Exercise 5.21   What function is *treefold F I*, where *F* is declared as follows?

```
fun F (v,f1,f2) vs = v :: f1 (f2 vs);
```

Exercise 5.22   Consider counting the *Fun* nodes in a term. Express this as a function modelled on *vars*, then as a function modelled on *accumVars* and finally without using functionals.

Exercise 5.23   Note that the result of *vars tm* mentions *x* twice. Write a function to compute the list of variables in a term without repetitions. Can you find a simple solution using functionals?

Sequences, or infinite lists

Lazy lists are one of the most celebrated features of functional programming. The elements of a lazy list are not evaluated until their values are required by the rest of the program; thus a lazy list may be infinite. In lazy languages like Haskell, all data structures are lazy and infinite lists are commonplace in programs. In ML, which is not lazy, infinite lists are rare. This section describes how to express infinite lists in ML, representing the tail of a list by a function in order to delay its evaluation.

It is important to recognize the hazards of programming with lazy lists. Hitherto we have expected every function, from the greatest common divisor to priority queues, to deliver its result in finite time. Recursion was used to reduce a problem to simpler subproblems. Every recursive function included a base case where it would terminate.

Now we shall be dealing with potentially infinite results. We may view any finite part of an infinite list, but never the whole. We may add two infinite lists element by element to form a list of sums, but may not reverse an infinite list or find its smallest element. We shall define recursions that go on forever, with no base case. Instead of asking whether the program terminates, we can only ask whether the program generates each finite part of its result in finite time.

ML functions on infinite lists are more complicated than their counterparts in a lazy language. By laying the mechanism bare, however, they may help us avoid some pitfalls. Mechanistic thinking should not be our only tool; computations over infinite values may exceed our powers of imagination. Domain theory gives a deeper view of such computations (Gunter, 1992; Winskel, 1993).

5.12   *A type of sequences*

Infinite lists are traditionally called *streams*, but let us call them *sequences*. (A 'stream' in ML is an input/output channel.) Like a list, a sequence either is empty or contains a head and tail. The empty sequence is *Nil* and a non-empty sequence has the form *Cons*(x, xf), where x is the head and xf is a function to compute the tail:[3]

```
datatype 'a seq = Nil
                | Cons of 'a * (unit -> 'a seq);
```

Starting from this declaration, we shall interactively develop a set of sequence primitives, by analogy with lists. Later, to avoid name clashes, we shall group them into an appropriate structure.

Functions to return the head and tail of a sequence are easily declared. As with lists, inspecting the empty sequence should raise an exception:

```
exception Empty;
fun hd (Cons(x,xf)) = x
  | hd Nil           = raise Empty;
> val hd = fn :  'a seq -> 'a
```

To inspect the tail, apply the function *xf* to (). The argument, the sole value of type *unit*, conveys no information; it merely forces evaluation of the tail.

```
fun tl (Cons(x,xf)) = xf()
  | tl Nil          = raise Empty;
> val tl = fn :  'a seq -> 'a seq
```

Calling *cons*(x, xq) combines a head x and tail sequence xq to form a longer sequence:

```
fun cons(x,xq)  = Cons(x, fn()=>xq);
> val cons = fn :  'a * 'a seq -> 'a seq
```

---

[3] Type *unit* was described in Section 2.8.

Note that *cons*(*x*, *E*) is not evaluated lazily. ML evaluates the expression *E*, yielding say *xq*, and returns *Cons* (*x*, fn()=>*xq*). So the fn inside *cons* does not delay the evaluation of the tail. Only use *cons* where lazy evaluation is not required, say to convert a list into a sequence:

```
fun fromList l = List.foldr cons Nil l;
> val fromList = fn : 'a list -> 'a seq
```

To delay the evaluation of *E*, write *Cons* (*x*, fn()=>*E*) instead of *cons*(*x*, *E*). Let us define the increasing sequence of integers starting from *k*:

```
fun from k = Cons(k, fn()=> from(k+1));
> val from = fn : int -> int seq
from 1;
> Cons (1, fn) : int seq
```

The sequence starts with 1; here are some more elements:

```
tl it;
> Cons (2, fn) : int seq
tl it;
> Cons (3, fn) : int seq
```

Calling *take*(*xq*, *n*) returns the first *n* elements of the sequence *xq* as a list:

```
fun take (xq, 0)          = []
  | take (Nil, n)         = raise Subscript
  | take (Cons(x,xf), n) = x :: take (xf(), n-1);
> val take = fn : 'a seq * int -> 'a list
take (from 30, 7);
> [30, 31, 32, 33, 34, 35, 36] : int list
```

How does it work? The computation of *take*(*from* 30, 2) goes as follows:

$$take(from\,30, 2)$$
$$\Rightarrow take(Cons(30, \text{fn}()=>from(30 + 1)), 2)$$
$$\Rightarrow 30 :: take(from(30 + 1), 1)$$
$$\Rightarrow 30 :: take(Cons(31, \text{fn}()=>from(31 + 1)), 1)$$
$$\Rightarrow 30 :: 31 :: take(from(31 + 1), 0)$$
$$\Rightarrow 30 :: 31 :: take(Cons(32, \text{fn}()=>from(32 + 1)), 0)$$
$$\Rightarrow 30 :: 31 :: []$$
$$\Rightarrow [30, 31]$$

Observe that the element 32 is computed but never used. Type *α seq* is not really lazy; the head of a non-empty sequence is always computed. What is worse, inspecting the tail repeatedly evaluates it repeatedly; we do not have call-by-need, only call-by-name. Such defects can be cured at the cost of considerable extra complication (see Section 8.4).

Exercise 5.24 Explain what is wrong with this version of *from*, describing the computation steps of *take*(*badfrom* 30, 2).

```
fun badfrom k = cons(k, badfrom(k+1));
```

Exercise 5.25 This variant of type α *seq* represents every non-empty sequence by a function, preventing premature evaluation of the first element (Reade, 1989, page 324). Code the functions *from* and *take* for this type of sequences:

```
datatype 'a seq = Nil
              | Cons of unit -> 'a * 'a seq;
```

Exercise 5.26 This variant of α *seq*, declared using mutual recursion, is even lazier than the one above. Every sequence is a function, delaying even the computation needed to tell if a sequence is non-empty. Code the functions *from* and *take* for this type of sequences:

```
datatype 'a seqnode = Nil
                  | Cons of 'a * 'a seq
and      'a seq     = Seq of unit -> 'a seqnode;
```

5.13   *Elementary sequence processing*

For a function on sequences to be computable, each finite part of the output must depend on at most a finite part of the input. Consider squaring a sequence of integers one by one. The tail of the output, when evaluated, applies *squares* to the tail of the input.

```
fun squares Nil : int seq = Nil
  | squares (Cons(x,xf)) = Cons(x*x, fn()=> squares(xf()));
> val squares = fn : int seq -> int seq
squares (from 1);
> Cons (1, fn) : int seq
take (it, 10);
> [1, 4, 9, 16, 25, 36, 49, 64, 81, 100] : int list
```

Adding corresponding elements of two sequences is similar. Evaluating the tail of the output evaluates the tails of the two inputs. If either input sequence becomes empty, then so does the output.

```
fun add  (Cons(x,xf),  Cons(y,yf))  =  Cons(x+y,
                                       fn()=> add(xf(),  yf()))
  | add _   : int seq             = Nil;
> val add = fn : int seq * int seq -> int seq
add (from 10000,  squares (from 1));
> Cons (10001, fn) : int seq
take (it, 5);
> [10001, 10005, 10011, 10019, 10029] : int list
```

The append function for sequences works like the one for lists. The elements of *xq* @ *yq* are first taken from *xq*; when *xq* becomes empty, elements are taken from *yq*.

```
fun Nil          @ yq = yq
  | (Cons(x,xf)) @ yq = Cons(x, fn()=> (xf()) @ yq);
> val @ = fn : 'a seq * 'a seq -> 'a seq
```

For a simple demonstration, let us build a finite sequence using *fromList*.

```
val finite = fromList [25,10];
> Cons (25, fn) : int seq
finite @ from 1415;
> Cons (25, fn) : int seq
take(it, 3);
> [25, 10, 1415] : int list
```

If *xq* is infinite then *xq* @ *yq* equals *xq*. A variant of append combines infinite sequences fairly. The elements of two sequences can be ***interleaved***:

```
fun interleave (Nil, yq)        = yq
  | interleave (Cons(x,xf), yq) =
        Cons(x, fn()=> interleave(yq, xf()));
> val interleave = fn : 'a seq * 'a seq -> 'a seq
take(interleave(from 0, from 50), 10);
> [0, 50, 1, 51, 2, 52, 3, 53, 4, 54] : int list
```

In its recursive call, *interleave* exchanges the two sequences so that neither can exclude the other.

Functionals for sequences. List functionals like *map* and *filter* can be generalized to sequences. The function *squares* is an instance of the functional *map*, which applies a function to every element of a sequence:

```
fun map f Nil          = Nil
  | map f (Cons(x,xf)) = Cons(f x, fn()=> map f (xf()));
> val map = fn : ('a -> 'b) -> 'a seq -> 'b seq
```

To filter a sequence, successive tail functions are called until an element is found to satisfy the given predicate. If no such element exists, the computation will never terminate.

```
fun filter pred Nil           = Nil
  | filter pred (Cons(x,xf)) =
        if pred x then Cons(x, fn()=> filter pred (xf()))
                  else filter pred (xf());
> val filter = fn : ('a -> bool) -> 'a seq -> 'a seq
filter (fn n => n mod 10 = 7) (from 50);
> Cons (57, fn) : int seq
take(it, 8);
> [57, 67, 77, 87, 97, 107, 117, 127] : int list
```

The function *from* is an instance of the functional *iterates*, which generates sequences of the form $[x, f(x), f(f(x)), \ldots, f^k(x), \ldots]$:

```
fun iterates f x = Cons(x, fn()=> iterates f (f x));
> val iterates = fn : ('a -> 'a) -> 'a -> 'a seq
iterates(secr op/ 2.0) 1.0;
> Cons (1.0, fn) : real seq
take(it, 5);
> [1.0, 0.5, 0.25, 0.125, 0.0625] : real list
```

A structure for sequences. Let us again gather up the functions we have explored, making a structure. As in the binary tree structure (Section 4.13), we leave the datatype declaration outside to allow direct reference to the constructors. Imagine that the other sequence primitives have been declared not at top level but in a structure *Seq* satisfying the following signature:

```
signature SEQUENCE =
  sig
  exception Empty
  val cons      : 'a * 'a seq -> 'a seq
  val null      : 'a seq -> bool
  val hd        : 'a seq -> 'a
  val tl        : 'a seq -> 'a seq
  val fromList  : 'a list -> 'a seq
  val toList    : 'a seq -> 'a list
  val take      : 'a seq * int -> 'a list
  val drop      : 'a seq * int -> 'a seq
  val @         : 'a seq * 'a seq -> 'a seq
  val interleave : 'a seq * 'a seq -> 'a seq
  val map       : ('a -> 'b) -> 'a seq -> 'b seq
  val filter    : ('a -> bool) -> 'a seq -> 'a seq
  val iterates  : ('a -> 'a) -> 'a -> 'a seq
  val from      : int -> int seq
  end;
```

Exercise 5.27   Declare the missing functions *null* and *drop* by analogy with the list versions. Also declare *toList*, which converts a finite sequence to a list.

Exercise 5.28   Show the computation steps of *add*(*from* 5, *squares*(*from* 9)).

Exercise 5.29   Declare a function that, given a positive integer k, transforms a sequence $[x_1, x_2, \ldots]$ into a new sequence by repeating each element k times:

$$[\underbrace{x_1, \ldots, x_1}_{k \text{ times}}, \underbrace{x_2, \ldots, x_2}_{k \text{ times}}, \ldots]$$

Exercise 5.30   Declare a function to add adjacent elements of a sequence, transforming $[x_1, x_2, x_3, x_4, \ldots]$ to $[x_1 + x_2, x_3 + x_4, \ldots]$.

Exercise 5.31   Which of the list functionals *takewhile*, *dropwhile*, *exists* and *all* can sensibly be generalized to infinite sequences? Code those that can be, and explain what goes wrong with the others.

5.14   *Elementary applications of sequences*

We can use structure *Seq* for making change, to express an infinite sequence of random numbers and to enumerate the prime numbers. These examples especially illustrate the sequence functionals.

Making change, revisited. The function *allChange* (Section 3.7) computes all possible ways of making change. It is not terribly practical: using British coin values, there are 4366 different ways of making change for 99 pence!

If the function returned a sequence, it could compute solutions upon demand, saving time and storage. Getting the desired effect in ML requires care. Replacing the list operations by sequence operations in *allChange* would achieve little. The new function would contain two recursive calls, with nothing to delay the second call's execution. The resulting sequence would be fully evaluated.

```
Seq.@ (allChange (c::coins, c::coinvals, amount-c),
        allChange (coins, coinvals, amount))
```

Better is to start with the solution of Exercise 3.14, where the append is replaced by an argument to accumulate solutions. An accumulator argument is usually a list. Should we change it to a sequence?

```
fun seqChange (coins, coinvals, 0, coinsf)            = Cons (coins, coinsf)
  | seqChange (coins, [], amount, coinsf)            = coinsf ()
  | seqChange (coins, c::coinvals, amount, coinsf) =
    if amount<0 then coinsf ()
    else seqChange(c::coins, c::coinvals, amount-c,
                   fn()=> seqChange (coins, coinvals, amount, coinsf));
> val seqChange = fn : int list * int list * int *
>                     (unit -> int list seq) -> int list seq
```

Instead of a sequence there is a tail function *coinsf* of type *unit → int list seq*. This allows us to use *Cons* in the first line, instead of the eager *Seq.cons*. And it requires a fn around the inner recursive call, delaying it. This sort of thing is easier in Haskell.

We can now enumerate solutions, getting each one instantly:

```
seqChange([], gb_coins, 99, fn ()=> Nil);
> Cons ([2, 2, 5, 20, 20, 50], fn) : int list seq
Seq.tl it;
> Cons ([1, 1, 2, 5, 20, 20, 50], fn) : int list seq
Seq.tl it;
> Cons ([1, 1, 1, 1, 5, 20, 20, 50], fn) : int list seq
```

The overheads are modest. Computing all solutions takes 354 msec, which is about 1/3 slower than the list version of the function and twice as fast as the original *allChange*.

Random numbers. In Section 3.18 we generated a list of 10,000 random numbers for the sorting examples. However, we seldom know in advance how many random numbers are required. Conventionally, a random number generator is a procedure that stores the 'seed' in a local variable. In a functional language, we can define an infinite sequence of random numbers. This hides the implementation details and generates the numbers as they are required.

```
local val a = 16807.0  and  m = 2147483647.0
      fun nextRand seed =
            let val t = a*seed
            in  t - m * real(floor(t/m))   end
in
   fun randseq s = Seq.map (secr op/ m)
                          (Seq.iterates nextRand (real s))
end;
> val randseq = fn : int -> real seq
```

Observe how *Seq.iterates* generates a sequence of numbers, which *Seq.map* divides by *m*. The random numbers are reals between 0 and 1, exclusive. Using *Seq.map* we convert them to integers from 0 to 9:

```
Seq.map (floor o secl(10.0) op* ) (randseq 1);
> Cons (0, fn) : int seq
Seq.take (it, 12);
> [0, 0, 1, 7, 4, 5, 2, 0, 6, 6, 9, 3] : int list
```

Prime numbers. The sequence of prime numbers can be computed by the Sieve of Eratosthenes.

- Start with the sequence [2, 3, 4, 5, 6, . . .].
- Take 2 as a prime. Delete all multiples of 2, since they cannot be prime. This leaves the sequence [3, 5, 7, 9, 11, . . .].
- Take 3 as a prime and delete its multiples. This leaves the sequence [5, 7, 11, 13, 17, . . .].
- Take 5 as a prime . . . .

At each stage, the sequence contains those numbers not divisible by any of the primes generated so far. Therefore its head is prime, and the process can continue indefinitely.

The function *sift* deletes multiples from a sequence, while *sieve* repeatedly sifts a sequence:

```
fun sift p = Seq.filter (fn n => n mod p <> 0);
> val sift = fn : int -> int seq -> int seq
fun sieve (Cons(p,nf)) = Cons(p, fn()=> sieve (sift p (nf())));
> val sieve = fn : int seq -> int seq
```

The sequence *primes* results from *sieve* [2, 3, 4, 5, . . .]. No primes beyond the first are generated until the sequence is inspected.

```
val primes = sieve (Seq.from 2);
> val primes = Cons (2, fn) : int seq
Seq.take (primes, 25);
> [2, 3, 5, 7, 11, 13, 17, 19, 23, 29, 31, 37, 41, 43,
>  47, 53, 59, 61, 67, 71, 73, 79, 83, 89, 97] : int list
```

When we write programs such as these, ML types help to prevent confusion between sequences and tail functions. A sequence has type τ *seq* while a tail function has type *unit* $\rightarrow$ τ *seq*. We can insert a function call $\cdots$ () or a function abstraction fn() =>$\cdots$ in response to type error messages.

5.15 *Numerical computing*

Sequences have applications in numerical analysis. This may seem surprising at first, but, after all, many numerical methods are based on infinite series. Why not express them literally?

Square roots are a simple example. Recall the Newton-Raphson method for computing the square root of some number a. Start with a positive approximation x_0. Compute further approximations by the rule

$$x_{k+1} = \left(\frac{a}{x_k} + x_k\right)/2 \,,$$

stopping when two successive approximations are sufficiently close. With sequences we can perform this computation directly.

The function *nextApprox* computes x_{k+1} from x_k. Iterating it computes the series of approximations.

```
fun nextApprox a x = (a/x + x) / 2.0;
> val nextApprox = fn : real -> real -> real
Seq.take(Seq.iterates (nextApprox 9.0) 1.0, 7);
> [1.0, 5.0, 3.4, 3.023529412, 3.000091554,
>   3.000000001, 3.0] : real list
```

The simplest termination test is to stop when the absolute difference between two approximations is smaller than a given tolerance $\epsilon > 0$ (written *eps* below).[4]

```
fun within (eps:real) (Cons(x,xf)) =
      let val Cons(y,yf) = xf()
      in  if Real.abs(x-y) < eps then y
          else within eps (Cons(y,yf))
      end;
> val within = fn : real -> real seq -> real
```

Putting 10^{-6} for the tolerance and 1 for the initial approximation yields a square root function:

```
fun qroot a = within 1E~6 (Seq.iterates (nextApprox a) 1.0);
> val qroot = fn : real -> real
qroot 5.0;
> 2.236067977 : real
it*it;
> 5.0 : real
```

Would not a Fortran program be better? This example follows Hughes (1989) and Halfant and Sussman (1988), who show how interchangeable parts involving sequences can be assembled into numerical algorithms. Each algorithm is tailor made to suit its application.

---

[4] The recursive call passes *Cons(y, yf)* rather than *xf*(), which denotes the same value, to avoid calling *xf*() twice. Recall that our sequences are not truly lazy, but employ a call-by-name rule.

For instance, there are many termination tests to choose from. The absolute difference ($|x - y| < \epsilon$) tested by *within* is too strict for large numbers. We could test relative difference ($|x/y - 1| < \epsilon$) or something fancier:

$$\frac{|x - y|}{(|x| + |y|)/2 + 1} < \epsilon$$

Sometimes it is prudent to test that three or more approximations are sufficiently close.

Each termination test can be packaged as a function from sequences to reals. Techniques like Richardson extrapolation (for accelerating the convergence of a series) can be packaged as functions from sequences to sequences. These functions can be combined to perform numerical differentiation, integration and so on.

Exercise 5.32 Compute the exponential function e^x by generating a sequence for the infinite sum

$$e^x = \frac{1}{0!} + \frac{x^1}{1!} + \frac{x^2}{2!} + \frac{x^3}{3!} + \cdots + \frac{x^k}{k!} + \cdots$$

Exercise 5.33 Write an ML function to take a value from a sequence using one of the other termination tests mentioned above. Declare a square root (or exponential) function using it.

5.16 Interleaving and sequences of sequences

Given infinite sequences *xq* and *yq*, consider forming the sequence of all pairs (x, y) with *x* from *xq* and *y* from *yq*. This problem illustrates the subtleties of computing with infinities.

As remarked above in Section 5.10, a list of lists can be generated using *map* with the curried pairing function *pair*. A sequence of sequences can be generated similarly:

```
fun makeqq (xq,yq) = Seq.map (fn x=> Seq.map (pair x) yq) xq;
> val makeqq = fn : 'a seq * 'b seq -> ('a * 'b) seq seq
```

A sequence of sequences can be viewed using *takeqq*(*xqq*, (*m*, *n*)). This list of lists is the $m \times n$ upper left rectangle of *xqq*.

```
fun takeqq (xqq, (m,n)) = map (secr Seq.take n) (Seq.take(xqq,m));
> val takeqq = fn
> : 'a seq seq * (int * int) -> 'a list list
```

```
makeqq (Seq.from 30, primes);
> Cons (Cons ((30, 2), fn), fn) : (int * int) seq seq
takeqq (it, (3,5));
> [[(30, 2), (30, 3), (30, 5), (30, 7), (30, 11)],
>  [(31, 2), (31, 3), (31, 5), (31, 7), (31, 11)],
>  [(32, 2), (32, 3), (32, 5), (32, 7), (32, 11)]]
> : (int * int) list list
```

The function *List . concat* appends the members of a list of lists, forming one list. Let us declare an analogous function *enumerate* to combine a sequence of sequences. Because the sequences may be infinite, we must use *interleave* instead of append.

Here is the idea. If the input sequence has head *xq* and tail *xqq*, recursively enumerate *xqq* and interleave the result with *xq*. If we take *List . concat* as a model we end up with faulty code:

```
fun enumerate Nil                  = Nil
  | enumerate (Cons(xq,xqf)) = Seq.interleave(xq, enumerate (xqf()));
> val enumerate = fn : 'a seq seq -> 'a seq
```

If the input to this function is infinite, ML will make an infinite series of recursive calls, generating no output. This version would work in a lazy functional language, but with ML we must explicitly terminate the recursive calls as soon as some output can be produced. This requires a more complex case analysis. If the input sequence is non-empty, examine its head; if that is also non-empty then it contains an element for the output.

```
fun enumerate Nil                         = Nil
  | enumerate (Cons(Nil,  xqf))           = enumerate (xqf())
  | enumerate (Cons(Cons(x,xf), xqf)) =
           Cons(x, fn()=> Seq.interleave(enumerate (xqf()), xf())));
> val enumerate = fn : 'a seq seq -> 'a seq
```

The second and third cases simulate the incorrect version's use of *interleave*, but the enclosing fn() =>··· terminates the recursive calls.

Here is the sequence of all pairs of positive integers.

```
val pairqq = makeqq (Seq.from 1, Seq.from 1);
> val pairqq = Cons (Cons ((1, 1), fn), fn)
> : (int * int) seq seq
Seq.take(enumerate pairqq, 18);
> [(1, 1), (2, 1), (1, 2), (3, 1), (1, 3), (2, 2), (1, 4),
>  (4, 1), (1, 5), (2, 3), (1, 6), (3, 2), (1, 7), (2, 4),
>  (1, 8), (5, 1), (1, 9), (2, 5)] : (int * int) list
```

We can be more precise about the order of enumeration. Consider the following declarations:

```
fun powof2 n = repeat double n 1;
> val powof2 = fn : int -> int
fun pack(i,j) = powof2(i-1) * (2*j - 1);
> val pack = fn : int * int -> int
```

This function, $pack(i, j) = 2^{i-1}(2j-1)$, establishes a one-to-one correspondence between positive integers and pairs (i, j) of positive integers. Thus, the Cartesian product of two countable sets is a countable set. Here is a small table of this function:

```
val nqq = Seq.map (Seq.map pack) pairqq;
> val nqq = Cons (Cons (1, fn), fn) : int seq seq
takeqq (nqq, (4,6));
> [[1,   3,   5,   7,   9,  11],
>  [2,   6,  10,  14,  18,  22],
>  [4,  12,  20,  28,  36,  44],
>  [8,  24,  40,  56,  72,  88]] : int list list
```

Our enumeration decodes the packing function, returning the sequence of positive integers in their natural order:

```
Seq.take (enumerate nqq, 12);
> [1, 2, 3, 4, 5, 6, 7, 8, 9, 10, 11, 12] : int list
```

It is not hard to see why this is so. Each interleaving takes half its elements from one sequence and half from another. Repeated interleaving distributes the places in the output sequence by powers of two, as in the packing function.

Exercise 5.34 Predict, or at least explain, ML's response to the following:

```
enumerate (Seq.iterates I Nil);
```

Exercise 5.35 Generate the sequence of all finite lists of positive integers. (Hint: first, declare a function to generate the sequence of lists having a given length.)

Exercise 5.36 Show that for every positive integer k there are unique positive integers i and j such that $k = pack(i, j)$. What is $pack(i, j)$ in binary notation?

Exercise 5.37 Adapt the definition of type α *seq* to declare a type of infinite binary trees. Write a function *itr* that, applied to an integer n, constructs the tree whose root has the label n and the two subtrees $itr(2n)$ and $itr(2n + 1)$.

Exercise 5.38 (Continuing the previous exercise.) Write a function to build a sequence consisting of all the labels in a given infinite binary tree. In what order are the labels enumerated? Then write an inverse function that constructs an infinite binary tree whose labels are given by a sequence.

Search strategies and infinite lists

Theorem proving, planning and other Artificial Intelligence applications require search. There are many search strategies:

- Depth-first search is cheap, but it may follow a blind alley and run forever without finding any solutions.
- Breadth-first search is *complete* — certain to find all the solutions — but it requires a huge amount of space.
- Depth-first iterative deepening is complete and requires little space, but can be slow.
- Best-first search must be guided by a function to estimate the distance from a solution.

By representing the set of solutions as a lazy list, the search strategy can be chosen independently from the process that consumes the solutions. The lazy list serves as a communication channel: the producer generates its elements and the consumer removes them. Because the list is lazy, its elements are not produced until the consumer requires them.

Figures 5.1 and 5.2 contrast the depth-first and breadth-first strategies, applying both to the same tree. The tree is portrayed at some point during the search, with subtrees not yet visited as wedges. Throughout this section, no tree node may have an infinite number of branches. Trees may have infinite depth.

In *depth-first search*, each subtree is fully searched before its brother to the right is considered. The numbers in the figure show the order of the visits. Node 5 is reached because node 4 is a leaf, while four subtrees remain to be visited. If the subtree below node 5 is infinite, the other subtrees will never be reached: the strategy is incomplete. Depth-first search is familiarly called backtracking.

Breadth-first search visits all nodes at the current depth before moving on to the next depth. In Figure 5.2 it has explored the tree to three levels. Because of finite branching, all nodes will be reached: the strategy is complete. But it is seldom practical, except in trivial cases. To reach a given depth, it visits an exponential number of nodes and uses an exponential amount of storage.

5.17   *Search strategies in ML*

Infinite trees could be represented rather like infinite lists, namely as an ML datatype containing functions to delay evaluation. For the search trees of this

Figure 5.1 *A depth-first search tree*

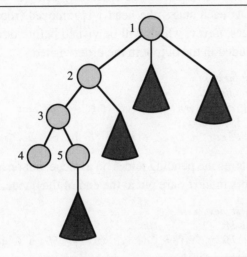

Figure 5.2 *A breadth-first search tree*

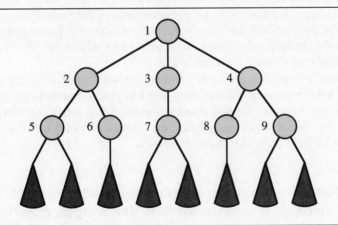

section, however, a node's subtrees can be computed from its label. Trees over type τ (with finite branching) are represented by a function $next : \tau \rightarrow \tau\ list$, where $next\ x$ is the list of the subtrees of x.

Depth-first search can be implemented efficiently using a stack to hold the nodes to visit next. At each stage, the head y is removed from the stack and replaced by its subtrees, $next\ y$, which will be visited before other nodes in the stack. Nodes are included in the output in the order visited.

```
fun depthFirst next x =
    let fun dfs []      = Nil
          | dfs(y::ys) = Cons(y, fn()=> dfs(next y @ ys))
    in  dfs [x]  end;
> val depthFirst = fn : ('a -> 'a list) -> 'a -> 'a seq
```

Breadth-first search stores the pending nodes on a queue, not on a stack. When y is visited, its successors in $next\ y$ are put at the end of the queue.[5]

```
fun breadthFirst next x =
    let fun bfs []      = Nil
          | bfs(y::ys) = Cons(y, fn()=> bfs(ys @ next y))
    in  bfs [x]  end;
> val breadthFirst = fn : ('a -> 'a list) -> 'a -> 'a seq
```

Both strategies simply enumerate all nodes in some order. Solutions are identified using the functional *Seq*.*filter* with a suitable predicate on nodes. Other search strategies can be obtained by modifying these functions.

ⓘ *Best-first search.* Searches in Artificial Intelligence frequently employ a heuristic distance function, which estimates the distance to a solution from any given node. The estimate is added to the known distance from that node to the root, thereby estimating the distance from the root to a solution via that node. These estimates impose an order on the pending nodes, which are stored in a priority queue. The node with the least estimated total distance is visited next.

If the distance function is reasonably accurate, best-first search converges rapidly to a solution. If it is a constant function, then best-first search degenerates to breadth-first search. If it overestimates the true distance, then best-first search may never find any solutions. The strategy takes many forms, the simplest of which is the A* algorithm. See Rich and Knight (1991) for more information.

Exercise 5.39 Write versions of *depthFirst* and *breadthFirst* with an additional argument: a predicate to recognize solutions. This is slightly more efficient than

---

[5] Stacks and queues are represented here by lists. Lists make efficient stacks but poor queues. Section 7.3 presents efficient queues.

the approach used in the text, as it avoids calling *Seq.filter* and copying the sequence of outputs.

Exercise 5.40   Implement best-first search, as described above. Your function must keep track of each node's distance from the root in order to add this to the estimated distance to a solution.

5.18   *Generating palindromes*

Let us generate the sequence of palindromes over the alphabet {*A*, *B*, *C*}. Each node of the search tree will be a list *l* of these letters, with 3 branches to nodes #"A"::*l*, #"B"::*l* and #"C"::*l*.

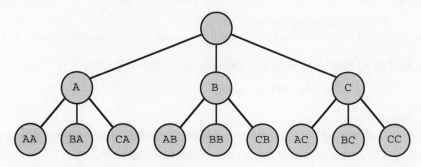

Function *nextChar* generates this tree.

```
fun nextChar l = [#"A"::l, #"B"::l, #"C"::l];
> val nextChar = fn : char list -> char list list
```

A *palindrome* is a list that equals its own reverse. Let us declare the corresponding predicate:

```
fun isPalin l = (l = rev l);
> val isPalin = fn : ''a list -> bool
```

There are, of course, more efficient ways of generating palindromes. Our approach highlights the differences between different search strategies. Let us declare a function to help us examine sequences of nodes (*implode* joins a list of characters to form a string):

```
fun show n csq = map implode (Seq.take(csq,n));
> val show = fn : int -> char list seq -> string list
```

Breadth-first search is complete and generates all the palindromes. Let us inspect the sequences before and after filtering:

```
show 8 (breadthFirst nextChar []);
> ["", "A", "B", "C", "AA", "BA", "CA", "AB"] : string list
show 8 (Seq.filter isPalin (breadthFirst nextChar []));
> ["", "A", "B", "C", "AA", "BB", "CC", "AAA"] : string list
```

Depth-first search fails to find all solutions. Since the tree's leftmost branch is infinite, the search never leaves it. We need not bother calling *Seq.filter*:

```
show 8 (depthFirst nextChar []);
> ["", "A", "AA", "AAA", "AAAA", "AAAAA", "AAAAAA",
>  "AAAAAAA"] : string list
```

If there is no solution on an infinite branch then depth-first search finds nothing at all. Let us start the search at the label *B*. There is only one palindrome of the form *AA*...*AB*:

```
show 5 (depthFirst nextChar [#"B"]);
> ["B", "AB", "AAB", "AAAB", "AAAAB"] : string list
```

The attempt to find more than one palindrome in this sequence ...

```
show 2 (Seq.filter isPalin (depthFirst nextChar [#"B"]));
```

... runs forever.

On the other hand, breadth-first search explores the entire subtree below *B*. Filtering yields the sequence of all palindromes ending in *B*:

```
show 6 (breadthFirst nextChar [#"B"]);
> ["B", "AB", "BB", "CB", "AAB", "BAB"] : string list
show 6 (Seq.filter isPalin (breadthFirst nextChar [#"B"]));
> ["B", "BB", "BAB", "BBB", "BCB", "BAAB"] : string list
```

Again, we see the importance of a complete search strategy.

5.19   *The Eight Queens problem*

A classic problem is to place 8 Queens on a chess board so that no Queen may attack another. No two Queens may share a row, column or diagonal. Solutions may be found by examining all safe ways of placing new Queens on successive columns. The root of the search tree contains an empty board. There are 8 positions for a Queen in the first column, so there are 8 branches from the root to boards holding one Queen. Once a Queen has been placed in the first column, there are fewer than 8 safe positions for a Queen in the second column; branching decreases with depth in the tree. A board containing 8 Queens must be a leaf node.

Since the tree is finite, depth-first search finds all solutions. Most published solutions to the problem, whether procedural or functional, encode depth-first search directly. A procedural program, recording the occupation of rows and diagonals using boolean arrays, can find all solutions quickly. Here, the Eight Queens problem simply serves to demonstrate the different search strategies.

We can represent a board position by a list of row numbers. The list $[q_1, \ldots, q_k]$ stands for the board having Queens in row q_i of column i for $i = 1, \ldots, k$. Function *safeQueen* tests whether a queen can safely be placed in row *newq* of the next column, forming the board $[newq, q_1, \ldots, q_k]$. (The other columns are essentially shifted to the left.) The new Queen must not be on the same row or diagonal as another Queen. Note that $|newq - q_i| = i$ exactly when *newq* and q_i share a diagonal.

```
fun safeQueen oldqs newq =
    let fun nodiag (i, []) = true
      | nodiag (i, q::qs) =
            Int.abs(newq-q)<>i andalso nodiag(i+1,qs)
    in  not (newq mem oldqs) andalso nodiag (1,oldqs)  end;
```

To generate the search tree, function *nextQueen* takes a board and returns the list of the safe board positions having a new Queen. Observe the use of the list functionals, *map* with a section and *filter* with a curried function. The Eight Queens problem is generalized to the n Queens problem, which is to place n Queens safely on an $n \times n$ board. Calling *upto* (declared in Section 3.1) generates the list $[1, \ldots, n]$ of candidate Queens.

```
fun nextQueen n qs =
    map (secr op:: qs) (List.filter (safeQueen qs) (upto(1,n)));
> val nextQueen = fn : int -> int list -> int list list
```

Let us declare a predicate to recognize solutions. Since only safe board positions are considered, a solution is any board having n Queens.

```
fun isFull n qs = (length qs=n);
> val isFull = fn : int -> 'a list -> bool
```

Function *depthFirst* finds all 92 solutions for 8 Queens. This takes 130 msec:

```
fun depthQueen n = Seq.filter (isFull n) (depthFirst (nextQueen n) []);
> val depthQueen = fn : int -> int list seq
Seq.toList (depthQueen 8);
> [[4, 2, 7, 3, 6, 8, 5, 1], [5, 2, 4, 7, 3, 8, 6, 1],
>  [3, 5, 2, 8, 6, 4, 7, 1], [3, 6, 4, 2, 8, 5, 7, 1],
>  [5, 7, 1, 3, 8, 6, 4, 2], [4, 6, 8, 3, 1, 7, 5, 2],
>  ...] : int list list
```

Since sequences are lazy, solutions can be demanded one by one. Depth-first search finds the first solution quickly (6.6 msec). This is not so important for the

Eight Queens problem, but the 15 Queens problem has over two million solutions. We can compute a few of them in one second:

```
Seq.take(depthQueen 15, 3);
> [[8, 11, 7, 15, 6, 9, 13, 4, 14, 12, 10, 2, 5, 3, 1],
>  [11, 13, 10, 4, 6, 8, 15, 2, 12, 14, 9, 7, 5, 3, 1],
>  [13, 11, 8, 6, 2, 9, 14, 4, 15, 10, 12, 7, 5, 3, 1]]
> : int list list
```

Imagine the design of a procedural program that could generate solutions upon demand. It would probably involve coroutines or communicating processes.

Function *breadthFirst* finds the solutions slowly.[6] Finding one solution takes nearly as long as finding all! The solutions reside at the same depth in the search tree; finding the first solution requires searching virtually the entire tree.

5.20   *Iterative deepening*

Depth-first iterative deepening combines the best properties of the other search procedures. Like depth-first search, it uses little space; like breadth-first search, it is complete. The strategy is to search the tree repeatedly, to finite but increasing depths. First it performs depth-first search down to some depth d, returning all solutions found. It then searches down to depth $2d$, returning all solutions found between depths d and $2d$. It then searches to depth $3d$, and so on. Since each search is finite, the strategy will eventually reach any depth.

The repeated searching is less wasteful than it may appear. Iterative deepening increases the time required to reach a given depth by no more than a constant factor, unless the tree branches very little. There are more nodes between depths kd and $(k + 1)d$ than above kd (Korf, 1985).

For simplicity, let us implement iterative deepening with $d = 1$. It yields the same result as breadth-first search, requiring more time but much less space.

Function *depthFirst* is not easily modified to perform iterative deepening because its stack contains nodes from various depths in the tree. The following search function has no stack; it visits each subtree in a separate recursive call. Argument *sf* of *dfs* accumulates the (possibly infinite!) sequence of solutions.

```
fun depthIter next x =
    let fun dfs k (y, sf) =
                if k=0 then fn()=> Cons(y,sf)
                else foldr (dfs (k-1)) sf (next y)
            fun deepen k = dfs k (x, fn()=> deepen (k+1)) ()
    in   deepen 0 end;
> val depthIter = fn : ('a -> 'a list) -> 'a -> 'a seq
```

---

[6] It takes 310 msec. A version using efficient queues takes 160 msec.

Let us examine this declaration in detail. Tail functions (of type *unit* → *α seq*) rather than sequences must be used in order to delay evaluation. The function call *dfs k* (*y, sf*) constructs the sequence of all solutions found at depth *k* below node *y*, followed by the sequence *sf*(). There are two cases to consider.

1 If *k* = 0 then *y* is included in the output.
2 If *k* > 0 then let *next y* = [*y₁, ..., yₙ*]. These nodes, the subtrees of *y*, are processed recursively via *foldr*. The resulting sequence contains all solutions found at depth *k* − 1 below *y₁, ..., yₙ*:

$$dfs(k-1)(y_1, \ldots dfs(k-1)(y_n, sf) \ldots)\,()$$

Calling *deepen k* creates a tail function to compute *deepen*(*k* + 1) and passes it to *dfs*, which inserts the solutions found at depth *k*.

Let us try it on the previous examples. Iterative deepening generates the same sequence of palindromes as breadth-first search:

```
show 8 (Seq.filter isPalin (depthIter nextChar []));
> ["", "A", "B", "C", "AA", "BB", "CC", "AAA"] : string list
```

It can also solve the Eight Queens problem, quite slowly (340 msec). With a larger depth interval *d*, iterative deepening recovers some of the efficiency of depth-first search, while remaining complete.

Exercise 5.41   A flaw of *depthIter* is that it explores ever greater depths even if the search space is finite. It can run forever, seeking the 93rd solution to the Eight Queens problem. Correct this flaw; is your version as fast as *depthIter*?

Exercise 5.42   Generalize function *depthIter* to take the depth interval *d* as a parameter. Generate palindromes using *d* = 5. How does the result differ from those obtained by other strategies?

Exercise 5.43   Declare a datatype of finite-branching search trees of possibly infinite depth, using a representation like that of sequences. Write a function to construct the tree generated by a parameter *next* : *α* → *α list*. Give an example of a tree that cannot be constructed in this way.

Summary of main points
- An ML expression can evaluate to a function.
- A curried function acts like a function of several arguments.
- Higher-order functions encapsulate common forms of computation, reducing the need for separate function declarations.

- A lazy list can contain an infinite number of elements, but only a finite number are ever evaluated.
- A lazy list connects a consumer to a producer, such that items are produced only when they have to be consumed.

6

Reasoning About Functional Programs

Most programmers know how hard it is to make a program work. In the 1970s, it became apparent that programmers could no longer cope with software projects that were growing ever more complex. Systems were delayed and cancelled; costs escalated. In response to this software crisis, several new methodologies have arisen — each an attempt to master the complexity of large systems.

Structured programming seeks to organize programs into simple parts with simple interfaces. An *abstract data type* lets the programmer view a data structure, with its operations, as a mathematical object. The next chapter, on modules, will say more about these topics.

Functional programming and *logic programming* aim to express computations directly in mathematics. The complicated machine state is made invisible; the programmer has to understand only one expression at a time.

Program correctness proofs are introduced in this chapter. Like the other responses to the software crisis, formal methods aim to increase our understanding. The first lesson is that a program only 'works' if it is *correct* with respect to its *specification*. Our minds cannot cope with the billions of steps in an execution. If the program is expressed in a mathematical form, however, then each stage of the computation can be described by a formula. Programs can be *verified* — proved correct — or *derived* from a specification. Most of the early work on program verification focused on Pascal and similar languages; functional programs are easier to reason about because they involve no machine state.

Chapter outline

The chapter presents proofs about functional programs, paying particular attention to induction. The proof methods are rigorous but informal. Their purpose is to increase our understanding of the programs.

The chapter contains the following sections:

Some principles of mathematical proof. A class of ML programs can be treated within elementary mathematics. Some integer functions are verified using mathematical induction.

213

Structural induction. This principle generalizes mathematical induction to finite lists and trees. Proofs about higher-order functions are presented.

A general induction principle. Some unusual inductive proofs are discussed. Well-founded induction provides a uniform framework for such proofs.

Specification and verification. The methods of the chapter are applied to an extended example: the verification of a merge sort function. Some limitations of verification are discussed.

Some principles of mathematical proof

The proofs in this chapter are conducted in a style typical of discrete mathematics. Most proofs are by induction. Much of the reasoning is equational, replacing equals by equals, although the logical connectives and quantifiers are indispensable.

6.1   *ML programs and mathematics*

Our proofs treat Standard ML programs as mathematical objects, subject to mathematical laws. A theory of the full language would be too complicated; let us restrict the form of programs. Only functional programs will be allowed; ML's imperative features will be forbidden. Types will be interpreted as sets, which restricts the form of datatype declarations. Exceptions are forbidden, although it would not be hard to incorporate them into our framework. We shall allow only well-defined expressions. They must be legally typed, and must denote terminating computations.

If all computations must terminate, recursive function definitions have to be restricted. Recall the function *facti*, declared as follows:

```
fun facti (n,p) =
        if n=0 then p  else  facti(n-1, n*p);
```

Recall from Section 2.11 that functional programs are computed by reduction:

$$facti(4, 1) \Rightarrow facti(4 - 1, 4 \times 1) \Rightarrow facti(3, 4) \Rightarrow \cdots \Rightarrow 24$$

Computing *facti*(n, p) yields a unique result for all $n \geq 0$; thus *facti* is a mathematical function satisfying these laws:

$$facti(0, p) = p$$
$$facti(n, p) = facti(n - 1, n \times p) \qquad \text{for } n > 0$$

If $n < 0$ then *facti*(n, p) produces a computation that runs forever; it is undefined. We may regard *facti*(n, p) as meaningful only for $n \geq 0$, which is the function's **precondition**.

For another example, consider the following declaration:

```
fun undef(x) = undef(x)-1;
```

Since *undef* (x) does not terminate for any x, we shall not regard it as meaningful. We may not adopt *undef* $(x) = undef(x) - 1$ as a law about numbers, for it is clearly false.

It is possible to introduce the value $\bot$ (called 'bottom') for the value of a non-terminating computation, and develop a ***domain theory*** for reasoning about arbitrary recursive function definitions. Domain theory interprets *undef* as the function satisfying *undef* $(x) = \bot$ for all x. It turns out that $\bot - 1 = \bot$, so *undef* $(x) = undef(x) - 1$ means simply $\bot = \bot$, which is valid. But domain theory is complex and difficult. The value $\bot$ induces a partial ordering on all types. All functions in the theory must be monotonic and continuous over this partial ordering; recursive functions denote least fixed points. By insisting upon termination, we can work within elementary set theory.

Restricting ourselves to terminating computations entails some sacrifices. It is harder to reason about programs that do not always terminate, such as interpreters. Nor can we reason about lazy evaluation — which is a pity, for using this sophisticated form of functional programming requires mathematical insights. Most functional programmers eventually learn some domain theory; there is no other way to understand what computation over an infinite list really means.

Logical notation. This chapter assumes you have some familiarity with formal proof. We shall adopt the following notation for logical formulæ:

$$
\begin{array}{ll}
\neg\phi & \text{not } \phi \\
\phi \wedge \psi & \phi \text{ and } \psi \\
\phi \vee \psi & \phi \text{ or } \psi \\
\phi \rightarrow \psi & \phi \text{ implies } \psi \\
\phi \leftrightarrow \psi & \phi \text{ if and only if } \psi \\
\forall x . \phi(x) & \text{for all } x, \phi(x) \\
\exists x . \phi(x) & \text{for some } x, \phi(x)
\end{array}
$$

From highest to lowest precedence, the connectives are $\neg, \wedge, \vee, \rightarrow, \leftrightarrow$. Here is an example of precedence in formulæ:

$$P \wedge Q \rightarrow P \vee \neg R \text{ abbreviates } (P \wedge Q) \rightarrow (P \vee (\neg R))$$

Quantifiers have the widest possible scope to the right:

$$\forall x . P \wedge \exists y . Q \rightarrow R \text{ abbreviates } \forall x . (P \wedge (\exists y . (Q \rightarrow R)))$$

Many logicians prefer a slightly different quantifier notation, omitting the dots. Then $\forall x\, P \land \exists y\, Q \rightarrow R$ abbreviates $((\forall x\, P) \land (\exists y\, Q)) \rightarrow R$. Our unconventional notation works well in proofs because typical formulæ have their quantifiers at the front.

Connectives and quantifiers are used to construct formulæ, not as a substitute for English. We may write 'for all x, the formula $\forall y . \phi(x, y)$ is true.'

ⓘ *Background reading.* Most textbooks on discrete mathematics cover predicate logic and induction. Mattson (1993) has extensive coverage of both topics. Reeves and Clarke (1990) have little to say about induction but describe logic in detail, including a chapter on natural deduction. Winskel (1993) includes chapters on basic logic, induction and domain theory. Gunter (1992) describes domain theory and other advanced topics related to lazy evaluation, ML and polymorphism.

6.2   *Mathematical induction and complete induction*

Let us begin with a review of mathematical induction. Suppose $\phi(n)$ is a property that we should like to prove for all natural numbers n (all non-negative integers). To prove it by induction, it suffices to prove two things: the ***base case***, namely $\phi(0)$, and the ***induction step***, namely that $\phi(k)$ implies $\phi(k+1)$ for all k.

The rule can be displayed as follows:

$$
\begin{array}{c}
[\phi(k)] \\
\dfrac{\phi(0) \quad \phi(k+1)}{\phi(n)}
\end{array}
\qquad
\begin{array}{l}
\text{proviso: } k \text{ must not occur in} \\
\text{other assumptions of } \phi(k+1).
\end{array}
$$

In this notation, the ***premises*** appear above the line and the ***conclusion*** below. These premises are the base case and the induction step. The formula $\phi(k)$, which appears in brackets, is the ***induction hypothesis***; it may be assumed while proving $\phi(k+1)$. The proviso means that k must be a new variable, not already present in other induction hypotheses (or other assumptions); thus k stands for an arbitrary value. This rule notation comes from ***natural deduction***, a formal theory of proofs.

In the induction step, we prove $\phi(k + 1)$ under the assumption $\phi(k)$. We assume the very property we are trying to prove, but of k only. This may look like circular reasoning, especially since n and k are often the same variable (to avoid having to write the induction hypothesis explicitly). Why is induction sound? If the base case and induction step hold, then we have $\phi(0)$ by the base case and $\phi(1), \phi(2), \dots$, by repeated use of the induction step. Therefore $\phi(n)$ holds for all n.

As a trivial example of induction, let us prove the following.

Theorem 1 *Every natural number is even or odd.*

Proof The inductive property is

> *n* is even or *n* is odd

which we prove by induction on *n*.

The base case, 0 is even or 0 is odd, is trivial: 0 is even.

In the induction step, we assume the induction hypothesis

> *k* is even or *k* is odd

and prove

> *k* + 1 is even or *k* + 1 is odd.

By the induction hypothesis, there are two cases: if *k* is even then *k* + 1 is odd; if *k* is odd then *k* + 1 is even. Since the conclusion holds in both cases, the proof is finished.   □

Notice that a box marks the end of a proof.

This proof not only tells us that every natural number is even or odd, but contains a method for testing a given number. The test can be formalized in ML as a recursive function:

```
datatype evenodd = Even | Odd;

fun test 0 = Even
  | test n = (case test (n-1) of
                    Even => Odd
                  | Odd  => Even);
```

In some formal theories of constructive mathematics, a recursive function can be extracted automatically from every inductive proof. We shall not study such theories here, but shall try to learn as much as possible from our proofs. Mathematics would be barren indeed if each proof gave us nothing but a single formula. By sharpening the statement of the theorem, we can obtain more information from its proof.

Theorem 2 *Every natural number has the form* 2*m* *or* 2*m* + 1 *for some natural number m.*

Proof Since this property is fairly complicated, let us express it in logical notation:

$$\exists m . n = 2m \lor n = 2m + 1$$

The proof is by induction on n.

The base case is

$$\exists m . 0 = 2m \vee 0 = 2m + 1.$$

This holds with $m = 0$ since $0 = 2 \times 0$.

For the induction step, assume the induction hypothesis

$$\exists m . k = 2m \vee k = 2m + 1$$

and show (renaming m as m' to avoid confusion)

$$\exists m' . k + 1 = 2m' \vee k + 1 = 2m' + 1.$$

By the induction hypothesis, there exists some m such that either $k = 2m$ or $k = 2m + 1$. In either case we can exhibit some m' such that $k + 1 = 2m'$ or $k + 1 = 2m' + 1$.

- If $k = 2m$ then $k + 1 = 2m + 1$, so $m' = m$.
- If $k = 2m + 1$ then $k + 1 = 2m + 2 = 2(m + 1)$, so $m' = m + 1$.

This concludes the proof.   □

The function contained in this more detailed proof does not just test whether a number is even or odd, but also yields the quotient after division by two. This is enough information to reconstruct the original number. Thus, we have a means of checking the result.

```
fun half 0 = (Even, 0)
  | half n = (case half (n-1) of
                (Even, m) => (Odd, m)
              | (Odd, m)  => (Even, m+1));
```

Complete induction. Mathematical induction reduces the problem $\phi(k)$ to the subproblem $\phi(k - 1)$, if $k > 0$. Complete induction reduces $\phi(k)$ to the k subproblems $\phi(0), \phi(1), \ldots , \phi(k - 1)$. It includes mathematical induction as a special case.

To prove $\phi(n)$ for all integer $n \geq 0$ by complete induction on n, it suffices to prove the following induction step:

$$\phi(k) \text{ assuming } \forall i < k . \phi(i)$$

The induction step comprises an infinite sequence of statements:

$$\phi(0)$$
$$\phi(1) \text{ assuming } \phi(0)$$
$$\phi(2) \text{ assuming } \phi(0) \text{ and } \phi(1)$$
$$\phi(3) \text{ assuming } \phi(0), \phi(1) \text{ and } \phi(2)$$
$$\vdots$$

Clearly it implies $\phi(n)$ for all n; complete induction is sound. The rule is portrayed as follows:

$$\frac{[\forall i < k . \phi(i)]}{\phi(n)} \qquad \text{proviso: } k \text{ must not occur in other}$$

proviso: k must not occur in other assumptions of the premise.

We now consider a simple proof.

Theorem 3 *Every natural number $n \geq 2$ can be written as a product of prime numbers, $n = p_1 \cdots p_k$.*

Proof By complete induction on n. There are two cases.

If n is prime then the result is trivial and $k = 1$.

If n is not prime then it is divisible by some natural number m such that $1 < m < n$. Since $m < n$ and $n/m < n$, we may appeal twice to the induction hypotheses of complete induction, writing these numbers as products of primes:

$$m = p_1 \cdots p_k \quad \text{and} \quad n/m = q_1 \cdots q_l$$

Now $n = m \times (n/m) = p_1 \cdots p_k q_1 \cdots q_l$. □

This is the easy part of the Fundamental Theorem of Arithmetic. The hard part is to show that the factorization into primes is unique, regardless of the choice of m in the proof (Davenport, 1952). As it stands, the proof provides a nondeterministic algorithm for factoring numbers into primes.

    Proofs as programs. There is a precise correspondence between constructive proofs and functional programs. If we can extract programs from proofs, then by proving theorems we obtain verified programs. Of course, not every proof is suitable. Not only must the proof be constructive (crucial parts of it at least), but it has to describe an efficient construction. The usual conception of the natural numbers corresponds to unary notation, which leads to hopelessly inefficient programs. The extracted programs contain computations that correspond to logical arguments; as they do not affect the result, they ought to be removed. Many people are investigating questions such as these. Thompson (1991) and Turner (1991) introduce this research area.

Exercise 6.1   Prove, by induction, the basic theorem of integer division: if n and d are natural numbers with $d \neq 0$, then there exist natural numbers q and r such that $n = dq + r$ and $0 \leq r < d$. Express the corresponding division function in ML. How efficient is it?

Exercise 6.2   Show that if $\phi(n)$ can be proved by mathematical induction on n, then it can also be proved by complete induction.

Exercise 6.3   Show that if $\phi(n)$ can be proved by complete induction on n, then it can also be proved using mathematical induction. (Hint: use a different induction formula.)

6.3   *Simple examples of program verification*

A *specification* is a precise description of the properties required of a program execution. It specifies the result of the computation, not the method. The specification of sorting states that the output contains the same elements as the input, arranged in increasing order. Any sorting algorithm satisfies this specification. A specification (for the present purposes, at least) says nothing about performance.

Program verification means proving that a program satisfies its specification. The complexity of a realistic specification makes verification difficult. Each of the programs verified below has a trivial specification: the result is a simple function of the input. We shall verify ML functions to compute factorials, Fibonacci numbers and powers.

The key step in these proofs is to formulate an induction suitable for the function. To be of any use, the induction hypothesis should be applicable to some recursive call of the function. The base case and induction step are simplified using function definitions, other mathematical laws and the induction hypothesis. If we are lucky, the simplified formula will be trivially true; if not, it may at least suggest a lemma to prove first.

Factorials.   The iterative function *facti* is intended to compute factorials. Let us prove that $facti(n, 1) = n!$ for all $n \geq 0$. Recall that $0! = 1$ and $n! = (n-1)! \times n$ for $n > 0$. The definition of *facti* was repeated in Section 6.1.

Induction on $facti(n, 1) = n!$ leads nowhere because it says nothing about argument p of *facti*. The induction hypothesis would be useless. We must find a relationship involving $facti(n, p)$ and $n!$ that implies $facti(n, 1) = n!$ and that can be proved by induction. A good try is $facti(n, p) = n! \times p$, but this will not quite do. It refers to some particular n and p, but p varies in the recursive calls.

The correct formulation has a universal quantifier:

$$\forall p \,.\, facti(n, p) = n! \times p$$

As an induction hypothesis about some fixed n, it asserts the equality for all p.

Theorem 4 *For every natural number n, facti(n, 1) = n!*

Proof This will follow by putting $p = 1$ in the following formula, which is proved by induction on n:

$$\forall p \,.\, facti(n, p) = n! \times p$$

By using n rather than k in the induction step, we can use this formula as the induction hypothesis.

For the base case we must show

$$\forall p \,.\, facti(0, p) = 0! \times p.$$

This holds because $facti(0, p) = p = 1 \times p = 0! \times p$.

For the induction step, the induction hypothesis is as stated above. We must show

$$\forall p \,.\, facti(n + 1, p) = (n + 1)! \times p.$$

Let us drop the universal quantifier and show the equality for arbitrary p. To simplify the equality, reduce the left side to the right side:

$$
\begin{aligned}
facti(n + 1, p) &= facti(n, (n + 1) \times p) & \text{[\textit{facti}]}\\
&= n! \times ((n + 1) \times p) & \text{[ind hyp]}\\
&= (n! \times (n + 1)) \times p & \text{[associativity]}\\
&= (n + 1)! \times p & \text{[factorial]}
\end{aligned}
$$

The comments in brackets are read as follows:

[*facti*] means 'by the definition of *facti*'
[ind hyp] means 'by the induction hypothesis'
[associativity] means 'by the associative law for $\times$'
[factorial] means 'by the definition of factorials'

Both sides are equal in the induction step. Observe that the quantified variable p of the induction hypothesis is replaced by $(n + 1) \times p$. □

Formal proofs should help us understand our programs. This proof explains the rôle of p in $facti(n, p)$. The induction formula is analogous to a **loop invariant** in procedural program verification. Since the proof depends on the associative law for $\times$, it suggests that $facti(n, 1)$ computes $n!$ by multiplying the same numbers in a different order. Later we shall generalize this to a theorem about transforming recursive functions into iterative functions (Section 6.9). Many of our theorems concern implementing some function efficiently.

Fibonacci numbers. Recall that the Fibonacci sequence is defined by $F_0 = 0$, $F_1 = 1$ and $F_n = F_{n-2} + F_{n-1}$ for $n \geq 2$. We shall prove that they can be computed by the function *itfib* (from Section 2.15):

```
fun itfib (n, prev, curr) : int =
    if n=1 then curr
    else itfib (n-1, curr, prev+curr);
```

Observing that $itfib(n, prev, curr)$ is defined for all $n \geq 1$, we set out to prove $itfib(n, 0, 1) = F_n$. As in the previous example, the induction formula must be generalized to say something about all the arguments of the function. There is no automatic procedure for doing this, but examining some computations of $itfib(n, 0, 1)$ reveals that *prev* and *curr* are always Fibonacci numbers. This suggests the relationship

$$itfib(n, F_k, F_{k+1}) = F_{k+n}.$$

Again, a universal quantifier must be inserted before induction.

Theorem 5 *For every integer $n \geq 1$, $itfib(n, 0, 1) = F_n$.*

Proof Put $k = 0$ in the following formula, which is proved by induction on n:

$$\forall k . itfib(n, F_k, F_{k+1}) = F_{k+n}$$

Since $n \geq 1$, the base case is to prove this for $n = 1$:

$$\forall k . itfib(1, F_k, F_{k+1}) = F_{k+1}$$

This is immediate by the definition of *itfib*.

For the induction step, the induction hypothesis is given above; we must show

$$\forall k . itfib(n + 1, F_k, F_{k+1}) = F_{k+(n+1)}.$$

We prove this by simplifying the left side:

$$
\begin{aligned}
itfib(n + 1, F_k, F_{k+1}) & \\
= itfib(n, F_{k+1}, F_k + F_{k+1}) & \qquad [itfib] \\
= itfib(n, F_{k+1}, F_{k+2}) & \qquad [\text{Fibonacci}] \\
= F_{(k+1)+n} & \qquad [\text{ind hyp}] \\
= F_{k+(n+1)} & \qquad [\text{arithmetic}]
\end{aligned}
$$

The induction hypothesis is applied with $k + 1$ in place of k, instantiating the quantifier.   □

This proof shows how pairs of Fibonacci numbers are generated successively. The induction formula is a key property of *itfib*, and is not at all obvious. It is good practice to state such a formula as a comment by the function declaration.

Powers. We now prove that $power(x, k) = x^k$ for every real number x and integer $k \geq 1$. Recall the definition of *power* (Section 2.14):

```
fun power(x,k) : real =
      if k=1 then x
      else if k mod 2 = 0 then      power(x*x, k div 2)
                          else x * power(x*x, k div 2);
> val power = fn : real * int -> real
```

The proof will assume that ML's real arithmetic is exact, ignoring roundoff errors. It is typical of program verification to ignore the limitations of physical hardware. To demonstrate that *power* is suitable for actual computers would require an error analysis as well, which would involve much more work.

We must check that $power(x, k)$ is defined for $k \geq 1$. The case $k = 1$ is obvious. If $k \geq 2$ then we need to examine the recursive calls, which replace k by $k \, div \, 2$. These terminate because $1 \leq k \, div \, 2 < k$.

Since x varies during the computation of $power(x, k)$, the induction formula must have a quantifier:

$$\forall x . power(x, k) = x^k$$

However, ordinary mathematical induction is not appropriate. In $power(x, k)$ the recursive call replaces k by $k \, div \, 2$, not $k - 1$. We use complete induction in order to have an induction hypothesis for $k \, div \, 2$.

Theorem 6 *For every integer $k \geq 1$, $\forall x . power(x, k) = x^k$.*

Proof The formula is proved by complete induction on k.

Although complete induction has no separate base case, we may perform case analysis on k. Since $k \geq 1$, let us consider $k = 1$ and $k \geq 2$ separately.

Case $k = 1$. We must prove

$$\forall x . power(x, 1) = x^1.$$

This holds because $power(x, 1) = x = x^1$.

Case $k \geq 2$. We consider subcases. If k is even then $k = 2j$, and if k is odd then $k = 2j + 1$, for some integer j (namely $k \, div \, 2$). In both cases $1 \leq j < k$, so there is an induction hypothesis for j:

$$\forall x . power(x, j) = x^j$$

If $k = 2j$ then $k \bmod 2 = 0$ and

$$
\begin{aligned}
power(x, 2j) &= power(x^2, j) && [power] \\
&= (x^2)^j && [\text{ind hyp}] \\
&= x^{2j}. && [\text{arithmetic}]
\end{aligned}
$$

If $k = 2j + 1$ then $k \bmod 2 = 1$ and

$$
\begin{aligned}
power(x, 2j + 1) &= x \times power(x^2, j) && [power] \\
&= x \times (x^2)^j && [\text{ind hyp}] \\
&= x^{2j+1}. && [\text{arithmetic}]
\end{aligned}
$$

In both of these cases, the induction hypothesis is applied with x^2 in place of x.

$\square$

Exercise 6.4   Verify that *introot* computes integer square roots (Section 2.16).

Exercise 6.5   Recall *sqroot* of Section 2.17, which computes real square roots by the Newton-Raphson method. Discuss the problems involved in verifying this function.

Structural induction

Mathematical induction establishes $\phi(n)$ for all natural numbers n by considering how a natural number is constructed. Although there are infinitely many natural numbers, they are constructed in just two ways:

- 0 is a number.
- If k is a number then so is $k + 1$.

Strictly speaking, we should introduce the successor function *suc* and reformulate the above:

- If k is a number then so is $suc(k)$.

Addition and other arithmetic functions are then defined recursively in terms of 0 and *suc*, which are essentially the constructors of an ML datatype. **Structural induction** is a generalization of mathematical induction to datatypes such as lists and trees.

6.4   *Structural induction on lists*

Suppose $\phi(xs)$ is a property that we should like to prove for all lists xs. Let xs have type τ *list* for some type τ. To prove $\phi(xs)$ by structural induction, it suffices to prove two premises:

- The base case is $\phi([])$.
- The induction step is that $\phi(ys)$ implies $\phi(y :: ys)$ for all y of type τ and ys of type τ *list*. The induction hypothesis is $\phi(ys)$.

The rule can be displayed as follows:

$$\frac{\phi([]) \quad \phi(y :: ys)}{\phi(xs)} \quad [\phi(ys)]$$

proviso: y and ys must not occur in other assumptions of $\phi(y :: ys)$.

Why is structural induction sound? We have $\phi([])$ by the base case. By the induction step, we have $\phi([y])$ for all y; the conclusion holds for all 1-element lists. Using the induction step again, the conclusion holds for all 2-element lists. Continuing this process, the conclusion $\phi(xs)$ holds for every n-element list xs; all lists are reached eventually. The rule can also be justified by mathematical induction on the length of the list.

To illustrate the rule, let us prove a fundamental property of lists.

Theorem 7 *No list equals its own tail.*

Proof The statement of the theorem can be formalized as follows:

$$\forall x . x :: xs \neq xs$$

This is proved by structural induction on the list xs.

The base case, $\forall x . [x] \neq []$, is trivial by the definition of equality on lists. Two lists are equal if they have the same length and the corresponding elements are equal.

In the induction step, assume the induction hypothesis

$$\forall x . x :: ys \neq ys$$

and show (for arbitrary y and ys)

$$\forall x . x :: (y :: ys) \neq y :: ys$$

By the definition of list equality, it is enough to show that the tails differ: to show $y :: ys \neq ys$. This follows by the induction hypothesis, putting y for the quantified variable x. Again, the quantifier in the induction formula is essential.   □

This theorem does not apply to infinite lists, for [1,1,1, ...] equals its own tail. The structural induction rules given here are sound for finite objects only. In domain theory, induction can be extended to infinite lists — but not for arbitrary formulæ! The restrictions are complicated; roughly speaking, the conclusion holds for infinite lists only if the induction formula is a conjunction of equations. So $x :: xs \neq xs$ cannot be proved for infinite lists.

Let us prove theorems about some of the list functions of Chapter 3. Each of these functions terminates for all arguments because each recursive call involves a shorter list.

The length of a list:

```
fun nlength []      = 0
  | nlength (x::xs) = 1 + nlength xs;
```

The infix operator @, which appends two lists:

```
fun []      @ ys = ys
  | (x::xs) @ ys = x :: (xs@ys);
```

The naïve reverse function:

```
fun nrev []      = []
  | nrev (x::xs) = (nrev xs) @ [x];
```

An efficient reverse function:

```
fun revAppend ([],    ys) = ys
  | revAppend (x::xs, ys) = revAppend (xs, x::ys);
```

Length and append. Here is an obvious property about the length of the concatenation of two lists.

Theorem 8 *For all lists xs and ys, nlength(xs @ ys) = nlength xs + nlength ys.*

Proof By structural induction on xs. We avoid renaming this variable; thus, the formula above also serves as the induction hypothesis.

The base case is

$$nlength([] @ ys) = nlength[] + nlength\,ys.$$

This holds because

$$
\begin{aligned}
nlength([] @ ys) &= nlength\,ys && \text{[@]} \\
&= 0 + nlength\,ys && \text{[arithmetic]} \\
&= nlength[] + nlength\,ys. && \text{[nlength]}
\end{aligned}
$$

For the induction step, assume the induction hypothesis and show, for all x and xs, that

$$nlength((x :: xs) \ @ \ ys) = nlength(x :: xs) + nlength \ ys.$$

This holds because

$$
\begin{aligned}
& nlength((x :: xs) \ @ \ ys) \\
& = nlength(x :: (xs \ @ \ ys)) && [@] \\
& = 1 + nlength(xs \ @ \ ys) && [nlength] \\
& = 1 + (nlength \ xs + nlength \ ys) && [\text{ind hyp}] \\
& = (1 + nlength \ xs) + nlength \ ys && [\text{associativity}] \\
& = nlength(x :: xs) + nlength \ ys. && [nlength]
\end{aligned}
$$

We could have written $1 + nlength \ xs + nlength \ ys$, omitting parentheses, instead of applying the associative law explicitly. □

The proof brings out the correspondence between inserting the list elements and counting them. Induction on xs works because the base case and induction step can be simplified using function definitions. Induction on ys leads nowhere: try it.

Efficient list reversal. The function *nrev* is a mathematical definition of list reversal, while *revAppend* reverses lists efficiently. The proof that they are equivalent is similar to Theorem 4, the correctness of *facti*. In both proofs, the induction formula is universally quantified over an accumulating argument.

Theorem 9 *For every list xs, we have* $\forall ys \ . \ revAppend(xs, ys) = nrev(xs) \ @ \ ys.$

Proof By structural induction on xs, taking the formula above as the induction hypothesis. The base case is

$$\forall ys \ . \ revAppend([], ys) = nrev[] \ @ \ ys.$$

It holds because $revAppend([], ys) = ys = [] \ @ \ ys = nrev[] \ @ \ ys$.
The induction step is to show, for arbitrary x and xs, the formula

$$\forall ys \ . \ revAppend(x :: xs, ys) = nrev(x :: xs) \ @ \ ys.$$

Simplifying the right side of the equality yields

$$nrev(x :: xs) \ @ \ ys = (nrev(xs) \ @ \ [x]) \ @ \ ys. \qquad [nrev]$$

Simplifying the left side yields

$$revAppend(x :: xs, ys) = revAppend(xs, x :: ys) \qquad [revAppend]$$
$$= nrev(xs) @ (x :: ys) \qquad [\text{ind hyp}]$$
$$= nrev(xs) @ ([x] @ ys). \qquad [@]$$

The induction hypothesis is applied with $x :: xs$ for the quantified variable ys.
Are we finished? Not quite: the parentheses do not agree. It remains to show

$$nrev(xs) @ ([x] @ ys) = (nrev(xs) @ [x]) @ ys.$$

This formula looks more complicated than the one we set out to prove. How shall we proceed? Observe that the formula is a special case of something simple and plausible: that @ is associative. We have only to prove

$$l_1 @ (l_2 @ l_3) = (l_1 @ l_2) @ l_3.$$

This routine induction is left as an exercise.   □

It would be tidier to prove each theorem in the correct order, making a flaw-less presentation. This example attempts to show how the need for a theorem is discovered. The hardest problem in a verification is recognizing what properties ought to be proved. The need here for the associative law may be obvious — but not if we are dazzled by the symbols, which happens all too easily.

Append and reverse. We now prove a relationship involving list concatenation and reversal.

Theorem 10 *For all lists xs and ys, $nrev(xs @ ys) = nrev\,ys @ nrev\,xs$.*

Proof By structural induction on xs. The base case is

$$nrev([] @ ys) = nrev\,ys @ nrev[].$$

This holds using the lemma $l @ [] = l$, which is left as an exercise.
The induction step is

$$nrev((x :: xs) @ ys) = nrev\,ys @ nrev(x :: xs).$$

This holds because

$$nrev((x :: xs) @ ys) = nrev(x :: (xs @ ys)) \qquad [@]$$
$$= nrev(xs @ ys) @ [x] \qquad [nrev]$$
$$= nrev\,ys @ nrev\,xs @ [x] \qquad [\text{ind hyp}]$$
$$= nrev\,ys @ nrev(x :: xs). \qquad [nrev]$$

In *nrev ys @ nrev xs @* [*x*] we have implicitly applied the associativity of @ by omitting parentheses. □

These last two theorems show that *nrev*, though inefficient to compute, is a good specification of reversal. It permits simple proofs. A literal specification, like

$$reverse[x_1, x_2, \ldots, x_n] = [x_n, \ldots, x_2, x_1],$$

would be most difficult to formalize. The function *revAppend* is not a good specification either; its performance is irrelevant and it is too complicated. But *nlength* is a good specification of the length of a list.

Exercise 6.6   Prove *xs @* [] = *xs* for every list *xs*, by structural induction.

Exercise 6.7   Prove l_1 @ (l_2 @ l_3) = (l_1 @ l_2) @ l_3 for all lists l_1, l_2 and l_3, by structural induction.

Exercise 6.8   Prove *nrev*(*nrev xs*) = *xs* for every list *xs*.

Exercise 6.9   Show that *nlength xs* = *length xs* for every list *xs*. (The function *length* was defined in Section 3.4.)

6.5   *Structural induction on trees*
        In Chapter 4 we studied binary trees defined as follows:

```
datatype 'a tree = Lf
               | Br of 'a * 'a tree * 'a tree;
```

Binary trees admit structural induction. In most respects, their treatment resembles that of lists. Suppose $\phi(t)$ is a property of trees, where *t* has type τ *tree*. To prove $\phi(t)$ by structural induction, it suffices to prove two premises:

- The base case is $\phi(Lf)$.
- The induction step is to show that $\phi(t_1)$ and $\phi(t_2)$ imply $\phi(Br(x, t_1, t_2))$ for all *x* of type τ and t_1, t_2 of type τ *tree*. There are two induction hypotheses: $\phi(t_1)$ and $\phi(t_2)$.

The rule can be portrayed thus:

$$\frac{[\phi(t_1),\ \phi(t_2)]}{\phi(Lf) \qquad \phi(Br(x, t_1, t_2))} {\phi(t)}$$

proviso: *x*, t_1 and t_2 must not occur in other assumptions of $\phi(Br(x, t_1, t_2))$.

This structural induction rule is sound because it covers all the ways of building a tree. The base case establishes $\phi(Lf)$. Applying the induction step once establishes $\phi(Br(x, Lf, Lf))$ for all x, covering all trees containing one Br node. Applying the induction step twice establishes $\phi(t)$ where t is any tree containing two Br nodes. Further applications of the induction step cover larger trees.

We can also justify the rule by complete induction on the number of labels in the tree, because every tree is finite and its subtrees are smaller than itself. Structural induction is not sound in general for infinite trees.

We shall prove some facts about the following functions on binary trees, from Section 4.10.

The number of labels in a tree:

```
fun size  Lf            = 0
  | size  (Br(v,t1,t2)) = 1 + size t1 + size t2;
```

The depth of a tree:

```
fun depth  Lf            = 0
  | depth  (Br(v,t1,t2)) = 1 + Int.max(depth t1, depth t2);
```

Reflection of a tree:

```
fun reflect  Lf            = Lf
  | reflect  (Br(v,t1,t2)) = Br(v, reflect t2, reflect t1);
```

The preorder listing of a tree's labels:

```
fun preorder  Lf            = []
  | preorder  (Br(v,t1,t2)) = [v] @ preorder t1 @ preorder t2;
```

The postorder listing of a tree's labels:

```
fun postorder  Lf            = []
  | postorder  (Br(v,t1,t2)) = postorder t1 @ postorder t2 @ [v];
```

Double reflection. We begin with an easy example: reflecting a tree twice yields the original tree.

Theorem 11 *For every binary tree t, reflect(reflect t) = t.*

Proof By structural induction on t. The base case is

$$reflect(reflect\, Lf) = Lf.$$

This holds by the definition of *reflect*: $reflect(reflect\, Lf) = reflect\, Lf = Lf$.

For the induction step we have the two induction hypotheses

$$reflect(reflect\, t_1) = t_1 \quad \text{and} \quad reflect(reflect\, t_2) = t_2$$

and must show

$$reflect(reflect(Br(x, t_1, t_2))) = Br(x, t_1, t_2).$$

Simplifying,

$$reflect(reflect(Br(x, t_1, t_2)))$$
$$= reflect(Br(x, reflect\, t_2, reflect\, t_1)) \qquad\qquad [reflect]$$
$$= Br(x, reflect(reflect\, t_1), reflect(reflect\, t_2)) \qquad [reflect]$$
$$= Br(x, t_1, reflect(reflect\, t_2)) \qquad\qquad [ind\ hyp]$$
$$= Br(x, t_1, t_2). \qquad\qquad [ind\ hyp]$$

Both induction hypotheses have been applied. We can observe the two calls of *reflect* cancelling each other. □

Preorder and postorder. If the concepts of preorder and postorder are obscure to you, then the following theorem may help. A key fact is Theorem 10, concerning *nrev* and @, which we have recently proved.

Theorem 12 *For every binary tree t, postorder(reflect t) = nrev(preorder t).*

Proof By structural induction on t. The base case is

$$postorder(reflect\, Lf) = nrev(preorder\, Lf).$$

This is routine; both sides are equal to [].
    For the induction step we have the induction hypotheses

$$postorder(reflect\, t_1) = nrev(preorder\, t_1)$$
$$postorder(reflect\, t_2) = nrev(preorder\, t_2)$$

and must show

$$postorder(reflect(Br(x, t_1, t_2))) = nrev(preorder(Br(x, t_1, t_2))).$$

First, we simplify the right-hand side:

$$nrev(preorder(Br(x, t_1, t_2)))$$
$$= nrev([x] @ preorder\, t_1 @ preorder\, t_2) \qquad\qquad [preorder]$$
$$= nrev(preorder\, t_2) @ nrev(preorder\, t_1) @ nrev[x] \qquad [Theorem\ 10]$$
$$= nrev(preorder\, t_2) @ nrev(preorder\, t_1) @ [x] \qquad\qquad [nrev]$$

Some steps have been skipped. Theorem 10 has been applied twice, to both occurrences of @, and *nrev*[x] is simplified directly to [x].

Now we simplify the left-hand side:

$postorder(reflect(Br(x, t_1, t_2)))$

$\quad = postorder(Br(x, reflect\ t_2, reflect\ t_1))$ [*reflect*]

$\quad = postorder(reflect\ t_2)\ @\ postorder(reflect\ t_1)\ @\ [x]$ [*postorder*]

$\quad = nrev(preorder\ t_2)\ @\ nrev(preorder\ t_1)\ @\ [x]$ [ind hyp]

Thus, both sides are equal.   □

Count and depth. We now prove a law relating the number of labels in a binary tree to its depth. The theorem is an inequality, reminding us that formal methods involve more than mere equations.

Theorem 13 *For every binary tree t, size $t \leq 2^{depth\ t} - 1$.*

Proof By structural induction on t. The base case is

$$size\ Lf \leq 2^{depth\ Lf} - 1.$$

It holds because $size\ Lf = 0 = 2^0 - 1 = 2^{depth\ Lf} - 1.$

In the induction step the induction hypotheses are

$$size\ t_1 \leq 2^{depth\ t_1} - 1 \quad \text{and} \quad size\ t_2 \leq 2^{depth\ t_2} - 1$$

and we must demonstrate

$$size(Br(x, t_1, t_2)) \leq 2^{depth(Br(x,t_1,t_2))} - 1.$$

First, simplify the right-hand side:

$2^{depth(Br(x,t_1,t_2))} - 1 = 2^{1+\max(depth\ t_1, depth\ t_2)} - 1$ [*depth*]

$\qquad\qquad\qquad = 2 \times 2^{\max(depth\ t_1, depth\ t_2)} - 1$ [arithmetic]

Next, show that the left side is less than or equal to this:

$size\ (Br(x, t_1, t_2)) = 1 + size\ t_1 + size\ t_2$ [*size*]

$\qquad \leq 1 + (2^{depth\ t_1} - 1) + (2^{depth\ t_2} - 1)$ [ind hyp]

$\qquad = 2^{depth\ t_1} + 2^{depth\ t_2} - 1$ [arithmetic]

$\qquad \leq 2 \times 2^{\max(depth\ t_1, depth\ t_2)} - 1$ [arithmetic]

Here we have identified max, the mathematical function for the maximum of two integers, with the library function $Int . max$.   □

Problematical datatypes. Our simple methods do not admit all ML datatypes. Consider this declaration:

```
datatype lambda = F of lambda -> lambda;
```

The mathematics in this chapter is based on set theory. Since there is no set A that is isomorphic to the set of functions $A \to A$, we can make no sense of this declaration. In domain theory, this declaration can be interpreted because there is a domain D isomorphic to $D \to D$, which is the domain of **continuous** functions from D to D. Even in domain theory, no induction rule useful for reasoning about D is known. This is because the type definition involves recursion to the left of the function arrow ($\to$). We shall not consider datatypes involving functions.

The declaration of type *term* (Section 5.11) refers to lists:

```
datatype term = Var of string
              | Fun of string * term list;
```

Type *term* denotes a set of finite terms and satisfies a structural induction rule. However, the involvement of lists in the type complicates the theory and proofs (Paulson, 1995, Section 4.4).

Exercise 6.10 Formalize and prove: *No binary tree equals its own left subtree.*

Exercise 6.11 Prove $size(reflect\ t) = size\ t$ for every binary tree t.

Exercise 6.12 Prove $nlength(preorder\ t) = size\ t$ for every binary tree t.

Exercise 6.13 Prove $nrev(inorder(reflect\ t)) = inorder\ t$ for every binary tree t.

Exercise 6.14 Define a function *leaves* to count the *Lf* nodes in a binary tree. Then prove $leaves\ t = size\ t + 1$ for all t.

Exercise 6.15 Verify the function *preord* of Section 4.11. In other words, prove $preord(t, []) = preorder\ t$ for every binary tree t.

6.6 *Function values and functionals*

Our mathematical methods extend directly to proofs about higher-order functions (functionals). The notion of 'functions as values' is familiar to mathematicians. In set theory, for example, functions are sets and are treated no differently from other sets.

We can prove many facts about functionals without using any additional rules. The laws of the λ-calculus could be introduced for reasoning about ML's fn notation, although this will not be done here. Our methods, needless to say, apply only to pure functions — not to ML functions with side effects.

Equality of functions. The **law of extensionality** states that functions f and g are equal if $f(x) = g(x)$ for all x (of suitable type). For instance, these three doubling functions are extensionally equal:

```
fun double1 (n)  =  2*n;
fun double2 (n)  =  n*2;
fun double3 (n)  =  (n-1)+(n+1);
```

The extensionality law is valid because the only operation that can be performed on an ML function is application to an argument. Replacing f by g, if these functions are extensionally equal, does not affect the value of any application of f.[1]

A different concept of equality, called **intensional equality**, regards two functions as equal only if their definitions are identical. Our three doubling functions are all distinct under intensional equality. This concept resembles function equality in Lisp, where a function value is a piece of Lisp code that can be taken apart.

There is no general, computable method of testing whether two functions are extensionally equal. Therefore ML has no equality test for function values. Lisp tests equality of functions by comparing their internal representations.

We now prove a few statements about function composition (the infix o) and the functional *map* (of Section 5.7).

```
fun (f o g) x = f (g x);

fun map f []      = []
  | map f (x::xs) = (f x) :: map f xs;
```

The associativity of composition. Our first theorem is trivial. It asserts that function composition is associative.

Theorem 14 *For all functions f, g and h (of appropriate type),*

$$(f \circ g) \circ h = f \circ (g \circ h).$$

Proof By the law of extensionality, it is enough to show

$$((f \circ g) \circ h)\, x = (f \circ (g \circ h))\, x$$

---

[1] The extensionality law relies on our global assumption that functions terminate. ML distinguishes $\bot$ (the undefined function value) from $\lambda x.\bot$ (the function that never terminates when applied) although both functions yield $\bot$ when applied to any argument.

for all x. This holds because

$$
\begin{aligned}
((f \circ g) \circ h) \, x &= (f \circ g)(h \, x) \\
&= f(g(h \, x)) \\
&= f((g \circ h) \, x) \\
&= (f \circ (g \circ h)) \, x.
\end{aligned}
$$

Each step holds by the definition of composition. □

As stated, the theorem holds only for functions of appropriate type; the equation must be properly typed. Typing restrictions apply to all our theorems and will not be mentioned again.

The list functional map. Functionals enjoy many laws. Here is a theorem about *map* and composition that can be used to avoid computing intermediate lists.

Theorem 15 *For all functions f and g, (map f) $\circ$ (map g) = map (f $\circ$ g).*

Proof By the extensionality law, this equality holds if

$$
((map f) \circ (map \, g)) \, xs = map \, (f \circ g) \, xs
$$

for all xs. Using the definition of $\circ$, this can be simplified to

$$
map f \, (map \, g \, xs) = map \, (f \circ g) \, xs
$$

Since xs is a list, we may use structural induction. This formula will also be our induction hypothesis. The base case is

$$
map f \, (map \, g \, []) = map \, (f \circ g) \, [].
$$

It holds because both sides equal []:

$$
map f \, (map \, g \, []) = map f \, [] = [] = map \, (f \circ g) \, []
$$

For the induction step, we assume the induction hypothesis and show (for arbitrary x and xs)

$$
map f \, (map \, g \, (x :: xs)) = map \, (f \circ g) \, (x :: xs).
$$

Straightforward reasoning yields

$$map f \; (map \; g \; (x :: xs))$$
$$= map f \; ((g\,x) :: (map \; g \; xs)) \qquad\qquad [map]$$
$$= f(g\,x) :: (map f \; (map \; g \; xs)) \qquad\qquad [map]$$
$$= f(g\,x) :: (map \; (f \circ g) \; xs) \qquad\qquad [\text{ind hyp}]$$
$$= (f \circ g)(x) :: (map \; (f \circ g) \; xs) \qquad\qquad [\circ]$$
$$= map \; (f \circ g) \; (x :: xs). \qquad\qquad [map]$$

Despite the presence of function values, the proof is a routine structural induction. □

The list functional foldl. The functional *foldl* applies a 2-argument function over the elements of a list. Recall its definition from Section 5.10:

```
fun foldl f e []      = e
  | foldl f e (x::xs) = foldl f  (f(x, e))  xs;
```

If $\oplus$ is an associative operator then *foldl* $(\mathrm{op}\oplus)\,(y\oplus z)\,xs = (foldl\,(\mathrm{op}\oplus)\,y\,xs)\oplus z$. For if $xs = [x_1, x_2, \ldots, x_n]$, this is equivalent to

$$x_n \oplus \cdots (x_2 \oplus (x_1 \oplus (y \oplus z))) \cdots = x_n \oplus \cdots (x_2 \oplus (x_1 \oplus y)) \oplus z.$$

Since $\oplus$ is associative we may erase the parentheses, reducing both sides to $x_n \oplus \cdots x_2 \oplus x_1 \oplus y \oplus z$. We see the notational advantage of working with an infix operator $\oplus$ instead of a function f. Now let us see the formal proof.

Theorem 16 *Suppose* $\oplus$ *is an infix operator that is associative, satisfying* $x \oplus (y \oplus z) = (x \oplus y) \oplus z$ *for all* x, y *and* z. *Then for all* y, z *and* xs,

$$\forall y \,.\, foldl\,(\mathrm{op}\oplus)\,(y \oplus z)\,xs = (foldl\,(\mathrm{op}\oplus)\,y\,xs) \oplus z.$$

Proof By structural induction on the list xs. The base case,

$$foldl\,(\mathrm{op}\oplus)\,(y \oplus z)\,[] = (foldl\,(\mathrm{op}\oplus)\,y\,[]) \oplus z,$$

is trivial; both sides reduce to $y \oplus z$.

For the induction step we show

$$foldl\,(\mathrm{op}\oplus)\,(y \oplus z)\,(x :: xs) = (foldl\,(\mathrm{op}\oplus)\,y\,(x :: xs)) \oplus z.$$

for arbitrary y, x and xs:

$$foldl\,(\text{op}\oplus)\,(y \oplus z)\,(x :: xs)$$
$$= foldl\,(\text{op}\oplus)\,(x \oplus (y \oplus z))\,xs \qquad\qquad [foldl]$$
$$= foldl\,(\text{op}\oplus)\,((x \oplus y) \oplus z)\,xs \qquad\qquad [\text{associativity}]$$
$$= (foldl\,(\text{op}\oplus)\,(x \oplus y)\,xs) \oplus z \qquad\qquad [\text{ind hyp}]$$
$$= (foldl\,(\text{op}\oplus)\,y\,(x :: xs)) \oplus z \qquad\qquad [foldl]$$

The induction hypothesis has been applied with $x \oplus y$ replacing the quantified variable y. □

Exercise 6.16 Prove $map\,f\,(xs \,@\, ys) = (map\,f\,xs) \,@\, (map\,f\,ys)$.

Exercise 6.17 Prove $(map\,f) \circ nrev = nrev \circ (map\,f)$.

Exercise 6.18 Declare a functional *maptree* on binary trees, satisfying the following equations (which you should prove):

$$(maptree\,f) \circ reflect = reflect \circ (maptree\,f)$$
$$(map\,f) \circ preorder = preorder \circ (maptree\,f)$$

Exercise 6.19 Prove $foldr\,(\text{op ::})\,ys\,xs = xs \,@\, ys$.

Exercise 6.20 Prove $foldl\,f\,z\,(xs \,@\, ys) = foldl\,f\,(foldl\,f\,z\,xs)\,ys)$.

Exercise 6.21 Suppose that $\odot$ and e satisfy, for all x, y and z,

$$x \odot (y \odot z) = (x \odot y) \odot z \quad \text{and} \quad e \odot x = x.$$

Let F abbreviate $foldr\,(\text{op}\odot)$. Prove that for all y and l, $(F\,e\,l) \odot y = F\,y\,l$.

Exercise 6.22 Let $\odot$, e and F be as in the previous exercise. Define the function G by $G(l, z) = F\,z\,l$. Prove that for all ls, $foldr\,G\,e\,ls = F\,e\,(map\,(F\,e)\,ls)$.

A general induction principle

In a structural induction proof on lists, we assume $\phi(xs)$ and then show $\phi(x :: xs)$. Typically the induction formula involves a recursive list function such as *nrev*. The induction hypothesis, $\phi(xs)$, says something about $nrev(xs)$. Since $nrev(x :: xs)$ is defined in terms of $nrev(xs)$, we can reason about $nrev(x :: xs)$ to show $\phi(x :: xs)$.

The list function *nrev* makes its recursive call on the tail of its argument. This kind of recursion is called **structural recursion** by analogy with structural induction. However, recursive functions can shorten the list in other ways. The function *maxl*, when applied to $m :: n :: ns$, may call itself on $m :: ns$:

```
fun maxl [m]        : int   = m
  | maxl (m::n::ns) = if m>n then maxl(m::ns)
                             else maxl(n::ns);
```

Quick sort and merge sort divide a list into two smaller lists and sort them recursively. Matrix transpose (Section 3.9) and Gaussian elimination make recursive calls on a smaller matrix obtained by deleting rows and columns.

Most functions on trees use structural recursion: their recursive calls involve a node's immediate subtrees. The function *nnf*, which converts a proposition into negation normal form, is not structurally recursive. We shall prove theorems about *nnf* in this section.

Structural induction works best with functions that are structurally recursive. With other functions, **well-founded induction** is often superior. Well-founded induction is a powerful generalization of complete induction. Because the rule is abstract and seldom required in full generality, our proofs will be done by a special case: induction on size. For instance, the function *nlength* formalizes the size of a list. In the induction step we have to prove $\phi(xs)$ under the induction hypothesis

$$\forall ys \, . \, nlength \, ys < nlength \, xs \rightarrow \phi(ys).$$

Thus, we may assume $\phi(ys)$ provided ys is a shorter list than xs.

6.7   *Computing normal forms*

Our tautology checker uses functions to compute normal forms of propositions (Section 4.19). These functions involve unusual recursions; structural induction seems inappropriate. First, let us recall some definitions.

The declaration of *prop*, the datatype of propositions, is

```
datatype prop = Atom of string
              | Neg  of prop
              | Conj of prop * prop
              | Disj of prop * prop;
```

Function *nnf* computes the negation normal form of a proposition. It is practically a literal rendering of the rewrite rules for this normal form, and has complex patterns.

```
fun nnf  (Atom a)          = Atom  a
  | nnf  (Neg (Atom a))     = Neg  (Atom a)
  | nnf  (Neg (Neg p))      = nnf p
  | nnf  (Neg (Conj(p,q)))  = nnf (Disj(Neg p, Neg q))
  | nnf  (Neg (Disj(p,q)))  = nnf (Conj(Neg p, Neg q))
  | nnf  (Conj(p,q))        = Conj(nnf p, nnf q)
  | nnf  (Disj(p,q))        = Disj(nnf p, nnf q) ;
```

The mutually recursive functions *nnfpos* and *nnfneg* compute the same normal form, but more efficiently:

```
fun nnfpos (Atom a)     = Atom  a
  | nnfpos (Neg p)       = nnfneg p
  | nnfpos (Conj(p,q)) = Conj(nnfpos p, nnfpos q)
  | nnfpos (Disj(p,q)) = Disj(nnfpos p, nnfpos q)
and nnfneg (Atom a)     = Neg  (Atom a)
  | nnfneg (Neg p)       = nnfpos p
  | nnfneg (Conj(p,q)) = Disj(nnfneg p, nnfneg q)
  | nnfneg (Disj(p,q)) = Conj(nnfneg p, nnfneg q) ;
```

We must verify that these functions terminate. The functions *nnfpos* and *nnfneg* are structurally recursive — recursion is always applied to an immediate constituent of the argument — and therefore terminate. For *nnf*, termination is not so obvious. Consider $nnf(Neg(Conj(p, q)))$, which makes a recursive call on a large expression. But this reduces in a few steps to

$$Disj(nnf(Neg p), nnf(Neg q)).$$

Thus the recursive calls after $Neg(Conj(p, q))$ involve the smaller propositions $Neg\,p$ and $Neg\,q$. The other complicated pattern, $Neg(Disj(p, q))$, behaves similarly. In every case, recursive computations in *nnf* involve smaller and smaller propositions, and therefore terminate.

Let us prove that *nnfpos* and *nnf* are equal. The termination argument suggests that theorems involving *nnf p* should be proved by induction on the size of *p*. Let us write $nodes(p)$ for the number of *Neg*, *Conj* and *Disj* nodes in *p*. This function can easily be coded in ML.

Theorem 17 *For all propositions p, nnf p = nnfpos p.*

Proof By mathematical induction on $nodes(p)$, taking as induction hypotheses $nnf\,q = nnfpos\,q$ for all q such that $nodes(q) < nodes(p)$. We consider seven cases, corresponding to the definition of *nnf*.

If $p = Atom\,a$ then $nnf(Atom\,a) = Atom\,a = nnfpos(Atom\,a)$.

If $p = Neg(Atom\,a)$ then

$$nnf(Neg(Atom\,a)) = Neg(Atom\,a) = nnfpos(Neg(Atom\,a)).$$

If $p = Conj(r, q)$ then

$$nnf(Conj(r, q)) = Conj(nnf\, r, nnf\, q) \qquad\qquad [nnf]$$
$$= Conj(nnfpos\, r, nnfpos\, q) \qquad\qquad \text{[ind hyp]}$$
$$= nnfpos(Conj(r, q)). \qquad\qquad [nnfpos]$$

The case $p = Disj(r, q)$ is similar.

If $p = Neg(Conj(r, q))$ then

$$nnf(Neg(Conj(r, q))) = nnf(Disj(Neg\, r, Neg\, q)) \qquad\qquad [nnf]$$
$$= Disj(nnf(Neg\, r), nnf(Neg\, q)) \qquad\qquad [nnf]$$
$$= Disj(nnfpos(Neg\, r), nnfpos(Neg\, q)) \qquad\qquad \text{[ind hyp]}$$
$$= nnfneg(Conj(r, q)) \qquad\qquad [nnfneg]$$
$$= nnfpos(Neg(Conj(r, q))). \qquad\qquad [nnfpos]$$

We have induction hypotheses for $Neg\, r$ and $Neg\, q$ because they are smaller, as measured by *nodes*, than $Neg(Conj(r, q))$.

The case $p = Neg(Disj(r, q))$ is similar.

If $p = Neg(Neg\, r)$ then

$$nnf(Neg(Neg\, r)) = nnf\, r \qquad\qquad [nnf]$$
$$= nnfpos\, r \qquad\qquad \text{[ind hyp]}$$
$$= nnfneg(Neg\, r) \qquad\qquad [nnfneg]$$
$$= nnfpos(Neg(Neg\, r)). \qquad\qquad [nnfpos]$$

An induction hypothesis applies since r contains fewer nodes than $Neg(Neg\, r)$.

$\square$

The conjunctive normal form. We now consider a different question: whether computing the conjunctive normal form preserves the meaning of a proposition. A **truth valuation** for propositions is a predicate that respects the connectives:

$$Tr(Neg\, p) \leftrightarrow \neg Tr(p)$$
$$Tr(Conj(p, q)) \leftrightarrow Tr(p) \wedge Tr(q)$$
$$Tr(Disj(p, q)) \leftrightarrow Tr(p) \vee Tr(q)$$

The predicate is completely determined by its valuation of atoms, $Tr(Atom\, a)$. To show that the normal forms preserve truth for all valuations, we make no assumptions about which atoms are true.

Most of the work of computing CNF is performed by *distrib*:

```
fun distrib  (p,  Conj(q,r))  = Conj(distrib(p,q),  distrib(p,r))
  | distrib  (Conj(q,r),  p)  = Conj(distrib(q,p),  distrib(r,p))
  | distrib  (p,  q)          = Disj(p,q)   (*no conjunctions*);
```

This function is unusual in its case analysis and its recursive calls.

The first two cases overlap if both arguments in $distrib(p, q)$ are conjunctions. Because ML tries the first case before the second, the second case cannot simply be taken as an equation. There seems to be no way of making the cases separate except to write nearly every combination of one *Atom*, *Neg*, *Disj* or *Conj* with another: at least 13 cases seem necessary. To avoid this, take the second case of *distrib* as a conditional equation; if p does not have the form $Conj(p_1, p_2)$ then

$$distrib(Conj(q, r), p) = Conj(distrib(q, p), distrib(r, p)).$$

The computation of $distrib(p, q)$ may make recursive calls affecting either p or q. It terminates because every call reduces the value of $nodes(p) + nodes(q)$. We shall use this measure for induction.

The task of $distrib(p, q)$ is to compute a proposition equivalent to $Disj(p, q)$, but in conjunctive normal form. Its correctness can be stated as follows.

Theorem 18 *For all propositions p, q and truth valuations Tr,*

$$Tr(distrib(p, q)) \leftrightarrow Tr(p) \lor Tr(q).$$

Proof We prove this by induction on $nodes(p) + nodes(q)$. The induction hypothesis is

$$Tr(distrib(p', q')) \leftrightarrow Tr(p') \lor Tr(q')$$

for all p' and q' such that $nodes(p') + nodes(q') < nodes(p) + nodes(q)$. The proof considers the same cases as in the definition of *distrib*.

If $q = Conj(q', r)$ then

$$
\begin{aligned}
&Tr(distrib(p, Conj(q', r))) \\
&\leftrightarrow Tr(Conj(distrib(p, q'), distrib(p, r))) && [distrib] \\
&\leftrightarrow Tr(distrib(p, q')) \land Tr(distrib(p, r)) && [Tr] \\
&\leftrightarrow (Tr(p) \lor Tr(q')) \land (Tr(p) \lor Tr(r)) && [\text{ind hyp}] \\
&\leftrightarrow Tr(p) \lor (Tr(q') \land Tr(r)) && [\text{distributive law}] \\
&\leftrightarrow Tr(p) \lor Tr(Conj(q', r)). && [Tr]
\end{aligned}
$$

The induction hypothesis has been applied twice using these facts:

$$nodes(p) + nodes(q') < nodes(p) + nodes(Conj(q', r))$$
$$nodes(p) + nodes(r) < nodes(p) + nodes(Conj(q', r))$$

We may now assume that q is not a *Conj*. If $p = Conj(p', r)$ then the conclusion follows as in the previous case. If neither p nor q is a *Conj* then

$$Tr(distrib(p, q)) \leftrightarrow Tr(Disj(p, q)) \qquad [distrib]$$
$$\leftrightarrow Tr(p) \vee Tr(q). \qquad [Tr]$$

The conclusion holds in every case.   □

   The proof exploits the distributive law of $\vee$ over $\wedge$, as might be expected. The overlapping cases in *distrib* do not complicate the proof at all. On the contrary, they permit a concise definition of this function and a simple case analysis.

Exercise 6.23   State and justify a rule for structural induction on values of type *prop*. To demonstrate it, prove the following formula by structural induction on p:

$$nnf\, p = nnfpos\, p \wedge nnf(Neg\, p) = nnfneg\, p$$

Exercise 6.24   Define a predicate *Isnnf* on propositions such that *Isnnf* (p) holds exactly when p is in negation normal form. Prove *Isnnf* $(nnf\, p)$ for every proposition p.

Exercise 6.25   Let *Tr* be an arbitrary truth valuation for propositions. Prove $Tr(nnf\, p) \leftrightarrow Tr(p)$ for every proposition p.

6.8   *Well-founded induction and recursion*

   Our treatment of induction is rigorous enough for the informal proofs we have been performing, but is not formal enough to be automated. Many induction rules can be formally derived from mathematical induction alone. A more uniform approach is to adopt the rule of **well-founded induction**, which includes most other induction rules as instances.

Well-founded relations.   The relation $\prec$ is **well-founded** if there exist no infinite decreasing chains

$$\cdots \prec x_n \prec \cdots \prec x_2 \prec x_1.$$

For instance, 'less than' ($<$) on the natural numbers is well-founded. 'Less than' on the integers is not well-founded: there exists the decreasing chain

$$\cdots < -n < \cdots < -2 < -1.$$

'Less than' on the rational numbers is not well-founded either; consider

$$\cdots < \frac{1}{n} < \cdots < \frac{1}{2} < \frac{1}{1}.$$

Observe that we have to state the domain of the relation — the set of values it is defined over — and not simply say that $<$ is well-founded.

Another well-founded relation is the **lexicographic ordering** of pairs of natural numbers, defined by

$$(i', j') \prec_{\text{lex}} (i, j) \quad \text{if and only if} \quad i' < i \vee (i' = i \wedge j' < j).$$

To see that $\prec_{\text{lex}}$ is well-founded, suppose there is an infinite decreasing chain

$$\cdots \prec_{\text{lex}} (i_n, j_n) \prec_{\text{lex}} \cdots \prec_{\text{lex}} (i_2, j_2) \prec_{\text{lex}} (i_1, j_1).$$

If $(i', j') \prec_{\text{lex}} (i, j)$ then $i' \leq i$. Since $<$ is well-founded on the natural numbers, the decreasing chain

$$\cdots \leq i_n \leq \cdots \leq i_2 \leq i_1$$

reaches some constant value i after say M steps: thus $i_n = i$ for all $n \geq M$. Now consider the strictly decreasing chain

$$\cdots < j_{M+n} < \cdots < j_{M+1} < j_M.$$

This must eventually terminate at some constant value j after say N steps: thus $(i_n, j_n) = (i, j)$ for all $n \geq M + N$. At this point the chain of pairs becomes constant, contradicting our assumption that it was decreasing under $\prec_{\text{lex}}$.

Similar reasoning shows that lexicographic orderings for triples, quadruples and so forth, are well-founded. The lexicographic ordering is not well-founded for lists of natural numbers; it admits an infinite decreasing chain:

$$\cdots \prec [1, 1, \ldots, 1, 2] \prec \cdots \prec [1, 2] \prec [2]$$

Another sort of well-founded relation is given by a **measure function**. If f is a function into the natural numbers, then there is a well-founded relation $\prec_f$ defined by

$$x \prec_f y \quad \text{if and only if} \quad f(x) < f(y).$$

Clearly, if there were an infinite decreasing chain

$$\cdots \prec_f x_n \prec_f \cdots \prec_f x_2 \prec_f x_1$$

then there would be an infinite decreasing chain

$$\cdots < f(x_n) < \cdots < f(x_2) < f(x_1)$$

in the natural numbers, which is impossible. Here f typically 'measures' the size of something. The well-founded relations $\prec_{nlength}$ and $\prec_{size}$ compare lists and trees by size. Our proof about *distrib* used the measure $nodes(p) + nodes(q)$ on pairs (p, q) of propositions.

The demonstration that $\prec_f$ is well-founded applies just as well if $<$ is replaced by any other well-founded relation. For instance, f could return pairs of natural numbers to be compared by $\prec_{lex}$. Similarly, the construction of $\prec_{lex}$ may be applied to any existing well-founded relations. There are several ways of constructing well-founded relations from others. Frequently we can show that a relation is well-founded by construction, without having to argue about decreasing chains.

Well-founded induction. Let $\prec$ be a well-founded relation over some type τ, and $\phi(x)$ a property to be proved for all x of type τ. To prove it by well-founded induction, it suffices to prove, for all y, the following induction step:

$$\text{if } \phi(y') \text{ for all } y' \prec y \text{ then } \phi(y)$$

The rule may be portrayed as follows:

$$\frac{[\forall y' \prec y . \phi(y')]}{\phi(y)} \qquad \text{proviso: } y \text{ must not occur in other}$$
$$\frac{}{\phi(x)} \qquad \text{assumptions of the premise.}$$

The rule is sound by contradiction: if $\phi(x)$ is false for any x then we obtain an infinite decreasing chain in $\prec$. By the induction step we know that $\forall y' \prec x . \phi(y')$ implies $\phi(x)$. If $\neg\phi(x)$ then $\neg\phi(y_1)$ for some $y_1 \prec x$. Repeating this argument for y_1, we get $\neg\phi(y_2)$ for some $y_2 \prec y_1$. We then get $y_3 \prec y_2$, and so forth.[2]

Complete induction is an instance of this rule, where $\prec$ is the well-founded relation $<$ (on the natural numbers). Our other induction rules are instances of well-founded induction for suitable choices of $\prec$.

The predecessor relation on the natural numbers, where $m \prec_N n$ just if $m+1 = n$, is obviously well-founded. Now consider proving $\phi(y)$ under the induction hypothesis $\forall y' \prec_N y . \phi(y')$. There are two cases:

- If $y = 0$ then, since $y' \prec_N 0$ never holds, we must prove $\phi(0)$ outright.
- If $y = k + 1$ then $y' \prec_N k + 1$ holds just if $y' = k$, so we may assume $\phi(k)$ when proving $\phi(k + 1)$.

---

[2] Infinite decreasing chains are intuitively appealing, but other definitions of well-foundedness permit simpler proofs. For instance, $\prec$ is well-founded just if every non-empty set contains a $\prec$-minimal element. There also exist definitions suited for constructive logic.

Therefore, well-founded induction over $\prec_N$ is precisely mathematical induction.

Structural induction is obtained similarly. Let $\prec_L$ be the relation on lists such that $xs \prec_L ys$ just if $x :: xs = ys$ for some x. Informally, $xs \prec_L ys$ means that xs is the tail of ys. Induction on $\prec_L$, which is clearly well-founded, yields structural induction on lists. Let $\prec_T$ be the relation on trees such that $t' \prec_T t$ just if $Br(x, t', t'') = t$ or $Br(x, t'', t') = t$ for some x and t''. Well-founded induction on this 'subtree of' relation yields structural induction on trees.

A well-founded relation given by a measure function yields induction on the size of an object. In reasoning about *distrib*, induction on the size of the pair (p, q) saves us from performing nested structural inductions on q and then p.

Well-founded induction can also simulate induction on a quantified formula, as when we proved

$$\forall p \,.\, facti(n, p) = n! \times p$$

by mathematical induction. It suffices to prove $facti(n, p) = n! \times p$ by well-founded induction on the pair (n, p) under the relation $\prec_{fst}$, where

$$(n', p') \prec_{fst} (n, p) \quad \text{if and only if} \quad n' + 1 = n.$$

Although many induction principles can be derived from mathematical induction alone, the derivations typically involve quantifiers. Well-founded induction makes significant proofs possible within quantifier-free logic.

Well-founded recursion. Let $\prec$ be a well-founded relation over some type τ. If f is a function with formal parameter x that makes recursive calls $f(y)$ only if $y \prec x$, then $f(x)$ terminates for all x. In this case, f is defined by ***well-founded recursion*** on $\prec$.

Informally, $f(x)$ terminates because $\prec$ has no infinite decreasing chains: there can be no infinite recursion. A formal justification of well-founded recursion is complex; besides termination, it must show that $f(x)$ is uniquely defined.

For most of our recursive functions, the well-founded relation is obvious. If $n > 0$ then $fact(n)$ recursively calls $fact(n - 1)$, so $fact$ is defined by well-founded recursion on the predecessor relation, $\prec_N$. When $facti(n, p)$ recursively calls $facti(n - 1, n \times p)$ it changes the second argument; its well-founded relation is $\prec_{fst}$. The list functions *nlength*, @ and *nrev* are recursive over the 'tail of' relation, $\prec_L$.

Proving that a function terminates suggests a useful form of induction for it — recall our proofs involving *nnf* and *distrib*. If a function is defined by well-founded recursion on $\prec$, then its properties can often be proved by well-founded induction on $\prec$.

ℹ️ *Well-founded relations in use.* Well-founded relations are central to the Boyer and Moore (1988) theorem prover, also called NQTHM. It accepts functions defined by well-founded recursion and employs elaborate heuristics to choose the right relation for well-founded induction. Its logic is quantifier-free, but as we have seen, this is not a fatal restriction. NQTHM is one of the most important theorem provers in existence. Demanding proofs in numerous areas of mathematics and computer science have been performed using it. The theorem prover Isabelle formally develops a theory of well-founded relations (Paulson, 1995, Section 3).

6.9   *Recursive program schemes*

Well-founded relations permit reasoning about program schemes. Suppose that p and g are functions and that $\oplus$ is an infix operator, and consider the ML declarations

```
fun f1(x)   = if p(x) then e else f1(g x) ⊕ x;
fun f2(x,y) = if p(x) then y else f2(g x, x ⊕ y);
```

Suppose that we are also given a well-founded relation $\prec$ such that $g(x) \prec x$ for all x such that $p(x) = false$. We then know that $f1$ and $f2$ terminate, and can prove theorems about them.

Theorem 19 *Suppose $\oplus$ is an infix operator that is associative and has identity e; that is, for all x, y and z,*

$$x \oplus (y \oplus z) = (x \oplus y) \oplus z$$
$$e \oplus x = x = x \oplus e.$$

Then for all x and a we have $f2(x, e) = f1(x)$.

Proof It suffices to prove the following formula, then put $y = e$:

$$\forall y . f2(x, y) = f1(x) \oplus y.$$

This holds by well-founded induction over $\prec$. There are two cases.
If $p(x) = true$ then

$$
\begin{aligned}
f2(x, y) &= y & [f2] \\
&= e \oplus y & [\text{identity}] \\
&= f1(x) \oplus y. & [f1]
\end{aligned}
$$

If $p(x) = false$ then

$$f2(x, y) = f2(g\,x, x \oplus y) \qquad\qquad [f2]$$
$$= f1(g\,x) \oplus x \oplus y \qquad\qquad [\text{ind hyp}]$$
$$= f1(x) \oplus y. \qquad\qquad [f1]$$

The induction hypothesis applies because $g(x) \prec x$. We have implicitly used the associativity of $\oplus$. $\square$

Thus we can transform a recursive function ($f1$) into an iterative function with an accumulator ($f2$). The theorem applies to the computation of factorials. Put

$$e = 1$$
$$\oplus = \times$$
$$g(x) = x - 1$$
$$p(x) = (x = 0)$$
$$\prec\; = \;\prec_N$$

Then $f1$ is the factorial function while $f2$ is the function *facti*. The theorem generalizes Theorem 4.

Our approach to program schemes is simpler than resorting to domain theory, but is less general. In domain theory it is simple to prove that any ML function of the form

```
fun h x = if p x then x else h(h(g x));
```

satisfies $h(h\,x) = h\,x$ for all x — regardless of whether the function terminates. Our approach cannot easily handle this. What well-founded relation should we use to demonstrate the termination of the nested recursive call in h?

Exercise 6.26 Recall the function *fst*, such that $fst(x, y) = x$ for all x and y. Give an example of a well-founded relation that uses *fst* as a measure function.

Exercise 6.27 Consider the function *ack*:

```
fun ack(0,n)  = n+1
  | ack(m,0)  = ack(m-1, 1)
  | ack(m,n)  = ack(m-1, ack(m,n-1));
```

Use a well-founded relation to show that $ack(m, n)$ is defined for all natural numbers m and n. Prove $ack(m, n) > m + n$ by well-founded induction.

Exercise 6.28 Give an example of a well-founded relation that is not transitive. Show that if $\prec$ is well-founded then so is $\prec^+$, its transitive closure.

Exercise 6.29   Consider the function *half*:

```
fun half 0 = 0
  | half n = half (n-2);
```

Show that this function is defined by well-founded recursion. Be sure to specify the domain of the well-founded relation.

Exercise 6.30   Show that well-founded induction on the 'tail of' relation $\prec_L$ is equivalent to structural induction for lists.

Specification and verification

Sorting is a good example for program verification: it is simple but not trivial. Considerable effort is required just to specify what sorting is. Most of our previous correctness proofs concerned the equivalence of two functions, and took little more than a page. Proving the correctness of the function *tmergesort* takes most of this section, even though many details are omitted.

First, consider a simpler specification task: the Greatest Common Divisor. If *m* and *n* are natural numbers then *k* is their GCD just if *k* divides both *m* and *n* exactly, and is the greatest number to do so. Given this specification, it is not hard to verify an ML function that computes the GCD by Euclid's Algorithm:

```
fun gcd (m,n) =
       if m=0 then   n   else gcd (n mod m, m);
```

The simplest approach is to observe that the specification defines a mathematical function:

$$GCD(m, n) = \max\{k \mid k \text{ divides both } m \text{ and } n\}$$

The value of $GCD(m, n)$ is uniquely defined unless $m = n = 0$, when the maximum does not exist; we need **not** know whether $GCD(m, n)$ is computable. Using simple number theory it is possible to prove these facts:

$$GCD(0, n) = n \qquad\qquad\qquad \text{for } n > 0$$
$$GCD(m, n) = GCD(n \bmod m, m) \qquad\qquad \text{for } m > 0$$

A trivial induction proves that $gcd(m, n) = GCD(m, n)$ for all natural numbers *m* and *n* not both zero. We thereby learn that $GCD(m, n)$ is computable.

A sorting function is not verified like this. It is not practical to define a mathematical function *sorting* and to prove $tmergesort(xs) = sorting(xs)$. Sorting involves two different correctness properties, which can be considered separately:

1 The output must be an ordered list.

2 The output must be some rearrangement of the elements of the input.

Too often in program verification, some of the correctness properties are ignored. This is dangerous. A function can satisfy property 1 by returning the empty list, or property 2 by returning its input unchanged. Either property alone is useless.

The specification does not have to specify the output uniquely. We might specify that a compiler generates correct code, but should not specify the precise code to generate. This would be too complicated and would forbid code optimizations. We might specify that a database system answers queries correctly, but should not specify the precise storage layout.

The next sections will prove that *tmergesort* is correct, in the sense that it returns an ordered rearrangement of its input. Let us recall some functions from Chapter 3. Proving that they terminate is left as an exercise.

The list utilities *take* and *drop*:

```
fun take ([], i)    = []
  | take (x::xs, i) = if i>0 then x::take(xs, i-1) else [];
fun drop ([], _)    = []
  | drop (x::xs, i) = if i>0 then drop (xs, i-1) else x::xs;
```

The merging function:

```
fun merge([],ys)         = ys : real list
  | merge(xs,[])         = xs
  | merge(x::xs, y::ys)  = if x<=y then x::merge(xs,  y::ys)
                                   else y::merge(x::xs,  ys);
```

The top-down merge sort:

```
fun tmergesort []  = []
  | tmergesort [x] = [x]
  | tmergesort xs  =
      let val k = length xs div 2
      in   merge (tmergesort (List.take(xs,k)),
                  tmergesort (List.drop(xs,k)))
      end;
```

6.10   *An ordering predicate*

The predicate *ordered* expresses that the elements of a list are in increasing order under $\leq$. Its properties include the following:

$$ordered([])$$

$$ordered([x])$$

$$ordered(x :: y :: ys) \leftrightarrow x \leq y \wedge ordered(y :: ys).$$

Note that *ordered*(*x* :: *xs*) implies *ordered*(*xs*). We now prove that merging two ordered lists yields another ordered list.

Theorem 20 *For all lists xs and ys,*

$$ordered(xs) \land ordered(ys) \rightarrow ordered(merge(xs, ys)).$$

Proof By induction on the value of *nlength xs* + *nlength ys*.

If *xs* = [] or *ys* = [] then the conclusion follows by the definition of *merge*. So assume *xs* = *x* :: *xs'* and *ys* = *y* :: *ys'* for some *xs'* and *ys'*. We may assume

$$ordered(x :: xs') \quad \text{and} \quad ordered(y :: ys')$$

and must show

$$ordered(merge(x :: xs', y :: ys')).$$

Consider the case where *x* ≤ *y*. (The case where *x* > *y* is similar and is left as an exercise.) By the definition of *merge*, it remains to show

$$ordered(x :: merge(xs', y :: ys')).$$

As we know *ordered*(*xs'*), we may apply the induction hypothesis, obtaining

$$ordered(merge(xs', y :: ys')).$$

Finally we have to show *x* ≤ *u*, where *u* is the head of *merge*(*xs'*, *y* :: *ys'*). Determining the head requires further case analysis.

If *xs'* = [] then *merge*(*xs'*, *y* :: *ys'*) = *y* :: *ys'*. Its head is *y* and we have already assumed *x* ≤ *y*.

If *xs'* = *v* :: *vs* then there are two subcases:

- If *v* ≤ *y* then *merge*(*xs'*, *y* :: *ys'*) = *v* :: *merge*(*vs*, *y* :: *ys'*). The head is *v* and *x* ≤ *v* follows from *ordered*(*xs*) since *xs* = *x* :: *v* :: *vs*.
- If *v* > *y* then *merge*(*xs'*, *y* :: *ys'*) = *y* :: *merge*(*xs'*, *ys'*). The head is *y* and we have assumed *x* ≤ *y*.   □

The proof is surprisingly tedious. Perhaps *merge* is less straightforward than it looks. Anyway, we are now ready to show that *tmergesort* returns an ordered list.

Theorem 21 *For every list xs, ordered*(*tmergesort xs*).

Proof By induction on the length of *xs*. If *xs* = [] or *xs* = [*x*] then the conclusion is obvious, so assume *nlength xs* ≥ 2.

Let $k = (nlength\,xs)\,div\,2$. Then $1 \le k < nlength\,xs$. It is easy to show these inequalities:

$$nlength(take(xs, k)) = k < nlength\,xs$$
$$nlength(drop(xs, k)) = nlength\,xs - k < nlength\,xs$$

By the induction hypotheses, we obtain corresponding facts:

$$ordered(tmergesort(take(xs, k)))$$
$$ordered(tmergesort(drop(xs, k)))$$

Since both arguments of *merge* are ordered, the conclusion follows by the previous theorem. □

Exercise 6.31   Fill in the details of the proofs in this section.

Exercise 6.32   Write another predicate to define the notion of ordered list, and prove that it is equivalent to *ordered*.

6.11   *Expressing rearrangement through multisets*

If the output of the sort is a rearrangement of the input, then there is a function, called a ***permutation***, that maps element positions in the input to the corresponding positions in the output. To show the correctness of sorting, we could provide a method of exhibiting the permutation. However, we do not need so much information; it would complicate the proof. This specification is too concrete.

We could show that the input and output of the sort contained the same set of elements, not considering where each element was moved. Unfortunately, this approach accepts [1,1,1,1,2] as a valid sorting of [2,1,2]. Sets do not take account of repeated elements. This specification is too abstract.

Multisets are a good way to specify sorting. A multiset is a collection of elements that takes account of their number but not of their order. The multisets $\langle 1, 1, 2 \rangle$ and $\langle 1, 2, 1 \rangle$ are equal; they differ from $\langle 1, 2 \rangle$. Multisets are often called ***bags***, for reasons that should be obvious. Here are some ways of forming multisets:

- Ø, the empty bag, contains no elements.
- $\langle u \rangle$, the singleton bag, contains one occurrence of u.
- $b_1 \uplus b_2$, the bag sum of b_1 and b_2, contains all elements in the bags b_1 and b_2 (accumulating repetitions of elements).

Rather than assume bags as primitive, let us represent them as functions into the natural numbers. If b is a bag then $b(x)$ is the number of occurrences of x in b. Thus, for all x,

$$\emptyset(x) = 0$$

$$\langle u \rangle(x) = \begin{cases} 0 & \text{if } u \neq x \\ 1 & \text{if } u = x \end{cases}$$

$$(b_1 \uplus b_2)(x) = b_1(x) + b_2(x).$$

These laws are easily checked:

$$b_1 \uplus b_2 = b_2 \uplus b_1$$

$$(b_1 \uplus b_2) \uplus b_3 = b_1 \uplus (b_2 \uplus b_3)$$

$$\emptyset \uplus b = b.$$

Let us define a function to convert lists into bags:

$$bag[] = \emptyset$$

$$bag(x :: xs) = \langle x \rangle \uplus bag\,xs.$$

The 'rearrangement' correctness property can finally be specified:

$$bag(tmergesort\,xs) = bag\,xs$$

A preliminary proof. To illustrate reasoning about multisets, let us work through a proof. It is a routine induction.[3]

Theorem 22 *For every list xs and integer k,*

$$bag(take(xs, k)) \uplus bag(drop(xs, k)) = bag\,xs.$$

Proof By structural induction on the list xs. In the base case,

$$
\begin{aligned}
bag(take([], k)) &\uplus bag(drop([], k)) \\
&= bag[] \uplus bag[] & [\textit{take,drop}] \\
&= \emptyset \uplus \emptyset & [bag] \\
&= \emptyset & [\uplus] \\
&= bag[]. & [bag]
\end{aligned}
$$

---

[3] It would be less routine if we adopted the standard library definitions of *take* and *drop*, where $take(xs, k)$ raises an exception unless $0 \leq k < length\,xs$. We should have to constrain k in the statement of the theorem and modify the proof accordingly.

For the induction step, we must prove

$$bag(take(x :: xs, k)) \uplus bag(drop(x :: xs, k)) = bag(x :: xs).$$

If $k > 0$ then

$$
\begin{aligned}
&bag(take(x :: xs, k)) \uplus bag(drop(x :: xs, k)) \\
&= bag(x :: take(xs, k-1)) \uplus \\
&\quad bag(drop(xs, k-1)) && [take, drop] \\
&= \langle x \rangle \uplus bag(take(xs, k-1)) \uplus \\
&\quad bag(drop(xs, k-1)) && [bag] \\
&= \langle x \rangle \uplus bag\, xs && [\text{ind hyp}] \\
&= bag(x :: xs). && [bag]
\end{aligned}
$$

If $k \leq 0$ then

$$
\begin{aligned}
&bag(take(x :: xs, k)) \uplus bag(drop(x :: xs, k)) \\
&= bag[] \uplus bag(x :: xs) && [take, drop] \\
&= \emptyset \uplus bag(x :: xs) && [bag] \\
&= bag(x :: xs). && [\uplus]
\end{aligned}
$$

Therefore, the conclusion holds for every integer k. □

The next step is to show that *merge* combines the elements of its arguments when forming its result.

Theorem 23 *For all lists xs and ys, $bag(merge(xs, ys)) = bag\, xs \uplus bag\, ys$.*

Proof By induction on the value of $nlength\, xs + nlength\, ys$.

If $xs = []$ or $ys = []$ then the conclusion is immediate, so assume $xs = x :: xs'$ and $ys = y :: ys'$ for some xs' and ys'. We must prove

$$bag(merge(x :: xs', y :: ys')) = bag(x :: xs') \uplus bag(y :: ys').$$

If $x \leq y$ then

$$
\begin{aligned}
&bag(merge(x :: xs', y :: ys')) \\
&= bag(x :: merge(xs', y :: ys')) && [merge] \\
&= \langle x \rangle \uplus bag(merge(xs', y :: ys')) && [bag] \\
&= \langle x \rangle \uplus bag\, xs' \uplus bag(y :: ys') && [\text{ind hyp}] \\
&= bag(x :: xs') \uplus bag(y :: ys'). && [bag]
\end{aligned}
$$

The case $x > y$ is similar. □

Finally, we prove that merge sort preserves the bag of elements given to it.

Theorem 24 *For every list xs, bag(tmergesort xs) = bag xs.*

Proof By induction on the length of xs. The only hard case is if $nlength\,xs \geq 2$. As in Theorem 21, the induction hypotheses apply to $take(xs, k)$ and $drop(xs, k)$:

$$bag(tmergesort(take(xs, k))) = bag(take(xs, k))$$
$$bag(tmergesort(drop(xs, k))) = bag(drop(xs, k))$$

Therefore

$$
\begin{aligned}
&bag(tmergesort\,xs)\\
&= bag(merge(tmergesort(take(xs, k)),\\
&\qquad\qquad\qquad tmergesort(drop(xs, k)))) \qquad\qquad [tmergesort]\\
&= bag(tmergesort(take(xs, k))) \uplus\\
&\qquad bag(tmergesort(drop(xs, k))) \qquad\qquad\qquad [\text{Theorem 23}]\\
&= bag(take(xs, k)) \uplus bag(drop(xs, k)) \qquad\qquad [\text{ind hyp}]\\
&= bag\,xs. \qquad\qquad\qquad\qquad\qquad\qquad\qquad [\text{Theorem 22}]
\end{aligned}
$$

This concludes the verification of *tmergesort*.   □

Exercise 6.33   Verify that $\uplus$ is commutative and associative. (Hint: recall the extensional equality of functions.)

Exercise 6.34   Prove that insertion sort preserves the bag of elements it is given. In particular, prove these facts:

$$bag(ins(x, xs)) = \langle x \rangle \uplus bag\,xs$$
$$bag(insort\,xs) = bag\,xs$$

Exercise 6.35   Modify merge sort to suppress repetitions: each input element should appear exactly once in the output. Formalize this property and state the theorems required to verify it.

6.12   *The significance of verification*

We could now announce that *tmergesort* has been verified — but would this mean anything? What, exactly, have we established about *tmergesort*? Formal verification has three fundamental limitations:

1 The model of computation may be too imprecise. Typically the hardware is assumed to be infallible. A model can be designed to cope with specific errors, like arithmetic overflow, rounding errors, or running out of store. However, a computer can fail in unanticipated ways. What if somebody takes an axe to it?

2 The specification may be incomplete or wrong. Design requirements are difficult to formalize, especially if they pertain to the real world. Satisfying a faulty specification will not satisfy the customer. Software engineers understand the difference between **verification** (did we build the product right?) and **validation** (did we build the right product?).

3 Proofs may contain errors. Automated theorem proving can reduce but not eliminate the likelihood of error. All human efforts may have flaws, even our principles of mathematics. This is not merely a philosophical problem. Many errors have been discovered in theorem provers, in proof rules and in published proofs.

Apart from these fundamental limitations, there is a practical one: formal proof is tedious. Look back over the proofs in this chapter; usually they take great pains to prove something elementary. Now consider verifying a compiler. The specification will be gigantic, comprising the syntax and semantics of a programming language along with the complete instruction set of the target machine. The compiler will be a large program. The proof should be divided into parts, separately verifying the parser, the type checker, the intermediate code generator and so forth. There may only be time to verify the most interesting part of the program: say, the code generator. So the 'verified' compiler could fail due to faulty parsing.

Let us not be too negative. Writing a formal specification reveals ambiguities and inconsistencies in the design requirements. Since design errors are far more serious than coding errors, writing a specification is valuable even if the code will not be verified. Many companies go to great expense to produce specifications that are rigorous, if not strictly formal.

The painstaking work of verification yields rewards. Most programs are incorrect, and an attempted proof often pinpoints the error. To see this, insert an error into any program verified in this chapter, and work through the proof again. The proof should fail, and the location of this failure should indicate the precise conditions under which the modified program fails.

A correctness proof is a detailed explanation of how the program or system works. If the proof is simple, we can go through it line by line, reading it as a series of snapshots of the execution. The inductive step traces what happens at a recursive function call. A large proof may consist of hundreds of theorems, examining every component or subsystem.

Specification and verification yield a fuller knowledge of the program and its task. This leads to increased confidence in the system. Formal proof does not eliminate the need for systematic testing, especially for a safety-critical system. Testing is the only way to investigate whether the computational model and the formal specification accurately reflect the real world. However, while testing can detect errors, it cannot guarantee success; nor does it provide insights into how a program works.

❶ *Further reading.* Bevier *et al.* (1989) have verified a tiny computer system consisting of several levels, both software and hardware. Avra Cohn (1989a) has verified some correctness properties of the Viper microprocessor. Taking her proofs as an example, Cohn (1989b) discusses the fundamental limitations of verification.

Fitzgerald *et al.* (1995) report a study in which two teams independently develop a trusted gateway. The control team uses conventional methods while the experimental team augments these methods by writing a formal specification. An unusually large study involves the AAMP5 pipelined microprocessor. This is a commercial product designed for use in avionics. It has been specified on two levels and some of its microcode proved correct (Srivas and Miller, 1995). Both studies suggest that writing formal specifications — whether or not they are followed up by formal proofs — uncovers errors.

A major study by Susan Gerhart *et al.* (1994) investigated 12 cases involving the use of formal methods. And in a famous philosophical monograph, Lakatos (1976) argues that we can learn from partial, even faulty, proofs.

Summary of main points
- Many functional programs can be given a meaning within elementary mathematics. Higher-order functions can be handled, but not lazy evaluation or infinite data structures.
- The proof that a function terminates has the same general form as most other proofs about the function.
- Mathematical induction applies to recursive functions over the natural numbers.
- Structural induction applies to recursive functions over lists and trees.
- Well-founded induction and recursion handle a wide class of terminating computations.
- Program proofs require precise and simple program specifications.
- Proofs can be fallible, but usually convey valuable information.

7

Abstract Types and Functors

Everyone accepts that large programs should be organized as hierarchical modules. Standard ML's structures and signatures meet this requirement. Structures let us package up declarations of related types, values and functions. Signatures let us specify what components a structure must contain. Using structures and signatures in their simplest form we have treated examples ranging from the complex numbers in Chapter 2 to infinite sequences in Chapter 5.

A modular structure makes a program easier to understand. Better still, the modules ought to serve as interchangeable parts: replacing one module by an improved version should not require changing the rest of the program. Standard ML's **abstract types** and **functors** can help us meet this objective too.

A module may reveal its internal details. When the module is replaced, other parts of the program that depend upon such details will fail. ML provides several ways of declaring an abstract type and related operations, while hiding the type's representation.

If structure B depends upon structure A, and we wish to replace A by another structure A', we could edit the program text and recompile the program. That is satisfactory if A is obsolete and can be discarded. But what if A and A' are both useful, such as structures for floating point arithmetic in different precisions?

ML lets us declare B to take a structure as a parameter. We can then invoke $B(A)$ and $B(A')$, possibly at the same time. A parametric structure, such as B, is called a **functor**. Functors let us treat A and A' as interchangeable parts.

The language of modules is distinct from the core language of types and expressions. It is concerned with program organization, not with computation itself. Modules may contain types and expressions, but not the other way around. The main module constructs have counterparts in the core language:

$$\text{structure} \sim \text{value}$$
$$\text{signature} \sim \text{type}$$
$$\text{functor} \sim \text{function}$$

257

This analogy is a starting point to understanding, but it fails to convey the full potential of ML modules.

Chapter outline

This chapter examines structures and signatures in greater depth, and introduces abstract types and functors. Many features of the module language are provided mainly to support functors. The chapter contains the following sections:

Three representations of queues. Three different structures implement queues, illustrating the idea of multiple data representations. But structures do not hide the representation of queues; it could be abused elsewhere in the program.

Signatures and abstraction. Signature constraints on the queue structures can hide details, declaring an abstract type of queues. The `abstype` declaration is a more flexible means of declaring abstract types. The three queue representations have their own concrete signatures.

Functors. Functors let us use the three queue implementations as interchangeable parts, first in a test harness and then for breadth-first search. Another example is generic matrix arithmetic, with numerical and graph applications. Functors allow dictionaries and priority queues to be expressed generically, for an arbitrary ordered type.

Building large systems using modules. A variety of deeper topics are covered: multiple arguments to functors, sharing constraints and the fully-functorial programming style. New declaration forms, such as `open` and `include`, help manage the deep hierarchies found in large programs.

Reference guide to modules. The full modules language is presented systematically and concisely.

Three representations of queues

A *queue* is a sequence whose elements may be inserted only at the end and removed only from the front. Queues enforce a first-in-first-out (FIFO) discipline. They provide the following operations:

- *empty*: the empty queue
- *enq(q, x)*: the queue obtained by inserting x on the end of q
- *null(q)*: the boolean-valued test of whether q is empty
- *hd(q)*: the front element of q
- *deq(q)*: the queue obtained by removing the front element of q
- *E*: the exception raised by *hd* and *deq* if the queue is empty

The queue operations are functional; *enq* and *deq* create new queues rather than modifying existing queues. We shall discuss several ways of representing queues and defining their operations as ML structures, eventually finding an efficient representation.

The names *enq* and *deq* abbreviate the words enqueue and dequeue, while *null* and *hd* clash with existing list operations. As we shall package the operations into structures, we can get away with short names without concern for clashes.

It is a simple exercise to write down the corresponding signature, but let us defer signatures until the next section. Then we shall also consider how to hide the representation of queues by declaring abstract data types.

7.1   *Representing queues as lists*

Representation 1, perhaps the most obvious, maintains a queue as the list of its elements. The structure *Queue*1 is declared as follows:

```
structure Queue1 =
  struct
  type 'a t = 'a list;
  exception E;

  val empty = [];

  fun enq(q,x) = q @ [x];

  fun null(x::q) = false
    | null _     = true;

  fun hd(x::q) = x
    | hd []     = raise E;

  fun deq(x::q) = q
    | deq []     = raise E;
  end;
```

The type of queues is simply $\alpha\ t$; outside the structure it is $\alpha\ Queue1.t$. The type abbreviation makes $\alpha\ Queue1.t$ a synonym for $\alpha\ list$. (Recall how in Section 2.7 we made *vec* a synonym for *real* $\times$ *real*.) Since a value of type $\alpha\ Queue1.t$ can be used with any list operations, the type name is little more than a comment.

Function *enq* uses append, while *deq* uses pattern-matching. The other queue operations are implemented easily and efficiently. But $enq(q, x)$ takes time proportional to the length of q: quite unsatisfactory.

Structures do not hide information. Declaring a structure hardly differs from declaring its items separately, except that a structure declaration is taken as a unit and introduces compound names. Each item behaves as if it were declared separately. Structure *Queue*1 makes no distinction between queues and lists:

```
Queue1.deq ["We","happy","few"];
> ["happy", "few"] : string list
```

7.2   *Representing queues as a new datatype*
Representation 2 declares a datatype with constructors *empty* and *enq*.
The operation *enq(q, x)* now takes constant time, independent of the length of *q*,
but *hd(q)* and *deq(q)* are slow. Calling *deq(q)* copies the remaining elements
of *q*. Even *hd(q)* requires recursive calls.

```
structure Queue2 =
  struct
  datatype 'a t = empty
                | enq of 'a t * 'a;
  exception E;

  fun null (enq _) = false
    | null empty   = true;

  fun hd (enq(empty,x)) = x
    | hd (enq(q,x))     = hd q
    | hd empty          = raise E;

  fun deq (enq(empty,x)) = empty
    | deq (enq(q,x))     = enq(deq q, x)
    | deq empty          = raise E;
  end;
```

Representation 2 gains little by defining a new datatype. It is essentially no different from representing a queue by a reversed list. Then

$$enq(q, x) = x :: q,$$

while *deq* is a recursive function to remove the last element from a list. We could
call this Representation 2a.

The type of queues, $\alpha\ Queue2.t$, is not abstract: it is a datatype with constructors *Queue2.empty* and *Queue2.enq*. Pattern-matching with the constructors
can remove the last element of the queue, violating its FIFO discipline:

```
fun last (Queue2.enq(q,x)) = x;
> val last = fn : 'a Queue2.t -> 'a
```

Such declarations abuse the data structure. Enough of them scattered throughout a program can make it virtually impossible to change the representation of
queues. The program can no longer be maintained.

Again, structures do not hide information. The differences between *Queue1*
and *Queue2* are visible outside. The function *Queue1.null* may be applied to any
list, while *Queue2.null* may only be applied to values of type $\alpha\ Queue2.t$. Both

*Queue*1 . *enq* and *Queue*2 . *enq* are functions, but *Queue*2 . *enq* is a constructor and may appear in patterns.

Our datatype declaration flouts the convention that constructor names start with a capital letter (Section 4.4). Within the confines of a small structure this is a minor matter, but to export such a constructor is questionable.

7.3 *Representing queues as pairs of lists*

Representation 3 (Burton, 1982) maintains a queue as a pair of lists. The pair

$$([x_1, x_2, \dots, x_m], [y_1, y_2, \dots, y_n])$$

denotes the queue

$$x_1 x_2 \cdots x_m y_n \cdots y_2 y_1.$$

The queue has a front part and a rear part. The elements of the rear part are stored in reverse order so that new ones can quickly be added to the end of the queue; $enq(q, y)$ modifies the queue thus:

$$(xs, [y_1, \dots, y_n]) \mapsto (xs, [y, y_1, \dots, y_n])$$

The elements of the front part are stored in correct order so that they can quickly be removed from the queue; $deq(q)$ modifies the queue thus:

$$([x_1, x_2, \dots, x_m], ys) \mapsto ([x_2, \dots, x_m], ys)$$

When the front part becomes empty, the rear part is reversed and moved to the front:

$$([], [y_1, y_2, \dots, y_n]) \mapsto ([y_n, \dots, y_2, y_1], [])$$

The rear part then accumulates further elements until the front part is again emptied. A queue is in ***normal form*** provided it does not have the form

$$([], [y_1, y_2, \dots, y_n])$$

for $n \geq 1$. The queue operations ensure that their result is in normal form. Therefore, inspecting the first element of a queue does not perform a reversal. A normal queue is empty if its front part is empty.

Here is a structure for this approach. The type of queues is declared as a datatype with one constructor, not as a type abbreviation. We used a similar technique for flexible arrays (page 158). The constructor costs nothing at run-time, while making occurrences of queues stand out in the code.

```
structure Queue3 =
  struct
  datatype 'a t = Queue of ('a list * 'a list);
  exception E;

  val empty = Queue([],[]);

  fun norm (Queue([],tails))  = Queue(rev tails,  [])
    | norm q                   = q;

  fun enq(Queue(heads,tails), x) = norm(Queue(heads, x::tails));

  fun null(Queue([],[]))  = true
    | null _               = false;

  fun hd(Queue(x::_,_))  = x
    | hd(Queue([],_))     = raise E;

  fun deq(Queue(x::heads,tails))  = norm(Queue(heads,tails))
    | deq(Queue([],_))             = raise E;
  end;
```

The function *norm* puts a queue into normal form by reversing the rear part, if necessary. It is called by *enq* and *deq*, since a queue must be put into normal form every time an element is added or removed.

Once again, none of the internal details are hidden. Users can tamper with the constructor *Queue3 . Queue* and the function *Queue3 . norm*. Pattern-matching with the constructor *Queue* exposes a queue as consisting of a pair of lists. Inside the structure, such access is essential; used outside, it could violate the queue's FIFO discipline. Calling *Queue3 . norm* from outside the structure can serve no purpose.

How efficient is this representation? The use of reverse may seem expensive. But the cost of an *enq* or *deq* operation is constant when averaged over the lifetime of the queue. At most two cons (::) operations are performed per queue element, one when it is put on the rear part and one when it is moved to the front part.

Measuring a cost over the lifetime of the data structure is called an ***amortized*** cost (Cormen *et al.*, 1990). Sleator and Tarjan (1985) present another data structure, self-adjusting trees, designed for a good amortized cost. The main drawback of such a data structure is that the costs are not evenly distributed. When normalization takes place, the reverse operation could cause an unexpected delay.

Also, the amortized cost calculation assumes that the queue usage follows an imperative style: is ***single-threaded***. Every time the data structure is updated, the previous value should be discarded. If we violate this assumption by repeatedly applying *deq* to a queue of the form

$$([x], [y_1, y_2, \dots, y_n])$$

then additional normalizations will result, incurring greater costs.

Flexible arrays can represent queues without these drawbacks. But the cost of each operation is greater, order log n where n is the number of elements in the queue. Representation 3 is simple and efficient, and can be recommended for most situations requiring functional queues.

Exercise 7.1   Under Representation 1, how much time does it take to build an n-element queue by applying *enq* operations to the empty queue?

Exercise 7.2   Discuss the relative merits of the three representations of functional queues. For example, are there any circumstances under which Representation 1 might be more efficient than Representation 3?

Exercise 7.3   Code Representation 2a in ML.

Exercise 7.4   Representation 4 uses flexible arrays, with *hiext* implementing *enq* and *lorem* implementing *deq*.   Code Representation 4 and compare its efficiency with Representation 3.

Exercise 7.5   A queue is conventionally represented using an array, with indices to its first and last elements. Are the functional arrays of Chapter 4 suitable for this purpose? How would it compare with the other representations of functional queues?

Signatures and abstraction

An *abstract type* is a type equipped with a set of operations, which are the only operations applicable to that type. Its representation can be changed — perhaps to a more efficient one — without affecting the rest of the program. Abstract types make programs easier to understand and modify. Queues should be defined as an abstract type, hiding internal details.

We can limit outside access to the components of a structure by constraining its signature. We can hide a type's representation by means of an `abstype` declaration. Combining these methods yields abstract structures.

7.4   *The intended signature for queues*

Although the structures *Queue*1, *Queue*2 and *Queue*3 differ, they each implement queues. Moreover they share a common interface, defined by signature *QUEUE*:

```
signature QUEUE =
  sig
  type 'a t                       (*type of queues*)
  exception E                     (*for errors in hd, deq*)
  val empty: 'a t                 (*the empty queue*)
  val enq  : 'a t * 'a -> 'a t    (*add to end*)
  val null : 'a t -> bool         (*test for empty queue*)
  val hd   : 'a t -> 'a           (*return front element*)
  val deq  : 'a t -> 'a t         (*remove from front*)
  end;
```

Each entry in a signature is called a ***specification***. The comments after each specification are optional, but make the signature more informative. A structure is an ***instance*** of this signature provided it declares, at least,

- a polymorphic type $\alpha\ t$ (which need not admit equality)
- an exception E
- a value *empty* of type $\alpha\ t$
- a value *enq* of type $\alpha\ t \times \alpha \to \alpha\ t$
- a value *null* of type $\alpha\ t \to bool$
- a value *hd* of type $\alpha\ t \to \alpha$
- a value *deq* of type $\alpha\ t \to \alpha\ t$

Consider each structure in turn. In *Queue*1, type $\alpha\ t$ abbreviates $\alpha\ list$, and the values have the correct types under this abbreviation. In *Queue*2, type $\alpha\ t$ is a datatype and *empty* and *enq* are constructors. In *Queue*3, type $\alpha\ t$ is again a datatype; the structure declares everything required by signature *QUEUE*, and the additional items *Queue* and *norm*. An instance of a signature may contain items not specified in the signature.

7.5   *Signature constraints*

Different views of a structure, with varying degrees of abstraction, can be obtained using different signatures. A structure can be constrained to a signature either when it is first defined or later. A constraint can be transparent or opaque.

Transparent signature constraints. The constraints we have used until now, indicated by a colon (:), are transparent. To see what this implies, let us constrain our existing queue structures using signature *QUEUE*:

```
structure S1: QUEUE = Queue1;
structure S2: QUEUE = Queue2;
structure S3: QUEUE = Queue3;
```

These declarations make *S1*, *S2* and *S3* denote the same structures as *Queue1*, *Queue2* and *Queue3*, respectively. However, the new structures are constrained to have the signature *QUEUE*. The types α *Queue2 . t* and α *S2 . t* are identical, yet *Queue2 . empty* is a constructor while *S2 . empty* may only be used as a value. The structures *Queue3* and *S3* are identical, yet *Queue3 . norm* is a function while *S3 . norm* means nothing.

A transparent signature constraint may hide components, but they are still present. This cannot be called abstraction. Structure *S1* does not hide its representation at all; type α *S1 . t* is identical to α *list*.

```
S1.deq ["We","band","of","brothers"];
> ["band", "of", "brothers"] : string S1.t
```

Structures *S2* and *S3* may seem more abstract, because they declare the type α *t* and hide its constructors. Without the constructors, pattern-matching is not available to take apart values of the type and disclose the representation. However, the constructor *Queue3 . Queue* may be used in a pattern to take apart a value of type α *S3 . t*:

```
val Queue3.Queue(heads,tails) =
        S3.enq(S3.enq(S3.empty,"Saint"), "Crispin");
> val heads = ["Saint"] : string list
> val tails = ["Crispin"] : string list
```

The concrete structure, *Queue3*, provides a loophole into its abstract view, *S3*.

Data abstraction is compromised in another way. For each of our queue structures, type α *t* admits equality testing. The equality test compares internal representations, not queues. Under Representation 3, the values $([1, 2], [])$ and $([1], [2])$ denote the same queue, but the equality test says they are different.

Opaque signature constraints. Using the symbol : > instead of a colon makes the constraint opaque. The constraint hides all information about the new structure except its signature. Let us create some truly abstract queue structures by constraining the concrete ones:

```
structure AbsQueue1 :> QUEUE = Queue1;
structure AbsQueue2 :> QUEUE = Queue2;
structure AbsQueue3 :> QUEUE = Queue3;
```

The components of the constrained structure are divorced from their counterparts in the original structure. Structure *AbsQueue1* represents queues by lists, but we cannot see this:

```
AbsQueue1.deq ["We","band","of","brothers"];
> Error: Type conflict:...
```

Type checking similarly forbids using the constructor *Queue3.Queue* to take apart the queues of structure *AbsQueue3*. Equality testing is forbidden too:

```
AbsQueue3.empty = AbsQueue3.empty;
> Error: type 'a AbsQueue3.t must be an equality type
```

Specifying a type by eqtype *t* instead of type *t* indicates that the type is to admit equality. Using eqtype in the signature allows you to export the type's equality test, even with an opaque signature constraint.

Limitations. An opaque signature constraint is perfect for declaring an abstract type of queues. The abstract structure can be made from an existing concrete structure, as in the *AbsQueue* declarations above, or we can simply constrain the original structure declaration:

```
structure Queue :> QUEUE = struct ... end;
```

But the two kinds of signature constraints give us an all-or-nothing choice, which is awkward for complex abstract types. Signature *DICTIONARY* specifies two types: *key* is the type of search keys; $\alpha\,t$ is the type of dictionaries (see Section 4.14). Type $\alpha\,t$ should be abstract, but *key* should be something concrete, like *string*. Otherwise, we should have no way to refer to keys; we should be unable to call *lookup* and *update*! The next section describes a more flexible approach to declaring abstract types.

Exercise 7.6   Assuming Representation 3, show how two different representations of the same queue value could be created using only the abstract queue operations.

Exercise 7.7   Extend signature *QUEUE* to specify the functions *length*, for returning the number of elements in a queue, and *equal*, for testing whether two queues consist of the same sequence of elements. Extend the structures *Queue1*, *Queue2* and *Queue3* with declarations of these functions.

7.6   The abstype *declaration*

Standard ML has a declaration form specifically intended for declaring abstract types. It hides the representation fully, including the equality test. The abstype declaration originates from the first ML dialect and reflects the early thinking of the structured programming school. Now it looks distinctly dated.

But it is more selective than an opaque constraint: it applies to chosen types instead of an entire signature.

A simple abstype declaration contains two elements, a datatype binding *DB* and a declaration *D*:

    abstype *DB* with *D* end

A datatype binding is a type name followed by constructor descriptions, exactly as they would appear in a datatype declaration. The constructors are visible within the declaration part, *D*, which must use them to implement all operations associated with the abstract type. Identifiers declared in *D* are visible outside, as is the type, but its constructors are hidden. Moreover, the type does not admit equality testing.

To illustrate the abstype declaration, let us apply it to queues. The declaration ought to be enclosed in a structure to prevent name clashes with the built-in list functions *null* and *hd*. But as a structure would complicate the example, those functions have instead been renamed. Exceptions are omitted to save space.

Queues as lists. We begin with Representation 1. Although *list* is already a datatype, the abstype declaration forces us to use a new constructor ($Q1$) in all the queue operations. This constructor is traditionally called the ***abstraction function***, as it maps concrete representations to abstract values.

```
abstype 'a queue1 = Q1 of 'a list
   with
   val empty = Q1 [];

   fun enq(Q1 q, x) = Q1 (q @ [x]);

   fun qnull(Q1 (x::q)) = false
     | qnull _          = true;

   fun qhd(Q1 (x::q)) = x;

   fun deq(Q1 (x::q)) = Q1 q;
   end;
```

In its response, ML echoes the names and types of the identifiers that have been declared:

```
> type 'a queue1
> val empty = - : 'a queue1
> val enq = fn : 'a queue1 * 'a -> 'a queue1
> val qnull = fn : 'a queue1 -> bool
> val qhd = fn : 'a queue1 -> 'a
> val deq = fn : 'a queue1 -> 'a queue1
```

The abstype declaration has hidden the connection between *queue*1 and *list*.

Queues as a new datatype. Now turn to Representation 2. Previously we called the constructors *empty* and *enq*, with lower case names, for use outside as values. And that was naughty. But the abstype declaration hides the constructors. We may as well give them capitalised names *Empty* and *Enq*, since we must now export their values explicitly:

```
abstype 'a queue2 = Empty
                  | Enq of 'a queue2 * 'a
  with
  val empty = Empty
  and enq   = Enq

  fun qnull (Enq _) = false
    | qnull Empty   = true;

  fun qhd (Enq(Empty,x)) = x
    | qhd (Enq(q,x))     = qhd q;

  fun deq (Enq(Empty,x)) = Empty
    | deq (Enq(q,x))     = Enq(deq q, x);
  end;
```

We do not need to declare a new constructor *Q2* because this representation requires its own constructors. ML's response is identical to its response to the declaration of *queue*1 except for the name of the queue type. An external user can operate on queues only by the exported operations.

These two examples illustrate the main features of abstype. We do not need to see the analogous declaration of *queue*3.

Abstract types in ML: summary. ML's treatment of abstract types is less straightforward than one might like, but it can be reduced to a few steps. If you would like to declare a type *t* and allow access only by operations you have chosen to export, here is how to proceed.

1 Consider whether to export the equality test for *t*. It is only appropriate if the representation admits equality, and if this equality coincides with equality of the abstract values. Also consider whether equality testing would actually be useful. Equality testing is appropriate for small objects such as dates and rational numbers, but not for matrices or flexible arrays.

2 Declare a signature *SIG* specifying the abstract type and its operations. The signature must specify *t* as an `eqtype` if it is to admit equality, and as a `type` otherwise.

3 Decide which sort of signature constraint to use with *SIG*. An opaque constraint is suitable only if all the types in the signatures are intended to be abstract.

4 Write the shell of a structure (or functor) declaration, attaching the constraint chosen in the previous step.

5 Within the brackets `struct` and `end`, declare type *t* and the desired operations. If you used a transparent signature constraint, this must be either a `datatype` declaration (to export equality) or an `abstype` declaration (to hide equality).

A `datatype` declaration can yield an abstract type because the signature constraint hides the constructors. An `abstype` or `datatype` declaration creates a fresh type, which ML regards as distinct from all others.

Functor *Dictionary* exemplifies the first approach (see page 282). The ring buffer structure *RingBuf* exemplifies the second (see page 333).

Exercise 7.8 Early papers on abstract types all considered the same example: stacks. The operations included *push* (which puts an item on top of the stack), *top* (which returns the top item) and *pop* (which discards the top item). At least two other operations are needed. Complete the design and code two distinct representations using `abstype`.

Exercise 7.9 Write an `abstype` declaration for the rational numbers, following Exercise 2.25 on page 63. Use a `local` declaration to keep any auxiliary functions private. Then modify your solution to obtain a structure matching signature *ARITH*.

Exercise 7.10 Design and code an `abstype` declaration for type *date*, which represents dates as a day and a month. (Assume it is not a leap year.) Provide a function *today* for converting a valid day and month to a date. Provide functions *tomorrow* and *yesterday*; they should raise an exception if the desired date lies outside the current year.

7.7   *Inferred signatures for structures*

A structure declaration can appear without a signature constraint, as in the declarations of *Queue*1, *Queue*2 and *Queue*3. ML then infers a signature fully describing the structure's internal details.

Signature *QUEUE1* is equivalent to the signature that is inferred for structure *Queue*1. It specifies $\alpha\ t$ as an `eqtype` — a type that admits equality — because lists can be compared for equality. Observe that the types of values involve type $\alpha\ list$ instead of $\alpha\ t$, as in signature *QUEUE*.

```
signature QUEUE1 =
  sig
  eqtype 'a t
  exception E
  val empty : 'a list
  val enq   : 'a list * 'a -> 'a list
  val null  : 'a list -> bool
  val hd    : 'a list -> 'a
  val deq   : 'a list -> 'a list
  end;
```

The signature inferred for *Queue*2 specifies $\alpha\ t$ as a `datatype` with constructors *empty* and *enq*; constructors are not specified again as values. The signature could be declared as follows:

```
signature QUEUE2 =
  sig
  datatype 'a t = empty | enq of 'a t * 'a
  exception E
  val null : 'a t -> bool
  val hd   : 'a t -> 'a
  val deq  : 'a t -> 'a t
  end;
```

The signature inferred for structure *Queue*3 again specifies $\alpha\ t$ as a `datatype` — not merely a type, as in signature *QUEUE*. All items in the structure are specified, including *Queue* and *norm*.

```
signature QUEUE3 =
  sig
  datatype 'a t = Queue of 'a list * 'a list
  exception E
  val empty : 'a t
  val enq   : 'a t * 'a -> 'a t
  val null  : 'a t -> bool
  val hd    : 'a t -> 'a
  val deq   : 'a t -> 'a t
  val norm  : 'a t -> 'a t
  end;
```

These signatures are more concrete and specific than *QUEUE*. No structure can be an instance of more than one of them. Consider *QUEUE1* and *QUEUE3*. Function *hd* must have type $\alpha\ list \to \alpha$ to satisfy *QUEUE1*; it must have type $\alpha\ t \to \alpha$

to satisfy *QUEUE3*, which also specifies that $\alpha\, t$ is a datatype clearly different from α *list*.

On the other hand, each signature has many different instances. A structure can satisfy the specification `val` x : *int* by declaring x to be any value of type *int*. It can satisfy the specification `type` t by declaring t to be any type. (However, it can satisfy a `datatype` specification only by an identical `datatype` declaration.) A structure may include items not specified in the signature. Thus, a signature defines a class of structures.

Interesting relationships hold among these classes. We have already seen that *QUEUE1*, *QUEUE2* and *QUEUE3* are disjoint. The latter two are contained in *QUEUE*; an instance of *QUEUE2* or *QUEUE3* is an instance of *QUEUE*. An instance of *QUEUE1* is an instance of *QUEUE* only if it makes type $\alpha\, t$ equivalent to α *list*. These containments can be shown in a Venn diagram:

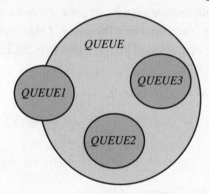

Exercise 7.11 Declare a structure that has signature *QUEUE1* and that implements queues by a different representation from that of *Queue*1.

Exercise 7.12 Declare a structure that has signature *QUEUE* but does not implement queues. After all, the signature specifies only the types of the queue operations, not their other properties.

Functors

An ML function is an expression that takes parameters. Applying it substitutes argument values for the parameters. The value of the resulting expression is returned. A function can only be applied to arguments of the correct type.

We have several implementations of queues. Could we write code that uses queues but is independent of any particular implementation? This seems to require taking a structure as a parameter.

Functions themselves can be parameters, for functions are values in ML. Records are also values. They are a bit like structures, but they cannot represent queue implementations because they cannot have types and exception constructors as components.

An ML *functor* is a structure that takes other structures as parameters. Applying it substitutes argument structures for the parameters. The bindings that arise from the resulting structure are returned. A functor can only be applied to arguments that match the correct signature.

Functors let us write program units that can be combined in different ways. A replacement unit can quickly be linked in, and the new system tested. Functors can also express generic algorithms. Let us see how they do so.

7.8   *Testing the queue structures*

Here is a simple test harness for queues. Given a queue structure, it returns a testing structure containing two functions. One converts a list to a queue; the other is the inverse operation. The test harness is declared as a functor with argument signature *QUEUE*:

```
functor TestQueue (Q: QUEUE) =
  struct
  fun fromList l = foldl (fn (x,q) => Q.enq(q,x)) Q.empty l;

  fun toList q   = if Q.null q then []
                   else Q.hd q :: toList (Q.deq q);
  end;
> functor TestQueue : <sig>
```

The functor body refers not to existing queue structures but to the argument *Q*. The two functions exercise the queue operations uniformly. Any queue structure can be tested and its efficiency measured. Let us start with *Queue*3. Applying the functor to this argument yields a new structure, which we name *TestQ*3. The components of *TestQ*3 are functions to test *Queue*3, as can be seen from their types:

```
structure TestQ3 = TestQueue (Queue3);
> structure TestQ3 :
>   sig
>     val fromList : 'a list -> 'a Queue3.t
>     val toList   : 'a Queue3.t -> 'a list
>   end
```

The test data is just the list of integers from 1 to 10,000:

```
val ns = upto(1,10000);
> val ns = [1, 2, 3, 4, ...] : int list
```

```
val q3 = TestQ3.fromList ns;
> val q3 = Queue ([1], [10000, 9999, 9998, 9997, ...])
> : int Queue3.t
val l3 = TestQ3.toList q3;
> val l3 = [1, 2, 3, 4, ...] : int list
l3 = ns;
> true : bool
```

*Queue*3 passes its first test: we get back the original list. It is also efficient, taking 10 msec to build *q*3 and 50 msec to convert it back to a list.

ML's response to the declaration of *q*3 reveals its representation as a pair of lists: *Queue*3 does not define an abstract type. We ought to try structure *Abs-Queue3*. Again we apply the functor and give the resulting structure a name:

```
structure TestAQ3 = TestQueue (AbsQueue3);
> structure TestAQ3 :
>    sig
>    val fromList : 'a list -> 'a AbsQueue3.t
>    val toList   : 'a AbsQueue3.t -> 'a list
>    end
val q = TestAQ3.fromList ns;
> val q = - : int AbsQueue3.t
```

Now ML reveals nothing about the representation. In terms of efficiency, *Queue*3 and *AbsQueue*3 are indistinguishable. Similar measurements reveal that *Abs-Queue3* is orders of magnitude faster than *Queue*1 and *Queue*2 and much faster than the balanced tree representation suggested in Exercise 7.4. Because *Queue*1 represents queues by lists, it could implement *fromList* and *toList* efficiently, but only operations specified in signature *QUEUE* are allowed in the functor body.

A more realistic test would involve an application of queues, such as breadth-first search. Function *breadthFirst* (Section 5.17) used lists instead of queues, for simplicity. A functor can express the search strategy independently from the implementation of queues.

```
functor BreadthFirst (Q: QUEUE) =
  struct
  fun enqlist q xs = foldl (fn (x,q) => Q.enq(q,x)) q xs;
  fun search next x =
    let fun bfs q =
            if Q.null q then Nil else
              let val y = Q.hd q
              in  Cons(y, fn()=> bfs (enqlist (Q.deq q) (next y)))
              end
    in  bfs (Q.enq(Q.empty, x))  end;
  end;
> functor BreadthFirst : <sig>
```

The function *enqlist* appends a list of elements to a queue. Let us apply the functor to an efficient queue structure:

```
structure Breadth = BreadthFirst (Queue3);
> structure Breadth :
>   sig
>     val enqlist : 'a Queue3.t -> 'a list -> 'a Queue3.t
>     val search  : ('a -> 'a list) -> 'a -> 'a seq
>   end
```

The function *Breadth . search* is equivalent to *breadthFirst*, but runs a lot faster.

Most languages have nothing comparable to functors. The C programmer obtains a similar effect using header and include files. Primitive methods such as these go a long way, but they do not forgive errors. Including the wrong file means the wrong code is compiled: we get a cascade of error messages. What happens if a functor is applied to the wrong sort of structure? Try applying *BreadthFirst* to the standard library structure *List*:

```
structure Wrong = BreadthFirst (List);
> Error: unmatched type spec: t
> Error: unmatched exception spec: E
> Error: unmatched val spec: empty
> Error: unmatched val spec: enq
> Error: unmatched val spec: deq
```

We get specific error messages describing what is missing from the argument. There is no complaint about the absence of *hd* and *null* because *List* has components with those names.

Taking the queue structure as a parameter may be a needless complication. *AbsQueue3* is the best queue structure; we may as well rename it *Queue* and use it directly, just as we use standard library structures such as *List*. But often we have a choice. There are several possible representations for dictionaries and priority queues. Even the standard library admits competing structures for real arithmetic. And when we consider generic operations, the case for functors becomes unassailable.

Exercise 7.13   Consider how you would obtain the effect of ML modules in another language of your choice. How would you express signatures such as *QUEUE*, alternative structures such as *Queue1* and *Queue2*, and functors such as *TestQueue*?

Exercise 7.14   To what extent is *TestQueue* a good test suite for queues?

7.9   *Generic matrix arithmetic*

Related structures can differ in other ways than performance. In Section 2.22 we considered the signature *ARITH*, which specifies the components *zero*, *sum*, *diff*, *prod*, etc. Suitable instances of this signature include structures that implement arithmetic on integers, reals, complex numbers and rational numbers. Chapter 3 mentioned further possibilities: binary numerals, matrices and polynomials.

To illustrate functors, let us code a generic structure for matrix arithmetic. For simplicity we shall treat only zero, sum and product:

```
signature ZSP =
    sig
    type t
    val zero : t
    val sum : t * t -> t
    val prod : t * t -> t
    end;
```

We shall declare a functor whose argument and result structures both match signature *ZSP*.

Declaring the matrix functor. Given a type *t* and the three arithmetic operations, functor *MatrixZSP* declares a type for matrices over *t* and the analogous matrix operations (Figure 7.1 on the following page). Before you study the functor body, reviewing Section 3.10 may be helpful.

In the functor heading, the second occurrence of : *ZSP* is a signature constraint on the result structure. Because the constraint is transparent, *MatrixZSP* does not return an abstract type. If it were opaque (using : >) then we could only operate on matrices using the exported operations of zero, sum and product: we could only express zero! As things stand, we can write matrices as lists of lists.

The result structure declares *t*, the type of matrices, in terms of the type of its elements, *Z* . *t*. The declaration is required by the result signature, which specifies a type *t*. The functor body never refers to it.

The structure then declares *zero*. In algebra, any $m \times n$ matrix of zeros is called a **zero matrix**. The specification *zero* : *t* in signature *ZSP* requires us to declare a single zero element. So the functor declares *zero* to be the empty list, and makes *sum* and *prod* satisfy the laws $0 + A = A + 0 = A$ and $0 \times A = A \times 0 = 0$.

The structure declares the function *sum* to compute the sum of two matrices. Two rows are added by adding corresponding elements, using the library functional *ListPair* . *map*. Two matrices are added similarly, by adding corresponding

Figure 7.1 *A functor for generic matrix arithmetic*

```
functor MatrixZSP (Z: ZSP) : ZSP =
  struct
  type t    = Z.t list list;

  val zero = [];

  fun sum  (rowsA,[])    = rowsA
    | sum  ([],rowsB)    = rowsB
    | sum  (rowsA,rowsB) = ListPair.map (ListPair.map Z.sum)
                                          (rowsA,rowsB);

  fun dotprod pairs = foldl Z.sum Z.zero (ListPair.map Z.prod pairs);

  fun transp ([]::_) = []
    | transp rows      = map hd rows :: transp (map tl rows);

  fun prod (rowsA,[])    = []
    | prod (rowsA,rowsB) =
        let val colsB = transp rowsB
        in  map (fn row => map (fn col => dotprod(row,col))
                                    colsB)
              rowsA
        end;
  end;
```

rows. There is no conflict between *sum* (matrix addition) and *Z* . *sum* (element addition).

Other functions in the structure support the declaration of *prod*. The dot product computation is also streamlined by *ListPair* . *map*, while matrix transpose is declared as in Section 5.7. As *transp* cannot handle the empty list, function *prod* catches this special case.

Because the *ListPair* functions discard unmatched list elements, there is no checking of matrix dimensions. Adding a 2×5 matrix to a 3×4 matrix yields a 2×4 matrix instead of an exception.

Numerical applications. Before applying the functor, we have to create some structures. We have already seen matrices of real numbers; now it is the integers' turn. Structure *IntZSP* contains just the specified operations specified by *ZSP*:

```
structure IntZSP =
   struct
   type t   = int;
   val zero = 0;
   fun sum (x,y) = x+y: t;
   fun prod (x,y) = x*y: t;
   end;
>  structure IntZSP :
>     sig
>     eqtype t
>     val prod : int * int -> t
>     val sum  : int * int -> t
>     val zero : int
>     end
```

Applying the functor to *IntZSP* builds a structure for arithmetic on integer matrices. Two examples are the sum $\left(\begin{smallmatrix}1&2\\3&4\end{smallmatrix}\right) + \left(\begin{smallmatrix}5&6\\7&8\end{smallmatrix}\right) = \left(\begin{smallmatrix}6&8\\10&12\end{smallmatrix}\right)$ and the product $\left(\begin{smallmatrix}1&2\\3&4\end{smallmatrix}\right) \times \left(\begin{smallmatrix}0&1\\1&0\end{smallmatrix}\right) = \left(\begin{smallmatrix}2&1\\4&3\end{smallmatrix}\right)$.

```
structure IntMatrix = MatrixZSP (IntZSP);
> structure IntMatrix : ZSP
IntMatrix.sum ([[1,2],[3,4]], [[5,6],[7,8]]);
> [[6, 8], [10, 12]] : IntMatrix.t
IntMatrix.prod ([[1,2],[3,4]], [[0,1],[1,0]]);
> [[2, 1], [4, 3]] : IntMatrix.t
```

The structure *Complex*, declared in Section 2.21, has several components not specified in *ZSP*. But signature matching ignores surplus components, so we may supply the structure as an argument to *MatrixZSP*. The result is a structure for arithmetic on matrices of complex numbers.

```
structure ComplexMatrix = MatrixZSP (Complex);
> structure ComplexMatrix : ZSP
```

This ability to use one structure for several purposes is a powerful tool for keeping programs simple. It requires, above all, careful design of signatures. Consistent naming conventions help ensure that different modules fit together.

Graph applications. The components *zero*, *sum* and *prod* do not have to be the obvious numerical interpretations. Many graph algorithms operate on matrices under surprising interpretations of 0, $+$ and $\times$.

A directed graph consisting of n nodes can be represented by an $n \times n$ **adjacency matrix**. The (i, j) element of the matrix is a boolean value, indicating the absence or presence of an edge from node i to node j. Typical matrix operations interpret *zero* as *false*, while *sum* is disjunction and *prod* is conjunction.

```
structure BoolZSP =
  struct
  type t   = bool;
  val zero = false;
  fun sum (x,y) = x orelse y;
  fun prod (x,y) = x andalso y;
  end;
> structure BoolZSP :
>   sig
>     eqtype t
>     val prod : bool * bool -> bool
>     val sum  : bool * bool -> bool
>     val zero : bool
>   end
```

If A is a boolean adjacency matrix, then $A \times A$ represents the graph having an edge from i to j precisely if there is a path of length two from i to j in the graph given by A. Matrix arithmetic can compute the transitive closure of a graph. However, bitwise operations (available in the standard library structure *Word8*) can perform such computations much faster, so let us turn to a more unusual example.

Define *zero* by infinity (∞), *sum* by minimum (*min*) and *prod* by sum ($+$). The other operations are extended to handle ∞ by $min(\infty, x) = min(x, \infty) = x$ and $\infty + x = x + \infty = \infty$. Thus the triple ($\infty$, *min*, $+$) satisfies more or less the same laws as $(0, +, \times)$. But what is this strange arithmetic good for?

Consider a directed graph whose edges are labelled with numbers, indicating the cost (possibly negative!) of travelling along that edge. The corresponding adjacency matrix has numeric elements. Element (i, j) is the cost of the edge from i to j, or infinity if no such edge exists. Let A be an adjacency matrix, and

use the strange arithmetic to compute $A \times A$. The (i, j) element of the product
is the minimum cost of the paths of length two from i to j. We have the necessary machinery to express a standard algorithm for computing the shortest paths
between all nodes of a graph.

Here is a structure implementing the strange arithmetic. It is based on type *int*.
It declares *zero* to be not infinity but some large integer.[1] It declares *sum* to be
the standard library's minimum function and *prod* to be an extended version of
addition.

```
structure PathZSP =
  struct
  type t = int;
  val SOME zero = Int.maxInt;
  val sum        = Int.min
  fun prod(m,n) = if m=zero orelse n=zero then zero
                     else m+n;
  end;
```

Applying our functor to this structure yields a structure for strange arithmetic
over matrices. The 'all-pairs shortest paths' algorithm can be coded in a few
lines:

```
structure PathMatrix = MatrixZSP (PathZSP);
> structure PathMatrix : ZSP

fun fast_paths mat =
  let val n = length mat
      fun f (m,mat) = if n-1 <= m then mat
                         else f(2*m, PathMatrix.prod(mat,mat))
  in f (1, mat)  end;
> val fast_paths = fn : PathMatrix.t -> PathMatrix.t
```

Cormen *et al.* (1990) discuss this algorithm (Section 26.1). Let us try it on one
of their worked examples. Given the adjacency matrix for a graph of five nodes,
fast paths returns the expected result:

```
val zz = PathZSP.zero;
> 1073741823 : int
fast_paths [[0,   3,   8,   zz,  ~4],
            [zz,  0,   zz,  1,   7],
            [zz,  4,   0,   zz,  zz],
            [2,   zz,  ~5,  0,   zz],
            [zz,  zz,  zz,  6,   0]];
```

[1] Component *maxInt* of standard library structure *Int* is either *SOME n*, where
     n is the maximum representable integer, or *NONE*. Any integer exceeding the
     sum of the absolute values of the edge labels could be used.

```
>  [[0,   1,  ~3,   2,  ~4],
>   [3,   0,  ~4,   1,  ~1],
>   [7,   4,   0,   5,   3],
>   [2,  ~1,  ~5,   0,  ~2],
>   [8,   5,   1,   6,   0]]  : PathMatrix.t
```

The argument of functor *MatrixZSP* is a structure consisting of only four components. Even smaller structures can be of use, as the next section shows.

ℹ   *An algebraic view.* Cormen *et al.* (1990) proceed to put the strange arithmetic on a sound foundation. They define (Section 26.4) the notion of **closed semiring** and describe its connection with path algorithms. A closed semiring involves operators analogous to 0, 1, + and × that satisfy a collection of algebraic laws: + and × should be commutative and associative, etc. A signature for closed semirings would need to augment *ZSP* with an additional component, *one*. ML modules are ideal for putting such abstractions to use.

Exercise 7.15   Declare a version of *PathZSP* that represents ∞ by a special value, not equal to any integer. Such a structure is appropriate for ML systems such as Poly/ML, where type *int* has no largest value.

Exercise 7.16   Matrices do not have to be lists of lists. Study the standard library structure *Vector*, then write a functor *VMatrixZSP* that represents matrices by vectors of vectors.

7.10   *Generic dictionaries and priority queues*

In Chapter 4 we implemented binary search trees for strings and priority queues for real numbers. Using functors we can lift the type restrictions, generalizing both data structures to arbitrary ordered types. The type and its ordering function will be packaged as a two-component structure.

Sorting can similarly be generalized — without using functors. Simply pass the ordering function as an argument, expressing sorting as a higher-order function. But this is only possible because sorting is an all-in-one operation. Turning the priority queue operations into higher-order functions would permit blunders such as adding items by one ordering and removing them by another.

Ordered types as structures. A mathematician defines an ordered set as a pair $(A, <)$, where A is a set and $<$ is a relation on A that is transitive and so forth. ML modules can express such mathematical concepts, although the notation is more cumbersome. The signature *ORDER* specifies a type t and an ordering function *compare*:

```
signature ORDER =
  sig
  type t
  val compare: t*t -> order
  end;
```

Recall that the ML library declares *order* as an enumeration type with constructors *LESS*, *EQUAL* and *GREATER*. The library structures such as *String*, *Int* and *Real* have a component *compare* that takes two operands of the corresponding type. For example, let us package up the string ordering:

```
structure StringOrder: ORDER =
  struct
  type t = string;
  val compare = String.compare
  end;
> structure StringOrder : ORDER
```

We may define our own ordering functions, but note that binary search trees need the ordering to be **linear**. An ordering $<$ is linear if for all x and y either $x < y$, $x = y$, or $x > y$. Here, it means that if the result of the comparison is *EQUAL* then the two operands really are equal. For priority queues, we could use a partial ordering: if two items are reported as *EQUAL* it means they have equal priority, even if the items themselves are different. (But see Exercise 7.23 below.)

A functor for dictionaries. Section 4.14 outlined the dictionary operations by declaring signature *DICTIONARY*, and implemented it using binary search trees. The implementation was flawed in two respects: keys were artificially restricted to type *string* and the tree representation was visible outside the structure.

Our new implementation (Figure 7.2) rectifies the first flaw by taking the ordering structure as a parameter, and the second flaw by means of an `abstype` declaration. It forbids equality testing because different binary search trees can represent the same dictionary.

The functor heading tells us that the only operation available for keys is comparison. The functor body resembles the previous, flawed structure. However, it compares keys using its parameter *Key . compare*, instead of *String . compare*. And it declares type *key* to be *Key . t* where the old structure declared it to be *string*.

Applying functor *Dictionary* to the structure *StringOrder* creates a structure of dictionaries with strings for keys.

```
structure StringDict = Dictionary (StringOrder);
> structure StringDict : DICTIONARY
```

Figure 7.2 *A functor for dictionaries as binary search trees*

```
functor Dictionary (Key: ORDER) : DICTIONARY =
  struct

  type key = Key.t;

  abstype 'a t = Leaf
               | Bran of key * 'a * 'a t * 'a t
    with

    exception E of key;

    val empty = Leaf;

    fun lookup (Leaf, b)                = raise E b
      | lookup (Bran(a,x,t1,t2), b) =
          (case Key.compare(a,b) of
                 GREATER => lookup(t1, b)
               | EQUAL   => x
               | LESS    => lookup(t2, b));

    fun insert (Leaf, b, y)              = Bran(b, y, Leaf, Leaf)
      | insert (Bran(a,x,t1,t2), b, y) =
          (case Key.compare(a,b) of
                 GREATER => Bran(a, x, insert(t1,b,y), t2)
               | EQUAL   => raise E b
               | LESS    => Bran(a, x, t1, insert(t2,b,y)));

    fun update (Leaf, b, y)              = Bran(b, y, Leaf, Leaf)
      | update (Bran(a,x,t1,t2), b, y) =
          (case Key.compare(a,b) of
                 GREATER => Bran(a, x, update(t1,b,y), t2)
               | EQUAL   => Bran(a, y, t1, t2)
               | LESS    => Bran(a, x, t1, update(t2,b,y)));

  end

  end;
```

Dictionaries can be created and searched. Here, an infix operator eliminates awkward nested calls to *update*:

```
infix |> ;
fun (d |> (k,x)) = StringDict.update(d,k,x);

val dict = StringDict.empty
                    |> ("Crecy",1346)
                    |> ("Poitiers",1356)
                    |> ("Agincourt",1415)
                    |> ("Trafalgar",1805)
                    |> ("Waterloo",1815);
> val dict = - : int StringDict.t
StringDict.lookup(dict,"Poitiers");
> 1356 : int
```

Priority queues: an example of a substructure. Section 4.16 outlined the priority queue operations by declaring signature *PRIORITY_QUEUE*, and implemented it using binary trees. The implementation had the same two flaws as that of dictionaries. Instead of covering the same ideas again, let us examine something new: substructures.

One difference between dictionaries and priority queues is the rôle of the ordering. The dictionary functor takes an ordering because it uses search trees; alternative implementations might take an equality test or a hashing function. But a priority queue is intrinsically concerned with an ordering: having accumulated items, it returns the smallest item first. So let us modify the result signature to make the ordering explicit:

```
signature PRIORITY_QUEUE =
  sig
  structure Item : ORDER
  type t
  val empty     : t
  val null      : t -> bool
  val insert    : Item.t * t -> t
  val min       : t -> Item.t
  val delmin     : t -> t
  val fromList  : Item.t list -> t
  val toList    : t -> Item.t list
  val sort      : Item.t list -> Item.t list
  end;
```

Signature *PRIORITY_QUEUE* specifies a substructure *Item* matching signature *ORDER*. The type of items is *Item*.*t*, while the type of priority queues is simply *t*. Thus *min*, which returns the smallest item in a queue, has type $t \rightarrow Item.t$.

Every priority queue structure carries the ordering with it. If *PQueue* is an instance of the signature, we may compare *x* with *y* by writing

> *PQueue . Item . compare* (*x*, *y*)

Under this approach, system components are specified as substructures. The previous version of *PRIORITY_QUEUE*, which many people prefer for its simplicity, specified a type *item* instead of a structure *Item*.

The corresponding functor has the following outline. Most of the body is omitted; it is similar to Figure 4.4 on page 163.

```
functor PriorityQueue (Item: ORDER) : PRIORITY_QUEUE =
  struct
  structure Item = Item;

  fun x <= y = (Item.compare(x,y) <> GREATER);

  abstype t = ...
    with
       ⋮
    end

  end;
```

The structure declaration of *Item* may seem to do nothing, because *Item* is already visible in the functor body. But the result signature requires this declaration. It is analogous to the many type declarations we have seen in structures and functors. Nested structure declarations do not have to be trivial; all the forms valid at top level are also valid inside another structure.

The functor redeclares the infix operator <= to denote 'less than or equal' on items. In Chapter 4, binary search trees used *compare* for their ordering, while priority queues used <=. It would be silly to declare distinct versions of signature *ORDER* for the two functors, or to specify all the different relational operators. Simple, uniform interfaces let modules fit together easily.

The abstype declaration can declare fresh tree constructors, as in *Dictionary*. Or it can use the existing constructors *Lf* and *Br* (declared at top level in Section 4.13) by declaring a dummy constructor, as in type *queue*1 above.

Exercise 7.17 Write a new version of functor *Dictionary*, representing a dictionary by a list of (*key*, *item*) pairs ordered by the keys.

Exercise 7.18 Complete the abstype declaration above, trying both alternatives. Which one do you prefer?

Exercise 7.19 Write a new version of functor *PriorityQueue*, representing a priority queue by an increasing list instead of a binary tree.

Exercise 7.20 Write a functor *Sorting* whose argument is an instance of signature *ORDER* and whose result implements both quick sort and merge sort. What is the point of providing more than one sorting algorithm?

Building large systems using modules

Through numerous small examples we have surveyed the basic features of the modules language. We have seen a variety of uses of structures:

- The library structure *List* holds related declarations, but more can be declared in terms of the list constructors.
- Structure *AbsQueue3* exports an abstract type together with all its primitive operations. Further queue operations can be expressed only in terms of those.
- The *ZSP* structures serve as the arguments or results of a functor. They have only a few components, namely those operations that are pertinent to the functor.

A large system ought be organized into hundreds of small structures such as those above. The organization should be hierarchical: major subsystems should be implemented as structures whose components are structures of the layer below. More chaotic programmers may find themselves presiding over a few huge structures, each consisting of hundreds or thousands of components.

A well-organized system will have many small signatures. Component specifications will obey strict naming conventions. In a group project, team members will have to agree upon each signature. Subsequent changes to signatures must be controlled rigorously.

The system will include some functors, possibly many. If the major subsystems are implemented independently, they will all have to be functors.

The modules language contains constructs, many of them obscure, that make all these working practices possible. So let us take a closer look at modules.

7.11 *Functors with multiple arguments*

An ML function takes only one argument. Multiple arguments are usually packaged as a tuple. Alternatively, they can be packaged as a record. Higher-order functions can express multiple arguments through the device of currying.

A functor also takes only one argument. Multiple arguments are packaged as a structure, which is analogous to passing a function's arguments as a record. The syntax is clumsy but workable. Some compilers extend Standard ML by providing higher-order functors, which allow currying.

A functor for lexicographic orderings. Our first example is a two-argument functor. If $<_\alpha$ is an ordering on type α and $<_\beta$ is an ordering on type β then the **lexicographic ordering** $<_{\alpha \times \beta}$ on type $\alpha \times \beta$ is defined by

$$(a', b') <_{\alpha \times \beta} (a, b) \text{ if and only if } a' <_\alpha a \text{ or } (a' = a \text{ and } b' <_\beta b).$$

The functor *LexOrder* has result signature *ORDER*. It takes two formal parameters: the structures *O1* and *O2*, also of signature *ORDER*. Its declaration illustrates ML's general syntax for functor headings:

```
functor LexOrder (structure O1: ORDER
                  structure O2: ORDER) : ORDER =
   struct
   type t = O1.t * O2.t;
   fun compare ((x1,y1), (x2,y2)) =
       (case O1.compare (x1,x2) of
            EQUAL => O2.compare (y1,y2)
          | ord    => ord)
   end;
```

The formal parameter list is simply a signature specification — a signature, but without the `sig` and `end` brackets. The specified components are visible in the functor body. The functor may be applied to any structure matching the specification: any structure containing two substructures *O1* and *O2* that match signature *ORDER*. The structure can be given by any structure expression, including another functor application.

Structure *StringOrder* has been declared above, and *IntegerOrder* can be declared similarly. We can supply those two arguments to the functor like this:

```
structure StringIntOrd = LexOrder(structure O1=StringOrder
                                  structure O2=IntegerOrder);
> structure StringIntOrd : ORDER
```

An argument consisting of a list of declarations is regarded as a structure expression. The multiple arguments form the body of the structure, and we may omit the `struct` and `end` brackets.

A demonstration will remind us of the functor's purpose. Combining the orderings on strings and integers yields an ordering on (string, integer) pairs. The ordering on strings takes precedence over that on integers.

Figure 7.3 *A dictionary functor using association lists*

```
functor AssocList (eqtype key) : DICTIONARY =
  struct
  type key  = key;
  type 'a t = (key * 'a) list;

  exception E of key;

  val empty = [];

  fun lookup ((a,x)::pairs, b) = if a=b then x
                                        else lookup(pairs, b)
    | lookup ([], b)           = raise E b;

  fun insert ((a,x)::pairs, b, y) = if a=b then raise E b
                                          else (a,x)::insert(pairs, b, y)
    | insert ([], b, y)           = [(b,y)];

  fun update (pairs, b, y) = (b,y)::pairs;

  end;
```

```
StringIntOrd.compare (("Edward", 3), ("Henry", 2));
> LESS : order
StringIntOrd.compare (("Henry", 6), ("Henry", 6));
> EQUAL : order
StringIntOrd.compare (("Henry", 6), ("Henry", 5));
> GREATER : order
```

Association lists; the `eqtype` *specification.* ML's functor syntax for multiple arguments does not require those arguments to be structures. They can be anything that a signature can specify, including types, values and exceptions.

The following example demonstrates the `eqtype` specification as well as the general functor syntax. We have previously implemented dictionaries as binary search trees. Lists of pairs are a simpler but slower representation. As in Section 3.16, the lookup operation compares keys using equality.

An `eqtype` specification may appear in any signature. It specifies types that admit equality. A structure only matches the signature if it declares actual types that really do admit equality. Within a functor body, equality testing is permitted on types specified by `eqtype`.

The functor's formal parameter list is a signature specification (Figure 7.3). It specifies one argument, an equality type. The general functor syntax lets us view *AssocList* as a functor whose formal parameter is a type. Because type *key* is specified as an `eqtype`, it admits equality testing within *AssocList*. Here are two functor applications:

```
structure StringIntAList = AssocList (type key = string*int);
> structure StringIntAList : DICTIONARY

structure FunctionAList = AssocList (type key = int->int);
> Error: type key must be an equality type
```

We may apply the functor to *string* × *int* because this type admits equality. The type *int* → *int* is rejected.

Functors with no arguments. The **empty structure** consists of no components:

```
struct end
```

Its signature is the **empty signature**:

```
sig end
```

The empty structure is mainly used as the argument of a functor. There it is analogous to the empty tuple (), which is mainly used when a function does not depend on the value of its argument. Recall the use of a function to represent the tail of a sequence (Section 5.12). Null arguments are also used with imperative programming. Our functor example involves references, which are discussed in Chapter 8.

Functor *MakeCell* takes a null argument. Its empty formal parameter list constitutes an empty signature. Every time *MakeCell* is called, it allocates a fresh reference cell and returns it as part of a structure. The cell initially contains 0:

```
functor MakeCell () =  struct  val cell = ref 0  end;
> functor MakeCell : <sig>
```

Here are two functor invocations. The empty actual parameter list constitutes the body of an empty structure.

```
structure C1 = MakeCell ()
and        C2 = MakeCell ();
> structure C1 : sig val cell : int ref end
> structure C2 : sig val cell : int ref end
```

Structures *C*1 and *C*2 have been created in the same way, but they contain distinct reference cells. Let us store a 1 in *C*1's cell, then inspect both of them:

```
C1.cell := 1;
> () : unit
C1.cell;
> ref 1 : int ref
C2.cell;
> ref 0 : int ref
```

The cells hold different integers. Because *MakeCell* is a functor, and not just a structure, it can allocate as many distinct cells as required.

⚠ *Functor syntax confusion.* The general functor syntax, with a signature specification in the functor heading, handles any number of arguments. But what if we have exactly one argument, a structure? We could use the primitive functor syntax; it is more concise and direct than the general syntax, which creates another structure. On the other hand, using both syntaxes in a program may lead to confusion. All our early examples used the primitive syntax:

```
functor TestQueue  (Q: QUEUE) ...
```

A different programmer might have used the general syntax:

```
functor TestQueue2 (structure Q: QUEUE) ...
```

These declarations differ only by the keyword `structure` in the formal parameter list, which might be overlooked. To avoid an error message, each functor should be invoked with the corresponding argument syntax:

```
TestQueue   (Queue3)
TestQueue2 (structure Q = Queue3)
```

For uniformity's sake, some programmers prefer to use the general syntax exclusively.

Exercise 7.21   Write a version of *AssocList* that does not involve `eqtype`. Instead, it should employ a signature similar to *ORDER*.

Exercise 7.22   Functor *AssocList* does not hide the representation of dictionaries; write a version that declares an abstract type.

Exercise 7.23   In a partial ordering, some pairs of elements may be unrelated. Signifying this outcome by *EQUAL* is not satisfactory in general; it would give the wrong results for the definition of lexicographic ordering. John Reppy suggests representing outcomes of comparisons by values of type *order option*, using *NONE* to signify 'unrelated.' Declare the signature *PORDER* for partial orderings, and the functor *LexPOrder* for combining partial orderings, by analogy with *ORDER* and *LexOrder*.

Exercise 7.24   (Continuing the previous exercise.) If α is a type and $<_\beta$ is a partial ordering on type β and f is a function of type $\alpha \to \beta$ then we can define a partial ordering $<$ over type α by $x' < x$ if and only if $f(x') <_\beta f(x)$. (Note that $f(x') = f(x)$ need not imply $x' = x$.) Declare a three-argument functor that implements this definition.

Exercise 7.25   Which structures are instances of the empty signature? In other words, which structures are legal arguments to functor *MakeCell*?

7.12   *Sharing constraints*

When modules are combined to form a larger one, special care may be needed to ensure that the components fit together. Consider the problem of combining dictionaries and priority queues, ensuring that their types agree.

Above we applied the functor *Dictionary* to the argument *StringOrder*, creating the structure *StringDict*. We then declared *dict* to be a dictionary indexed by strings. We can similarly apply *PriorityQueue* to *StringOrder*, creating a structure for priority queues of strings.

```
structure StringPQueue = PriorityQueue (StringOrder);
> structure StringPQueue : PRIORITY_QUEUE
```

Let us now declare *pq* to be a priority queue of strings:

```
StringPQueue.insert("Agincourt", StringPQueue.empty);
> - : StringPQueue.t
StringPQueue.insert("Crecy", it);
> - : StringPQueue.t
val pq = StringPQueue.insert("Poitiers", it);
> val pq = - : StringPQueue.t
```

Since elements of *pq* are strings, and *dict* is indexed by strings, the least element of *pq* may serve as a search key into *dict*.

```
StringDict.lookup(dict, StringPQueue.min pq);
> 1356 : int
```

We have used dictionaries and priority queues together, but only for type *string*. Generalizing this expression to an arbitrary ordered type requires a functor. In the functor body, the expression has the form

```
Dict.lookup(dict, PQueue.min pq)
```

where *PQueue* and *Dict* are structures matching signatures *PRIORITY_QUEUE* and *DICTIONARY*, respectively. But do the types agree?

$$PQueue.min : PQueue.t \rightarrow PQueue.Item.t$$

$$Dict.lookup : \alpha\ Dict.t \times Dict.key \rightarrow \alpha$$

The call of *Dict . lookup* is permissible only if *PQueue . Item . t* is the same type as *Dict . key*. One way to ensure this is for the functor to build the structures *PQueue* and *Dict* itself. The following functor takes an ordered type as an argument, and supplies it to functors *PriorityQueue* and *Dictionary*. Our expression appears as the body of function *lookmin*:

```
functor Join1 (Order: ORDER) =
  struct
  structure PQueue = PriorityQueue (Order);
  structure Dict   = Dictionary   (Order);

  fun lookmin(dict, pq) = Dict.lookup(dict, PQueue.min pq);

  end;
```

It is often useful for one functor to call another. But functor *Join*1 does not combine existing structures: it makes new ones. This approach could create many duplicate structures.

Our functor should take existing structures *PQueue* and *Dict*, checking that their types are compatible. A ***sharing constraint*** can compel types to agree:

```
functor Join2 (structure PQueue :  PRIORITY_QUEUE
               structure Dict   :  DICTIONARY
               sharing type PQueue.Item.t = Dict.key) =
  struct
  fun lookmin(dict, pq) = Dict.lookup(dict, PQueue.min pq);
  end;
```

We have reverted to the multiple-argument functor syntax; sharing constraints are a form of signature specification. In the body of the functor, the constraint guarantees that the two types are identical. The type checker therefore accepts the declaration of *lookmin*. When the functor is applied to actual structures, the ML compiler insists that the two types really are the same.

To demonstrate the functor, we shall need priority queues and dictionaries of integers:

```
structure IntegerPQueue = PriorityQueue (IntegerOrder);
> structure IntegerPQueue : PRIORITY_QUEUE
structure IntegerDict = Dictionary (IntegerOrder);
> structure IntegerDict : DICTIONARY
```

Two string-based structures can be combined, and so can two integer-based structures. In each case, function *lookmin* takes a dictionary and a priority queue based on the same type.

```
structure StringCom = Join2 (structure PQueue = StringPQueue
                             structure Dict   = StringDict);
> structure StringCom
> : sig
>     val lookmin: 'a StringDict.t * StringPQueue.t -> 'a
>   end

structure IntegerCom = Join2 (structure PQueue = IntegerPQueue
                              structure Dict   = IntegerDict);
> structure IntegerCom
> : sig
>     val lookmin: 'a IntegerDict.t * IntegerPQueue.t -> 'a
>   end
```

But if we try to mix the types, the compiler rejects the declaration:

```
structure Bad = Join2 (structure PQueue = IntegerPQueue
                       structure Dict   = StringDict);
> Error: type sharing violation
>    StringDict.key # IntegerPQueue.Item.t
```

Sharing constraints on structures. When functors combine system components, common substructures may need sharing constraints. Here is a sketch of a typical situation. Structure *In* inputs problems; structure *Out* outputs solutions. The two components communicate via a priority queue of goals, in structure *PQueue*. Structure *Main* coordinates the program via *In* and *Out*.

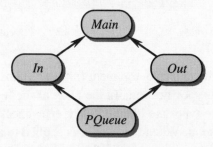

Suppose that *In* and *Out* match the following signatures:

```
signature IN =
  sig
  structure PQueue: PRIORITY_QUEUE
  type problem
  val  goals: problem -> PQueue.t
  end;
```

```
signature OUT =
  sig
  structure PQueue: PRIORITY_QUEUE
  type solution
  val   solve: PQueue.t -> solution
  end;
```

A functor to combine *In* and *Out* might look like this:

```
functor MainFunctor (structure In: IN and Out: OUT
                     sharing In.PQueue = Out.PQueue) =
  struct
  fun tackle(p) = Out.solve(In.goals p)
  end;
```

Because the structures *In . PQueue* and *Out . PQueue* are declared as sharing, the types *In . PQueue . t* and *Out . PQueue . t* are identical in the functor body. (Observe the use of and to specify two structures concisely.)

When building the system, put the same structure *PQueue* into *In* and *Out*. The functor *MainFunctor* will then accept *In* and *Out* as arguments, since they will satisfy the sharing constraint.

Understanding sharing constraints. Sharing is one of the most difficult aspects of ML modules. Although sharing constraints may appear in any signature, they are only necessary if the signature specifies a functor argument. The more functors you use, the more sharing constraints you will need.

A type error is the usual warning that a sharing constraint might be necessary. In our previous example, omitting the constraint might cause the error 'type conflict: expected *In . PQueue . t*, found *Out . PQueue . t*.' Unfortunately, some compilers produce cryptic error messages.

The type error could be eliminated by imposing a sharing constraint on those types:

```
sharing type In.PQueue.t = Out.PQueue.t
```

The structure sharing constraint actually used in *MainFunctor* is stronger: it implies type sharing all the way down. It implies that the types *In . PQueue . Item . t* and *Out . PQueue . Item . t* are also shared.

ML enforces sharing constraints by comparing the types' identities. Each new datatype or abstract type is regarded as distinct from all previously existing types.

```
structure DT1 = struct datatype t = C end;
structure DT2 = struct datatype t = C end;
structure DT3 = struct type t = DT1.t end;
```

The types *DT*1.*t* and *DT*2.*t* are distinct, even though they arise from identical `datatype` declarations. Type abbreviations preserve the identity, so types *DT*1.*t* and *DT*3.*t* are the same.

Exercise 7.26   Explain ML's response to the following declarations.

```
signature TYPE = sig type t end;
functor Funny (structure A: TYPE and B: TYPE
               sharing A=B) = A;
structure S1 = Funny (structure A=DT1 and B=DT1);
structure S2 = Funny (structure A=DT2 and B=DT2);
structure S3 = Funny (structure A=S1  and B=S2);
```

Exercise 7.27   Suppose that the functors *Input* and *Output* are declared as follows:

```
functor Input (structure PQueue: PRIORITY_QUEUE): IN =
  struct
  structure PQueue = PQueue;
  fun goals ... ;
  end;
functor Output (structure PQueue: PRIORITY_QUEUE): OUT =
  struct
  structure PQueue = PQueue;
  fun solve ... ;
  end;
```

By applying these functors, declare structures that may be given to *MainFunctor*. Then declare structures that have the required signatures but violate the functor's sharing constraint.

Exercise 7.28   The functors *Input* and *Output* declared above incorporate the formal parameter *PQueue* into the result structure. Modify them to generate a fresh instance of *PRIORITY_QUEUE* instead. How will this affect *MainFunctor*?

7.13   *Fully-functorial programming*

It is a truism that one should never declare a procedure that is called only once. We have never declared a functor to be called only once. Each formal parameter has had a choice of actual parameters; for example, the parameter *Order* could be instantiated by *StringOrder* or *IntegerOrder*. Non-generic program units have been coded as structures, not as functors.

But declaring procedures is now regarded as good style, even if they are called only once. There are good reasons for declaring more functors than are strictly necessary. Some programmers code almost entirely with functors, writing structures only to supply as arguments to functors. Their functors and signatures are self-contained: they refer only to other signatures and to components of the standard library.

If all program units are coded as functors then they can be written and compiled separately. First, the signatures are declared; then, the functors are coded. When a functor is compiled, error messages may reveal mistakes and omissions in the signatures. Revised signatures can be checked by recompiling the functors.

The functors may be coded in any order. Each functor refers to signatures, but not to structures or other functors. Some people prefer to code from the top down, others from the bottom up. Several programmers can code their functors independently.

Once all the functors have been written and compiled, applying them generates a structure for each program unit. The final structure contains the executable program. A functor can be modified, recompiled and a new system built, without recompiling the other functors, provided no signatures have changed. Applying the functors amounts to linking the program units. Different configurations of a system can be built.

Functors for binary trees. From Section 4.13 onwards we declared structures for binary trees, flexible arrays, etc. We even declared *tree* as a top level datatype. The fully-functorial style requires every program unit to be specified by a self-contained signature.

We must now declare a signature for binary trees. The signature must specify the datatype *tree*, as it will not be declared at top level.

```
signature TREE =
  sig
  datatype 'a tree = Lf  |  Br of 'a * 'a tree * 'a tree
  val size   : 'a tree -> int
  val depth  : 'a tree -> int
  val reflect : 'a tree -> 'a tree
    ⋮
  end;
```

We must declare a signature for the Braun array operations. The signature specifies *Tree* as a substructure to provide access to type *tree*.[2]

---

[2] It could instead specify type *tree* directly; see Section 7.15.

```
signature BRAUN =
  sig
  structure Tree: TREE
  val sub    : 'a Tree.tree * int -> 'a
  val update : 'a Tree.tree * int * 'a -> 'a Tree.tree
  val delete : 'a Tree.tree * int -> 'a Tree.tree
    ⋮
  end;
```

Signature *FLEXARRAY* (Section 4.15) is self-contained, as it depends only on the standard type *int*. Signatures *ORDER* and *PRIORITY_QUEUE* (Section 7.10) are also self-contained. Since a signature may refer to others, the declarations must be made in a correct order: *TREE* must be declared before *BRAUN*, and *ORDER* before *PRIORITY_QUEUE*.

Since our functors do not refer to each other, they can be declared in any order. The functor *PriorityQueue* can be declared now, even if its implementation relies on binary trees. The functor is self-contained: it takes a binary tree structure as a formal parameter, *Tree*, and uses it for access to the tree operations:

```
functor PriorityQueue (structure Order : ORDER
                        structure Tree  : TREE)
        : PRIORITY_QUEUE =
    ⋮
  abstype t = PQ of Item.t Tree.tree
    ⋮
```

The structure *Flex* (see page 158) can be turned into a functor *FlexArray* taking *Braun* as its formal parameter. The body of the functor resembles the original structure declaration. But the tree operations are now components of the substructure *Braun . Tree*.

```
functor FlexArray (Braun: BRAUN) : FLEXARRAY =
    ⋮
  val empty = Array(Braun.Tree.Lf,0);
    ⋮
```

The structure *Braun* can similarly be turned into a functor *BraunFunctor* taking *Tree* as its formal parameter.

```
functor BraunFunctor (Tree: TREE) : BRAUN = ...
```

Even structure *Tree* can be made into a functor: taking the null parameter.

```
functor TreeFunctor () : TREE = struct ...   end;
```

Now all the functors have been declared.

Linking the functors together. The final phase, after all the code has been written, is to apply the functors. Each structure is built by applying a functor to previously created structures. To begin, applying *TreeFunctor* to the empty argument list generates the structure *Tree*.

```
structure Tree = TreeFunctor ();
> structure Tree : TREE
```

Functor applications create the structures *Braun* and *Flex*:

```
structure Braun = BraunFunctor (Tree);
structure Flex  = FlexArray (Braun);
```

The structure *StringOrder* is declared as it was above:

```
structure StringOrder = ... ;
```

Now structure *StringPQ* can be declared, as before, by functor application:

```
structure StringPQueue =
    PriorityQueue (structure Item = StringOrder
                   structure Tree = Tree);
```

Figure 7.4 portrays the complete system, with structures as rounded boxes and functors as rectangles. Most of the structures were created by functors; only *StringOrder* was written directly.

The drawbacks of the fully-functorial style should be evident. All the functor declarations clutter the code; even inventing names for them is hard. Sharing constraints multiply. If we continue this example, we can expect many constraints to ensure that structures share the same *Tree* substructure. With some ML systems, your compiled code may be twice as large as it should be, because it exists both as functors and as structures.

A good compromise is to use functors for all major program units: those that must be coded independently. Many of them will be generic anyway. Lower-level units can be declared as structures. Biagioni *et al.* (1994) have organized the layers of a large networking system using signatures and functors; components can be joined in various ways to meet specialized requirements.

ⓘ *When is a signature self-contained?* Names introduced by a specification become visible in the rest of the signature. Signature *TREE* specifies the type *tree* and then uses it, and type *int*, to specify the type of *size*. Predefined names like *int* and the standard library structures are said to be **pervasive**: they are visible everywhere. A name that occurs in a signature and that has not been specified there is said to be *free* in that signature. The only name occurring free in *TREE* is *int*.

Figure 7.4 *Structures and functors involving trees*

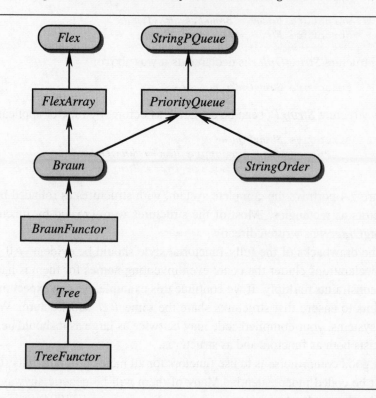

David MacQueen wrote the original proposal for Standard ML modules (in Harper *et al.* (1986)). He proposed that signatures could not refer to names declared elsewhere in a program, except names of other signatures. A signature could refer to structures specified within the same signature, but not to free-standing structures. Thus, every signature was completely self-contained, and every structure carried with it the structures and types it depended upon. This restriction, the ***signature closure rule***, was eventually relaxed to give programmers greater freedom.

In the fully-functorial style, the structures are declared last of all. Signatures will naturally obey the signature closure rule, as there will be no structures for them to refer to. The only names free in *BRAUN* are the pervasive type *int* and the signature *TREE*. If the line

```
    structure Tree: TREE
```

were removed, the signature would depend on some structure *Tree* already declared, since it mentions *Tree.tree* in the types of the functions. This is an acceptable programming style, but it is not the fully-functorial style, and it violates the signature closure rule.

ℹ️ *Functors and signature constraints.* In the fully-functorial style of programming, each functor refers to structures only as formal parameters. Nothing is known about an argument structure except its signature, just as when an actual structure is given an opaque signature constraint.

Suppose a functor's formal parameters include a structure *Dict* of signature *DICTIONARY*. In the functor body, type α *Dict.t* behaves like an abstract type: it has no constructors to allow pattern-matching, and equality testing is forbidden. Type *Dict.key* is similarly abstract; unless a sharing constraint equates it with some other type, we shall be unable to call *Dict.lookup*.

Exercise 7.29 Write a functor with no formal parameters and result signature *QUEUE*, implementing Representation 3 of queues.

Exercise 7.30 Specify a signature *SEQUENCE* for an abstract type of lazy lists, and implement the type by writing a functor with result signature *SEQUENCE*. Write a functor that takes instances of *QUEUE* and *SEQUENCE*, and declares search functions like *depthFirst* and *breadthFirst* (Section 5.17).

Exercise 7.31 List which names appear free in signatures *QUEUE1*, *QUEUE2*, *QUEUE3*, *DICTIONARY* (Section 4.14) and *FLEXARRAY* (Section 4.15).

7.14   *The open declaration*

Compound names get cumbersome when structures are nested. In the body of functor *FlexArray*, the type of binary trees is called *Braun.Tree.tree* and its constructors are called *Braun.Tree.Lf* and *Braun.Tree.Br*. The type and its constructors behave in the normal manner, but any patterns written using the constructor notation are likely to be unreadable.

Although the fully-functorial style makes the problem worse, long compound names can arise in any large program. Fortunately there are many ways of abbreviating such names.

Opening a structure declares its items so that they are known by their simple names. The syntax of an open declaration is

$$\texttt{open}\ \ Id$$

where *Id* is the (possibly compound) name of a structure. Only one level of a structure is opened at a time. After declaring

```
open Braun;
```

we may write *Tree* and *Tree.Lf* instead of *Braun.Tree* and *Braun.Tree.Lf*. If we go on to declare

```
open Tree;
```

then we may write *Lf* and *Br* instead of *Tree.Lf* and *Tree.Br*. In the scope of this open declaration, *Lf* and *Br* denote constructors and may not be redeclared as values.

Local open declarations. Since open is a declaration, a let or local construct can restrict its scope. Recall that let makes a declaration that is private to an expression, while local (Section 2.18) makes a declaration that is private to another declaration.

Here is an example of a local open declaration that also demonstrates how open can be misused. Functor *FlexArray* might use local as follows:

```
functor FlexArray (Braun: BRAUN) : FLEXARRAY =
  struct
    local open Braun Braun.Tree
    in
    datatype 'a array = Array of 'a tree * int;
    val empty = Array(Lf,0);
    fun length (Array(_,n)) = n;
    fun sub    ...
    fun update ...
    fun delete ...
    fun loext  ...
    fun lorem  ...
  end
end;
```

The open declaration makes the components of *Braun* and *Braun . Tree* visible, while local restricts their scope to the functor body. We no longer need to write compound names.

Or do we? Recall that the functor implements flexible arrays in terms of Braun arrays. Subscripting on flexible arrays uses subscripting on Braun arrays. Both operations are called *sub*; to avoid a name clash we must write a compound name:

```
fun sub (Array(t,n), k) =
    if 0<=k andalso k<n then Braun.sub(t,k+1)
    else raise Subscript;
```

Omitting the prefix *Braun .* above would create a spurious recursive call to *sub*, and a type error. So opening *Braun* does not accomplish anything. There is no need to open *Braun . Tree* either, as the functor body uses this prefix only twice.

Structure expressions using let. A better candidate for open is *BraunFunctor*, which uses the tree constructors extensively (see Figure 7.5 on the following page). Opening structure *Tree* spares us from writing compound names for the constructors in expressions such as *Br* (*w* , *Lf* , *Lf*) .

The functor uses a new let construct, one that operates on structures. Suppose the *Str* is a structure expression requiring the declaration *D*. Then evaluating the structure expression

```
let D in Str end
```

yields the result of evaluating *Str*, while delimiting the scope of *D*. If *Str* has the form struct ... end, as does the body of *BraunFunctor*, then we can equivalently write (as in the previous example)

```
struct
local D in ... end
end
```

However, we can use let with other structure expressions, such as functor applications. It is especially useful when a structure is used more than once:

```
functor QuadOrder (O: ORDER) : ORDER =
    let structure OO = LexOrder (structure O1 = O
                                 structure O2 = O)
    in   LexOrder (structure O1 = OO
                   structure O2 = OO)
    end;
```

Figure 7.5 *Example of* let *open in a functor body*

```
functor BraunFunctor (Tree: TREE) : BRAUN =
  let open Tree in
    struct
    structure Tree = Tree;

    fun sub (Lf, _)            = raise Subscript
      | sub (Br(v,t1,t2), k) =
          if k = 1 then v
          else if k mod 2 = 0
                  then sub (t1, k div 2)
                  else sub (t2, k div 2);

    fun update (Lf, k, w)         =
          if k = 1 then Br (w, Lf, Lf)
          else raise Subscript
      | update (Br(v,t1,t2), k, w) =
          if k = 1 then Br (w, t1, t2)
          else if k mod 2 = 0
                  then Br (v,  update(t1, k div 2, w),  t2)
                  else Br (v,  t1,  update(t2, k div 2, w));

    fun delete (Lf, n)          = raise Subscript
      | delete (Br(v,t1,t2), n) =
          if n = 1 then Lf
          else if n mod 2 = 0
                  then Br (v,  delete(t1, n div 2),  t2)
                  else Br (v,  t1,  delete(t2, n div 2));

    fun loext (Lf, w)          = Br(w, Lf, Lf)
      | loext (Br(v,t1,t2), w) = Br(w, loext(t2,v),  t1);

    fun lorem Lf                            = raise Size
      | lorem (Br(_,Lf,_))                 = Lf
      | lorem (Br(_, t1 as Br(v,_,_),  t2)) = Br(v,  t2, lorem t1);

    end
  end;
```

Functor *QuadOrder* takes an ordered structure and returns the lexicographic ordering for quadruples of the form $((w, x), (y, z))$. Internally it creates the structure *OO*, which defines the ordering for pairs.

⚠️ *Infix operators in structures.* Infix directives issued inside a structure have no effect outside. When a structure is opened, its names are made visible as ordinary identifiers, not as infix operators; restoring their infix status requires new infix directives. A compound name can never become an infix operator; only simple names are permitted in an infix directive.

Top level infix directives, issued outside any structure, have global scope. Opening a structure can bind or re-bind these top level operators.

⚠️ *Re-binding identifiers using* open. Opening several structures can declare hundreds of names at a stroke. Unless these names are descriptive, we may not be able to remember which structure they belong to. Using open to override existing bindings can be particularly confusing.

ML systems may provide the library structures *Real32*, *Real64*, *Real96*, etc., which implement the standard floating point operations in various precisions. The structures match signature *REAL*, which specifies a type *real* and operators such as +, -, * and /.

Compound names make these structures hard to use. The 64-bit version of $(a/x+x)/y$ is incomprehensible:

```
Real64./ (Real64.+ (Real64./(a,x), x), y)
```

A local open declaration restores readability:

```
let open Real64 in (a/x + x) / y end
```

Unfortunately, opening *Real64* redeclares all the numeric operators, obliterating their overloading. We can no longer write integer expressions such as $n+1$. The integer operations are still accessible via their home structure: we can still write `Int.+(n,1)`. But is this an improvement?

Opening *Real64* at top level is plainly wrong. There is no way of restoring the overloading. It is better to open *Real64* with a small scope, as above, or to declare new infix operators and bind them to the 64-bit functions.

Alternatives to open. As these examples show, open can cause obscurity. Our structures have been designed to take advantage of compound names. The simple names of the items are too short. Compound names like *Braun.sub* and *Flex.sub* do not merely avoid clashes; they are informative and reinforce our knowledge of the program's organization.

We can shorten compound names by declaring abbreviations, without using open. Our declaration of functor *FlexArray* can be improved:

```
functor FlexArray (Braun: BRAUN) : FLEXARRAY =
  struct
    local structure T = Braun.Tree
    in
    datatype 'a array = Array of 'a T.tree * int;
    val empty = Array(T.Lf,0);
    end
      ⋮
  end;
```

Instead of opening *Braun . Tree*, we declare structure *T* to abbreviate it. Having to write *T . tree* is perfectly acceptable, and patterns expressed using *T . Lf* and *T . Br* can be succinct.

Some programmers will regard compound identifiers as unacceptable, at least for heavily used items. But there is no need to open a large module if only a few of the items are really needed. An open declaration can be replaced by separate abbreviations:

```
type 'a queue     = 'a Queue.t;
val hd            = Queue.hd;
exception QEmpty  = Queue.E;
```

The last line makes *QEmpty* a synonym for *Queue . E*; it is a constructor and may even appear in exception handlers. In such exception bindings, the right-hand side must be the name of an exception constructor.

Selective use of open. In Section 4.13 we declared datatype *tree* at top level to avoid having compound constructor names. That was poor style; every type and variable ought to belong to a home structure. Opening the full tree structure is equally undesirable. And there is no analogue of exception bindings for exporting individual datatype constructors.

We must use open, but we can do so selectively. Core declarations — in this case, the datatype *tree* and the function *depth* — can be declared in a substructure:

```
structure Tree =
  struct

  structure Export =
    struct
    datatype 'a tree = Lf
                     | Br of 'a * 'a tree * 'a tree;

    fun depth Lf              = 0
      | depth (Br(v,t1,t2)) = 1 + Int.max (depth t1, depth t2);
    end;
```

```
open Export;

fun size Lf           = 0
  | size (Br(v,t1,t2)) = 1 + size t1 + size t2;
    ⋮
end;
```

The substructure *Export* contains the items that are to be exported to top level. It is immediately opened, exporting the items to the main structure. Later we can export the core items, leaving the others accessible only by compound names:

```
open Tree.Export;
depth Lf;
> 0 : int
Tree.size Lf;
> 0 : int
```

A variation on this idea is to declare the structure of core items at top level. It might be called *TreeCore*, with its own signature *TREECORE*. Other structures and signatures for trees could refer to the core ones.

Exercise 7.32 Explain why the declaration of *StrangePQueue* is valid.

```
functor StrangePQueue () =
    let structure UsedTwice = struct open StringOrder Tree end
    in  PriorityQueue (structure Item = UsedTwice
                       structure Tree = UsedTwice)
    end;
```

Exercise 7.33 What is the effect of the following declaration?

```
open Queue3;   open Queue2;
```

Exercise 7.34 What is wrong with the following attempt at multiple-precision arithmetic?

```
functor MultiplePrecision (F: REAL) =
    struct
    fun half x = F./(x, 2.0)
    end;
```

7.15   Signatures and substructures

Complex programs require complex signatures. When structures are nested, their signatures can become cluttered with excessively long compound names. Suppose we declare a signature for pairs of Braun arrays, specifying a substructure matching signature *BRAUN*:

```
signature BRAUNPAIR0 =
  sig
  structure Braun: BRAUN
  val zip: 'a Braun.Tree.tree * 'b Braun.Tree.tree ->
            ('a*'b) Braun.Tree.tree
    ⋮
  end;
```

The compound names render the type of *zip* unreadable. As with structures, there are a number of approaches to simplifying such signatures.

Avoiding substructures. Strictly speaking, a signature need never specify substructures, even if it must be self-contained. Instead, it can specify all the types appearing in its `val` specifications. Omitting structure *Braun* from our signature makes it more readable:

```
signature BRAUNPAIR1 =
  sig
  type 'a tree
  val zip: 'a tree * 'b tree -> ('a*'b) tree
    ⋮
  end;
```

This signature specifies considerably less than *BRAUNPAIR0*. All the components of *Braun* are missing, and *tree* is specified as a mere `type`. Specifying *tree* as a `datatype` would have required copying its entire specification from signature *TREE*, an unpleasant duplication.

A signature should be as small as possible, so *BRAUNPAIR1* may be ideal. It is, provided the components it specifies can be used independently of those in *Braun*; in other words, it should be self-contained in use, rather than in the formal sense of having no free identifiers.

Sharing constraints in a signature. A signature should be as small as possible, but it should not be even smaller. If every instance of *BRAUNPAIR1* must be accompanied by an instance of *BRAUN*, then identifying their *tree* components will require a sharing constraint. Every functor heading of the form

```
functor PairFunctor0 (BP: BRAUNPAIR0)
```

could become more than twice as long:

```
functor PairFunctor1 (structure Braun: BRAUN
                      structure BP: BRAUNPAIR1
                      sharing type Braun.Tree.tree = BP.tree)
```

The solution is to specify both substructure *Braun* and type *tree* in the same signature, with a sharing constraint to relate them:

```
signature BRAUNPAIR2 =
  sig
  structure Braun: BRAUN
  type 'a tree
  sharing type tree = Braun.Tree.tree
  val zip: 'a tree * 'b tree -> ('a*'b) tree
    ⋮
  end;
```

A structure that matches this signature must declare type α *tree* to satisfy the sharing constraint:

```
type 'a tree = 'a Braun.Tree.tree
```

We have the advantages of both the previous approaches. The signature is readable and complete, allowing simple functor headings like that of *PairFunctor*0.

Type abbreviations in signatures. Type sharing constraints are adequate for the present purpose, namely to shorten compound names in signatures. But they cannot specify arbitrary type abbreviations. Sharing constraints apply to identifiers, not to types; the sharing specification is

```
tree = Braun.Tree.tree
```

and not

```
'a tree = 'a Braun.Tree.tree
```

Signatures may make type abbreviations. This is yet another way of shortening those compound names:

```
signature BRAUNPAIR3 =
  sig
  structure Braun: BRAUN
  type 'a tree = 'a Braun.Tree.tree
  val zip: 'a tree * 'b tree -> ('a*'b) tree
  end;
```

For a structure to match this signature, it must declare an equivalent type abbreviation.

The `include` *specification.* **Including** a signature means specifying its components as belonging directly to the current signature, not to a substructure. The specification

```
include SIG
```

has the effect of writing out the contents of *SIG* without the surrounding `sig ...` `end` brackets. Our example now becomes

```
signature BRAUNPAIR4 =
  sig
  include BRAUN
  val zip: 'a Tree.tree * 'b Tree.tree -> ('a*'b) Tree.tree
  end;
```

There are compound names, but they are acceptably short because substructure *Braun* has vanished. All its components have been incorporated into the new signature. So instances of *BRAUNPAIR4* match signature *BRAUN* as well.

Including yourself in trouble. Multiple inclusion can be a powerful structuring technique. It can be combined with sharing constraints to get a limited effect of renaming. If the included signature specifies, say, types *to* and *from*, then sharing constraints can identify these types with other types in the signature (Biagioni *et al.*, 1994). The standard library uses sharing constraints in a similar fashion, sometimes to rename the components of substructures.

Avoid including signatures that have names in common: this could give an identifier repeated or conflicting specifications. Excessive use of `include` can lead to large, flat signatures, obscuring the module hierarchy. If signature *BRAUN* had itself specified

```
include TREE
```

instead of

```
structure Tree: TREE
```

then we should have no compound names at all. In a superficial sense, this would aid readability. But all the components of three different structures would be thrown together without any organization.

Reference guide to modules

This section collects the concepts of structures, signatures and functors, summarizing the modules language as a whole. It describes practically the entire language, including some of the more obscure features. First, let us review the basic definitions.

A *structure* is a collection of declarations, typically of items that serve a common purpose. These may include types, values and other structures. Since structures may be grouped into larger structures, a software system can be designed as a hierarchy. A structure can be treated as a unit, no matter how complex it is internally.

A *signature* consists of type checking information about each item declared in a structure. It lists the types; it lists the values, with their types; it lists the substructures, with their signatures. Sharing constraints identify common components of substructures. Just as different values can have the same type, different structures can have the same signature.

A *functor* is a mapping from structures to structures. The body of the functor defines a structure in terms of a formal parameter, which is specified by a signature. Applying the functor substitutes an actual structure into the body. Functors allow program units to be coded separately and can express generic units.

A *module* is either a structure or a functor.

7.16   *The syntax of signatures and structures*

This book aims to teach programming techniques, not to describe Standard ML in full. Modules involve a great deal of syntax, however; here is a systematic description of their main features.

In the syntax definitions, an optional phrase is enclosed in square brackets. A repeatable phrase (occurring at least once) is indicated informally using three dots (...). For example, in

$$\text{exception } Id_1 \left[\text{of } T_1\right] \text{ and } \dots \text{ and } Id_n \left[\text{of } T_n\right]$$

the 'of T_1' phrases are optional. The keyword and separates simultaneous declarations.

Syntax of signatures. A signature has the form

        sig *Spec* end

where a *Spec* is a specification of types, values, exceptions, structures and sharing constraints.

A value specification of the form

        val $Id_1 : T_1$ and ... and $Id_n : T_n$

specifies values named $Id_1, \dots , Id_n$ with types $T_1, \dots , T_n$, respectively. Several values and their types can be specified simultaneously.

Types may be specified (simultaneously) by

$$\text{type } \left[\mathit{TypeVars}_1\right]Id_1 \left[= T_1\right] \text{ and } \dots \text{ and } \left[\mathit{TypeVars}_n\right]Id_n \left[= T_n\right]$$

If T_i is present, for $i = 1, \dots , n$, then Id_i is specified as a type abbreviation.

Types that admit equality may be specified by

$$\texttt{eqtype} \; \left[\textit{TypeVars}_1\right]\textit{Id}_1 \; \texttt{and} \; \dots \; \texttt{and} \; \left[\textit{TypeVars}_n\right]\textit{Id}_n$$

In both `type` and `eqtype` specifications, a type is given by optional type variables (*TypeVars*) followed by an identifier, exactly as may appear on the left side of a type declaration. A `datatype` specification has the same syntax as a `datatype` declaration.

Exceptions, with optional types, can be specified by

$$\texttt{exception} \; \textit{Id}_1 \; \left[\texttt{of} \; T_1\right] \; \texttt{and} \; \dots \; \texttt{and} \; \textit{Id}_n \; \left[\texttt{of} \; T_n\right]$$

Structures, with their signatures, are specified by

$$\texttt{structure} \; \textit{Id}_1 : \textit{Sig}_1 \; \texttt{and} \; \dots \; \texttt{and} \; \textit{Id}_n : \textit{Sig}_n$$

Sharing constraints have the form

$$\texttt{sharing} \; \left[\texttt{type}\right] \; \textit{Id}_1 \; = \; \textit{Id}_2 \; = \; \dots \; = \; \textit{Id}_n$$

The identifiers $\textit{Id}_1, \dots, \textit{Id}_n$ are specified to share. If the keyword `type` is present then they must be type identifiers; otherwise they must be structure identifiers. Sharing constraints may appear in any signature; they most frequently appear in a functor's formal parameter list, which is given as a signature specification. Sharing of two structures implies sharing of their corresponding named types.

Include specifications have the form

$$\texttt{include} \; \textit{SigId}_1 \; \dots \; \textit{SigId}_n$$

Each *SigId* should be a signature identifier, and specifies the components of that signature.

ⓘ *The `where type` qualification.* A new signature form has recently been proposed, which allows us to constrain type identifiers $\textit{Id}_i$ to existing types T_i in a signature *Sig*:

$$\textit{Sig} \; \texttt{where type} \; \left[\textit{TypeVars}_1\right]\textit{Id}_1 \; = \; T_1 \; \texttt{and} \; \left[\textit{TypeVars}_n\right]\textit{Id}_n \; = \; T_n$$

This construct can be used wherever signatures are combined in elaborate ways. In conjunction with an opaque signature constraint, it provides another way of declaring abstract types. Consider this functor heading:

```
functor Dictionary (Key: ORDER)
          :> DICTIONARY where type key = Key.t
```

The functor's result signature is an abstract view of *DICTIONARY*, but with *key* constrained to be the type of sort keys specified by the argument structure *Key*. This corrects the 'all-or-nothing' limitation of opaque constraints mentioned at the end of Section 7.5. The functor body no longer has to use `abstype`.

Syntax of structures. A structure can be created by a declaration (which may declare substructures) enclosed by the brackets struct and end:

> struct *D* end

A structure can also be given by a functor application:

> *FunctorId* (*Str*)

The functor named *FunctorId* is applied to the structure *Str*. This is the primitive syntax for functor application, used in our first examples, which allows only one argument. Passing multiple arguments requires the general form of functor application, where the argument is a declaration:

> *FunctorId* (*D*)

This abbreviates the functor application

> *FunctorId* (struct *D* end)

and is analogous to writing a tuple as the argument of a function for the effect of multiple arguments.

Local declarations in a structure have the form

> let *D* in *Str* end

Evaluation performs the declaration *D* and yields the value of the structure expression *Str*. The scope of *D* is restricted to *Str*.

A structure may have a transparent or opaque signature constraint:

> *Str* : *Sig*
> *Str* :> *Sig*

7.17 *The syntax of module declarations*

Signature, structure and functor declarations are not allowed within expressions. Structures may be declared inside other structures, but functor declarations must not be nested.

Signature constraints are given in the form :>*Sig* but :*Sig* is also allowed.

A signature declaration makes the identifiers $Id_1, \ldots, Id_n$ denote the signatures $Sig_1, \ldots, Sig_n$, respectively:

> signature Id_1=Sig_1 and ... and Id_n=Sig_n

A structure declaration makes the identifier Id_i denote the structure Str_i (optionally specifying the signature Sig_i), for $1 \leq i \leq n$:

$$\texttt{structure}\ Id_1\Big[:>Sig_1\Big]=Str_1\ \texttt{and}\ \dots\ \texttt{and}\ Id_n\Big[:>Sig_n\Big]=Str_n$$

The primitive syntax for a functor declaration is

$$\texttt{functor}\ Id\ (Id':Sig')\ \Big[:>Sig\Big]\ =\ Str$$

where Id is the name of the functor, Id' and Sig' are the name and signature of the formal parameter, structure Str is the body and Sig is an optional signature constraint.

The general syntax for a functor declaration, which gives the effect of multiple arguments, has the form

$$\texttt{functor}\ Id\ (Spec)\ \Big[:>Sig\Big]\ =\ Str$$

The formal parameter list is given by the specification $Spec$. The functor still takes one argument, a structure whose signature is determined by $Spec$. The formal parameter is implicitly opened in the body of the functor, making its components visible.

Summary of main points

- Structures do not hide internal representations.
- The `abstype` declaration can be combined with structures and signatures to hide the internal details of an abstract data type.
- A functor is a structure that takes other structures as parameters.
- Functors can express generic algorithms and permit program units to be combined freely.
- Sharing constraints may be necessary to ensure that certain subcomponents of a system are identical.
- Compound names can be abbreviated by careful use of `open` declarations, among other methods.

8

Imperative Programming in ML

Functional programming has its merits, but imperative programming is here to stay. It is the most natural way to perform input and output. Some programs are specifically concerned with managing state: a chess program must keep track of where the pieces are! Some classical data structures, such as hash tables, work by updating arrays and pointers.

Standard ML's imperative features include references, arrays and commands for input and output. They support imperative programming in full generality, though with a flavour unique to ML. Looping is expressed by recursion or using a `while` construct. References behave differently from Pascal and C pointers; above all, they are secure.

Imperative features are compatible with functional programming. References and arrays can serve in functions and data structures that exhibit purely functional behaviour. We shall code sequences (lazy lists) using references to store each element. This avoids wasteful recomputation, which is a defect of the sequences of Section 5.12. We shall code functional arrays (where updating creates a new array) with the help of mutable arrays. This representation of functional arrays can be far more efficient than the binary tree approach of Section 4.15.

A typical ML program is largely functional. It retains many of the advantages of functional programming, including readability and even efficiency: garbage collection can be faster for immutable objects. Even for imperative programming, ML has advantages over conventional languages.

Chapter outline

This chapter describes reference types and arrays, with examples of their use in data structures. ML's input and output facilities are presented.

The chapter contains the following sections:

Reference types. References stand for storage locations and can be created, updated and inspected. Polymorphic references cannot be created, but polymorphic functions can use references.

References in data structures. Three large examples are presented. We modify our type of sequences to store computed elements internally. Ring buffers illustrate how references can represent linked data structures. *V*-arrays exploit imperative programming techniques in a functional data structure.

Input and output. Library functions convert between strings and basic types, such as *real*. Channels, carrying streams of characters, connect an ML program to input and output devices. Examples include date scanning, conversion to HTML, and pretty printing.

Reference types

References in ML are essentially store addresses. They correspond to the variables of C, Pascal and similar languages, and serve as pointers in linked data structures. For control structures, ML provides while-do loop commands; the if-then-else and case expressions also work for imperative programming. The section concludes by explaining the interaction between reference types and polymorphism.

8.1   *References and their operations*

All values computed during the execution of an ML program reside for some time in the machine store. To functional programmers, the store is nothing but a device inside the computer; they never have to think about the store until they run out of it. With imperative programming the store is visible. An ML reference denotes the address of a location in the store. Each location contains a value, which can be replaced using an assignment. A reference is itself a value; if x has type τ then a reference to x is written *ref x* and has type τ *ref*.

The constructor *ref* creates references. When applied to a value v, it allocates a new address with v for its initial contents, and returns a reference to this address. Although *ref* is an ML function, it is not a function in the mathematical sense because it returns a new address every time it is called.

The function !, when applied to a reference, returns its contents. This operation is called **dereferencing**. Clearly ! is not a mathematical function; its result depends upon the store.

The assignment $E_1 := E_2$ evaluates E_1, which must return a reference p, and E_2. It stores at address p the value of E_2. Syntactically, := is a function and $E_1 := E_2$ is an expression, even though it updates the store. Like most functions that change the machine's state, it returns the value () of type *unit*.

Here is a simple example of these primitives:

```
val p = ref 5 and q = ref 2;
> val p = ref 5 : int ref
> val q = ref 2 : int ref
```

The references *p* and *q* are declared with initial contents 5 and 2.

```
(!p,!q);
> (5, 2) : int * int
p := !p + !q;
> () : unit
(!p,!q);
> (7, 2) : int * int
```

The assignment changes the contents of *p* to 7. Note the word 'contents'! The assignment does not change the value of *p*, which is a fixed address in the store; it changes the contents of that address. We may use *p* and *q* like integer variables in Pascal, except that dereferencing is explicit. We must write ! *p* to get the contents of *p*, since *p* by itself denotes an address.

References in data structures. Because references are ML values, they may belong to tuples, lists, etc.

```
val refs = [p,q,p];
> val refs = [ref 7, ref 2, ref 7] : int ref list
q := 1346;
> () : unit
refs;
> [ref 7, ref 1346, ref 7] : int ref list
```

The first and third elements of *refs* denote the same address as *p*, while the second element is the same as *q*. ML compilers print the value of a reference as *ref c*, where *c* is its contents, rather than printing the address as a number. So assigning to *q* affects how *refs* is printed. Let us assign to the head of the list:

```
hd refs := 1415;
> () : unit
refs;
> [ref 1415, ref 1346, ref 1415] : int ref list
(!p,!q);
> (1415, 1346) : int * int
```

Because the head of *refs* is *p*, assigning to *hd refs* is the same as assigning to *p*.

References to references are also allowed:

```
val refp = ref p and refq = ref q;
> val refp = ref (ref 1415) : int ref ref
> val refq = ref (ref 1346) : int ref ref
```

The assignment below updates the contents (*q*) of *refq* with the contents (1415) of the contents (*p*) of *refp*. Here *refp* and *refq* behave like Pascal pointer variables.

```
!refq := !(!refp);
> () : unit
(!p,!q);
> (1415, 1415) : int * int
```

Equality of references. The ML equality test is valid for all reference types. Two references of the same type are equal precisely if they denote the same address. The following tests verify that *p* and *q* are distinct references, and that the head of *refs* equals *p*, not *q*:

```
p=q;
> false : bool
hd refs = p;
> true : bool
hd refs = q;
> false : bool
```

In Pascal, two pointer variables are equal if they happen to contain the same address; an assignment makes two pointers equal. The ML notion of reference equality may seem peculiar, for if *p* and *q* are distinct references then nothing can make them equal (short of redeclaring them). In imperative languages, where all variables can be updated, a pointer variable really involves two levels of reference. The usual notion of pointer equality is like comparing the contents of *refp* and *refq*, which are references to references:

```
!refp = !refq;
> false : bool
refq := p;
> () : unit
!refp = !refq;
> true : bool
```

At first, *refp* and *refq* contain different values, *p* and *q*. Assigning the value *p* to *refq* makes *refp* and *refq* have the same contents; both 'pointer variables' refer to *p*.

When two references are equal, like *p* and *hd refs*, assigning to one affects the contents of the other. This situation, called **aliasing**, can cause great confusion. Aliasing can occur in procedural languages; in a procedure call, a global variable and a formal parameter may denote the same address.

ⓘ *Cyclic data structures.* Circular chains of references arise in many situations. Suppose that we declare *cp* to refer to the successor function on the integers, and dereference it in the function *cFact*.

```
val cp = ref (fn k => k+1);
> val cp = ref fn : (int -> int) ref
fun cFact n =  if n=0  then  1  else  n * !cp(n-1);
> val cFact = fn : int -> int
```

Each time *cFact* is called, it takes the current contents of *cp*. Initially this is the successor function, and $cFact(8) = 8 \times 8 = 64$:

```
cFact 8;
> 64 : int
```

Let us update *cp* to contain *cFact*. Now *cFact* refers to itself via *cp*. It becomes a recursive function and computes factorials:

```
cp := cFact;
> () : unit
cFact 8;
> 40320 : int
```

Updating a reference to create a cycle is sometimes called 'tying the knot.' Many functional language interpreters implement recursive functions exactly as shown above, creating a cycle in the execution environment.

Exercise 8.1   True or false: if $E_1 = E_2$ then *ref* $E_1 = $ *ref* E_2.

Exercise 8.2   Declare the function + : = such that + : = *Id E* has the same effect as *Id* : = !*Id* + *E*, for integer *E*.

Exercise 8.3   With *p* and *q* declared as above, explain ML's response when these expressions are typed at top level:

```
p:=!p+1        2*!q
```

8.2   *Control structures*

ML does not distinguish commands from expressions. A command is an expression that updates the state when evaluated. Most commands have type *unit* and return (). Viewed as an imperative language, ML provides only basic control structures.

The conditional expression

```
if E then E₁ else E₂
```

can be viewed as a conditional command. It evaluates E, possibly updating the state. If the resulting boolean value is *true* then it executes E_1; otherwise it executes E_2. It returns the value of E_1 or E_2, though with imperative programming that value is normally ().

Note that this behaviour arises from ML's treatment of expressions in general; ML has only one `if` construct.

Similarly, the `case` expression can serve as a control structure:

$$\text{case } E \text{ of } P_1 \Rightarrow E_1 \mid \cdots \mid P_n \Rightarrow E_n$$

First E is evaluated, perhaps changing the state. Then pattern-matching selects some expression E_i in the usual way. It is evaluated, again perhaps changing the state, and the resulting value is returned.

In the function call $E_1 \, E_2$ and the n-tuple $(E_1, E_2, \ldots, E_n)$, the expressions are evaluated from left to right. If E_1 changes the state, it could affect the outcome of E_2.

A series of commands can also be executed by the expression

$$(E_1; E_2; \ldots; E_n)$$

When this expression is evaluated, the expressions $E_1, E_2, \ldots, E_n$ are evaluated from left to right. The result is the value of E_n; the values of the other expressions are discarded. Because of the other uses of the semicolon in ML, this construct must always be enclosed in parentheses unless it forms the body of a `let` expression:

$$\text{let } D \text{ in } E_1; E_2; \ldots; E_n \text{ end}$$

For iteration, ML has a `while` command:

$$\text{while } E_1 \text{ do } E_2$$

If E_1 evaluates to *false* then the `while` is finished; if E_1 evaluates to *true* then E_2 is evaluated and the `while` is executed again. To be precise, the `while` command satisfies the recursion

$$\text{while } E_1 \text{ do } E_2 \equiv \text{if } E_1 \text{ then } (E_2; \text{ while } E_1 \text{ do } E_2)$$
$$\text{else } ()$$

The value returned is (), so E_2 is evaluated just for its effect on the state.

Simple examples. ML can imitate procedural programming languages. The following procedures, apart from the explicit dereferencing (the `!` operation), could have been written in Pascal or C. The function *impFact* computes factorials using local references *resultp* and *ip*, returning the final contents of *resultp*. Observe the use of a `while` command to execute the body n times:

```
fun impFact n =
  let val resultp = ref 1
      and ip      = ref 0
  in  while !ip < n do (ip      := !ip + 1;
                        resultp := !resultp * !ip);
      !resultp
  end;
> val impFact = fn : int -> int
```

The body of the while contains two assignments. At each iteration it adds one to the contents of *ip*, then uses the new contents of *ip* to update the contents of *resultp*.

Although calling *impFact* allocates new references, this state change is invisible outside. The value of *impFact*(*E*) is a mathematical function of the value of *E*.

```
impFact 6;
> 720 : int
```

In procedural languages, a procedure may have reference parameters in order to modify variables in the calling program. In Standard ML, a reference parameter is literally a formal parameter of reference type. We can transform *impFact* into a procedure *pFact* that takes *resultp* as a reference parameter.

```
fun pFact (n, resultp) =
  let val ip = ref 0
  in  resultp := 1;
      while !ip < n do (ip      := !ip + 1;
                        resultp := !resultp * !ip)
  end;
> val pFact = fn : int * int ref -> unit
```

Calling *pFact*(*n*, *resultp*) assigns the factorial of *n* to *resultp*:

```
pFact (5,p);
> () : unit
p;
> ref 120 : int ref
```

These two functions demonstrate the imperative style, but a pure recursive function is the clearest and probably the fastest way to compute factorials. More realistic imperative programs appear later in this chapter.

Supporting library functions. The standard library declares some top level functions for use in imperative programs. The function *ignore* ignores its argument and returns (). Here is a typical situation:

```
if !skip then ignore (TextIO.inputLine file)
          else skip := true;
```

The input/output command returns a string, while the assignment returns (). Calling *ignore* discards the string, preventing a clash between types *string* and *unit*. The argument to *ignore* is evaluated only for its side-effects, here to skip the next line of a file.

Sometimes we must retain an expression's value before executing some command. For instance, if *x* contains 0.5 and *y* contains 1.2, we could exchange their contents like this:

```
y := #1 (!x, x := !y);
> () : unit
(!x, !y);
> (1.2, 0.5) : real * real
```

The exchange works because the arguments of the pair are evaluated in order. The function #1 returns the first component,[1] which is the original contents of *x*. The library infix *before* provides a nicer syntax for this trick. It simply returns its first argument.

```
y := (!x before x := !y);
```

The list functional *app* applies a command to every element of a list. For example, here is a function to assign the same value to each member of a list of references:

```
fun initialize rs x = app (fn r => r:=x) rs;
> val initialize = fn : 'a ref list -> 'a -> unit
initialize refs 1815;
> () : unit
refs;
> [ref 1815, ref 1815, ref 1815] : int ref list
```

Clearly *app f l* is similar to *ignore* (*map f l*), but avoids building a list of results. The top level version of *app* comes from structure *List*. Other library structures, including *ListPair* and *Array*, declare corresponding versions of *app*.

Exceptions and commands. When an exception is raised, the normal flow of execution is interrupted. An exception handler is chosen, as described in Section 4.8, and control resumes there. This could be dangerous; an exception could occur at any time, leaving the state in an abnormal condition. The following exception

---

[1] Section 2.9 explains selector functions of the form #*k*.

handler traps any exception, tidies up the state, and re-raises the exception. The variable *e* is a trivial pattern (of type *exn*) to match all exceptions:

```
handle e => ( ... (*tidy up actions*) ... ; raise e)
```

Note: Most commands return the value () of type *unit*. From now on, our sessions will omit the boring response

```
> () : unit
```

Exercise 8.4 Expressions $(E_1; E_2; \ldots; E_n)$ and while E_1 do E_2 are derived forms in ML, which means they are defined by translation to other expressions. Describe suitable translations.

Exercise 8.5 Write an imperative version of the function *sqroot*, which computes real square roots by the Newton-Raphson method (Section 2.17).

Exercise 8.6 Write an imperative version of the function *fib*, which computes Fibonacci numbers efficiently (Section 2.15).

Exercise 8.7 The simultaneous assignment

$$V_1, V_2, \ldots, V_n := E_1, E_2, \ldots, E_n$$

first evaluates the expressions, then assigns their values to the corresponding references. For instance $x, y := \ !y, \ !x$ exchanges the contents of *x* and *y*. Write an ML function to perform simultaneous assignments. It should have the polymorphic type $(\alpha \ ref)list \times \alpha \ list \to unit$.

8.3   *Polymorphic references*

References have been a notorious source of insecurity ever since they were introduced to programming languages. Often, no type information was kept about the contents of a reference; a character code could be interpreted as a real number. Pascal prevents such errors, ensuring that each reference contains values of one fixed type, by having a distinct type 'pointer to τ' for each type τ. In ML, the problem is harder: what does the type $\tau \ ref$ mean if τ is polymorphic? Unless we are careful, the contents of this reference could change over time.

An imaginary session. This illegal session demonstrates what could go wrong if references were naïvely added to the type system. We begin by declaring the identity function:

```
fun I x = x;
> val I = fn : 'a -> 'a
```

Since *I* is polymorphic, it may be applied to arguments of any types. Now let us create a reference to *I*:

```
val fp = ref I;
> val fp = ref fn : ('a -> 'a) ref
```

With its polymorphic type $(\alpha \to \alpha)ref$, we should be able to apply the contents of *fp* to arguments of any types:

```
(!fp true, !fp 5);
> (true, 5) : bool * int
```

And its polymorphic type lets us assign a function of type *bool* → *bool* to *fp*:

```
fp := not;
!fp 5;
```

Applying *not* to the integer 5 is a run-time type error, but ML is supposed to detect all type errors at compile-time. Obviously something has gone wrong, but where?

Polymorphism and substitution. In the absence of imperatives, evaluating an expression repeatedly always yields the same result. The declaration val *Id* = *E* makes *Id* a synonym for this one result. Ignoring efficiency, we could just as well substitute *E* for *Id* everywhere.

For example, here are two polymorphic declarations, of a function and a list of lists:

```
let val I = fn x => x  in  (I true, I 5) end;
> (true, 5) : bool * int
let val nill = [[]]  in  (["Exeter"]::nill, [1415]::nill) end;
> ([["Exeter"], []], [[1415], []])
> : string list list * int list list
```

Substituting the declarations away affects neither the value returned nor the typing:

```
((fn x => x) true, (fn x => x) 5);
> (true, 5) : bool * int
(["Exeter"]::[[]], [1415]::[[]]);
> ([["Exeter"], []], [[1415], []])
> : string list list * int list list
```

Now let us see how ML reacts to our imaginary session above, when packaged as a `let` expression:

```
let val fp = ref I
in   ((!fp true, !fp 5), fp := not, !fp 5)  end;
> Error: Type conflict: expected int, found bool
```

ML rejects it, thank heavens — and with a meaningful error message too. What happens if we substitute the declarations away?

```
((!(ref I)  true,  !(ref I)  5),  (ref I)  := not,  !(ref I)  5);
> ((true, 5), (), 5) : (bool * int) * unit * int
```

The expression is evaluated without error. But the substitution has completely altered its meaning. The original expression allocates a reference *fp* with initial contents *I*, extracts its contents twice, updates it and finally extracts the new value. The modified expression allocates four different references, each with initial contents *I*. The assignment is pointless, updating a reference used nowhere else.

The crux of the problem is that repeated calls to *ref* always yield different references. We declare `val` *fp* = *ref I* expecting that each occurrence of *fp* will denote the same reference: the same store address. Substitution does not respect the sharing of *fp*. Polymorphism treats each identifier by substituting the type of its defining expression, thereby assuming that substitution is valid.

The culprit is sharing, not side effects. We must regulate the creation of polymorphic references, not assignments to them.

Polymorphic value declarations. **Syntactic values** are expressions that are too simple to create references. They come in several forms:

- A literal constant such as 3 is a syntactic value.
- An identifier is one also, as it refers to some other declaration that has been dealt with already.
- A syntactic value can be built up from others using tupling, record notation and constructors (excluding *ref*, of course).
- A function in `fn` notation is a syntactic value, even if its body uses *ref*, as the body is not executed until the function is called.

Calls to *ref* and other functions are not syntactic values.

If *E* is a syntactic value then the polymorphic declaration `val` *Id* = *E* is equivalent to a substitution. The declaration is polymorphic in the usual way: each occurrence of *Id* may have a different instance of *E*'s type. Every `fun` declaration is treated like this, for it is shorthand for a `val` declaration with `fn` notation, which is a syntactic value.

If *E* is not a syntactic value then the declaration `val` *Id* = *E* might create references. To respect sharing, each occurrence of *Id* must have the same type. If the declaration occurs inside a `let` expression, then each type variable in the type of *E* is frozen throughout the `let` body. The expression

```
let val fp = ref I
in  fp := not;  !fp 5   end;
```

is illegal because *ref I* involves the type variable α, which cannot stand for *bool* and *int* at the same time. The expression

```
let val fp = ref I
in  (!fp true,  !fp 5)   end;
```

is illegal for the same reason. Yet it is safe: if we could evaluate it, the result would be (*true*, 5) with no run-time error. A monomorphic version is legal:

```
let val fp = ref I
in  fp := not;  !fp true   end;
> false : bool
```

A top level polymorphic declaration is forbidden unless *E* is a syntactic value; the type checker cannot predict how future occurrences of *Id* will be used:

```
val fp = ref I;
> Error: Non-value in polymorphic declaration
```

A monomorphic type constraint makes the top level declaration legal. The expression no longer creates polymorphic references:

```
val fp = ref (I: bool -> bool);
> val fp = ref fn : (bool -> bool) ref
```

Imperative list reversal. We now consider an example with real polymorphism. The function *irev* reverses a list imperatively. It uses one reference to scan down the list and another to accumulate the elements in reverse.

```
fun irev l =
   let val resultp = ref []
       and lp      = ref l
   in  while not (null (!lp)) do
              (resultp := hd(!lp) :: !resultp;
               lp      := tl(!lp));
           !resultp
   end;
> val irev = fn : 'a list -> 'a list
```

The variables *lp* and *resultp* have type (α *list*)*ref*; the type variable α is frozen in the body of the `let`. ML accepts *irev* as a polymorphic function because it is declared using `fun`.

As we can verify, *irev* is indeed polymorphic:

```
irev [25,10,1415];
> [1415, 10, 25] : int list
irev (explode("Montjoy"));
> [#"y", #"o", #"j", #"t", #"n", #"o", #"M"]
> : char list
```

It can be used exactly like the standard function *rev*.

Polymorphic exceptions. Although exceptions do not involve the store, they require a form of sharing. Consider the following nonsense:

```
exception Poly of 'a;          (* illegal!! *)
(raise Poly true) handle Poly x => x+1;
```

If this expression could be evaluated, it would attempt to evaluate *true* + 1, a run-time error. When a polymorphic exception is declared, ML ensures that it is used with only one type, just like a restricted value declaration. The type of a top level exception must be monomorphic and the type variables of a local exception are frozen.

Limitations of value polymorphism. As noted in Section 5.4, the restriction to syntactic values bans some natural polymorphic declarations. In most cases they can be corrected easily, say by using `fun` instead of `val`:

```
val length   = foldl (fn (_,n) => n+1) 0;    (*rejected*)
fun length l = foldl (fn (_,n) => n+1) 0 l;  (*accepted*)
```

Compile-time type checking must make conservative assumptions about what could happen at run-time. Type checking rejects many programs that could execute safely. The expression *hd*[5, *true*]+3 evaluates safely to 8 despite being ill-typed. Most modern languages employ compile-time type checking; programmers accept these restrictions in order to be free from type errors at run-time.

ⓘ   *The history of polymorphic references.* Many people have studied polymorphic references, but Mads Tofte is generally credited with cracking the problem. Early ML compilers forbade polymorphic references altogether: the function *ref* could have only monomorphic types. Tofte's original proposal, adopted in the ML *Definition*, was more liberal than the one used now. Special 'weak' type variables tracked the use of imperative features, and only they were restricted in `val` declarations. Standard ML of New Jersey used an experimental approach where weak type variables had numerical degrees of weakness.

Weak type variables result in complicated, unintuitive types. They assign different types to *irev* and *rev*, and prevent their being used interchangeably. Worst of all, they make it hard to write signatures before implementing the corresponding structures.

Wright (1995) proposed treating all `val` declarations equally — in effect, making all type variables weak. Purely functional code would be treated like imperative code. Could programmers tolerate such restrictions? Using a modified type checker, Wright examined an immense body of ML code written by others. The restrictions turned out to cause very few errors, and those could be repaired easily. And so, after due consideration, this proposal has been recommended for ML.

The type checking of polymorphic references in Standard ML is probably safe. Tofte (1990) proved its correctness for a subset of ML and there is no reason to doubt that it is correct for the full language. Greiner (1996) has investigated a simplification of the New Jersey system. Harper (1994) describes a simpler approach to such proofs. Standard ML has been defined with great care to avoid insecurities and other semantic defects; in this regard, the language is practically in a class by itself.

Exercise 8.8   Is this expression legal? What does *WI* do?

```
let fun WI x = !(ref x)
in  (WI false, WI "Clarence")  end
```

Exercise 8.9   Which of these declarations are legal? Which could, if evaluated, lead to a run-time type error?

```
val funs = [hd];
val l    = rev [];
val l'   = tl [3];
val lp   = let fun nilp x = ref [] in  nilp() end;
```

References in data structures

Any textbook on algorithms describes recursive data structures such as lists and trees. These differ from ML recursive datatypes (as seen in Chapter 4) in one major respect: the recursion involves explicit link fields, or pointers. These pointers can be updated, allowing re-linking of existing data structures and the creation of cycles.

Reference types, in conjunction with recursive datatypes, can implement such linked data structures. This section presents two such examples: doubly-linked circular lists and a highly efficient form of functional array. We begin with a simpler use of references: not as link fields, but as storage for previously computed results.

8.4   *Sequences, or lazy lists*

Under the representation given in Section 5.12, the tail of a sequence is a function to compute another sequence. Each time the tail is inspected, a possibly expensive function call is repeated. This inefficiency can be eliminated. Represent the tail of a sequence by a reference, which initially contains a function and is later updated with the function's result. Sequences so implemented exploit the mutable store, but when viewed from outside are purely functional.

An abstract type of sequences. Structure *ImpSeq* implements lazy lists; see Figure 8.1 on the next page. Type $\alpha\ t$ has three constructors: *Nil* for the empty sequence, *Cons* for non-empty sequences, and *Delayed* to permit delayed evaluation of the tail. A sequence of the form

$$Cons(x, ref(Delayed\ xf)),$$

where *xf* has type *unit* $\rightarrow \alpha\ t$, begins with x and has the sequence *xf*() for its remaining elements. Note that *Delayed xf* is contained in a reference cell. Applying *force* updates it to contain the value of *xf*(), removing the *Delayed*. Some overhead is involved, but if the sequence element is revisited then there will be a net gain in efficiency.

The function *null* tests whether a sequence is empty, while *hd* and *tl* return the head and tail of a sequence. Because *tl* calls *force*, a sequence's outer constructor cannot be *Delayed*. Inside structure *ImpSeq*, functions on sequences may exploit pattern-matching; outside, they must use *null*, *hd* and *tl* because the constructors are hidden. An opaque signature constraint ensures that the structure yields an abstract type:

```
signature IMP_SEQUENCE =
  sig
  type 'a t
  exception Empty
  val empty     : 'a t
  val cons      : 'a * (unit -> 'a t) -> 'a t
  val null      : 'a t -> bool
  val hd        : 'a t -> 'a
  val tl        : 'a t -> 'a t
  val take      : 'a t * int -> 'a list
  val toList    : 'a t -> 'a list
  val fromList  : 'a list -> 'a t
  val @         : 'a t * 'a t -> 'a t
  val interleave : 'a t * 'a t -> 'a t
  val concat    : 'a t t -> 'a t
  val map       : ('a -> 'b) -> 'a t -> 'b t
```

Figure 8.1 *Lazy lists using references*

```
structure ImpSeq :> IMP_SEQUENCE =
  struct
  datatype 'a t = Nil
                | Cons    of 'a * ('a t) ref
                | Delayed of unit -> 'a t;

  exception Empty;

  fun delay xf = ref(Delayed xf);

  val empty = Nil;

  fun cons(x,xf) = Cons(x, delay xf);

  fun force xp =
          case !xp of
            Delayed f => let val s = f()
                          in  xp := s;  s  end
          | s => s;

  fun null Nil         = true
    | null (Cons _)    = false;

  fun hd Nil           = raise Empty
    | hd (Cons(x,_))   = x;

  fun tl Nil           = raise Empty
    | tl (Cons(_,xp))  = force xp;

  fun take (xq, 0)          = []
    | take (Nil, n)         = []
    | take (Cons(x,xp), n)  = x :: take (force xp, n-1);

  fun        Nil @ yq = yq
    | (Cons(x,xp)) @ yq =
          Cons(x, delay(fn()=> (force xp) @ yq));

  fun map f Nil          = Nil
    | map f (Cons(x,xp)) =
          Cons(f x, delay(fn()=> map f (force xp)));

  fun cycle seqfn =
      let val knot = ref Nil
      in  knot := seqfn (fn()=> !knot);  !knot  end;
  end;
```

```
val filter    : ('a -> bool) -> 'a t -> 'a t
val cycle     : ((unit -> 'a t) -> 'a t) -> 'a t
end;
```

Cyclic sequences. The function *cycle* creates cyclic sequences by tying the knot. Here is a sequence whose tail is itself:

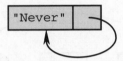

This behaves like the infinite sequence "Never", "Never",..., but occupies a tiny amount of space in the computer. It is created by

```
ImpSeq.cycle(fn xf => ImpSeq.cons("Never", xf));
> - : string ImpSeq.t
ImpSeq.take(5, it);
> ["Never", "Never", "Never", "Never", "Never"]
> : string list
```

When *cycle* is applied to some function *seqfn*, it creates the reference *knot* and supplies it to *seqfn* (packaged as a function). The result of *seqfn* is a sequence that, as its elements are computed, eventually refers to the contents of *knot*. Updating *knot* to contain this very sequence creates a cycle.

Cyclic sequences can compute Fibonacci numbers in an amusing fashion. Let *add* be a function that adds two sequences of integers, returning a sequence of sums. To illustrate reference polymorphism, *add* is coded in terms of a function to join two sequences into a sequence of pairs:

```
fun pairs(xq,yq) =
        ImpSeq.cons((ImpSeq.hd xq, ImpSeq.hd yq),
                     fn()=>pairs(ImpSeq.tl xq, ImpSeq.tl yq));
> val pairs = fn
> : 'a ImpSeq.t * 'b ImpSeq.t -> ('a * 'b) ImpSeq.t
fun add (xq,yq) = ImpSeq.map Int.+ (pairs(xq,yq));
> val add = fn
> : int ImpSeq.t * int ImpSeq.t -> int ImpSeq.t
```

The sequence of Fibonacci numbers can be defined using *cycle*:

```
val fib = ImpSeq.cycle(fn fibf =>
    ImpSeq.cons(1, fn()=>
        ImpSeq.cons(1, fn()=>
            add(fibf(), ImpSeq.tl(fibf())))));
> val fib = - : int ImpSeq.t
```

This definition is cyclic. The sequence begins 1, 1, and the remaining elements are obtained by adding the sequence to its tail:

$$add(fib, \ ImpSeq.tl \ fib)$$

Initially, *fib* can be portrayed as follows:

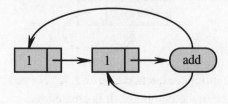

When the third element of *fib* is inspected by *tl* (*tl fib*), the *add* call computes a 2 and *force* updates the sequence as follows:

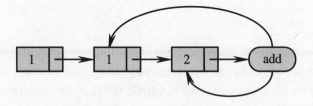

When the next element is inspected, *fib* becomes

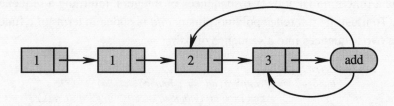

Because the sequence is cyclic and retains computed elements, each Fibonacci number is computed only once. This is reasonably fast. If Fibonacci numbers were defined recursively using the sequences of Section 5.12, the cost of computing the *n*th element would be exponential in *n*.

Exercise 8.10   The Hamming problem is to enumerate all integers of the form $2^i 3^j 5^k$ in increasing order. Declare a cyclic sequence consisting of these numbers. Hint: declare a function to merge increasing sequences, and consider the following diagram:

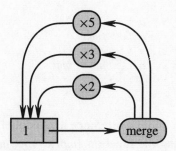

Exercise 8.11 Implement the function *iterates*, which given *f* and *x* creates a cyclic representation of the sequence $[x, f(x), f(f(x)), \dots, f^k(x), \dots]$.

Exercise 8.12 Discuss the difficulty of showing whether a cyclic sequence is correct — that it generates a sequence of values satisfying a given specification. Comment on the following sequence:

```
val fib2 = ImpSeq.cycle(fn fibf =>
    ImpSeq.cons(1, fn()=> add(fibf(), ImpSeq.tl(fibf()))));
```

Exercise 8.13 Code the functions omitted from structure *ImpSeq* but specified in its signature, namely *toList*, *fromList*, *interleave*, *concat* and *filter*.

8.5   *Ring buffers*

A doubly-linked list can be read forwards or backwards, and allow elements to be inserted or deleted at any point. It is cyclic if it closes back on itself:

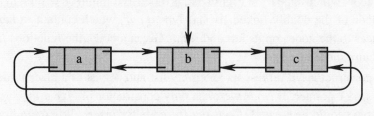

This mutable data structure, sometimes called a **ring buffer**, should be familiar to most programmers. We implement it here to make a comparison between references in Standard ML and pointer variables in procedural languages. Let us define an abstract type with the following signature:

```
signature RINGBUF =
  sig
  eqtype 'a t
  exception Empty
  val empty    :   unit -> 'a t
  val null     :   'a t -> bool
```

```
val label    :   'a t -> 'a
val moveLeft :   'a t -> unit
val moveRight :  'a t -> unit
val insert   :   'a t * 'a -> unit
val delete   :   'a t -> 'a
end;
```

A ring buffer has type $\alpha\ t$ and is a reference into a doubly-linked list. A new ring buffer is created by calling the function *empty*. The function *null* tests whether a ring buffer is empty, *label* returns the label of the current node, and *moveLeft/moveRight* move the pointer to the left/right of the current node. As shown below, *insert(buf, e)* inserts a node labelled *e* to the left of the current node. Two links are redirected to the new node; their initial orientations are shown by dashed arrows and their final orientations by shaded arrows:

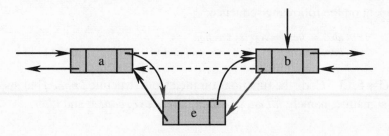

The function *delete* removes the current node and moves the pointer to the right. Its value is the label of the deleted node.

The code, which appears in Figure 8.2, is much as it might be written in Pascal. Each node of the doubly-linked list has type $\alpha\ buf$, which contains a label and references to the nodes on its left and right. Given a node, the functions *left* and *right* return these references.

The constructor *Nil* represents an empty list and serves as a placeholder, like Pascal's `nil` pointer. If *Node* were the only constructor of type $\alpha\ buf$, no value of that type could be created. Consider the code for *insert*. When the first node is created, its left and right pointers initially contain *Nil*. They are then updated to contain the node itself.

Bear in mind that reference equality in ML differs from the usual notion of pointer equality. The function *delete* must check whether the only node of a buffer is about to be deleted. It cannot determine whether *Node(lp, x, rp)* is the only node by testing whether $lp = rp$, as a Pascal programmer might expect. That equality will always be false in a properly constructed buffer; each link field must be a distinct reference so that it can be updated independently. The test $left(!lp) = lp$ is correct. If the node on the left (namely $!lp$) and the current node

Figure 8.2 *Ring buffers as doubly-linked lists*

```
structure RingBuf :> RINGBUF =
  struct
  datatype 'a buf = Nil | Node of 'a buf ref * 'a * 'a buf ref;
  datatype 'a t   = Ptr of 'a buf ref;
  exception Empty;

  fun left  (Node(lp,_,_)) = lp
    | left Nil             = raise Empty;

  fun right  (Node(_,_,rp)) = rp
    | right Nil             = raise Empty;

  fun empty() = Ptr(ref Nil);

  fun null (Ptr p) = case !p of
          Nil          => true
        | Node(_,x,_) => false;

  fun label (Ptr p) = case !p of
          Nil          => raise Empty
        | Node(_,x,_) => x;

  fun moveLeft  (Ptr p)  = (p := !(left(!p)));
  fun moveRight (Ptr p)  = (p := !(right(!p)));

  fun insert (Ptr p, x) =
      case !p of
          Nil          =>
                let val lp   = ref Nil
                    and rp   = ref Nil
                    val new  = Node(lp,x,rp)
                in  lp := new;  rp := new;  p := new  end
        | Node(lp,_,_) =>
                let val new = Node(ref(!lp), x, ref(!p))
                in  right(!lp) := new;  lp := new  end;

  fun delete  (Ptr p) =
      case !p of
          Nil          => raise Empty
        | Node(lp,x,rp) =>
                (if left(!lp) = lp then p := Nil
                 else (right(!lp) := !rp;  left (!rp) := !lp;  p := !rp);
                 x)
  end;
```

---

have the same left link, then they are the same node and that is the only node in the buffer.

Here is a small demonstration of ring buffers. First, let us create an empty buffer. Because the call to *empty* is not a syntactic value, we must constrain its result to some monotype, here *string*. (Compare with the empty sequence *ImpSeq.empty*, which contains no references and is polymorphic.)

```
val buf: string RingBuf.t = RingBuf.empty();
> val buf = - : string RingBuf.t
RingBuf.insert(buf, "They");
```

If only *insert* and *delete* are performed, then a ring buffer behaves like a mutable queue; elements can be inserted and later retrieved in the same order.

```
RingBuf.insert(buf, "shall");
RingBuf.delete buf;
> "They" : string
RingBuf.insert(buf, "be");
RingBuf.insert(buf, "famed");
RingBuf.delete buf;
> "shall" : string
RingBuf.delete buf;
> "be" : string
RingBuf.delete buf;
> "famed" : string
```

Exercise 8.14   Modify *delete* to return a boolean value instead of a label: *true* if the modified buffer is empty and otherwise *false*.

Exercise 8.15   Which of the equalities below are suitable for testing whether *Node*(*lp*, *x*, *rp*) is the only node in a ring buffer?

$$!lp = !rp \qquad right(!lp) = lp \qquad right(!lp) = rp$$

Exercise 8.16   Compare the following insertion function with *insert*; does it have any advantages or disadvantages?

```
fun insert2 (Ptr p, x) =
    case !p of
        Nil              => p := Node(p,x,p)
      | Node(lp,_,_) =>
            let val new = Node(lp,x,p)
            in   right(!lp) := new;   lp := new end;
```

Exercise 8.17   Code a version of *insert* that inserts the new node to the right of the current point, rather than to the left.

Exercise 8.18   Show that if a value of type α *RingBuf . t* (with a strong type variable) could be declared, a run-time type error could ensue.

Exercise 8.19   What good is equality testing on type α *RingBuf . t?*

8.6   *Mutable and functional arrays*
        The Definition of Standard ML says nothing about arrays, but the standard library provides a structure *Array* with the following signature:

```
signature ARRAY =
  sig
  eqtype 'a array
  val array       :  int * 'a -> 'a array
  val fromList    :  'a list -> 'a array
  val tabulate    :  int * (int -> 'a) -> 'a array
  val sub         :  'a array * int -> 'a
  val update      :  'a array * int * 'a -> unit
  val length      :  'a array -> int
    ⋮
  end;
```

Each array has a fixed size. An n-element array admits subscripts from 0 to $n-1$. The operations raise exception *Subscript* if the array bound is exceeded and raise *Size* upon any attempt to create an array of negative (or grossly excessive) size.[2]
   Here is a brief description of the main array operations:

   • *array*(n, x) creates an n-element array with x stored in each cell.
   • *fromList*$[x_0, x_1, \ldots, x_{n-1}]$ creates an n-element array with x_k stored in cell k, for $k = 0, \ldots, n-1$.
   • *tabulate*(n, f) creates an n-element array with $f(k)$ stored in cell k, for $k = 0, \ldots, n-1$.
   • *sub*(A, k) returns the contents of cell k of array A.
   • *update*(A, k, x) updates cell k of array A to contain x.
   • *length*(A) returns the size of array A.

Array are mutable objects and behave much like references. They always admit equality: two arrays are equal if and only if they are the same object. Arrays of arrays may be created, as in Pascal, to serve as multi-dimensional arrays.

ⓘ   *Standard library aggregate structures.* Arrays of type α *array* can be updated.
     Immutable arrays provide random access to static data, and can make functional programs more efficient. The library structure *Vector* declares a type α *vector* of

---
[2] These exceptions are declared in the library structure *General*.

immutable arrays. It provides largely the same operations as *Array*, excluding *update*. Functions *tabulate* and *fromList* create vectors, while *Array . extract* extracts a vector from an array.

Because types α *array* and α *vector* are polymorphic, they require an additional indirection for every element. Monomorphic arrays and vectors can be represented more compactly. The library signature *MONO_ARRAY* specifies the type *array* of mutable arrays over another type *elem*. Signature *MONO_VECTOR* is analogous, specifying a type *vector* of immutable arrays. Various standard library structures match these signatures, giving arrays of characters, floating point numbers, etc.

The library regards arrays, vectors and even lists as variations on one concept: aggregates. The corresponding operations agree as far as possible. Arrays, like lists, have *app* and fold functionals. The function *Array . fromList* converts a list to an array, and the inverse operation is easy to code:

```
fun toList l = Array.foldr op:: [] l;
```

Lists, like arrays, have a *tabulate* function. They both support subscripting, indexed from zero, and both raise exception *Subscript* if the upper bound is exceeded.

Representing functional arrays. Holmström and Hughes have developed a hybrid representation of functional arrays, exploiting mutable arrays and association lists. An association list consisting of (*index*, *contents*) pairs has a functional update operation: simply add a new pair to the front of the list. Update is fast, but lookup requires an expensive search. Introducing a mutable array, called the **vector**, makes lookups faster (Aasa *et al.*, 1988).

Initially, a functional array is represented by a vector. Update operations build an association list in front of the vector, indicating differences between the current contents of the vector and the values of various arrays. Consider two cells i and j of a functional array A, with $i \neq j$, and suppose $A[i] = u$ and $A[j] = v$. Now perform some functional updates. Obtain B from A by storing x in position i; obtain C from B by storing y in position j:

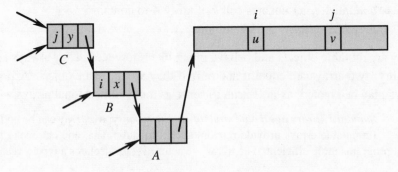

Other links into A, B and C are shown; these come from arrays created by further updating. The arrays form a tree, called a ***version tree*** since its nodes are 'versions' of the vector. Unlike ordinary trees, its links point towards the root rather than away from it. The root of the tree is *A*, which is a dummy node linked to the vector. The dummy node contains the only direct link into the vector, in order to simplify the re-rooting operation.

Re-rooting the version tree. Although *C* has the correct value, with $C[i] = x$, $C[j] = y$ and the other elements like in *A*, lookups to *C* are slower than they could be. If *C* is the most heavily used version of the vector, then the root of the version tree ought to be moved to *C*. The links from *C* to the vector are reversed; the updates indicated by those nodes are executed in the vector; the previous contents of those vector cells are recorded in the nodes.

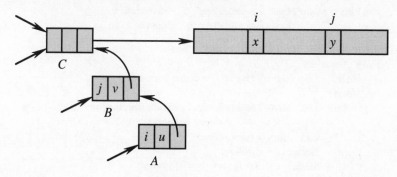

This operation does not affect the values of the functional arrays, but lookups to *A* become slower while lookups to *C* become faster. The dummy node is now *C*. Nodes of the version tree that refer to *A*, *B*, or *C* likewise undergo a change in lookup time, but not in value. Re-rooting does not require locating those other nodes. If there are no other references to *A* or *B* then the ML storage allocator will reclaim them.

An implementation. Figure 8.3 shows an ML structure declaration for version tree arrays, called *v*-arrays for short. It matches the following signature:

```
signature VARRAY =
  sig
  type 'a t
  val array     :   int * 'a -> 'a t
  val reroot    :   'a t -> 'a t
  val sub       :   'a t * int -> 'a
  val justUpdate:   'a t * int * 'a -> 'a t
  val update    :   'a t * int * 'a -> 'a t
  end;
```

Figure 8.3 *Functional arrays as version trees*

```
structure Varray :> VARRAY =
  struct
  datatype 'a t = Modif of {limit  : int,
                            index  : int ref,
                            elem   : 'a ref,
                            next   : 'a t ref}
                 | Main of 'a Array.array;

  fun array (n,x) =
        if n < 0 then raise Size
        else  Modif{limit=n, index=ref 0, elem=ref x,
                    next=ref(Main(Array.array(n,x)))};

  fun reroot (va as Modif{index, elem, next,...}) =
      case !next of
          Main _ => va   (*have reached root*)
        | Modif _ =>
            let val Modif{index=bindex,elem=belem,next=bnext,...} =
                               reroot (!next)
                val Main ary = !bnext
            in  bindex := !index;
                belem  := Array.sub(ary, !index);
                Array.update(ary, !index, !elem);
                next   := !bnext;
                bnext  := va;
                va
            end;

  fun sub (Modif{index,elem,next,...}, i) =
      case !next of
          Main ary => Array.sub(ary,i)
        | Modif _  => if !index = i then !elem
                                    else sub(!next,i);

  fun justUpdate (va as Modif{limit,...}, i, x) =
        if  0<=i andalso i<limit
        then Modif{limit=limit, index= ref i, elem=ref x, next=ref va}
        else raise Subscript;

  fun update (va,i,x) = reroot(justUpdate(va,i,x));
  end;
```

An opaque signature constraint hides the representation of *v*-arrays, including their equality test. The underlying equality compares identity of stored objects, which is not functional behaviour.

The type of *v*-arrays is $\alpha\ t$, which has constructors *Modif* and *Main*. A *Modif* (for modification) node is a record with four fields. The upper limit of the *v*-array is stored for subscript checking. The other fields are references to an index, an element and the next *v*-array; these are updated during re-rooting. A *Main* node contains the mutable array.

Calling *array*(*n*, *x*) constructs a *v*-array consisting of a vector and a dummy node. The recursive function *reroot* performs re-rooting. The subscript operation *sub*(*va*, *i*) searches in the nodes for *i* and if necessary looks up that subscript in the vector. The function *justUpdate* simply creates a new node, while *update* follows this operation by re-rooting at the new array. The library exceptions *Subscript* and *Size* can be raised explicitly and from the *Array* operations.

Programs frequently use functional arrays in a single-threaded fashion, discarding the previous value of the array after each update. In this case, we should re-root after each update. If many versions of a functional array are active then version trees could be inefficient; only one version can be represented by the vector. In this case, we should represent functional arrays by binary trees, as in Section 4.15. Binary trees would also allow an array to grow and shrink.

ⓘ *Experimental results for v-arrays.* The code above is based upon Aasa *et al.* (1988). For several single-threaded algorithms, they found *v*-arrays to be more efficient than other representations of functional arrays. At best, *v*-arrays can perform lookups and updates in constant time, although more slowly than mutable arrays. Quick sort on *v*-arrays turns out to be no faster than quick sort on lists, suggesting that arrays should be reserved for tasks requiring random access. Lists are efficient for processing elements sequentially.

Exercise 8.20 Recall the function *allChange* of Section 3.7. With the help of arrays, write a function that can efficiently determine the value of

> *length* (*allChange* ([], [5,2], 16000));

Exercise 8.21 Add a function *fromList* to structure *Varray*, to create a *v*-array from a non-empty list.

Exercise 8.22 Add a function *copy* to structure *Varray*, such that *copy*(*va*) creates a new *v*-array having the same value as *va*.

Exercise 8.23 Declare a structure *Array2* for mutable arrays of 2 dimensions, with components analogous to those of *Array*.

Exercise 8.24   Declare a structure *Varray*2 for *v*-arrays of 2 dimensions, with components analogous to those of *Varray*.

Exercise 8.25   What are the contents of the dummy node? Could an alternative representation of *v*-arrays eliminate this node?

Input and output

Input/output can be a tiresome subject. Reading data in and printing results out seems trivial compared with the computation lying in between — especially as the operations must conform to the arbitrary features of common operating systems. Input/output brings our secure, typed and mainly functional world into contact with byte-oriented, imperative devices. Small wonder that the ML *Definition* specified a parsimonious set of primitives. The Algol 60 definition did not bother with input/output at all.

The ML library rectifies this omission, specifying several input/output models and dozens of operations. It also provides string processing functions for scanning inputs and formatting outputs. We shall examine a selection of these.

Input/output of linked data structures such as trees poses special difficulties. Flattening them to character strings destroys the usually extensive sharing of subtrees, causing exponential blowup. A persistent store, like the one in Poly/ML, can save arbitrary data structures efficiently. Such facilities are hard to find and can be inflexible.

8.7   *String processing*

The library provides extensive functions for processing strings and substrings. Structures *Int*, *Real* and *Bool* (among others) contain functions for translating between basic values and strings. The main functions are *toString*, *fromString*, *fmt* and *scan*. Instead of overloading these functions at top level, the library declares specialized versions in every appropriate structure. You might declare these functions in some of your own structures.

Converting to strings. The function *toString* expresses its argument as a string according to a default format:

```
Int.toString (~23 mod 10);
> "7" : string
Real.toString Math.pi;
> "3.14159265359" : string
Bool.toString (Math.pi = 22.0/7.0);
> "false" : string
```

Structure *StringCvt* supports more elaborate formatting. You can specify how many decimal places to display, and pad the resulting string to a desired length. You even have a choice of radix. For example, the DEC PDP-8 used octal notation, and padded integers to four digits:

```
Int.fmt StringCvt.OCT 31;
> "37" : string
StringCvt.padLeft #"0" 4 it;
> "0037" : string
```

Operations like *String.concat* can combine formatted results with other text.

Converting from strings. The function *fromString* converts strings to basic values. It is permissive; numeric representations go well beyond what is valid in ML programs. For instance, the signs + and − are accepted as well as ~:

```
Real.fromString "+.6626e-33";
> SOME 6.626E~34 : real option
```

The string is scanned from left to right and trailing characters are ignored. User errors may go undetected:

```
Int.toString "1o24";
> SOME 1 : int option
Bool.fromString "falsetto";
> SOME false : bool option
```

Not every string is meaningful, no matter how permissive we are:

```
Int.fromString "My master's mind";
> NONE : int option
```

Splitting strings apart. Since *fromString* ignores leftover characters, how are we to translate a series of values in a string? The library structures *String* and *Substring* provide useful functions for scanning. The function *String.tokens* extracts a list of tokens from a string. Tokens are non-empty substrings separated by one or more delimiter characters. A predicate of type *char* → *bool* defines the delimiter characters; structure *Char* contains predicates for recognizing letters (*isAlpha*), spaces (*isSpace*) and punctuation (*isPunct*). Here are some sample invocations:

```
String.tokens Char.isSpace
     "What is thy name?  I know thy quality.";
> ["What", "is", "thy", "name?",
>  "I", "know", "thy", "quality."] : string list
```

Figure 8.4 *Scanning dates from strings*

```
val months = ["JAN", "FEB", "MAR", "APR", "MAY", "JUN",
              "JUL", "AUG", "SEP", "OCT", "NOV", "DEC"];

fun dateFromString s =
  let val sday::smon::syear::_ = String.tokens (fn c => c = #"-") s
      val SOME day  = Int.fromString sday
      val mon       = String.substring (smon, 0, 3)
      val SOME year = Int.fromString syear
  in  if List.exists (fn m => m=mon) months
      then SOME (day, mon, year)
      else NONE
  end
  handle Subscript => NONE
       | Bind      => NONE;
```

```
String.tokens Char.isPunct
    "What is thy name?  I know thy quality.";
> ["What is thy name", "  I know thy quality"]
> : string list
```

We thus can split a string of inputs into its constituent parts, and pass them to *fromString*. Function *dateFromString* (Figure 8.4) decodes dates of the form *dd-MMM-yyyy*. It takes the first three hyphen-separated tokens of the input. It parses the day and year using *Int.fromString*, and shortens the month to three characters using *String.substring*. It returns *NONE* if the month is unknown, or if exceptions are raised; *Bind* could arise in three places.

```
dateFromString "25-OCTOBRE-1415-shall-live-forever";
> SOME (25, "OCT", 1415) : (int * string * int) option
dateFromString "2L-DECX-18o5";
> SOME (2, "DEC", 18) : (int * string * int) option
```

We see that *dateFromString* is as permissive as the other *fromString* functions.

Scanning from character sources. The *scan* functions, found in several library structures, give precise control over text processing. They accept any functional character source, not just a string. If you can write a function

$$getc : \sigma \rightarrow (char \times \sigma)option$$

then type σ can be used as a character source. Calling *getc* either returns *NONE* or else packages the next character with a further character source.

The *scan* functions read a basic value, consuming as many characters as possible and leaving the rest for subsequent processing. For example, let us define lists as a character source:

```
fun listGetc (x::l) = SOME (x,l)
  | listGetc []      = NONE;
> val listGetc = fn : 'a list -> ('a * 'a list) option
```

The *scan* functions are curried, taking the character source as their first argument. The integer *scan* function takes, in addition, the desired radix; *DEC* means decimal. Let us scan some faulty inputs:

```
Bool.scan listGetc (explode "mendacious");
> NONE : (bool * char list) option
Bool.scan listGetc (explode "falsetto");
> SOME (false, [#"t", #"t", #"o"])
> : (bool * char list) option
Real.scan listGetc (explode "6.626x-34");
> SOME (6.626, [#"x", #"-", #"3", #"4"])
> : (real * char list) option
Int.scan StringCvt.DEC listGetc (explode "1o24");
> SOME (1, [#"o", #"2", #"4"])
> : (int * char list) option
```

The mis-typed characters x and o do not prevent numbers from being scanned, but they remain in the input. Such errors can be detected by checking that the input has either been exhausted or continues with an expected delimiter character. In the latter case, delimiters can be skipped and further values scanned.

The *fromString* functions are easy to use but can let errors slip by. The *scan* functions form the basis for robust input processing.

Exercise 8.26 Declare function *writeCheque* for printing amounts on cheques. Calling *writeCheque w* (*dols*, *cents*) should express the given sum in dollars and cents to fit a field of width *w*. For instance, *writeCheque* 9 (57,8) should return the string "$***57.08"

Exercise 8.27 Write a function *toUpper* for translating all the letters in a string to upper case, leaving other characters unchanged. (Library structures *String* and *Char* have relevant functions.)

Exercise 8.28   Repeat the examples above using substrings instead of lists as the source of characters. (The library structure *Substring* declares useful functions including *getc*.)

Exercise 8.29   Use the *scan* functions to code a function for scanning dates. It should accept an arbitrary character source. (Library structure *StringCvt* has relevant functions.)

8.8   *Text input/output*

ML's simplest input/output model supports imperative operations on text files. A **stream** connects an external file (or device) to the program for transmitting characters. An **input** stream is connected to a producer of data, such as the keyboard; characters may be read from it until the producer terminates the stream. An **output** stream is connected to a consumer of data, such as a printer; characters may be sent to it until the program terminates the stream.

The input and output operations belong to structure *TextIO*, whose signature is in effect an extension of the following:

```
signature TEXT_IO =
  sig
  type instream and outstream
  exception Io of {name: string, function: string, cause: exn}
  val stdIn        : instream
  val stdOut       : outstream
  val openIn       : string -> instream
  val openOut      : string -> outstream
  val closeIn      : instream -> unit
  val closeOut     : outstream -> unit
  val inputN       : instream * int -> string
  val inputLine    : instream -> string
  val inputAll     : instream -> string
  val lookahead    : instream -> char option
  val endOfStream  : instream -> bool
  val output       : outstream * string -> unit
  val flushOut     : outstream -> unit
  val print        : string -> unit
  end;
```

Here are brief descriptions of these items. Consult the library documentation for more details.

- Input streams have type *instream* while output streams have type *outstream*. These types do not admit equality.
- Exception *Io* indicates that some low-level operation failed. It bundles

up the name of the affected file, a primitive function and the primitive exception that was raised.

- *stdIn* and *stdOut*, the standard input and output streams, are connected to the terminal in an interactive session.
- *openIn*(*s*) and *openOut*(*s*) create a stream connected to the file named *s*.
- *closeIn*(*is*) and *closeOut*(*os*) terminate a stream, disconnecting it from its file. The stream may no longer transmit characters. An input stream may be closed by its device, for example upon end of file.
- *inputN*(*is*, *n*) removes up to *n* characters from stream *is* and returns them as a string. If fewer than *n* characters are present before the stream closes then only those characters are returned.
- *inputLine*(*is*) reads the next line of text from stream *is* and returns it as a string ending in a newline character. If stream *is* has closed, then the empty string is returned.
- *inputAll*(*is*) reads the entire contents of stream *is* and returns them as a string. Typically it reads in an entire file; it is not suitable for interactive input.
- *lookahead*(*is*) returns the next character, if it exists, without removing it from the stream *is*.
- *endOfStream*(*is*) is *true* if the stream *is* has no further characters before its terminator.
- *output*(*os*, *s*) writes the characters of string *s* to the stream *os*, provided it has not been closed.
- *flushOut*(*os*) sends to their ultimate destination any characters waiting in system buffers.
- *print*(*s*) writes the characters in *s* to the terminal, as might otherwise be done using *output* and *flushOut*. Function *print* is available at top level.

The input operations above may **block**: wait until the required characters appear or the stream closes.

Suppose the file Harry holds some lines by Henry V, from his message to the French shortly before the battle of Agincourt:

```
My people are with sickness much enfeebled,
my numbers lessened, and those few I have
almost no better than so many French ...
But, God before, we say we will come on!
```

Let *infile* be an input stream to Harry. We peek at the first character:

```
val infile = TextIO.openIn ("Harry");
> val infile = ? : TextIO.instream
```

```
TextIO.lookahead infile;
> SOME #"M" : char option
```

Calling *lookahead* does not advance into the file. But now we extract ten characters as a string, then read the rest of the line.

```
TextIO.inputN (infile,10);
> "My people " : string
TextIO.inputLine infile;
> "are with sickness much enfeebled;\n" : string
```

Calling *inputAll* gets the rest of the file as a long and unintelligible string, which we then output to the terminal:

```
TextIO.inputAll infile;
> "my numbers lessened, and those few I have\nalmo#
print it;
> my numbers lessened, and those few I have
> almost no better than so many French ...
> But, God before, we say we will come on!
```

A final peek reveals that we are at the end of the file, so we close it:

```
TextIO.lookahead infile;
> NONE : char option
TextIO.inputLine infile;
> "" : string
TextIO.closeIn infile;
```

Closing streams when you are finished with them conserves system resources.

8.9   *Text processing examples*

A few small examples will demonstrate how to process text files in ML. The amount of actual input/output is surprisingly small; string processing functions such as *String*.*tokens* do most of the work.

Batch input/output. Our first example is a program to read a series of lines and print the initial letters of each word. Words are tokens separated by spaces; subscripting gets their initial characters and *implode* joins them to form a string:

```
fun firstChar s = String.sub (s,0);
> val firstChar = fn : string -> char
val initials = implode o (map firstChar) o
             (String.tokens Char.isSpace);
> val initials = fn : string -> string
initials "My ransom is this frail and worthless trunk";
> "Mritfawt" : string
```

The function *batchInitials*, given input and output streams, repeatedly reads a line from the input and writes its initials to the output. It continues until the input stream is exhausted.

```
fun batchInitials (is, os) =
  while not (TextIO.endOfStream is)
  do TextIO.output(os, initials (TextIO.inputLine is) ^ "\n");
> val batchInitials = fn
> : TextIO.instream * TextIO.outstream -> unit
```

Let *infile* be a fresh input stream to `Harry`. We apply *batchInitials* to it:

```
val infile = TextIO.openIn("Harry");
> val infile = ? : TextIO.instream
batchInitials(infile, TextIO.stdOut);
> Mpawsme
> mnlatfIh
> anbtsmF.
> BGbwswwco
```

The output appears at the terminal because *stdOut* has been given as the output stream.

Interactive input/output. We can make *batchInitials* read from the terminal just by passing *stdIn* as its first argument. But an interactive version ought to display a prompt before it pauses to accept input. A naïve attempt calls *output* just before calling *inputLine*:

```
while not (TextIO.endOfStream is)
do (TextIO.output(os, "Input line? ");
    TextIO.output(os, initials(TextIO.inputLine is) ^ "\n"));
```

But this does not print the prompt until after it has read the input! There are two mistakes. (1) We must call *flushOut* to ensure that the output really appears, instead of sitting in some buffer. (2) We must print the prompt before calling *endOfStream*, which can block; therefore we must move the prompting code between the `while` and `do` keywords. Here is a better version:

```
fun promptInitials (is, os) =
  while (TextIO.output(os, "Input line? ");
         TextIO.flushOut os;
         not (TextIO.endOfStream is))
  do TextIO.output(os, "Initials:   " ^
                       initials(TextIO.inputLine is) ^ "\n");
> val promptInitials = fn
> : TextIO.instream * TextIO.outstream -> unit
```

Recall that evaluating the expression $(E_1; E_2; \ldots; E_n)$ evaluates $E_1, E_2, \ldots, E_n$ in that order and returns the value of E_n. We can execute any commands before the testing the loop condition. In this sample execution, text supplied to the standard input is underlined:

```
promptInitials (TextIO . stdIn,  TextIO . stdOut) ;
> Input line? If we may pass, we will;
> Initials:   Iwmpww
> Input line? If we be hindered ...
> Initials:   Iwbh.
> Input line?
```

The final input above was Control-D, which terminates the input stream. That does not prevent our reading further characters from *stdIn* in the future. Similarly, after we reach the end of a file, some other process could extend the file. Calling *endOfStream* can return *true* now and *false* later.

If the output stream is always the terminal, using *print* further simplifies the while loop:

```
while (print "Input line? ";  not  (TextIO . endOfStream is))
do print ("Initials:    " ^ initials (TextIO . inputLine is) ^ "\n");
```

Translating into HTML. Our next example performs only simple input/output, but illustrates the use of substrings. A value of type *substring* is represented by a string s and two integers i and n; it stands for the n-character segment of s starting at position i. Substrings support certain forms of text processing efficiently, with minimal copying and bounds checking. A substring can be divided into tokens or scanned from the left or right; the results are themselves substrings.

Our task is to translate plays from plain text into HTML, the HyperText Markup Language used for the World Wide Web. Figure 8.5 shows a typical input. Blank lines separate paragraphs. Each speech is a paragraph; the corresponding output must insert the <P> markup tag. The first line of a paragraph gives the character's name, followed by a period; the output must emphasize this name by enclosing it in the <EM> and </EM> tags. To preserve line breaks, the translation should attach the <BR> tag to subsequent lines of each paragraph.

Function *firstLine* deals with the first line of a paragraph, separating the name from the rest of line. It uses three components of the library structure *Substring*, namely *all*, *splitl* and *string*. Calling *all s* creates a substring representing the whole of string s. The call to *splitl* scans this substring from left to right, returning in *name* the substring before the first period, and in *rest* the remainder of the original substring. The calls to *string* convert these substrings to strings so that they can be concatenated with other strings containing the markup tags.

Figure 8.5 *Raw input prior to conversion*

```
Westmoreland. Of fighting men they have full three score thousand.

Exeter. There's five to one; besides, they all are fresh.

Westmoreland. O that we now had here
But one ten thousand of those men in England
That do no work to-day!

King Henry V. What's he that wishes so?
My cousin Westmoreland? No, my fair cousin:
If we are marked to die, we are enough
To do our country loss; and if to live,
The fewer men, the greater share of honour.
```

Figure 8.6 *Displayed output from* HTML

Westmoreland. Of fighting men they have full three score thousand.

Exeter. There's five to one; besides, they all are fresh.

Westmoreland. O that we now had here
But one ten thousand of those men in England
That do no work to-day!

King Henry V. What's he that wishes so?
My cousin Westmoreland? No, my fair cousin:
If we are marked to die, we are enough
To do our country loss; and if to live,
The fewer men, the greater share of honour.

```
fun firstLine s =
    let val (name, rest) =
            Substring.splitl (fn c => c <> #".") (Substring.all s)
    in  "\n<P><EM>" ^ Substring.string name ^
        "</EM>"      ^ Substring.string rest
    end;
> val firstLine = fn : string -> string
```

In this example, observe the placement of the markup tags:

```
firstLine "King Henry V. What's he that wishes so?";
> "\n<P><EM>King Henry V</EM>. What's he that wishes so?"
> : string
```

Function *htmlCvt* takes a filename and opens input and output streams. Its main loop is the recursive function *cvt*, which translates one line at a time, keeping track of whether or not it is the first line of a paragraph. An empty string indicates the end of the input, while an empty line (containing just the newline character) starts a new paragraph. Other lines are translated according as whether or not they are the first. The translated line is output and the process repeats.

```
fun htmlCvt fileName =
    let val is = TextIO.openIn fileName
        and os = TextIO.openOut (fileName ^ ".html")
        fun cvt _ ""   = ()
          | cvt _ "\n" = cvt true (TextIO.inputLine is)
          | cvt first s   =
                    (TextIO.output (os,
                                    if first then firstLine s
                                    else "<BR>" ^ s);
                     cvt false (TextIO.inputLine is));
    in  cvt true "\n";  TextIO.closeIn is;  TextIO.closeOut os
    end;
> val htmlCvt = fn : string -> unit
```

Finally, *htmlCvt* closes the streams. Closing the output stream ensures that text held in buffers actually reaches the file. Figure 8.6 on the page before shows how a Web browser displays the translated text.

ℹ️ *Input/output and the standard library.* Another useful structure is *BinIO*, which supports input/output of binary data in the form of 8-bit bytes. Characters and bytes are not the same thing: characters occupy more than 8 bits on some systems, and they assign special interpretations to certain codes. Binary input/output has no notion of line breaks, for example.

The functors *ImperativeIO*, *StreamIO* and *PrimIO* support input/output at lower levels. (The library specifies them as optional, but better ML systems will provide them.) *ImperativeIO* supports imperative operations, with buffering. *StreamIO* provides functional operations for input: items are not removed from an instream, but yield a new instream. *PrimIO* is the most primitive level, without buffering and implemented in terms of operating system calls. The functors can be applied to support specialized input/output, say for extended character sets.

Andrew Appel designed this input/output interface with help from John Reppy and Dave Berry.

Exercise 8.30   Write an ML program to count how many lines, words and characters are contained in a file. A word is a string of characters delimited by spaces, tabs, or newlines.

Exercise 8.31   Write a procedure to prompt for the radius of a circle, print the corresponding area (using $A = \pi r^2$) and repeat. If the attempt to decode a real number fails, it should print an error message and let the user try again.

Exercise 8.32   The four characters < > & " have special meanings in HTML. Occurrences of them in the input should be replaced by the escape sequences `&lt; &gt; &amp; &quot;` (respectively). Modify *htmlCvt* to do this.

8.10   *A pretty printer*

Programs and mathematical formulæ are easier to read if they are laid out with line breaks and indentation to emphasize their structure. The tautology checker of Section 4.19 includes the function *show*, which converts a proposition to a string. If the string is too long to fit on one line, we usually see something like this (for a margin of 30):

```
((((landed | saintly) | ((~lan
ded) | (~saintly))) & (((~rich
) | saintly) | ((~landed) | (~
saintly)))) & (((landed | rich
) | ((~landed) | (~saintly)))
& (((~rich) | rich) | ((~lande
d) | (~saintly)))))
```

Figure 8.7 shows the rather better display produced by a pretty printer. Two propositions (including the one above) are formatted to margins of 30 and 60. Finding the ideal presentation of a formula may require judgement and taste, but a simple scheme for pretty printing gives surprisingly good results. Some ML systems provide pretty-printing primitives similar to those described below.

The pretty printer accepts a piece of text decorated with information about nesting and allowed break points. Let us indicate nesting by angle brackets ($\langle\rangle$) and possible line breaks by a vertical bar ($|$). An expression of the form $\langle e_1 \ldots e_n\rangle$ is called a ***block***.

Figure 8.7 *Output of the pretty printer*

```
((~((((~landed) | rich) &
    (~(saintly & rich)))) |
 ((~landed) | (~saintly)))

((((landed | saintly) |
  ((~landed) | (~saintly))) &
 ((((~rich) | saintly) |
  ((~landed) |
   (~saintly)))) &
 (((landed | rich) |
  ((~landed) | (~saintly))) &
 ((((~rich) | rich) |
  ((~landed) | (~saintly)))))

((~((((~landed) | rich) & (~(saintly & rich)))) |
 ((~landed) | (~saintly)))

(((((landed | saintly) | ((~landed) | (~saintly))) &
  ((((~rich) | saintly) | ((~landed) | (~saintly)))) &
 (((landed | rich) | ((~landed) | (~saintly))) &
  ((((~rich) | rich) | ((~landed) | (~saintly)))))
```

For instance, the block

$$\left\langle\!\!\left\langle \; a \; * \; \Big| \; b \; \right\rangle - \Big|\Big\langle \; (\; \Big\langle \; c \; + \; \Big| \; d \; \Big\rangle \;) \; \right\rangle\!\!\right\rangle$$

represents the string a*b-(c+d). It allows line breaks after the characters *, –
and +.

When parentheses are suppressed according to operator precedences, correct
pretty printing is essential. The nesting structure of the block corresponds to the
formula

$$(a \times b) - (c + d) \quad \text{rather than} \quad a \times (b - (c + d)).$$

If a*b-(c+d) does not fit on one line, then it should be broken after the – character; outer blocks are broken before inner blocks.

The pretty printing algorithm keeps track of how much space remains on the
current line. When it encounters a break, it determines how many characters
there are until the next break in the same block or in an enclosing block. (Thus it
ignores breaks in inner blocks.) If that many characters will not fit on the current
line, then the algorithm prints a new line, indented to match the beginning of the
current block.

The algorithm does not insist that a break should immediately follow every
block. In the previous example, the block

$$\Big\langle \; c \; + \; \Big| \; d \; \Big\rangle$$

is followed by a) character; the string d) cannot be broken. Determining the
distance until the next break is therefore somewhat involved.

The pretty printer has the signature

```
signature PRETTY =
  sig
  type t
  val blo  :  int * t list -> t
  val str  :  string -> t
  val brk  :  int -> t
  val pr   :  TextIO.outstream * t * int -> unit
  end;
```

and provides slightly fancier primitives than those just described:

- *t* is the type of symbolic expressions, namely blocks, strings and breaks.
- $blo(i, [e_1, \dots, e_n])$ creates a block containing the given expressions, and
  specifies that the current indentation be increased by i. This indentation
  will be used if the block is broken.

- *str*(*s*) creates an expression containing the string *s*.
- *brk*(*l*) creates a break of length *l*; if no line break is required then *l* spaces will be printed instead.
- *pr*(*os*, *e*, *m*) prints expression *e* on stream *os* with a right margin of *m*.

Figure 8.8 presents the pretty printer. Observe that *Block* stores the total size of a block, as computed by *blo*. Also, *after* holds the distance from the end of the current block to the next break.

The output shown above in Figure 8.7 was produced by augmenting our tautology checker as follows:

```
local open Pretty
  in

  fun prettyshow  (Atom a)      = str a
    | prettyshow  (Neg p)       =
          blo(1, [str"(~", prettyshow p, str")"])
    | prettyshow  (Conj(p,q))  =
          blo(1, [str"(", prettyshow p, str" &",
                  brk 1, prettyshow q, str")"])
    | prettyshow  (Disj(p,q))   =
          blo(1, [str"(", prettyshow p, str" |",
                  brk 1, prettyshow q, str")"]);

  end;
> val prettyshow = fn : prop -> Pretty.t
```

Calling *Pretty.pr* with the result of *prettyshow* does the pretty printing.

ⓘ *Further reading.* The pretty printer is inspired by Oppen (1980). Oppen's algorithm is complicated but requires little storage; it can process an enormous file, storing only a few linefuls. Our pretty printer is adequate for displaying theorems and other computed results that easily fit in store. Kennedy (1996) presents an ML program for drawing trees.

Exercise 8.33   Give an example of how a block of the form

$$\Big\langle\!\!\Big\langle E_1 \ * \ \Big| E_2 \Big\rangle - \Big|\Big\langle \ (\ \Big\langle E_3 \ + \ \Big| E_4 \Big\rangle \ ) \ \Big\rangle\!\!\Big\rangle$$

could be pretty printed with a line break after the * character and none after the − character. How serious is this problem? Suggest a modification to the algorithm to correct it.

Exercise 8.34   Implement a new kind of block, with 'consistent breaks': unless the entire block fits on the current line, all of its breaks are forced. For instance,

Figure 8.8 *The pretty printer*

```
structure Pretty : PRETTY =
  struct
  datatype t = Block of t list * int * int
             | String of string
             | Break of int;

  fun breakdist (Block(_,_,len)::es, after) = len + breakdist (es,after)
    | breakdist (String s :: es, after)     = size s + breakdist (es,after)
    | breakdist (Break _ :: es, after)      = 0
    | breakdist ([], after)                 = after;

  fun pr (os, e, margin) =
   let val space = ref margin

        fun blanks n = (TextIO.output(os, StringCvt.padLeft #" " n "");
                        space := !space - n)

        fun newline () = (TextIO.output(os,"\n"); space := margin)

        fun printing ([], _, _)                = ()
          | printing (e::es, blockspace, after) =
            (case e of
                 Block(bes,indent,len) =>
                     printing(bes, !space-indent, breakdist (es,after))
               | String s  => (TextIO.output(os,s);  space := !space - size s)
               | Break len =>
                     if len + breakdist (es,after) <= !space
                     then blanks len
                     else (newline(); blanks(margin-blockspace));
             printing (es, blockspace, after))
   in  printing([e], margin, 0);  newline() end;

  fun length (Block(_,_,len)) = len
    | length (String s)       = size s
    | length (Break len)      = len;

  val str = String and brk = Break;

  fun blo (indent,es) =
    let fun sum ([],   k) = k
          | sum (e::es, k) = sum(es, length e + k)
    in  Block(es, indent, sum(es,0))  end;
  end;
```

consistent breaking of

$$\Big\langle \ \texttt{if} \ E \ \Big| \ \texttt{then} \ E_1 \ \Big| \ \texttt{else} \ E_2 \Big\rangle$$

would produce
```
if E
then E₁
else E₂
```
and never
```
if E then E₁
else E₂
```

Exercise 8.35   Write a purely functional version of the pretty printer. Instead of writing to a stream, it should return a list of strings. Does the functional version have any practical advantages?

Exercise 8.36   The Fortran statement

```
FORMAT (' Input =', I6, '  Output =', F8.2)
```

describes a line of text beginning with the string ' Input =', followed by an integer taking up 6 characters, followed by the string ' Output =', followed by a floating point (real) number taking up 8 characters, with 2 digits to the right of the decimal point. A file written under a Fortran format can be read under the same format. Discuss how this kind of formatted input/output could be implemented in ML. How would formats and data be represented?

Summary of main points
- References denote mutable cells in the store, like the variables and pointers of procedural languages.
- In ML, variables cannot be updated; only references and arrays can be updated.
- To prevent polymorphic references from causing run-time type errors, the expression in a polymorphic `val` declaration must be a syntactic value.
- Cyclic data structures, like ring buffers, can be constructed using references.
- A function can exploit imperative features while exhibiting purely functional behaviour.
- Input and output commands transmit characters between the program and external devices.

9

Writing Interpreters for the λ-Calculus

This chapter brings together all the concepts we have learned so far. For an extended example, it presents a collection of modules to implement the λ-calculus as a primitive functional programming language. Terms of the λ-calculus can be parsed, evaluated and the result displayed. It is hardly a practical language. Trivial arithmetic calculations employ unary notation and take minutes. However, its implementation involves many fundamental techniques: parsing, representing bound variables and reducing expressions to normal form. These techniques can be applied to theorem proving and computer algebra.

Chapter outline

We consider parsing and two interpreters for λ-terms, with an overview of the λ-calculus. The chapter contains the following sections:

A functional parser. An ML functor implements top-down recursive descent parsing. Parsers can be combined using infix operators that resemble the symbols for combining grammatical phrases.

Introducing the λ-calculus. Terms of this calculus can express functional programs. They can be evaluated using either the call-by-value or the call-by-name mechanism. Substitution must be performed carefully, avoiding variable name clashes.

Representing λ-terms in ML. Substitution, parsing and pretty printing are implemented as ML structures.

The λ-calculus as a programming language. Typical data structures of functional languages, including infinite lists, are encoded in the λ-calculus. The evaluation of recursive functions is demonstrated.

A functional parser

Before discussing the λ-calculus, let us consider how to write scanners and parsers in a functional style. The parser described below complements the pretty printer of the previous chapter. Using these tools, ML programs can read and write λ-terms, ML types and logical formulæ.

357

9.1   *Scanning, or lexical analysis*

A parser seldom operates directly on a string of characters. The characters are first **scanned**: processed into **tokens** such as keywords, identifiers, special symbols and numbers. The parser is supplied a list of tokens.

This two-level approach simplifies the grammar used for parsing. The scanner removes spaces, line breaks and comments in some uniform fashion, leaving the parser to deal with more complex matters of syntax. Scanning can be performed by a finite-state machine. Such a machine, driven by character-indexed arrays, can run extremely fast. For small inputs, the scanning functions in the library structure *Substring* do the job quite well.

A lexical analyser, or lexer, is a structure with the following signature:

```
signature LEXICAL =
  sig
  datatype token = Id of string | Key of string
  val scan : string -> token list
  end;
```

A *token* is either an identifier or a keyword. This simple scanner does not recognize numbers. Calling *scan* performs lexical analysis on a string and returns the resulting list of tokens.

Before we can parse a language, we must specify its vocabulary. To classify tokens as identifiers or keywords, the scanner must be supplied with an instance of the signature *KEYWORD*:

```
signature KEYWORD =
  sig
  val alphas  : string list
  and symbols : string list
  end;
```

The list *alphas* defines the alphanumeric keywords like "if" and "let", while *symbols* lists symbolic keywords like "(" and ")". The two kinds of keywords are treated differently:

- A string of alphanumeric characters is scanned as far as possible — until it is not followed by another letter or digit. It is classified as a keyword if it belongs to *alphas*, and as an identifier otherwise.
- A string of symbolic characters is scanned until it matches some element of *symbols*, or until it is not followed by another symbolic character. It is always classified as a keyword. For instance, if "(" belongs to *symbols* then the string "((" is scanned as two "(" tokens, and as one "((" token otherwise.

Figure 9.1 *The lexical analysis functor*

```
functor Lexical (Keyword: KEYWORD) : LEXICAL =
  struct
  datatype token = Key of string   |   Id of string;

  fun member (x:string, l) = List.exists (fn y => x=y) l;

  fun alphaTok a =
      if member(a, Keyword.alphas) then Key(a) else Id(a);

  (*scanning of a symbolic keyword*)
  fun symbolic (sy, ss) =
      case Substring.getc ss of
          NONE          => (Key sy, ss)
        | SOME (c,ss1) =>
              if member(sy, Keyword.symbols)
                  orelse not (Char.isPunct c)
              then  (Key sy, ss)
              else  symbolic (sy ^ String.str c, ss1);

  (*Scanning a substring into a list of tokens*)
  fun scanning (toks, ss) =
      case Substring.getc ss of
          NONE          => rev toks       (*end of substring*)
        | SOME (c,ss1) =>
              if Char.isAlphaNum c
                  then (*identifier or keyword*)
                  let val (id, ss2) = Substring.splitl Char.isAlphaNum ss
                      val tok       = alphaTok (Substring.string id)
                  in  scanning (tok::toks, ss2)
                  end
              else if Char.isPunct c
              then (*special symbol*)
                  let val (tok, ss2) = symbolic (String.str c, ss1)
                  in  scanning (tok::toks, ss2)
                  end
              else (*ignore spaces, line breaks, control characters*)
                  scanning (toks, Substring.dropl (not o Char.isGraph) ss);

  fun scan a = scanning([], Substring.all a);
  end;
```

Functor *Lexical* (Figure 9.1 on the preceding page) implements the scanner using several *Substring* functions: *getc*, *splitl*, *string*, *dropl* and *all*. The function *getc* splits a substring into its first character, paired with the rest of the substring; if the substring is empty, the result is *NONE*. In Section 8.9 we met the functions *all* and *string*, which convert between strings and substrings. We also met *splitl*, which scans a substring from the left, splitting it into two parts. The function *dropl* is similar but returns only the second part of the substring; the scanner uses it to ignore spaces and other non-printing characters. The library predicate *Char.isAlphaNum* recognizes letters and digits, while *Char.isGraph* recognizes all printing characters and *Char.isPunct* recognizes punctuation symbols.

The code is straightforward and efficient, as fast as the obvious imperative implementation. The *Substring* functions yield functional behaviour, but they work by incrementing indices. This is better than processing lists of characters.

The functor declares function *member* for internal use. It does not depend upon the infix *mem* declared in Chapter 3, or on any other top level functions not belonging to the standard library. The membership test is specific to type *string* because polymorphic equality can be slow.

The lexical analyser is implemented as a functor because the information in signature *KEYWORD* is static. We only need to change the list of keywords or special symbols when parsing a new language. Applying the functor to some instance of *KEYWORD* packages that information into the resulting structure. We could have implemented the lexer as a curried function taking similar information as a record, but this would complicate the lexer's type in exchange for needless flexibility.

Exercise 9.1   Modify the scanner to recognize decimal numerals in the input. Let a new constructor *Num : integer → token* return the value of a scanned integer constant.

Exercise 9.2   Modify the scanner to ignore comments. The comment brackets, such as " (*" and "*) ", should be supplied as additional components of the structure *Keyword*.

9.2   *A toolkit for top-down parsing*

A top-down recursive descent parser closely resembles the grammar that it parses. There are procedures for all the syntactic phrases, and their mutually recursive calls precisely mirror the grammar rules.

The resemblance is closer in functional programming. Higher-order functions can express syntactic operations such as concatenation of phrases, alternative phrases and repetition of a phrase. With an appropriate choice of infix operators, a functional parser can be coded to look almost exactly like a set of grammar rules. Do not be fooled; the program has all the limitations of top-down parsing. In particular, a **left-recursive** grammar rule such as

$$exp = exp \ "*"$$

makes the parser run forever! Compiler texts advise on coping with these limitations.

Outline of the approach. Suppose that the grammar includes a certain class of phrases whose meanings can be represented by values of type τ. A **parser** for such phrases must be a function of type

$$token\ list \rightarrow \tau \times token\ list,$$

henceforth abbreviated as type τ *phrase*. When the parser is given a list of tokens that begins with a valid phrase, it removes those tokens and computes their meaning as a value of type τ. The parser returns the pair of this meaning and the remaining tokens. If the token list does not begin with a valid phrase, then the parser rejects it by raising exception *SyntaxErr*.

Not all functions of type τ *phrase* are parsers. A parser must only remove tokens from the front of the token list; it must not insert tokens, or modify the token list in any other way.

To implement complex parsers, we define some primitive parsers and some operations for combining parsers.

Parsing primitive phrases. The trivial parsers recognize an identifier, a specific keyword, or the empty phrase. They remove no more than one token from their input:

- The parser *id*, of type *string phrase*, removes an *Id* token from its input and returns this identifier as a string (paired with the tail of the token list).
- The parser $\$a$ has type *string phrase* if a is a string. It removes the keyword token *Key a* from its input and returns a paired with the tail of the token list.
- The parser *empty* has the polymorphic type $(\alpha\ list)\ phrase$. It returns [] paired with the original token list.

The first two of these reject their input unless it begins with the required token, while *empty* always succeeds.

Alternative phrases. If *ph*1 and *ph*2 have type τ *phrase* then so does *ph*1 | |*ph*2. The parser *ph*1 | |*ph*2 accepts all the phrases that are accepted by either of the parsers *ph*1 or *ph*2. This parser, when supplied with a list of tokens, passes them to *ph*1 and returns the result if successful. If *ph*1 rejects the tokens then *ph*2 is attempted.

The parser ! !*ph* is the same as *ph*, except that if *ph* rejects the tokens then the entire parse fails with an error message. This prevents an enclosing | | operator from attempting to parse the phrase in another way. The operator ! ! is typically used in phrases that start with a distinguishing keyword, and therefore have no alternative parse; see $-- below.

Consecutive phrases. The parser *ph*1--*ph*2 accepts a *ph*1 phrase followed by a *ph*2 phrase. This parser, when supplied with a list of tokens, passes them to *ph*1. If *ph*1 parses a phrase and returns (*x*, *toks*2) then the remaining tokens (*toks*2) are passed to *ph*2. If *ph*2 parses a phrase and returns (*y*, *toks*3) then *ph*1--*ph*2 returns ((*x*, *y*), *toks*3). Note that *toks*3 consists of the tokens remaining after both parses. If either parser rejects its input then so does *ph*1--*ph*2.

Thus, the meaning of *ph*1--*ph*2 is the pair of the meanings of *ph*1 and *ph*2, applied to consecutive segments of the input. If *ph*1 has type τ_1 *phrase* and *ph*2 has type τ_2 *phrase* then *ph*1--*ph*2 has type $(\tau_1 \times \tau_2)$ *phrase*.

The operator $-- covers a common case. The parser *a* $-- *ph* resembles $*a* -- *ph*; it parses a phrase that begins with the keyword token *a* and continues as *ph*. But it returns the meaning of *ph*, not paired with *a*. Moreover, if *ph* rejects its tokens then (using ! !) it fails with an error message. The operator $-- is appropriate if only one grammar rule starts with the symbol *a*.

Modifying the meaning. The parser *ph*>>*f* accepts the same inputs as *ph*, but returns (*f*(*x*), *toks*) when *ph* returns (*x*, *toks*). Thus, it assigns the meaning *f*(*x*) when *ph* assigns the meaning *x*. If *ph* has type σ *phrase* and *f* has type σ → τ then *ph*>>*f* has type τ *phrase*.

Repetition. To illustrate these operators, let us code a parsing functional. If *ph* is any parser then *repeat ph* will parse zero or more repetitions of *ph*:

```
fun repeat ph toks = (    ph -- repeat ph >> (op::)
                     || empty    ) toks;
```

The precedences of the infix operators are `--`, `>>`, `||` from highest to lowest. The body of *repeat* consists of two parsers joined by `||`, resembling the obvious grammatical definition: a repetition of *ph* is either a *ph* followed by a repetition of *ph*, or is empty.

The parser *ph* `--` *repeat ph* returns $((x, xs), toks)$, where *xs* is a list. The operator `>>` applies a list 'cons' (the operator `::`), converting the pair (x, xs) to $x ::$ *xs*. In the second line, *empty* yields [] as the meaning of the empty phrase. In short, *repeat ph* constructs the list of the meanings of the repeated phrases. If *ph* has type τ *phrase* then *repeat ph* has type $(\tau\ list)\ phrase$.

Beware of infinite recursion. Can the declaration of *repeat* be simplified by omitting *toks* from both sides? No — calling *repeat ph* would immediately produce a recursive call to *repeat ph*, resulting in disaster:

```
fun repeat ph = ph -- repeat ph >> (op::)   ||   empty;
```

Mentioning the formal parameter *toks* is a device to delay evaluation of the body of *repeat* until it is given a token list; the inner *repeat ph* is normally given a shorter token list and therefore terminates. Lazy evaluation would eliminate the need for this device.

9.3   *The ML code of the parser*

Infix directives for the operators `$--`, `--`, `>>` and `||` assign appropriate precedences to them. The exact numbers are arbitrary, but `$--` must have higher precedence than `--` in order to attract the string to its left. Also `>>` must have lower precedence than `--` in order to encompass an entire grammar rule. Finally, `||` must have the lowest precedence so that it can combine grammar rules.

```
infix 6 $--;
infix 5 --;
infix 3 >>;
infix 0 ||;
```

These directives have global effect because they are made at top level. We should also open the structure containing the parsing operators: compound names cannot be used as infix operators.

Functor *Parsing* (Figure 9.3 on page 365) implements the parser. The functor declaration has the primitive form that takes exactly one argument structure, in this case *Lex*. Its result signature is *PARSE* (Figure 9.2).

You may notice that many of the types in this signature differ from those given in the previous section. The type abbreviation

$$\alpha\ phrase = token\ list \rightarrow \alpha \times token\ list$$

Figure 9.2 *Signature for functional parsers*

```
signature PARSE =
  sig
  exception SyntaxErr of string
  type token
  val id     : token list -> string * token list
  val $      : string -> token list -> string * token list
  val empty  : 'a -> 'b list * 'a
  val ||     : ('a -> 'b) * ('a -> 'b) -> 'a -> 'b
  val !!     : ('a -> 'b * 'c) -> 'a -> 'b * 'c
  val --     : ('a -> 'b * 'c) * ('c -> 'd * 'e) -> 'a -> ('b * 'd) * 'e
  val $--    : string * (token list -> 'a * 'b) -> token list -> 'a * 'b
  val >>     : ('a -> 'b * 'c) * ('b -> 'd) -> 'a -> 'd * 'c
  val repeat : ('a -> 'b * 'a) -> 'a -> 'b list * 'a
  val infixes :
        (token list -> 'a * token list) * (string -> int) *
        (string -> 'a -> 'a -> 'a) -> token list -> 'a * token list
  val reader : (token list -> 'a * 'b list) -> string -> 'a
  end;
```

---

is not used; more importantly, some of the types in the signature are more general than is necessary for parsing. They are not restricted to token lists.

ML often assigns a function a type that is more polymorphic than we expect. If we specify the signature prior to coding the functor — which is a disciplined style of software development — then any additional polymorphism is lost. When designing a signature, it is sometimes useful to consult the ML top level and note what types it suggests.

Signature *PARSE* specifies the type *token* in order to specify the types of *id* and other items. Accordingly, *Parsing* declares the type *token* to be equivalent to *Lex . token*.

The function *reader* packages a parser for outside use. Calling *reader ph a* scans the string *a* into tokens and supplies them to the parsing function *ph*. If there are no tokens left then *reader* returns the meaning of the phrase; otherwise it signals a syntax error.

Parsing infix operators. The function *infixes* constructs a parser for infix operators, when supplied with the following arguments:

• *ph* accepts the atomic phrases that are to be combined by the operators.

Figure 9.3 *The parsing functor*

```
functor Parsing (Lex: LEXICAL) : PARSE =
  struct
  type token = Lex.token;

  exception SyntaxErr of string;

  fun id (Lex.Id a :: toks) = (a,toks)
    | id toks                = raise SyntaxErr "Identifier expected";

  fun $a (Lex.Key b :: toks) = if a=b then (a,toks)
                                       else raise SyntaxErr a
    | $a _                   = raise SyntaxErr "Symbol expected";

  fun empty toks = ([],toks);

  fun (ph1 || ph2) toks = ph1 toks   handle SyntaxErr _ => ph2 toks;

  fun !! ph toks = ph toks   handle SyntaxErr msg =>
                            raise Fail ("Syntax error: " ^ msg);

  fun (ph1 -- ph2) toks =
      let val (x,toks2) = ph1 toks
          val (y,toks3) = ph2 toks2
      in  ((x,y), toks3)  end;

  fun (ph>>f) toks =
      let val (x,toks2) = ph toks
      in  (f x, toks2)  end;

  fun (a $-- ph) = ($a -- !!ph >> #2);

  fun repeat ph toks = (   ph -- repeat ph >> (op::)
                        || empty         ) toks;

  fun infixes (ph,prec_of,apply) =
    let fun over k toks = next k (ph toks)
        and next k (x, Lex.Key(a)::toks) =
                if prec_of a < k then (x, Lex.Key a :: toks)
                else next k ((over (prec_of a) >> apply a x) toks)
          | next k (x, toks) = (x, toks)
    in  over 0  end;

  (*Scan and parse, checking that no tokens remain*)
  fun reader ph a =
          (case ph (Lex.scan a) of
               (x, [])    => x
             | (_, _::_) => raise SyntaxErr "Extra characters in phrase");
  end;
```

- *prec_of* gives the precedences of the operators, returning -1 for all key-words that are not infix operators.
- *apply* combines the meanings of phrases; *apply a x y* applies the operator *a* to operands *x* and *y*.

The resulting parser recognizes an input like

$$ph \oplus ph \otimes ph \ominus ph \oslash ph$$

and groups the atomic phrases according to the precedences of the operators. It employs the mutually recursive functions *over* and *next*.

Calling *over k* parses a series of phrases, separated by operators of precedence *k* or above. In *next k (x, toks)* the argument *x* is the meaning of the preceding phrase and *k* is the governing precedence. The call does nothing unless the next token is an operator *a* of precedence *k* or above; in this case, tokens are recursively parsed by *over(prec_of a)* and their result combined with *x*. The result and the remaining tokens are then parsed under the original precedence *k*.

The algorithm does not handle parentheses; this should be done by *ph*. Section 10.6 demonstrates the use of *infixes*.

Writing a backtracking parser. A grammar is **ambiguous** if some token list admits more than one parse. Our method is easily modified such that each parsing function returns a sequence (lazy list) of successful outcomes. Inspecting elements of this sequence causes backtracking over all parses of the input.

The parser *ph1--ph2* returns the sequence of all possible ways of parsing a *ph1* followed by a *ph2*. It applies *ph1* to the input, which yields a sequence of (*x, toks2*) pairs. For each element of this sequence it applies *ph2* to *toks2*, obtaining a sequence of (*y, toks3*) pairs. Finally it returns the sequence of all successful outcomes ((*x, y*), *toks3*). For each outcome, the meaning (*x, y*) consists of a pair of meanings returned by *ph1* and *ph2*.

A parser rejects its input by returning the empty sequence rather than by raising an exception. Note that if *ph1* rejects its input or if *ph2* rejects each of the outcomes of *ph1* then *ph1--ph2* yields the empty sequence, rejecting its input.

This is an enjoyable exercise in sequence processing, but it suffers from the drawbacks of backtracking parsers: it is slow and handles errors poorly. It can take exponential time to parse the input; bottom-up parsing would be much faster. If the input contains a syntax error, a backtracking parser returns no information other than an empty sequence. Our parser can easily be made to pinpoint syntax errors. Modify type *token* so that each token carries its position in the input string, and make ! ! include that information in its error messages.

Backtracking is valuable in theorem proving. A 'tactic' for finding proofs can be expressed as a function that takes a goal and returns a sequence of solutions. Tactics can be combined to form effective search procedures. The next chapter presents this technique, which is related to our treatment of parsing functions.

Exercise 9.3   Give an example of a parser *ph* such that, for all inputs, *ph* terminates successfully but *repeat ph* runs forever.

Exercise 9.4   A *parse tree* is a tree representing the structure of a parsed token list. Each node stands for a phrase, with branches to its constituent symbols and sub-phrases. Modify our parsing method so that it constructs parse trees. Declare a suitable type *partree* of parse trees such that each parsing function can have type

$$token\ list \rightarrow partree \times token\ list.$$

Code the operators | |, --, *id*, $, *empty* and *repeat*; note that >> no longer serves any purpose.

Exercise 9.5   Modify the parsing method to generate a sequence of successful results, as described above.

Exercise 9.6   Code the parsing method in a procedural style, where each parsing 'function' has type *unit* $\rightarrow \alpha$ and updates a reference to a token list by removing tokens from it. Does the procedural approach have any drawbacks, or is it superior to the functional approach?

Exercise 9.7   Modify signature *PARSE* to specify a substructure *Lex* of signature *LEXICAL* rather than a type *token*, so that other signature items can refer to the type *Lex . token*. Modify the functor declaration accordingly.

Exercise 9.8   When an expression contains several infix operators of the same precedence, does *infixes* associate them to the left or to the right? Modify this function to give the opposite association. Describe an algorithm to handle a mixture of left and right-associating operators.

9.4   *Example: parsing and displaying types*

The parser and pretty printer will now be demonstrated using a grammar for ML types. For purposes of the example, ML's type system can be simplified by dropping record and product types. There are two forms of type to consider:

Types such as *int*, *bool list* and (α *list*) $\rightarrow$ (β *list*) consist of a ***type constructor*** applied to zero or more ***type arguments***. Here the type constructor *int* is applied to zero arguments; *list* is applied to the type *bool*; and $\rightarrow$ is applied to the types α *list* and β *list*. ML adopts a postfix syntax for most type constructors, but $\rightarrow$ has an infix syntax. Internally, such types can be represented by a string paired with a list of types.

A type can consist merely of a type variable, which can be represented by a string. Our structure for types has the following signature:

```
signature TYPE =
  sig
  datatype t = Con of string * t list | Var of string
  val pr   : t -> unit
  val read : string -> t
  end;
```

It specifies three components:

- The datatype *t* comprises the two forms of type, with *Con* for type constructors and *Var* for type variables.
- Calling *pr ty* prints the type *ty* at the terminal.
- The function *read* converts a string to a type.

We could implement this signature using a functor whose formal parameter list would contain the signatures *PARSE* and *PRETTY*. But it is generally simpler to avoid writing functors unless they will be applied more than once. Let us therefore create structures for the lexical analyser and the parser, for parsing types. They will be used later to implement the λ-calculus.

Structure *LamKey* defines the necessary symbols. Structure *LamLex* provides lexical analysis for types and the λ-calculus, while *LamParsing* provides parsing operators.

```
structure LamKey =
    struct val alphas  = []
              and symbols = ["(", ")", "/", "->"]
       end;
structure LamLex     = Lexical (LamKey);
structure LamParsing = Parsing (LamLex);
```

Structure *Type* (Figure 9.4) matches signature *TYPE*. For simplicity, it only treats the $\rightarrow$ symbol; the other type constructors are left as an exercise. The grammar defines types and atomic types in mutual recursion. An atomic type is either a

Figure 9.4 *Parsing and displaying* ML *types*

```
structure Type : TYPE =
  struct

  datatype t = Con of string * t list
             | Var of string;

  local (** Parsing **)
    fun makeFun (ty1,ty2) = Con("->",[ty1,ty2]);
    open LamParsing

    fun typ toks =
      (    atom  --  "->" $-- typ              >> makeFun
      ||  atom
      ) toks
    and atom toks =
      (    $"'"  --  id                        >> (Var o op^)
      ||  "(" $-- typ -- $")"                  >> #1
      ) toks;
  in
    val read = reader typ;
  end;

  local (** Display **)
    fun typ (Var a)                = Pretty.str a
      | typ (Con("->",[ty1,ty2])) = Pretty.blo(0,  [atom ty1,
                                                    Pretty.str " ->",
                                                    Pretty.brk 1,
                                                    typ ty2])

    and atom (Var a) = Pretty.str a
      | atom ty      = Pretty.blo(1, [Pretty.str"(",
                                      typ ty,
                                      Pretty.str")"]);
  in
    fun pr ty = Pretty.pr (TextIO.stdOut, typ ty, 50)
  end

end;
```

---

type variable or any type enclosed in parentheses:

$$Type \; = \; Atom \; \text{->} \; Type$$
$$| \; Atom$$

$$Atom \; = \; ' \; Id$$
$$| \; (\; Type \;)$$

This grammar treats → as an infix operator that associates to the right. It interprets `'a->'b->'c` as `'a->('b->'c)` rather than `('a->'b)->'c` because
`'a -> 'b` is not an *Atom*.

The structure contains two `local` declarations, one for parsing and one for
pretty printing. Each declares mutually recursive functions *typ* and *atom* corresponding to the grammar. Opening structure *LamParsing* makes its operations
available at top level; recall that the infix directives were global.

Parsing of types. Using the top-down parsing operators, the function definitions
in the parser are practically identical to the grammar rules. The operator >>,
which applies a function to a parser's result, appears three times. Function *typ*
uses >> to apply *makeFun* to the result of the first grammar rule, combining two
types to form a function type. Using $--$ in the rule prevents the arrow symbol
from being returned as a constituent of the phrase.

Both cases of *atom* involve >>, with two mysterious functions. During parsing of the type variable `'a`, in the first case, >> applies *Var o* `op^` to the pair
(`"'"`, `"a"`). This function consists of *Var* composed with string concatenation;
it concatenates the strings to `"'a"` and returns the type *Var* `"'a"`.

In the second case of *atom*, parsing the phrase (*Type*) calls the function #1,
which selects the first component of its argument. Here it takes the pair (*ty*, `")"`)
and yields *ty*. Had we not used $--$ to parse the left parenthesis, we should have
needed the even more mysterious function (#2 *o* #1).

The parsing functions mention the argument *toks* to avoid looping (like *repeat*
above) and because a `fun` declaration must mention an argument.

Pretty printing of types. The same mutual recursion works for displaying as for
parsing. Functions *typ* and *atom* both convert a type into a symbolic expression
for the pretty printer, but *atom* encloses its result in parentheses unless it is just
an identifier. Parentheses appear only when necessary; too many parentheses are
confusing.

The functions *blo*, *str* and *brk* of structure *Pretty* are used in typical fashion
to describe blocks, strings and breaks. Function *atom* calls *blo* with an inden-

tation of one to align subsequent breaks past the left parenthesis. Function *typ* calls *blo* with an indentation of zero, since it includes no parentheses; after the string " ->", it calls *brk* 1 to make a space or a line break.

The function *pr* writes to the terminal (stream *TextIO . stdOut*), with a right margin of fifty.

Trying some examples. We can enter types, note their internal representations (as values of *Type . t*) after parsing, and check that they are displayed correctly:

```
Type.read"'a->'b->'c";
> Con ("->", [Var "'a",
>               Con ("->", [Var "'b", Var "'c"])])
> : Type.t
Type.pr it;
> 'a -> 'b -> 'c
Type.read"('a->'b)->'c";
> Con ("->", [Con ("->", [Var "'a", Var "'b"]),
>             Var "'c"])
> : Type.t
Type.pr it;
> ('a -> 'b) -> 'c
```

Our parsing of types is naïve. A string of the form (*Type*) must be parsed twice. The first grammar rule for *Type* fails: there is no -> token after the right parenthesis. The second grammar rule parses it successfully as an *Atom*. We could modify the grammar to remove the repeated occurrence of *Atom*.

ⓘ *More on parsing.* LR parsing is the method of choice for complicated grammars, like those of programming languages. This bottom-up technique is reliable, efficient and general; it supports good error recovery. LR parsers are not written by hand but generated using a tool such as Yacc (yet another compiler-compiler). The tool accepts a grammar, constructs parsing tables and outputs the parser in source form. Each syntax rule may be augmented with a *semantic action*: code to be executed whenever that rule applies. Most parser generators are based upon the C language.

ML-Yacc (Tarditi and Appel, 1994) uses ML for semantic actions and for the generated parser. ML-Yacc is fairly complicated to set up, but it is worth considering for any nontrivial grammar. You must supply ML-Yacc with a lexical analyser, which might be hand-coded or generated using a tool such as ML-Lex (Appel *et al.*, 1994).

The functional approach to top-down parsing has been understood for a long time. Burge (1975) contains one of the earliest published descriptions, including the use of lazy lists for backtracking. Reade (1989) gives a more modern account. Frost and Launchbury (1989) use the method to parse a subset of English for a question-answering system. Tobias Nipkow, who suggested ! ! and $--, has used the approach to parse Isabelle theory files.

Aho *et al.* (1986) describes lexical analysis and parsing extremely well. It covers both the top-down approach implemented here using functions, and the bottom-up approach that underlies ML-Yacc.

Exercise 9.9   Implement parsing and pretty printing of arbitrary type constructors. First, define a grammar for ML's postfix syntax, as in the examples

```
'c list list              (string,int) sum
('a -> 'b) list           'a list -> 'b list
```

Parentheses are optional when a type constructor is applied to one argument not involving the arrow; thus `'a -> 'b list` stands for `'a -> (('b) list)` rather than `('a -> 'b) list`.

Exercise 9.10   Use the parsing primitives, or alternatively ML-Yacc, to implement a parser for propositions — type *prop* of Section 4.17.

Introducing the λ-calculus

Turing machines, recursive functions and register machines are formal models of computation. The λ-calculus, developed by Alonzo Church, is one of the earliest models and perhaps the most realistic. It can express computations over pairs, lists, trees (even infinite ones) and higher-order functions. Most functional languages are nothing more than elaborated forms of the λ-calculus, and their implementations are founded in λ-calculus theory.

Church's thesis asserts that the effectively computable functions are precisely those functions that can be computed in the λ-calculus. Because 'effective' is a vague notion, Church's thesis cannot be proved, but the λ-calculus is known to have the same power as the other models of computation. Functions coded in these models can be computed effectively, given sufficient time and space, and nobody has exhibited a computable function that cannot be coded in these models.

9.5   *λ-terms and λ-reductions*

The λ-calculus is a simple formal theory of functions. Its terms, called λ-terms, are constructed recursively from variables $x, y, z, \ldots$ and other λ-terms. Let $t, u, \ldots$ stand for arbitrary λ-terms. They may take one of three forms:

$$x \quad \text{a variable}$$
$$(\lambda x.t) \quad \text{functional } \textbf{\textit{abstraction}}$$
$$(t\,u) \quad \text{function } \textit{application}$$

A term t_1 is a *subterm* of t_2 if t_1 is contained in t_2 or is identical to it. For instance, y is a subterm of $(\lambda z.(z\,y))$.

In the abstraction $(\lambda x.t)$, we call x the *bound variable* and t the *body*. Every occurrence of x in t is *bound* by the abstraction. Conversely, an occurrence of a variable y is *free* if it is not bound — if it is not contained within the body of some abstraction $(\lambda y.u)$. For example, x occurs bound and y occurs free in $(\lambda z.(\lambda x.(y\,x)))$. From now on, let $a, b, c, \ldots$ denote free variables.

The names of bound variables have little significance. If they are renamed consistently in an abstraction, the new abstraction is essentially the same as the old. This principle is known throughout mathematics. In the integral $\int_a^b f(x)dx$, the variables a and b are free while x is bound. In the product $\Pi_{k=0}^n p(k)$, the variable n is free while k is bound.

The abstraction $(\lambda x.t)$ represents the function f with $f(x) = t$ for all x. Applying $(\lambda x.t)$ to an argument u yields the term that results when u is substituted for all free occurrences of x in t. Write the result of this substitution as $t[u/x]$. Substitution involves some delicate points, but let us leave them for later.

λ-conversions. These are rules for transforming a λ-term while preserving its intuitive meaning. Conversions should not be confused with equations such as $x + y = y + x$, which are statements about known arithmetic operations. The λ-calculus is not concerned with previously existing mathematical objects. The λ-terms themselves are the objects, and the λ-conversions are symbolic transformations upon them.

Most important is *β-conversion*, which transforms a function application by substituting the argument into the body:

$$((\lambda x.t)u) \Rightarrow_\beta t[u/x]$$

In this example, the argument is $(g\,a)$:

$$((\lambda x.((f\,x)x))(g\,a)) \Rightarrow_\beta ((f(g\,a))(g\,a))$$

Here is an example of two successive β-conversions:

$$((\lambda z.(z\,a))(\lambda x.x)) \Rightarrow_\beta ((\lambda x.x)a) \Rightarrow_\beta a$$

An *α-conversion* renames the bound variable in an abstraction:

$$(\lambda x.t) \Rightarrow_\alpha (\lambda y.t[y/x])$$

The abstraction over x is transformed into an abstraction over y, and x is replaced by *y*. Examples:

$$(\lambda x.a\,x) \Rightarrow_\alpha (\lambda y.a\,y)$$
$$(\lambda x.(x(\lambda y.(y\,x)))) \Rightarrow_\alpha (\lambda z.(z(\lambda y.(y\,z))))$$

Two λ-terms are **congruent** if one can be transformed into the other using α-conversions (possibly applied to subterms). Intuitively, we may regard congruent terms as being the same, renaming bound variables whenever necessary. Free variables are significant, however; thus *a* is distinct from *b* while $(\lambda x.x)$ is congruent to $(\lambda y.y)$.

Notation. Nested abstractions and applications can be abbreviated:

$$(\lambda x_1.(\lambda x_2.\ldots(\lambda x_n.t)\ldots)) \quad \text{as} \quad (\lambda x_1 x_2 \ldots x_n.t)$$
$$(\ldots(t_1 t_2)\ldots t_n) \quad \text{as} \quad (t_1 t_2 \ldots t_n)$$

The outer parentheses are dropped when the term is not enclosed in another term or is the body of an abstraction. For example,

$$(\lambda x.(x(\lambda y.(y\,x)))) \text{ can be written as } \lambda x.x(\lambda y.y\,x).$$

Reduction to normal form. A **reduction step** $t \Rightarrow u$ transforms *t* to *u* by applying a β-conversion to any subterm of *t*. If a term admits no reductions then it is in **normal form**. To **normalize** a term means to apply reductions until a normal form is reached.

Some terms can be reduced in more than one way. The **Church-Rosser Theorem** states that different reduction sequences starting from a term can always be brought together again. In particular, no two sequences of reductions can reach distinct (non-congruent) normal forms. The normal form of a term can be regarded as its value; it is independent of the order in which reductions are performed.

For instance, $(\lambda x.a\,x)((\lambda y.b\,y)c)$ has two different reduction sequences, both leading to the same normal form. The affected subterm is underlined at each step:

$$\underline{(\lambda x.a\,x)}((\lambda y.b\,y)c) \Rightarrow a(\underline{(\lambda y.b\,y)c}) \Rightarrow a(b\,c)$$
$$(\lambda x.a\,x)(\underline{(\lambda y.b\,y)c}) \Rightarrow \underline{(\lambda x.a\,x)(b\,c)} \Rightarrow a(b\,c)$$

Many λ-terms have no normal form. For instance, $(\lambda x.x\,x)(\lambda x.x\,x)$ reduces to itself by β-conversion. Any attempt to normalize this term must fail to terminate:

$$\underline{(\lambda x.x\,x)(\lambda x.x\,x)} \Rightarrow \underline{(\lambda x.x\,x)(\lambda x.x\,x)} \Rightarrow \cdots$$

A term t can have a normal form even though certain reduction sequences never terminate. Typically, t contains a subterm u that has no normal form, but u can be erased by a reduction step. For example, the reduction sequence

$$(\lambda y.a)((\lambda x.xx)(\lambda x.xx)) \Rightarrow a$$

reaches normal form directly, erasing the term $(\lambda x.xx)(\lambda x.xx)$. This corresponds to a **call-by-name** treatment of functions: the argument is not evaluated but simply substituted into the body of the function. Attempting to normalize the argument generates a nonterminating reduction sequence:

$$(\lambda y.a)((\lambda x.xx)(\lambda x.xx)) \Rightarrow (\lambda y.a)((\lambda x.xx)(\lambda x.xx)) \Rightarrow \cdots$$

Evaluating the argument prior to substitution into the function body corresponds to a **call-by-value** treatment of function application. In this example, the call-by-value strategy never reaches the normal form. The reduction strategy corresponding to call-by-name evaluation always reaches a normal form if one exists.

You may well ask, in what sense is $\lambda x.xx$ a function? It can be applied to any object and applies that object to itself! In classical mathematics, a function can only be defined over some previously existing set of values. The λ-calculus does not deal with functions as they are classically understood.[1]

9.6 *Preventing variable capture in substitution*

Substitution must be defined carefully: otherwise the conversions could go wrong. For instance, the term $\lambda xy.yx$ ought to behave like a curried function that, when applied to arguments t and u, returns ut as its result. For all λ-terms t and u, we should expect to have the reductions

$$(\lambda xy.yx)tu \Rightarrow (\lambda y.yt)u \Rightarrow ut.$$

The following reduction sequence is certainly wrong:

$$(\lambda xy.yx)yb \Rightarrow (\lambda y.yy)b \Rightarrow bb \ \ ???$$

The β-conversion of $(\lambda xy.yx)y$ to $\lambda y.yy$ is incorrect because the free variable y has become bound. The substitution has **captured** this free variable. By first renaming the bound variable y to z, the reduction can be performed safely:

$$(\lambda xz.zx)yb \Rightarrow (\lambda z.zy)b \Rightarrow by$$

---

[1] Dana Scott has constructed models in which every abstraction, including $\lambda x.xx$, denotes a function (Barendregt, 1984). However, this chapter regards the λ-calculus from a purely syntactic point of view.

In general, the substitution $t[u/x]$ will not capture any variables provided no free variable of u is bound in t.

If bound variables are represented literally, then substitution must sometimes rename bound variables of t to avoid capturing free variables. Renaming is complicated and can be inefficient. It is essential that the new names do not appear elsewhere in the term. Preferably they should be similar to the names that they replace; nobody wants to see a variable called G6620094.

A name-free representation. Changing the representation of λ-terms can simplify the substitution algorithm. The name x of a bound variable serves only to match each occurrence of x with its binding λx so that reductions can be performed correctly. If these matches can be made by other means, then the names can be abolished.

We can achieve this using the nesting depth of abstractions. Each occurrence of a bound variable is represented by an index, giving the number of abstractions lying between it and its binding abstraction. Two λ-terms are congruent — differing only by α-conversions — if and only if their name-free representations are identical.

In the name-free notation, no variable name appears after the λ symbol and bound variable indices appear as numbers. The first occurrence of x in the body of $\lambda x.(\lambda y.x)x$ is represented by 1 because it is enclosed in an abstraction over y. The second occurrence of x is not enclosed in any other abstraction and is represented by 0. Therefore the name-free representation of $\lambda x.(\lambda y.x)x$ is $\lambda.(\lambda.1)0$.

Here is a term where the bound variables occur at several nesting depths:

$$\lambda x.x(\lambda y.x\,y(\lambda z.x\,y\,z))$$

Viewing the term as a tree emphasizes its nesting structure:

In the name-free notation, the three occurrences of x are represented by 0, 1 and 2:

$$\lambda.0(\lambda.1\,0(\lambda.2\,1\,0))$$

Operations such as abstraction and substitution are easily performed in the name-free representation. It is a good data structure for variable binding, but is unreadable as a notation. The original variable names should be retained for later display, so that the user sees the traditional notation.

Abstraction. Suppose that t is a λ-term that we would like to abstract over all free occurrences of the variable x, constructing the abstraction $\lambda x.t$. Take, for instance, $x(\lambda y.a\,x\,y)$, which in the name-free notation is

$$x(\lambda.a\,x\,0).$$

To bind all occurrences of x, we must replace them by the correct indices, here 0 and 1, and insert a λ symbol:

$$\lambda.0(\lambda.a\,1\,0)$$

This can be performed by a recursive function on terms that keeps count of the nesting depth of abstractions. Each occurrence of x is replaced by an index equal to its depth.

Substitution. To perform the β-conversion

$$(\lambda x.t)u \Rightarrow_\beta t[u/x],$$

the term t must be recursively transformed, replacing all the occurrences of x by u. In the name-free notation, x could be represented by several different indices. The index is initially 0 and increases with the depth of abstractions in t. For instance, the conversion

$$(\lambda x.x(\lambda y.a\,x\,y))b \Rightarrow_\beta b(\lambda y.a\,b\,y)$$

becomes

$$(\lambda.0(\lambda.a\,1\,0))b \Rightarrow_\beta b(\lambda.a\,b\,0)$$

in the name-free notation. Observe that x has index 0 in the outer abstraction and index 1 in the inner one.

Performing β-conversion on a subterm $(\lambda x.t)u$ is more complex. The argument u may contain variables bound outside, namely indices with no matching abstraction in u. These indices must be increased by the current nesting depth before substitution into t; this ensures that they refer to the same abstractions afterwards.

For instance, in

$$\lambda z.(\lambda x.x(\lambda y.x))(a\,z) \Rightarrow_\beta \lambda z.a\,z(\lambda y.a\,z),$$

the argument $a\,z$ is substituted in two places, one of which lies in the scope of λy. In the name-free approach, $a\,z$ receives two different representations:

$$\lambda.(\lambda.0(\lambda.1))(a\,0) \Rightarrow_\beta \lambda.a\,0(\lambda.a\,1)$$

Exercise 9.11   Show all the reduction sequences for normalizing the term

$$(\lambda f.f(f\,a))((\lambda x.x\,x)((\lambda y.y)(\lambda y.y))).$$

Exercise 9.12   For each term, show its normal form or demonstrate that it has none:

$$(\lambda f\,x\,y.f\,x\,y)(\lambda u\,v.u)$$
$$(\lambda x.f(x\,x))(\lambda x.f(x\,x))$$
$$(\lambda x\,y.y\,x)(\lambda x.f(f\,x))(\lambda x.f(f(f(f\,x))))$$
$$(\lambda x.x\,x)(\lambda x.x)$$

Exercise 9.13   Give the name-free representations of the following terms:

$$\lambda x\,y\,z.x\,z(y\,z)$$
$$\lambda x\,y.(\lambda z.x\,y\,z)y\,x$$
$$\lambda f.(\lambda x.f(\lambda y.x\,x\,y))(\lambda x.f(\lambda y.x\,x\,y))$$
$$(\lambda p\,x\,y.p\,x\,y)(\lambda x\,y.y)\,a\,b$$

Exercise 9.14   Consider a representation of λ-terms that designates bound variables internally by unique integers. Give algorithms for constructing λ-terms and for performing substitution.

Representing λ-terms in ML

Implementing the λ-calculus in ML is straightforward under the name-free representation. The following sections present ML programs for abstraction and substitution, and for parsing and pretty printing λ-terms.

We shall need *StringDict*, the dictionary structure declared in Section 7.10. It allows us to associate any information, in this case λ-terms, with strings. We can evaluate λ-terms with respect to an **environment** of defined identifiers.

9.7   *The fundamental operations*

Here is the signature for the name-free representation:

```
signature LAMBDA =
  sig
  datatype t = Free   of string
             | Bound of int
             | Abs    of string * t
             | Apply of t * t;
  val abstract  : int -> string -> t -> t
  val absList   : string list * t -> t
  val applyList : t * t list -> t
  val subst     : int -> t -> t -> t
  val inst      : t StringDict.t -> t -> t
  end;
```

Datatype *t* comprises free variables (as strings), bound variables (as indices), abstractions and applications. Each *Abs* node stores the bound variable name for use in printing.

Calling *abstract i b t* converts each occurrence of the free variable b in t to the index i (or a greater index within nested abstractions). Usually $i = 0$ and the result is immediately enclosed in an abstraction to match this index. Recursive calls over abstractions in t have $i > 0$.

Calling *absList*($[x_1, \ldots, x_n], t$) creates the abstraction $\lambda x_1 \ldots x_n.t$.

Calling *applyList*($t, [u_1, \ldots, u_n]$) creates the application $t\, u_1 \ldots u_n$.

Calling *subst i u t* substitutes u for the bound variable index i in t. Usually $i = 0$ and t is the body of an abstraction in the β-conversion $(\lambda x.t)u$. The case $i > 0$ occurs during recursive calls over abstractions in t. All indices exceeding i are decreased by one to compensate for the removal of that index.

Calling *inst env t* copies t, replacing all occurrences of variables defined in *env* by their definitions. The dictionary *env* represents an environment, and *inst* expands all the definitions in a term. This process is called **instantiation**. Definitions may refer to other definitions; instantiation continues until defined variables no longer occur in the result.

Signature *LAMBDA* is concrete, revealing all the internal details. Many values of type *t* are **improper**: they do not correspond to real λ-terms because they contain unmatched bound variable indices. No term has the representation *Bound i*, for any i. Moreover, *abstract* returns improper terms and *subst* expects them. An abstract signature for the λ-calculus would provide operations upon λ-terms themselves, hiding their representation.

Structure *Lambda* (Figure 9.5) implements the signature. Function *shift* is private to the structure because it is called only by *subst*. Calling *shift i d u* adds i to all the unmatched indices j in u such that $j \geq d$. Initially $d = 0$ and d is in-

Figure 9.5 *The name-free representation of λ-terms*

```
structure Lambda : LAMBDA =
  struct
  datatype t = Free  of string
             | Bound of int
             | Abs   of string * t
             | Apply of t * t;

  (*Convert occurrences of b to bound index i in a term*)
  fun abstract i b (Free a)     = if a=b then  Bound i  else  Free a
    | abstract i b (Bound j)    = Bound j
    | abstract i b (Abs(a,t))   = Abs(a, abstract (i+1) b t)
    | abstract i b (Apply(t,u)) = Apply(abstract i b t, abstract i b u);

  (*Abstraction over several free variables*)
  fun absList (bs,t) = foldr (fn (b,u) => Abs(b, abstract 0 b u)) t bs;

  (*Application of t to several terms*)
  fun applyList (t0,us) = foldl (fn (u,t) => Apply(t,u)) t0 us;

  (*Shift a term's non-local indices by i*)
  fun shift 0 d u           = u
    | shift i d (Free a)    = Free a
    | shift i d (Bound j)   = if j>=d then Bound(j+i) else Bound j
    | shift i d (Abs(a,t))  = Abs(a, shift i (d+1) t)
    | shift i d (Apply(t,u)) = Apply(shift i d t, shift i d u);

  (*Substitute u for bound variable i in a term t*)
  fun subst i u (Free a)     = Free a
    | subst i u (Bound j)    =
          if j<i then        Bound j            (*locally bound*)
          else if j=i then   shift i 0 u
          else (*j>i*)       Bound(j-1)         (*non-local to t*)
    | subst i u (Abs(a,t))   = Abs(a, subst (i+1) u t)
    | subst i u (Apply(t1,t2)) = Apply(subst i u t1, subst i u t2);

  (*Substitution for free variables*)
  fun inst env (Free a)      = (inst env (StringDict.lookup(env,a))
                                  handle StringDict.E _ => Free a)
    | inst env (Bound i)     = Bound i
    | inst env (Abs(a,t))    = Abs(a, inst env t)
    | inst env (Apply(t1,t2)) = Apply(inst env t1, inst env t2);
  end;
```

---

creased in recursive calls over abstractions in *u*. Before substituting some term *u* into another term, any unmatched indices in *u* must be shifted.

Function *inst* substitutes for free variables, not bound variables. It expects to be given proper λ-terms having no unmatched indices. It therefore does not keep track of the nesting depth or call *shift*.

Exercise 9.15 Explain the use of the fold functionals in the declarations of *abs-List* and *applyList*.

Exercise 9.16 Declare a signature for the λ-calculus that hides its internal representation. It should specify predicates to test whether a λ-term is a variable, an abstraction or an application, and specify functions for abstraction and substitution. Sketch the design of two structures, employing two different representations of λ-terms, that would have this signature.

9.8   *Parsing λ-terms*

In order to apply the parser and pretty printer, we require a grammar for λ-terms, including the abbreviations for nested abstractions and applications. The following grammar distinguishes between ordinary terms and atomic terms. A per cent sign (%) serves as the λ symbol:

$$Term = \text{\% } Id \ Id^* \ Term$$
$$| \ Atom \ Atom^*$$

$$Atom = Id$$
$$| \ (\ Term \ )$$

Note that *phrase** stands for zero or more repetitions of *phrase*. A term consisting of several Atoms in a row, such as *a b c d*, abbreviates the nested application $(((a\,b)c)d)$. A more natural grammar would define the phrase class *Applic*:

$$Applic = Atom$$
$$| \ Applic \ Atom$$

Then we could replace the *Atom Atom** in *Term* by *Applic*. But the second grammar rule for *Applic* is left-recursive and would cause our parser to loop. Eliminating this left recursion in the standard way yields our original grammar.

Structure *ParseTerm* (Figure 9.6) uses structures *Parse* and *Lambda*, containing the parser and the λ-term operations, to satisfy signature *PARSE_TERM*:

```
signature PARSE_TERM =
   sig  val read: string -> Lambda.t  end;
```

Figure 9.6 *The λ-calculus parser*

```
structure ParseTerm : PARSE_TERM =
  struct

  fun makeLambda ((b,bs),t) = Lambda.absList (b::bs, t);

  open LamParsing

  fun term toks =
    (   "%" $-- id -- repeat id -- "." $-- term >> makeLambda
     || atom -- repeat atom                      >> Lambda.applyList
    ) toks
  and atom toks =
    (   id                                       >> Lambda.Free
     || "(" $-- term -- $")"                      >> #1
    ) toks;
  val read = reader term;

  end;
```

The structure's only purpose is to parse λ-terms. Its signature specifies just one component: the function *read* converts a string to a λ-term. Its implementation is straightforward, using components *absList* and *applyList* of structure *Lambda*.

Exercise 9.17 In function *makeLambda*, why does the argument pattern have the form it does?

Exercise 9.18 What is the result of parsing `"%x x.x(%x x.x)"`?

9.9   *Displaying λ-terms*

Structure *DisplayTerm* (Figure 9.7 on the facing page) implements pretty printing for λ-terms. Using structures *Pretty* and *Lambda* — the pretty printer and the term operations — it satisfies signature *DISPLAY_TERM*:

```
signature DISPLAY_TERM =
  sig
  val rename  : string list * string -> string
  val stripAbs : Lambda.t -> string list * Lambda.t
  val pr      : Lambda.t -> unit
  end;
```

The signature specifies several components:

Figure 9.7 *The λ-calculus pretty printer*

```
structure DisplayTerm : DISPLAY_TERM =
  struct

  (*Free variable in a term*)
  fun vars (Lambda.Free a)       = [a]
    | vars (Lambda.Bound i)      = []
    | vars (Lambda.Abs(a,t))     = vars t
    | vars (Lambda.Apply(t1,t2)) = vars t1 @ vars t2;

  (*Rename variable "a" to avoid clashes*)
  fun rename (bs,a) =
      if List.exists (fn x => x=a) bs  then  rename (bs, a ^ "'")  else  a;

  (*Remove leading lambdas; return bound variable names*)
  fun strip (bs, Lambda.Abs(a,t)) =
        let val b = rename (vars t, a)
        in  strip (b::bs, Lambda.subst 0 (Lambda.Free b) t)
        end
    | strip (bs, u)               = (rev bs, u);

  fun stripAbs t = strip ([],t);

  fun spaceJoin (b,z) = " " ^ b ^ z;

  fun term (Lambda.Free a)       = Pretty.str a
    | term (Lambda.Bound i)      = Pretty.str "??UNMATCHED INDEX??"
    | term (t as Lambda.Abs _) =
        let val (b::bs,u) = stripAbs t
            val binder    = "%" ^ b ^ (foldr spaceJoin ". " bs)
        in  Pretty.blo(0, [Pretty.str binder, term u])
        end
    | term t                     = Pretty.blo(0, applic t)
  and applic (Lambda.Apply(t,u)) = applic t @ [Pretty.brk 1, atom u]
    | applic t                   = [atom t]
  and atom (Lambda.Free a)       = Pretty.str a
    | atom t                     = Pretty.blo(1, [Pretty.str"(",
                                                  term t,
                                                  Pretty.str")"]);

  fun pr t = Pretty.pr (TextIO.stdOut, term t, 50);
  end;
```

- *rename*($[a_1, \ldots, a_n]$, a) appends prime ($'$) characters to a to make it differ from each of $a_1, \ldots, a_n$.
- *stripAbs* analyses an abstraction into its bound variables and body, as described below.
- Calling *pr t* prints the term t at the terminal.

Even with the name-free representation, bound variables may have to be renamed when a term is displayed. The normal form of $(\lambda xy.x)y$ is shown as %y$'$. y, not as %y. y. Function *stripAbs* and its auxiliary function *strip* handle abstractions. Given $\lambda x_1 \ldots x_m.t$, the bound variables are renamed to differ from all free variables in t. The new names are substituted into t as free variables. Thus, all indices are eliminated from a term as it is displayed.

The mutually recursive functions *term*, *applic* and *atom* prepare λ-terms for pretty printing. A *Free* variable is displayed literally. A *Bound* variable index should never be encountered unless it has no matching *Abs* node (indicating that the term is improper). For an *Abs* node, the bound variables are renamed; then *foldleft* joins them into a string, separated by spaces. An *Apply* node is displayed using *applic*, which corresponds to the grammatical phrase *Applic* mentioned in the previous section. Finally, *atom* encloses a term in parentheses unless it is simply an identifier.

Exercise 9.19   How will the normal form of $(\lambda x\, y.x)(\lambda y.y)$ be displayed? Modify *DisplayTerm* to ensure that, when a term is displayed, no variable name is bound twice in overlapping scopes.

Exercise 9.20   Terms can be displayed without substituting free variables for bound variables. Modify *DisplayTerm* to keep a list of the variables bound in the abstractions enclosing the current subterm. To display the term *Bound i*, locate the *i*th name in the list.

The λ-calculus as a programming language

Despite its simplicity, the λ-calculus is rich enough to model the full range of functional programming. Data structures such as pairs and lists can be processed under either call-by-value or call-by-name evaluation strategies. After a brief discussion of these topics we shall demonstrate them using ML. First, we must make some definitions.

Write $t \Rightarrow^* u$ whenever t can be transformed into u by zero or more reduction steps. If u is in normal form then $t \Rightarrow^* u$ can be viewed as evaluating t to obtain the result u. Not every evaluation strategy will succeed in finding this normal form.

Write $t_1 = t_2$ whenever there is some term u (not necessarily in normal form!) such that $t_1 \Rightarrow^* u$ and $t_2 \Rightarrow^* u$. If $t_1 = t_2$ then both terms have the same normal form, if any. Viewing normal forms as values, $t_1 = t_2$ means that t_1 and t_2 have the same value.

Write $a \equiv t$, where a is a free variable, to mean 'a abbreviates t by definition.'

9.10   *Data structures in the λ-calculus*

We now consider how to encode boolean values, ordered pairs, natural numbers and lists. The codings given below are arbitrary; all that matters is that the data structures and their operations satisfy certain standard properties. An encoding of the booleans must define the truth values *true* and *false* and the conditional operator *if* as λ-terms, satisfying (for all t and u)

$$if\ true\ t\ u = t$$
$$if\ false\ t\ u = u$$

Once we have two distinct truth values and the conditional operator, we can define negation, conjunction and disjunction. Analogously, the ML compiler may represent *true* and *false* by any bit patterns provided the operations behave properly.

The booleans. The booleans can be coded by defining

$$true \equiv \lambda x\ y.x$$
$$false \equiv \lambda x\ y.y$$
$$if \equiv \lambda p\ x\ y.p\ x\ y$$

The necessary properties are easily verified. For instance:

$$
\begin{aligned}
if\ true\ t\ u &\equiv (\lambda p\ x\ y.p\ x\ y)true\ t\ u \\
&\Rightarrow (\lambda x\ y.true\ x\ y)t\ u \\
&\Rightarrow (\lambda y.true\ t\ y)u \\
&\Rightarrow true\ t\ u \\
&\Rightarrow (\lambda y.t)u \\
&\Rightarrow t
\end{aligned}
$$

This establishes *if true t u* $\Rightarrow^*$ *t* and therefore *if true t u* $= t$.

Ordered pairs. An encoding must specify a function *pair* (to construct pairs) and projection functions *fst* and *snd* (to select the components of a pair). The usual encoding is

$$pair \equiv \lambda x\ y\ f.f\ x\ y$$
$$fst \equiv \lambda p.p\ true$$
$$snd \equiv \lambda p.p\ false$$

where *true* and *false* are defined as above. These reductions, and the corresponding equations, are easily verified for all *t* and *u*:

$$fst(pair\ t\ u) \Rightarrow^* t$$
$$snd(pair\ t\ u) \Rightarrow^* u$$

The natural numbers. Of the several known encodings of the natural numbers, Church's is the most elegant. Underlined numbers $\underline{0}, \underline{1}, \ldots$, denote the **Church numerals**:

$$\underline{0} \equiv \lambda f\ x.x$$
$$\underline{1} \equiv \lambda f\ x.f\ x$$
$$\underline{2} \equiv \lambda f\ x.f(f\ x)$$
$$\vdots$$
$$\underline{n} \equiv \lambda f\ x.f^n(x)$$

Here $f^n(x)$ abbreviates $\underbrace{f(\cdots(f\ x)\cdots)}_{n \text{ times}}$.

The function *suc* computes the successor of a number, and *iszero* tests whether a number equals zero:

$$suc \equiv \lambda n\ f\ x.n\ f\ (f\ x)$$
$$iszero \equiv \lambda n.n(\lambda x.false)true$$

It is not difficult to verify the following reductions, where $\underline{n}$ is an arbitrary Church numeral:

$$suc\ \underline{n} \Rightarrow^* \underline{n+1}$$
$$iszero\ \underline{0} \Rightarrow^* true$$
$$iszero(suc\ \underline{n}) \Rightarrow^* false$$

Church numerals allow wonderfully succinct definitions of addition, multiplication and exponentiation:

$$add \equiv \lambda m\ n\ f\ x.m\ f(n\ f\ x)$$

$$mult \equiv \lambda m\ n\ f.m(n\ f)$$

$$expt \equiv \lambda m\ n\ f\ x.n\ m\ f\ x$$

These can be formally verified by induction, and their underlying intuitions are simple. Each Church numeral $\underline{n}$ is an operator to apply a function n times. Note that

$$add\ \underline{m}\ \underline{n}\ f\ x = f^m(f^n(x)) = f^{m+n}(x);$$

the others are understood similarly.

An encoding of the natural numbers must also specify a predecessor function *pre* such that

$$pre(suc\ \underline{n}) = \underline{n}$$

for all numbers $\underline{n}$. With Church numerals, computing $\underline{n}$ from $\underline{n+1}$ is complex (and slow!); given f and x, we must compute $f^n(x)$ from $g^{n+1}(y)$ for some g and y. A suitable g is a function on pairs such that $g(z, z') = (f(z), z)$ for all (z, z'); then

$$g^{n+1}(x, x) = (f^{n+1}(x), f^n(x))$$

and we take the second component. To formalize this, define *prefn* to construct g. Then define the predecessor function *pre* and the subtraction function *sub*:

$$prefn \equiv \lambda f\ p.pair(f(fst\ p))\ (fst\ p)$$

$$pre \equiv \lambda n\ f\ x.snd(n(prefn\ f)(pair\ x\ x))$$

$$sub \equiv \lambda m\ n.n\ pre\ m$$

For subtraction, $sub\ \underline{m}\ \underline{n} = pre^n(\underline{m})$; this computes the nth predecessor of $\underline{m}$.

Lists. Lists are encoded using pairing and the booleans. A non-empty list with head x and tail y is coded as $(false, (x, y))$. The empty list *nil* could be coded as $(true, true)$, but a simpler definition happens to work:

$$nil \equiv \lambda z.z$$

$$cons \equiv \lambda x\ y.pair\ false\ (pair\ x\ y)$$

$$null \equiv fst$$

$$hd \equiv \lambda z.fst(snd\ z)$$

$$tl \equiv \lambda z.snd(snd\ z)$$

The essential properties are easy to check for all *t* and *u*:

$$null \; nil \Rightarrow^* true$$
$$null(cons \; t \; u) \Rightarrow^* false$$
$$hd(cons \; t \; u) \Rightarrow^* t$$
$$tl(cons \; t \; u) \Rightarrow^* u$$

A call-by-name evaluation reduces *hd(cons t u)* to *t* without evaluating *u*, and can process infinite lists.

Exercise 9.21   Define an encoding of ordered pairs in terms of an arbitrary encoding of the booleans. Demonstrate it by encoding the booleans with *true* = λ*x y.y* and *false* = λ*x y.x*.

Exercise 9.22   Verify, for all Church numerals $\underline{m}$ and $\underline{n}$:

$$iszero(suc \; \underline{n}) = false$$
$$add \; \underline{m} \; \underline{n} = \underline{m+n}$$
$$mult \; \underline{m} \; \underline{n} = \underline{m \times n}$$
$$expt \; \underline{m} \; \underline{n} = \underline{m^n}$$

Exercise 9.23   Define an encoding of the natural numbers that has a simple predecessor function.

Exercise 9.24   Define an encoding of labelled binary trees.

Exercise 9.25   Write an ML function *numeral* of type *int* → *Lambda.t* such that *numeral n* constructs the Church numeral $\underline{n}$, for all $n \geq 0$.

9.11   *Recursive definitions in the λ-calculus*
        There is a λ-term *fact* that computes factorials of Church numerals by the recursion

$$fact \; n = if \; (iszero \; n) \; \underline{1} \; (mult \; n \; (fact(pre \; n))).$$

There is a λ-term *append* that joins two lists by the recursion

$$append \; z \; w = if \; (null \; z) \; w \; (cons(hd \; z)(append(tl \; z)w)).$$

There even is a λ-term *inflist* satisfying the recursion

$$inflist = cons \; MORE \; inflist,$$

encoding the infinite list [*MORE, MORE,* ...].

Recursive definitions are encoded with the help of the λ-term *Y*:

$$Y \equiv \lambda f.(\lambda x.f(x\,x))(\lambda x.f(x\,x))$$

Although the intuition behind *Y* is obscure, a simple calculation verifies that *Y* satisfies the *fixed point property*

$$Y f = f(Y f)$$

for all λ-terms *f*. We can exploit this property to expand the body of a recursive object repeatedly. Define

$$fact \equiv Y(\lambda g\; n.if\; (iszero\; n)\; \underline{1}\; (mult\; n\; (g(pre\; n))))$$
$$append \equiv Y(\lambda g\; z\; w.if\; (null\; z)\; w\; (cons(hd\; z)(g(tl\; z)w)))$$
$$inflist \equiv Y(\lambda g.cons\; MORE\; g)$$

In each definition, the recursive occurrence is replaced by the bound variable *g* in *Y*(λ*g.* ...). Let us verify the recursion equation for *inflist*; the others are similar. The first and third lines hold by definition, while the second line uses the fixed point property:

$$inflist \equiv Y(\lambda g.cons\; MORE\; g)$$
$$= (\lambda g.cons\; MORE\; g)(Y(\lambda g.cons\; MORE\; g)))$$
$$\equiv (\lambda g.cons\; MORE\; g)inflist$$
$$\Rightarrow cons\; MORE\; inflist$$

Recursive functions coded using *Y* execute correctly under call-by-name reduction. In order to use call-by-value reduction, recursive functions must be coded using a different fixed point operator (discussed below); otherwise execution will not terminate.

9.12 *The evaluation of λ-terms*

The structure *Reduce* (Figure 9.8) implements the call-by-value and call-by-name reduction strategies. Its signature is *REDUCE*:

```
signature REDUCE =
  sig
  val eval    : Lambda.t -> Lambda.t
  val byValue : Lambda.t -> Lambda.t
  val headNF  : Lambda.t -> Lambda.t
  val byName  : Lambda.t -> Lambda.t
  end;
```

Figure 9.8 *Reduction of λ-terms*

```
structure Reduce : REDUCE =
  struct

  fun eval (Lambda.Apply(t1,t2)) =
                (case eval t1 of
                     Lambda.Abs(a,u)  => eval(Lambda.subst 0 (eval t2) u)
                   | u1               => Lambda.Apply(u1, eval t2))
    | eval t                      = t;

  fun byValue t                    = bodies (eval t)
  and bodies (Lambda.Abs(a,t))     = Lambda.Abs(a, byValue t)
    | bodies (Lambda.Apply(t1,t2)) = Lambda.Apply(bodies t1, bodies t2)
    | bodies t                     = t;

  fun headNF (Lambda.Abs(a,t))     = Lambda.Abs(a, headNF t)
    | headNF (Lambda.Apply(t1,t2)) =
                (case headNF t1 of
                     Lambda.Abs(a,t) => headNF(Lambda.subst 0 t2 t)
                   | u1              => Lambda.Apply(u1, t2))
    | headNF t                     = t;

  fun byName t                     = args (headNF t)
  and args (Lambda.Abs(a,t))       = Lambda.Abs(a, args t)
    | args (Lambda.Apply(t1,t2))   = Lambda.Apply(args t1, byName t2)
    | args t                       = t;
  end;
```

The signature specifies four evaluation functions:

- *eval* evaluates a term using a call-by-value strategy resembling ML's. Its result need not be in normal form.
- *byValue* normalizes a term using call-by-value.
- *headNF* reduces a term to **head normal form**, which is discussed below.
- *byName* normalizes a term using call-by-name.

Call-by-value. In ML, evaluating the abstraction fn x => E does not evaluate E, for there is no general way to evaluate E without having a value for x. We have often exploited ML's treatment of abstractions, writing fn () => E to delay the evaluation of E. This allows a kind of lazy evaluation.

The situation in the λ-calculus is different. The abstraction $\lambda x.(\lambda y.a\,y)x$ reduces to the normal form $\lambda x.a\,x$ with no question of whether x has a value. Even so, it is advantageous not to reduce the bodies of abstractions. This permits the delaying of evaluation, like in ML. It is essential for handling recursion.

The function *eval*, given the application $t_1\,t_2$, evaluates t_1 to u_1 and t_2 to u_2. (Assume these evaluations terminate.) If u_1 is the abstraction $\lambda x.u$ then *eval* calls itself on $u[u_2/x]$, substituting the value of the argument into the body; if u_1 is anything else then *eval* returns u_1u_2. Given an abstraction or variable, *eval* returns its argument unchanged. Although *eval* performs most of the work of reduction, its result may contain abstractions not in normal form.

The function *byValue* uses *eval* to reduce a term to normal form. It calls *eval* on its argument, then recursively scans the result to normalize the abstractions in it.

Suppose that t equals *true*. When *eval* is given *if* $t\,u_1\,u_2$, it evaluates both u_1 and u_2 although only u_1 is required. If this is the body of a recursive function then it will run forever, as discussed in Section 2.12. We should insert abstractions to delay evaluation. Choose any variable x and code the conditional expression as

$$(\textit{if } t\,(\lambda x.u_1)\,(\lambda x.u_2))\,x.$$

Given this term, *eval* will return $\lambda x.u_1$ as the result of the *if* and then apply it to x. Thus it will evaluate u_1 but not u_2. If t equals *false* then only u_2 will be evaluated. Conditional expressions must be coded this way under call-by-value.

Recursive definitions encoded using Y fail under call-by-value because the evaluation of $Y\,f$ never terminates. Abstractions may be inserted into Y to delay evaluation. The operator

$$YV \equiv \lambda f.(\lambda x.f(\lambda y.x\,x\,y))(\lambda x.f(\lambda y.x\,x\,y))$$

enjoys the fixed point property and can express recursive functions for evaluation using *byValue*.

Call-by-name. A λ-term is in **head normal form** if, for $m \geq 0$ and $n \geq 0$, it can be viewed as follows:

$$\lambda x_1 \ldots x_m.x\, t_1 \ldots t_n.$$

The variable x may either be free or bound (one of $x_1, \ldots, x_m$).

Observe that the term's normal form (if it exists) must be

$$\lambda x_1 \ldots x_m.x\, u_1 \ldots u_n,$$

where u_i is the normal form of t_i for $i = 1, \ldots, n$. Head normal form describes a term's outer structure, which cannot be affected by reductions. We can normalize a term by computing its head normal form, then recursively normalizing the subterms $t_1, \ldots, t_n$. This procedure will reach the normal form if one exists, because every term that has a normal form also has a head normal form.

For example, the term $\lambda x.a((\lambda z.z)x)$ is in head normal form and its normal form is $\lambda x.a\, x$. A term not in head normal form can be viewed as

$$\lambda x_1 \ldots x_m.(\lambda x.t)\, t_1 \ldots t_n,$$

where $n > 0$. It admits a reduction in the leftmost part of the body. For instance, $(\lambda x\, y.y\, x)t$ reduces to the head normal form $\lambda y.y\, t$, for any term t. Many terms without a normal form have a head normal form; consider

$$Y = \lambda f.f(Y f).$$

A few terms, such as $(\lambda x.x\, x)(\lambda x.x\, x)$, lack even a head normal form. Such terms can be regarded as undefined.

The function *headNF* computes the head normal form of $t_1\, t_2$ by recursively computing *headNF* t_1 and then, if an abstraction results, doing a β-conversion. The argument t_2 is not reduced before substitution; this is call-by-name.[2]

Function *byName* normalizes a term by computing its *headNF* and then normalizing the arguments of the outermost application. This achieves call-by-name reduction with reasonable efficiency.

Exercise 9.26   Show that $YV f = f(\lambda y.YV f\, y)$.

---

[2] *headNF* exploits Proposition 8.3.13 of Barendregt (1984): if $t\, u$ has a head normal form then so does t.

Exercise 9.27 Derive a head normal form of *Y Y*, or demonstrate that none exists.

Exercise 9.28 Derive a head normal form of *inflist*, or demonstrate that none exists.

Exercise 9.29 Describe how *byValue* and *byName* would compute the normal form of *fst(pair t u)*, for arbitrary λ-terms *t* and *u*.

9.13   *Demonstrating the evaluators*

To demonstrate our implementation of the λ-calculus, we create an environment *stdEnv*. It defines the λ-calculus encodings of the booleans, ordered pairs and so forth (Figure 9.9 on the next page). Function *insert* of *StringDict* adds a definition to a dictionary, provided that string is not already defined there.

Function *stdRead* reads a term and instantiates it using *stdEnv*, expanding the definitions. Note that "2" expands to something large, derived from *suc(suc 0)*:

```
fun stdRead a = inst stdEnv (ParseLam.read a);
> val stdRead = fn : string -> term
DisplayTerm.pr (stdRead "2");
> (%n f x. n f (f x))
> ((%n f x. n f (f x)) (%f x. x))
```

This term could do with normalization. We define a function *try* such that *try evfn* reads a term, applies *evfn* to it, and displays the result. Using call-by-value, we reduce "2" to a Church numeral:

```
fun try evfn = DisplayTerm.pr o evfn o stdRead;
> val try = fn : (term -> term) -> string -> unit
try Reduce.byValue "2";
> %f x. f (f x)
```

Call-by-value can perform simple arithmetic on Church numerals: $2 + 3 = 5$, $2 \times 3 = 6$, $2^3 = 8$:

```
try Reduce.byValue "add 2 3";
> %f x. f (f (f (f (f x))))
try Reduce.byValue "mult 2 3";
> %f x. f (f (f (f (f (f x)))))
try Reduce.byValue "expt 2 3";
> %f x. f (f (f (f (f (f (f (f x)))))))
```

The environment defines *factV*, which encodes a recursive factorial function using *YV* and with abstractions to delay evaluation of the arguments of the *if*. It works under call-by-value reduction, computing $3! = 6$:

Figure 9.9 *Constructing the standard environment*

```
fun insertEnv ((a,b),env) =
    StringDict.insert (env, a, ParseTerm.read b);

val stdEnv = foldl insertEnv StringDict.empty
[    (*booleans*)
 ("true", "%x y.x"),                ("false",  "%x y.y"),
 ("if", "%p x y. p x y"),
     (*ordered pairs*)
 ("pair", "%x y f.f x y"),
 ("fst", "%p.p true"),              ("snd", "%p.p false"),
     (*natural numbers*)
 ("suc", "%n f x. n f (f x)"),
 ("iszero", "%n. n (%x.false) true"),
 ("0", "%f x. x"),                  ("1", "suc 0"),
 ("2", "suc 1"),                    ("3", "suc 2"),
 ("4", "suc 3"),                    ("5", "suc 4"),
 ("6", "suc 5"),                    ("7", "suc 6"),
 ("8", "suc 7"),                    ("9", "suc 8"),
 ("add", "%m n f x. m f (n f x)"),
 ("mult", "%m n f. m (n f)"),
 ("expt", "%m n f x. n m f x"),
 ("prefn", "%f p. pair (f (fst p)) (fst p)"),
 ("pre", "%n f x. snd (n (prefn f) (pair x x))"),
 ("sub", "%m n. n pre m"),
     (*lists*)
 ("nil", "%z.z"),
 ("cons", "%x y. pair false (pair x y)"),
 ("null", "fst"),
 ("hd", "%z. fst(snd z)"),      ("tl", "%z. snd(snd z)"),
     (*recursion for call-by-name*)
 ("Y", "%f. (%x.f(x x))(%x.f(x x))"),
 ("fact", "Y(%g n. if (iszero n) 1 (mult n (g (pre n))))"),
 ("append", "Y(%g z w.if (null z) w (cons (hd z) (g(tl z)w)))"),
 ("inflist", "Y(%z. cons MORE z)"),
     (*recursion for call-by-value*)
 ("YV", "%f. (%x.f(%y.x x y)) (%x.f(%y.x x y))"),
 ("factV",
  "YV (%g n.(if (iszero n) (%y.1) (%y.mult n (g (pre n))))y)")
];
```

```
try Reduce.byValue "factV 3";
> %f x. f (f (f (f (f (f x)))))
```

Call-by-name reduction can do the same computations as call-by-value can, and more. It handles recursive definitions involving *Y* and *if*, without needing any tricks to delay evaluation. Here, we *append* the lists [*FARE, THEE*] and [*WELL*]:

```
try Reduce.byName
   "append (cons FARE (cons THEE nil)) (cons WELL nil)";
> %f. f (%x y. y)
>      (%f. f FARE
>          (%f. f (%x y. y)
>              (%f. f THEE
>                  (%f. f (%x y. y)
>                      (%f. f WELL (%z. z))))))
```

Let us take the head of the infinite list [*MORE, MORE, . . .*]:

```
try Reduce.byName "hd inflist";
> MORE
```

Execution is extremely slow, especially with call-by-name. Computing *fact* 3 takes 330 msec, compared with 60 msec for *factV* 3. Computing *fact* 4 takes forty seconds! This should hardly be surprising when arithmetic employs unary notation and recursion works by copying. Even so, we have all the elements of functional programming.

With a little more effort, we can obtain a real functional language. Rather than encoding data structures in the pure λ-calculus, we can take numbers, arithmetic operations and ordered pairs as primitive. Rather than interpreting the λ-terms, we can compile them for execution on an abstract machine. For call-by-value reduction, the SECD machine is suitable. For call-by-name reduction we can compile λ-terms into combinators and execute them by graph reduction. The design and implementation of a simple functional language makes a challenging project.

ⓘ *Further reading.* M. J. C. Gordon (1988) describes the λ-calculus from the perspective of a computer scientist; he discusses ways of representing data and presents Lisp code for reducing and translating λ-expressions. Barendregt (1984) is the comprehensive reference on the λ-calculus. Boolos and Jeffrey (1980) introduce the theory of computability, including Turing machines, register machines and the general recursive functions.

N. G. de Bruijn (1972) developed the name-free notation for the λ-calculus, and used it in his AUTOMATH system (Nederpelt *et al.*, 1994). It is also used in Isabelle (Paulson, 1994) and in Hal, the theorem prover of Chapter 10.

Field and Harrison (1988) describe basic combinator reduction. Modern implementations of lazy evaluation use more sophisticated techniques (Peyton Jones, 1992).

Exercise 9.30   What is the result when *try Reduce . byName* is applied to these strings?

```
"hd (tl (Y (%z. append (cons MORE (cons AND nil)) z)))"
"hd (tl (tl (Y (%g n. cons n (g (suc n))) 0)))"
```

Summary of main points
- Top-down parsers can be expressed in a natural way using higher-order functions.
- The λ-calculus is a theoretical model of computation with close similarities to functional programming.
- The name-free representation of variable binding is easily implemented on the computer.
- Data structures such as numbers and lists, with their operations, can be encoded as λ-terms.
- The λ-term *Y* encodes recursion by repeated copying.
- There exist call-by-value and call-by-name evaluation strategies for the λ-calculus.

10

A Tactical Theorem Prover

ML was originally designed to serve as the programming language for a theorem prover, Edinburgh LCF. So it is fitting that a book on ML should conclude by describing a theorem prover, called Hal, inspired by LCF.[1] Hal constructs a proof by refinement steps, working backwards from a goal. At its simplest, this is proof checking: at each step, an inference rule is matched to a goal, reducing it to certain subgoals. If we are ever to prove anything significant, we shall require more automation. Hal provides *tactics* and *tacticals*, which constitute a high-level language for expressing search procedures. A few primitive tactics, applied using a tactical for depth-first search, implement a general tactic that can prove many theorems automatically, such as

$$\neg(\exists x . \forall y . \phi(x, y) \leftrightarrow \neg\phi(y, y))$$

$$\exists xy . \phi(x, y) \rightarrow \forall xy . \phi(x, y)$$

$$\exists x . \forall yz . (\phi(y) \rightarrow \psi(z)) \rightarrow (\phi(x) \rightarrow \psi(x))$$

For raw power Hal cannot compete with specialized theorem provers. What Hal lacks in power it makes up in flexibility. A typical resolution theorem prover supports pure classical logic with equality, but without induction. Tactical theorem provers allow a mixture of automatic and interactive working, in virtually any logic.

Hal works in classical logic for familiarity's sake, but it can easily be extended to include induction, modal operators, set theory or whatever. Its tactics must be changed to reflect the new inference rules; the tacticals remain the same, ready to express search procedures for the new logic.

Chapter outline

The chapter contains the following sections:

A sequent calculus for first-order logic. The semantics of first-order logic is

---

[1] Hal is named after King Henry V, who was a master tactician.

397

sketched and the sequent calculus is described. Quantifier reasoning involves parameters and meta-variables.

Processing terms and formulæ in ML. Hal's representation of first-order logic borrows techniques from previous chapters. A major new technique is unification.

Tactics and the proof state. Hal implements the sequent calculus as a set of transformations upon an abstract type of proof states. Each inference rule is provided as a tactic.

Searching for proofs. A crude user interface allows the tactics to be demonstrated. Tacticals add control structures to tactics, and are used to code automatic tactics for first-order logic.

A sequent calculus for first-order logic

We begin with a quick overview of first-order logic. The syntax of first-order logic has been presented in Section 6.1. *Propositional logic* concerns formulæ built by the connectives $\land$, $\lor$, $\neg$, $\to$ and $\leftrightarrow$. First-order logic introduces the quantifiers $\forall$ and $\exists$, with variables and terms. A *first-order language* augments the logical symbols with certain constants a, b, ... , function symbols f, g, ... and predicate symbols P, Q, ... Let ϕ, ψ, χ, ... stand for arbitrary formulæ.

The *universe* is a non-empty set containing the possible values of terms. Constants denote elements of the universe; function symbols denote functions over the universe; predicate symbols denote relations over the universe. A *structure* defines the semantics of a first-order language by specifying a universe and giving the interpretations of the constants, function symbols and predicate symbols. An ML structure is analogous to a logical structure.

The meaning of a formula depends on the values of its free variables. An *assignment* is a mapping from free variables to elements of the universe. Given a structure and an assignment, every formula is either true or false. The formula $\forall x . \phi$ is true if and only if ϕ is true for every possible value that could be assigned to x (leaving the other variables unchanged). The connectives are defined by truth tables; for instance, $\phi \land \psi$ is true if and only if ϕ is true and ψ is true.

A *valid* formula is one that is true in all structures and assignments. Since there are infinitely many structures, exhaustive testing can never show that a formula is valid. Instead, we can attempt to show that a formula is valid by formal proof using inference rules, each of which is justified by the semantics of the logic. Each rule accepts zero or more premises and yields a conclusion; a sound rule must yield a valid conclusion provided its premises are valid. A set of inference rules for a logic is called a **proof system** or a **formalization**.

Of the many proof systems for classical first-order logic, easiest to automate is the **sequent calculus**. The tableau method, which is sometimes used to automate first-order logic, is a compact notation for the sequent calculus.

10.1   *The sequent calculus for propositional logic*

To keep matters simple, let us temporarily restrict attention to propositional logic. A **sequent** has the form

$$\phi_1, \ldots, \phi_m \vdash \psi_1, \ldots, \psi_n$$

where $\phi_1, \ldots, \phi_m$ and $\psi_1, \ldots, \psi_n$ are multisets of formulæ. As discussed above in Chapter 6, a multiset is a collection of elements whose order is insignificant. Traditionally a sequent contains lists of formulæ, and the logic includes rules for exchanging adjacent formulæ; multisets make such rules unnecessary.

Given a structure and an assignment, the sequent above is true if and only if some of the formulæ $\phi_1, \ldots, \phi_m$ are false or some of the formulæ $\psi_1, \ldots, \psi_n$ are true. In other words, the sequent has the same meaning as the formula

$$\phi_1 \wedge \cdots \wedge \phi_m \rightarrow \psi_1 \vee \cdots \vee \psi_n.$$

As a special case, $\vdash \psi$ has the same meaning as ψ. A sequent is not a formula, however; the $\vdash$ symbol (the 'turnstile') is not a logical connective.

For convenience in writing the rules, Γ and Δ will stand for multisets of formulæ. The comma will denote multiset union; thus Γ, Δ stands for the union of Γ and Δ. A formula appearing where a multiset is expected (like ϕ in $\Gamma \vdash \phi$) will stand for a singleton multiset. Thus Γ, ϕ is a multiset containing an occurrence of ϕ, where Γ denotes its other elements.

Validity and basic sequents. A **valid** sequent is one that is true under every structure and assignment. The theorems of our sequent calculus will be precisely the valid sequents.

A sequent is called **basic** if both sides share a common formula ϕ. This can be formalized as the axiom

$$\phi, \Gamma \vdash \Delta, \phi.$$

In the notation just described, ϕ, Γ and Δ, ϕ are multisets containing ϕ. Such sequents are clearly valid.

The other formulæ, those contained in Γ and Δ, play no part in the inference. The sequent calculus is sometimes formulated such that a basic sequent must

have the form $\phi \vdash \phi$. Then sequents of the form $\phi, \Gamma \vdash \Delta, \phi$ can be derived
with the help of 'weakening' rules, which insert arbitrary formulæ into a sequent.

Sequent rules for the connectives. Sequent calculus rules come in pairs, to introduce each connective on the left or right of the $\vdash$ symbol. For example, the rule
$\wedge$:left introduces a conjunction on the left, while $\wedge$:right introduces a conjunction on the right. Here is the latter rule in the usual notation, with its premises
above the line and its conclusion below:

$$\frac{\Gamma \vdash \Delta, \phi \quad \Gamma \vdash \Delta, \psi}{\Gamma \vdash \Delta, \phi \wedge \psi} \wedge\text{:right}$$

To show that $\wedge$:right is a sound rule, let us assume that its premises are valid and
demonstrate that its conclusion is valid. Suppose that, under some structure and
assignment, every formula in Γ is true; we must demonstrate that some formula
in $\Delta, \phi \wedge \psi$ is true. If no formula in Δ is true, then both ϕ and ψ are true by the
premises. Therefore $\phi \wedge \psi$ is true.

Now let us justify the rule $\wedge$:left.

$$\frac{\phi, \psi, \Gamma \vdash \Delta}{\phi \wedge \psi, \Gamma \vdash \Delta} \wedge\text{:left}$$

To show that this rule is sound, we proceed as above. Suppose that every formula
in $\Gamma, \phi \wedge \psi$ is true. Then both ϕ and ψ are true. Assuming that the premise is
valid, some formula of Δ must be true, and this establishes the conclusion.

Figure 10.1 presents the rules for the propositional connectives $\wedge$, $\vee$, $\rightarrow$, $\leftrightarrow$
and $\neg$. All the rules are justified similarly.

Exercise 10.1   Which formula is equivalent to $\phi_1, \ldots, \phi_m \vdash$, a sequent whose
right side is empty?

Exercise 10.2   Justify the rules $\vee$:left and $\vee$:right.

Exercise 10.3   Justify the rules $\leftrightarrow$:left and $\leftrightarrow$:right.

10.2   *Proving theorems in the sequent calculus*
     Inference rules are often viewed in a forward direction, from premises
to conclusion. Thus, $\wedge$:right accepts premises $\Gamma \vdash \Delta, \phi$ and $\Gamma \vdash \Delta, \psi$, yielding
the conclusion $\Gamma \vdash \Delta, \phi \wedge \psi$. Applying another rule to this sequent yields another conclusion, and so forth. A formal proof is a tree constructed by applying

Figure 10.1 *Sequent rules for the propositional connectives*

:left	:right

$$\frac{\phi, \psi, \Gamma \vdash \Delta}{\phi \wedge \psi, \Gamma \vdash \Delta} \qquad \frac{\Gamma \vdash \Delta, \phi \quad \Gamma \vdash \Delta, \psi}{\Gamma \vdash \Delta, \phi \wedge \psi}$$

$$\frac{\phi, \Gamma \vdash \Delta \quad \psi, \Gamma \vdash \Delta}{\phi \vee \psi, \Gamma \vdash \Delta} \qquad \frac{\Gamma \vdash \Delta, \phi, \psi}{\Gamma \vdash \Delta, \phi \vee \psi}$$

$$\frac{\Gamma \vdash \Delta, \phi \quad \psi, \Gamma \vdash \Delta}{\phi \rightarrow \psi, \Gamma \vdash \Delta} \qquad \frac{\phi, \Gamma \vdash \Delta, \psi}{\Gamma \vdash \Delta, \phi \rightarrow \psi}$$

$$\frac{\phi, \psi, \Gamma \vdash \Delta \quad \Gamma \vdash \Delta, \phi, \psi}{\phi \leftrightarrow \psi, \Gamma \vdash \Delta} \qquad \frac{\phi, \Gamma \vdash \Delta, \psi \quad \psi, \Gamma \vdash \Delta, \phi}{\Gamma \vdash \Delta, \phi \leftrightarrow \psi}$$

$$\frac{\Gamma \vdash \Delta, \phi}{\neg \phi, \Gamma \vdash \Delta} \qquad \frac{\phi, \Gamma \vdash \Delta}{\Gamma \vdash \Delta, \neg \phi}$$

inference rules. Here is a proof of the sequent $\phi \wedge \psi \vdash \psi \wedge \phi$:

$$\frac{\dfrac{\phi, \psi \vdash \psi \qquad \phi, \psi \vdash \phi}{\phi, \psi \vdash \psi \wedge \phi}}{\phi \wedge \psi \vdash \psi \wedge \phi} \begin{array}{l} \wedge\text{:right} \\[4pt] \wedge\text{:left} \end{array} \qquad (*)$$

Viewed in the forward direction, two basic sequents are combined by ∧:right and the result transformed by ∧:left. However, the forward reading does not help us find a proof of a given sequent.

For the purpose of finding proofs, rules should be viewed in the backward direction, from a goal to subgoals. Thus, ∧:right accepts the goal $\Gamma \vdash \Delta, \phi \wedge \psi$ and returns the subgoals $\Gamma \vdash \Delta, \phi$ and $\Gamma \vdash \Delta, \psi$. If these subgoals can be proved as theorems, then so can the goal. The subgoals are refined by further rule applications until all the remaining subgoals are basic sequents, which are immediately valid. The proof tree is constructed from the root upwards; the process is called *refinement* or *backward proof*.

Viewed in the backward direction, the proof (*) begins with the sequent to be proved, namely $\phi \wedge \psi \vdash \psi \wedge \phi$. This goal is refined by ∧:left to $\phi, \psi \vdash \psi \wedge \phi$; this subgoal is refined by ∧:right to $\phi, \psi \vdash \psi$ and $\phi, \psi \vdash \phi$. These two subgoals are basic sequents, so the proof is finished.

Under the backward reading, each rule attacks a formula in the goal. Applying ∧:left breaks down a conjunction on the left side, while ∧:right breaks down a conjunction on the right. If all the resulting subgoals are basic sequents, then the initial goal has been proved. For propositional logic, this procedure must terminate.

A sequent may have several different proofs, depending on which formulæ are broken down first. The proof (∗) first breaks down the conjunction on the left in $\phi \wedge \psi \vdash \psi \wedge \phi$. For a different proof, begin by breaking down the conjunction on the right:

$$\dfrac{\phi, \psi \vdash \psi}{\phi \wedge \psi \vdash \psi} \text{ ∧:left} \qquad \dfrac{\dfrac{\phi, \psi \vdash \phi}{\phi \wedge \psi \vdash \phi} \text{ ∧:left}}{\phi \wedge \psi \vdash \psi \wedge \phi} \text{ ∧:right}$$

This is larger than the proof (∗) in that ∧:left is applied twice. Applying ∧:right to the initial goal produced two subgoals, each with a conjunction on the left. Shorter proofs usually result if the rule that produces the fewest subgoals is chosen at each step.

To summarize, we have the following proof procedure:

- Take the sequent to be proved as the initial goal. The root of the proof tree, and its only leaf, is this goal.
- Select some subgoal that is a leaf of the proof tree and apply a rule to it, turning the leaf into a branch node with one or more leaves.
- Stop whenever all the leaves are basic sequents (success), or when no rules can be applied to a leaf (failure).

This procedure is surprisingly effective, though its search is undirected. Both ∨:left and ∧:right may be applied to the subgoal $p \vee q, r \vdash r \wedge r$. The former rule performs case analysis on the irrelevant formula $p \vee q$; the latter rule yields two basic subgoals, succeeding immediately.

Exercise 10.4   Construct proofs of the sequents $\phi \vee \psi \vdash \psi \vee \phi$ and $\phi_1 \wedge (\phi_2 \wedge \phi_3) \vdash (\phi_1 \wedge \phi_2) \wedge \phi_3$.

Exercise 10.5   Construct a proof of the sequent

$$\vdash (\phi_1 \wedge \phi_2) \vee \psi \leftrightarrow (\phi_1 \vee \psi) \wedge (\phi_2 \vee \psi).$$

Exercise 10.6   Show that any sequent containing both ϕ and $\neg\phi$ to the left of the $\vdash$ symbol is provable.

10.3 Sequent rules for the quantifiers

Propositional logic is decidable; our proof procedure can determine, in finite time, whether any formula is a theorem. With quantifiers, no such decision procedure exists. Quantifiers, moreover, introduce many syntactic complications.

Each quantifier binds a variable; thus x and y occur bound and z occurs free in $\forall x . \exists y . R(x, y, z)$. Renaming the bound variables does not affect the meaning of a formula; the previous example is equivalent to $\forall y . \exists w . R(y, w, z)$. Some of the inference rules involve substitution, and $\phi[t/x]$ will stand for the result of substituting t for every free occurrence of x in ϕ. Less formally, $\phi(x)$ stands for a formula involving x and $\phi(t)$ stands for the result of substituting t for free occurrences of x. The name-free representation of bound variables (Section 9.6) works as well for quantifier syntax as it does for the λ-calculus.

The universal quantifier has these two sequent rules:

$$\frac{\phi[t/x],\ \forall x . \phi,\ \Gamma \vdash \Delta}{\forall x . \phi,\ \Gamma \vdash \Delta} \quad \forall\text{:left} \qquad\qquad \frac{\Gamma \vdash \Delta,\ \phi}{\Gamma \vdash \Delta,\ \forall x . \phi} \quad \forall\text{:right}$$

proviso: x must not occur free in the conclusion

The rule $\forall$:left is easy to justify; if $\forall x . \phi$ is true then so is $\phi[t/x]$, where t is any term.

To justify $\forall$:right, which is the more complicated rule, let us assume that its premise is valid and demonstrate that its conclusion is valid. Given some structure and assignment, suppose that every formula in Γ is true and that no formula in Δ is true; then we must show that $\forall x . \phi$ is true. It suffices to show that ϕ is true for every possible assignment to x that leaves the other variables unchanged. By the proviso of $\forall$:right, changing the value of x does not affect the truth of any formula of Γ or Δ; since the premise is valid, ϕ must be true.

Ignoring the proviso can yield unsound inferences:

$$\frac{P(x) \vdash P(x)}{P(x) \vdash \forall x . P(x)} \quad \forall\text{:right ???}$$

The conclusion is false if $P(x)$ stands for the predicate $x = 0$ over the integers and x is assigned the value 0.

The existential quantifier has these two sequent rules:

$$\frac{\phi,\ \Gamma \vdash \Delta}{\exists x . \phi,\ \Gamma \vdash \Delta} \quad \exists\text{:left} \qquad\qquad \frac{\Gamma \vdash \Delta,\ \exists x . \phi,\ \phi[t/x]}{\Gamma \vdash \Delta,\ \exists x . \phi} \quad \exists\text{:right}$$

proviso: x must not occur free in the conclusion

They are dual to the rules for the universal quantifier and can be justified similarly. Note that $\exists x . \phi$ is equivalent to $\neg \forall x . \neg \phi$.

The rules $\forall$:left and $\exists$:right have one feature that is not present in any of the other rules: in backward proof, they do not remove any formulæ from the goal. They expand a quantified formula, substituting a term into its body; and they retain the formula to allow repeated expansion. It is impossible to determine in advance how many expansions of a quantified formula are required for a proof. Because of this, our proof procedure can fail to terminate; first-order logic is undecidable.

Exercise 10.7   If the premise of $\forall$:right is ignored, can a proof involving this rule reach an inconsistent conclusion? (This means a sequent $\vdash \phi$ such that $\neg\phi$ is a valid formula.)

10.4   *Theorem proving with quantifiers*

Our backward proof procedure is reasonably effective with quantifiers, at least for tackling simple problems that do not require a more discriminating search. Let us begin with an easy proof involving universal quantification:

$$\frac{\dfrac{\dfrac{\phi(x), \; \forall x . \phi(x) \vdash \phi(x), \; \psi(x)}{\forall x . \phi(x) \vdash \phi(x), \; \psi(x)}}{\dfrac{\forall x . \phi(x) \vdash \phi(x) \vee \psi(x)}{\forall x . \phi(x) \vdash \forall x . \phi(x) \vee \psi(x)}}}{} \quad \begin{array}{l} \forall\text{:left} \\ \vee\text{:right} \\ \vee\text{:right} \\ \forall\text{:right} \end{array}$$

The proviso of $\forall$:right holds; x is not free in the conclusion. In a backward proof, this conclusion is the initial goal.

If we first applied $\forall$:left, inserting the formula $\phi(x)$, then x would be free in the resulting subgoal. Then $\forall$:right could not be applied without renaming the quantified variable:

$$\frac{\dfrac{\dfrac{\phi(x), \; \forall x . \phi(x) \vdash \phi(y), \; \psi(y)}{\phi(x), \; \forall x . \phi(x) \vdash \phi(y) \vee \psi(y)}}{\dfrac{\phi(x), \; \forall x . \phi(x) \vdash \forall x . \phi(x) \vee \psi(x)}{\forall x . \phi(x) \vdash \forall x . \phi(x) \vee \psi(x)}}}{} \quad \begin{array}{l} \vee\text{:right} \\ \vee\text{:right} \\ \forall\text{:left} \end{array}$$

The topmost sequent is not basic; to finish the proof we must again apply $\forall$:left. The first application of this rule has accomplished nothing. We have a general heuristic: never apply $\forall$:left or $\exists$:right to a goal if a different rule can usefully be applied.

The following proof illustrates some of the difficulties of using quantifiers.[2]

$$
\frac{\dfrac{\dfrac{\dfrac{\dfrac{\phi(x),\ \phi(z) \vdash \exists z.\phi(z) \to \forall x.\phi(x),\ \phi(x),\ \forall x.\phi(x)}{\phi(z) \vdash \exists z.\phi(z) \to \forall x.\phi(x),\ \phi(x),\ \phi(x) \to \forall x.\phi(x)}}{\phi(z) \vdash \exists z.\phi(z) \to \forall x.\phi(x),\ \phi(x)}}{\phi(z) \vdash \exists z.\phi(z) \to \forall x.\phi(x),\ \forall x.\phi(x)}}{\vdash \exists z.\phi(z) \to \forall x.\phi(x),\ \phi(z) \to \forall x.\phi(x)}}{\vdash \exists z.\phi(z) \to \forall x.\phi(x)}
$$

$$
\begin{array}{l}
\to\text{:right} \\
\exists\text{:right} \\
\forall\text{:right} \\
\to\text{:right} \\
\exists\text{:right}
\end{array}
$$

Working upwards from the goal, $\exists$:right is applied, introducing z as a free variable. Although the existential formula remains in the subgoal, it remains dormant until we again reach a goal where no other rule is applicable. The next inference, $\to$:right, moves $\phi(z)$ to the left. Since x is not free in the subgoal, $\forall$:right can be applied, replacing $\forall x.\phi(x)$ by $\phi(x)$. In the resulting subgoal, $\exists$:right is again applied (there is no alternative), substituting x for z. The final subgoal after $\to$:right is a basic sequent containing $\phi(x)$ on both sides.

Observe that $\exists z.\phi(z) \to \forall x.\phi(x)$ is expanded twice by $\exists$:right. The sequent cannot be proved otherwise. Sequents requiring n expansions of a quantifier, for any given n, are not hard to devise.

Unification. When reasoning about quantifiers, we have a difficulty: how do we choose the term t in the rules $\exists$:right and $\forall$:left? This amounts to predicting which term will ultimately generate basic subgoals and a successful proof. In the proof above, choosing z in the first $\exists$:right was arbitrary; any term would have worked. Choosing x in the second $\exists$:right was crucial — but perhaps not obvious.

We can postpone choosing the term in such rules. Introduce **meta-variables** $?a, ?b, \ldots$ as placeholders for terms. When a goal can be solved by substituting appropriate terms for its meta-variables, perform this substitution — throughout the proof. For instance, the subgoal $P(?a), \Gamma \vdash \Delta, P(f(?b))$ becomes basic if we replace $?a$ by $f(?b)$; observe that $?a$ has still not been fully determined, only its outer form $f(\cdots)$. We solve for unknowns incrementally. **Unification**, the process of determining the appropriate substitutions, is the key to automated reasoning about quantifiers.

The rule $\forall$:left now takes the following form, where $?a$ stands for any meta-

---

[2] To see that $\exists z.\phi(z) \to \forall x.\phi(x)$ is a theorem, first note that in fully parenthesized form it is $\exists z.[\phi(z) \to (\forall x.\phi(x))]$. Pushing the existential quantifier inside the implication changes it to a universal quantifier. The formula is thus equivalent to $(\forall z.\phi(z)) \to (\forall x.\phi(x))$, which is trivially true.

variable:

$$\frac{\phi[?a/x], \forall x . \phi, \Gamma \vdash \Delta}{\forall x . \phi, \Gamma \vdash \Delta} \quad \forall\text{:left}$$

Enforcing provisos. Meta-variables cause difficulties of their own. Recall that ∀:right and ∃:left have the proviso 'x not free in conclusion.' What shall we do when the conclusion contains meta-variables, which could be replaced by any terms? Our approach is to label each free variable with a list of forbidden meta-variables. The free variable $b_{?a_1,...,?a_k}$ must never be contained in a term substituted for the meta-variables $?a_1, \ldots , ?a_k$. The unification algorithm can enforce this.

Let us simplify the terminology. Labelled free variables will be called *parameters*. Meta-variables will be called *variables*.

Using parameters, the rule ∀:right becomes

$$\frac{\Gamma \vdash \Delta, \phi[b_{?a_1,...,?a_k}/x]}{\Gamma \vdash \Delta, \forall x . \phi} \quad \forall\text{:right}$$

proviso: b must not occur in the conclusion and $?a_1, \ldots , ?a_k$ must be all the variables in the conclusion.

The first part of the proviso ensures that the parameter b is not already in use, while the second part ensures that b is not slipped in later by a substitution. The treatment of ∃:left is the same.

Parameters ensure correct quantifier reasoning. For example, $\forall x . \phi(x, x)$ does not, in general, imply $\exists y . \forall x . \phi(x, y)$. Consider an attempted proof of the corresponding sequent:

$$\frac{\dfrac{\dfrac{\phi(?c, ?c), \forall x.\phi(x, x) \vdash \exists y.\forall x.\phi(x, y), \phi(b_{?a}, ?a)}{\forall x.\phi(x, x) \vdash \exists y.\forall x.\phi(x, y), \phi(b_{?a}, ?a)}}{\forall x.\phi(x, x) \vdash \exists y.\forall x.\phi(x, y), \forall x.\phi(x, ?a)}}{\forall x.\phi(x, x) \vdash \exists y.\forall x.\phi(x, y)}} \begin{array}{l} \forall\text{:left} \\ \\ \forall\text{:right} \\ \\ \exists\text{:right} \end{array}$$

The topmost sequent cannot be made basic. To make $\phi(?c, ?c)$ and $\phi(b_{?a}, ?a)$ identical, a substitution would have to replace both $?c$ and $?a$ by $b_{?a}$. However, the parameter $b_{?a}$ is forbidden from occurring in a term substituted for $?a$. The attempted proof may continue to grow upwards through applications of ∀:right and ∃:left, but no basic sequent will ever be generated.

For a contrasting example, let us prove that $\forall x.\phi(x, x)$ implies $\forall x.\exists y.\phi(x, y)$:

$$\frac{\dfrac{\dfrac{\phi(?c, ?c), \forall x.\phi(x, x) \vdash \exists y.\phi(a, y), \phi(a, ?b)}{\forall x.\phi(x, x) \vdash \exists y.\phi(a, y), \phi(a, ?b)}}{\forall x.\phi(x, x) \vdash \exists y.\phi(a, y)}}{\forall x.\phi(x, x) \vdash \forall x.\exists y.\phi(x, y)} \begin{array}{l} \forall\text{:left} \\ \\ \exists\text{:right} \\ \\ \forall\text{:right} \end{array}$$

Replacing $?b$ and $?c$ by a transforms both $\phi(?c, ?c)$ and $\phi(a, ?b)$ into $\phi(a, a)$, completing the proof. The parameter a is not labelled with any variables because there are none in the goal supplied to ∀:right.

ℹ️ *Further reading.* A number of textbooks present logic from the viewpoint of computer science. They emphasize proof procedures and unification, avoiding the more traditional concerns of mathematical logic, such as model theory. See Galton (1990) or Reeves and Clarke (1990) for a gentle introduction to logic. Gallier (1986) gives a more technical treatment centred around the sequent calculus.

Exercise 10.8 Reconstruct the first three quantifier proofs above, this time using (meta) variables and parameters.

Exercise 10.9 Falsify the sequent $\forall x . P(x, x) \vdash \exists y . \forall x . P(x, y)$ by letting P denote a suitable relation in a structure.

Exercise 10.10 If the attempted proof of $\forall x . \phi(x, x) \vdash \exists y . \forall x . \phi(x, y)$ is continued, will parameters allow it to succeed?

Exercise 10.11 Demonstrate that $\vdash \exists z . \phi(z) \rightarrow \forall x . \phi(x)$ has no proof that applies ∃:right only once.

Exercise 10.12 For each of the following, construct a proof or demonstrate that no proof exists (a and b are constants):

$$\vdash \exists z . \phi(z) \rightarrow \phi(a) \wedge \phi(b)$$
$$\forall x . \exists y . \phi(x, y) \vdash \exists y . \forall x . \phi(x, y)$$
$$\exists y . \forall x . \phi(x, y) \vdash \forall x . \exists y . \phi(x, y)$$

Processing terms and formulæ in ML

Let us code an infrastructure for theorem proving. Terms and formulæ must be represented; abstraction, substitution, parsing and pretty printing must be implemented. Thanks to the methods we have accumulated in recent chapters, none of this programming is especially difficult.

10.5 *Representing terms and formulæ*

The techniques we have developed for the λ-calculus (in Section 9.7) work for first-order logic. In some respects, first-order logic is simpler. An inference can affect only the outermost variable binding; there is nothing corresponding to a reduction within a λ-term.

The signature. Signature *FOL* defines the representation of first-order terms and formulæ:

```
signature FOL =
  sig
  datatype term = Var      of string
                | Param    of string * string list
                | Bound    of int
                | Fun      of string * term list
  datatype form = Pred     of string * term list
                | Conn     of string * form list
                | Quant    of string * string * form
  type goal          = form list * form list
  val precOf       : string -> int
  val abstract     : int -> term -> form -> form
  val subst        : int -> term -> form -> form
  val termVars     : term * string list -> string list
  val goalVars     : goal *string list -> string list
  val termParams   : term * (string * string list) list
                       -> (string * string list) list
  val goalParams   : goal * (string * string list) list
                       -> (string * string list) list
  end;
```

Type *term* realizes the methods described in the previous section. A variable (constructor *Var*) has a name. A *Bound* variable has an index. A *Fun* application has a function's name and argument list; a function taking no arguments is simply a constant. A parameter (*Param*) has a name and a list of forbidden variables.

Type *form* is elementary. An atomic formula (*Pred*) has a predicate's name and argument list. A connective application (*Conn*) has a connective and a list of formulæ, typically "~", "&", "|", "-->", or "<->" paired with one or two formulæ. A *Quant* formula has a quantifier (either "ALL" or "EX"), a bound variable name and a formula for the body.

Type *goal* abbreviates the type of pairs of formula lists. Some older ML compilers do not allow type abbreviations in signatures. We could specify *goal* simply as a type: its declaration inside the structure would be visible outside.

The function *precOf* defines the precedences of the connectives, as required for parsing and printing.

Functions *abstract* and *subst* resemble their namesakes of the previous chapter, but operate on formulæ. Calling *abstract i t p* replaces each occurrence of *t* in *p* by the index *i* (which is increased within quantifications); typically $i = 0$ and *t* is an atomic term. Calling *subst i t p* replaces the index *i* (increased within quantifications) by *t* in the formula *p*.

The function *termVars* collects the list of variables in a term (without repetitions); *termVars*(*t*, *bs*) inserts all the variables of *t* into the list *bs*. The argument *bs* may appear to be a needless complication, but it eliminates costly list appends while allowing *termVars* to be extended to formulæ and goals. This will become clear when we examine the function definitions.

The function *goalVars*, which also takes two arguments, collects the list of variables in a goal. A goal in Hal is a sequent. Although sequents are represented in ML using formula lists, not multisets, we shall be able to implement the style of proof discussed above.

The functions *termParams* and *goalParams* collect the list of parameters in a term or goal, respectively. Each parameter consists of its name paired with a list of variable names.

The structure. Structure *Fol* (Figure 10.2) implements signature *FOL*. The da-tatype declarations of *term* and *form* are omitted to save space; they are identical to those in the signature. The structure declares several functions not specified in the signature.

Calling *replace* (*u*1, *u*2) *t* replaces the term *u*1 by *u*2 throughout the term *t*. This function is called by *abstract* and *subst*.

Functionals *accumForm* and *accumGoal* demonstrate higher-order programming. Suppose that *f* has type *term* $\times \tau \rightarrow \tau$, for some type τ, where *f*(*t*, *x*) accumulates some information about *t* in *x*. (For instance, *f* could be *termVars*, which accumulates the list of free variables in a term.) Then *foldr f* extends *f* to lists of terms. The function *accumForm f* has type *form* $\times \tau \rightarrow \tau$, extending *f* to operate on formulæ. It lets *foldr f* handle the arguments of a predicate $P(t_1, \ldots, t_n)$; it recursively lets *foldr* (*accumForm f*) handle the formula lists of connectives. The functional *accumGoal* calls *foldr* twice, extending a function of type *form* $\times \tau \rightarrow \tau$ to one of type (*form list* $\times$ *form list*) $\times \tau \rightarrow \tau$. It extends a function involving formulæ to one involving goals.

Functionals *accumForm* and *accumGoal* provide a uniform means of traversing formulæ and goals. They define the functions *goalVars* and *goalParams* and could have many similar applications. Moreover, they are efficient: they create no lists or other data structures.

The functions *termVars* and *termParams* are defined by recursion, scanning a term to accumulate its variables or parameters. They use *foldr* to traverse argument lists. The function *insert* (omitted to save space) builds an ordered list of strings without repetitions. Note that *termVars* does not regard the parameter $b_{?a_1,\ldots,?a_k}$ as containing $?a_1, \ldots, ?a_k$; these forbidden variables are not logically part of the term and perhaps ought to be stored in a separate table.

Figure 10.2 *First-order logic: representing terms and formulæ*

```
structure Fol : FOL =
  struct
  datatype term = ... ;   datatype form = ...
  type goal = form list * form list;

  fun replace (u1,u2) t =
      if t=u1 then u2 else
        case t of Fun(a,ts) => Fun(a, map (replace(u1,u2)) ts)
                | _         => t;

  fun abstract i t (Pred(a,ts))      = Pred(a, map (replace(t, Bound i)) ts)
    | abstract i t (Conn(b,ps))      = Conn(b, map (abstract i t) ps)
    | abstract i t (Quant(qnt,b,p))  = Quant(qnt, b, abstract (i+1) t p);

  fun subst i t (Pred(a,ts))      = Pred(a, map (replace(Bound i, t)) ts)
    | subst i t (Conn(b,ps))      = Conn(b, map (subst i t) ps)
    | subst i t (Quant(qnt,b,p))  = Quant(qnt, b, subst (i+1) t p);

  fun precOf "~"    = 4
    | precOf "&"    = 3
    | precOf "|"    = 2
    | precOf "<->"  = 1
    | precOf "-->"  = 1
    | precOf _      = ~1      (*means not an infix*);

  fun accumForm f (Pred(_,ts), z)    = foldr f z ts
    | accumForm f (Conn(_,ps), z)    = foldr (accumForm f) z ps
    | accumForm f (Quant(_,_,p), z)  = accumForm f (p,z);

  fun accumGoal f ((ps,qs), z) = foldr f (foldr f z qs) ps;

  fun insert ...

  fun termVars (Var a, bs)      = insert(a,bs)
    | termVars (Fun(_,ts), bs)  = foldr termVars bs ts
    | termVars (_, bs)          = bs;

  val goalVars = accumGoal (accumForm termVars);

  fun termParams (Param(a,bs), pairs) = (a,bs) :: pairs
    | termParams (Fun(_,ts), pairs)   = foldr termParams pairs ts
    | termParams (_, pairs)           = pairs;

  val goalParams = accumGoal (accumForm termParams);
  end;
```

Exercise 10.13 Sketch how *FOL* and *Fol* can be modified to adopt a new representation of terms. Bound variables are identified by name, but are syntactically distinct from parameters and meta-variables. Would this representation work for the λ-calculus?

Exercise 10.14 Change the declaration of type *form*, replacing *Conn* by separate constructors for each connective, say *Neg, Conj, Disj, Imp, Iff*. Modify *FOL* and *Fol* appropriately.

Exercise 10.15 The function *accumGoal* is actually more polymorphic than was suggested above. What is its most general type?

10.6   *Parsing and displaying formulæ*

Our parser and pretty printer (from Chapters 9 and 8, respectively) can implement the syntax of first-order logic. We employ the following grammar for terms (*Term*), optional argument lists (*TermPack*), and non-empty term lists (*TermList*):

$$TermList \ = \ Term\{,\ \ Term\}*$$

$$TermPack \ = \ (\ \ TermList\ \ )$$

$$|\ \ Empty$$

$$Term \ = \ Id\ TermPack$$

$$|\ \ ?\ \ Id$$

Formulæ (*Form*) are defined in mutual recursion with primaries, which consist of atomic formulæ and their negations:

$$Form \ = \ \text{ALL}\ \ Id\ \ .\ \ Form$$

$$|\ \ \text{EX}\ \ \ Id\ \ .\ \ Form$$

$$|\ \ Form\ Conn\ Form$$

$$|\ \ Primary$$

$$Primary \ = \ \tilde{}\ \ Primary$$

$$|\ \ (\ \ Form\ \ )$$

$$|\ \ Id\ TermPack$$

The quantifiers are rendered into ASCII characters as ALL and EX; the following table gives the treatment of the connectives:

Usual symbol: ¬ ∧ ∨ → ↔
ASCII *version*: ~ & | --> <->

The formula $\exists z . \phi(z) \to \forall x . \phi(x)$ might be rendered as

```
EX z. P(z) --> (ALL x. P(x))
```

since ASCII lacks Greek letters. Hal requires a quantified formula to be enclosed in parentheses if it is the operand of a connective.

Parsing. The signature for parsing is minimal. It simply specifies the function *read*, for converting strings to formulæ:

```
signature PARSE_FOL =
  sig
  val read: string -> Fol.form
  end;
```

Before we can implement this signature, we must build structures for the lexical analysis and parsing of first-order logic. Structure *FolKey* defines the lexical syntax. Let us apply the functors described in Chapter 9:

```
structure FolKey    =
    struct val alphas  = ["ALL","EX"]
             and symbols = ["(", ")", ".", ",", "?", "~",
                            "&", "|", "<->", "-->", "|-"]
    end;
structure FolLex    = Lexical (FolKey);
structure FolParsing = Parsing (FolLex);
```

Figure 10.3 presents the corresponding structure. It is fairly simple, but a few points are worth noting.

Functions *list* and *pack* express the grammar phrases *TermList* and *TermPack*. They are general enough to define 'lists' and 'packs' of arbitrary phrases.

The parser cannot distinguish constants from parameters or check that functions have the right number of arguments: it keeps no information about the functions and predicates of the first-order language. It regards any identifier as a constant, representing x by *Fun*("x", []). When parsing the quantification $\forall x . \phi(x)$, it abstracts the body $\phi(x)$ over its occurrences of the 'constant' x.

As discussed in the previous chapter, our parser cannot accept left-recursive grammar rules such as

$$Form = Form\ Conn\ Form.$$

Figure 10.3 *Parsing for first-order logic*

```
structure ParseFol : PARSE_FOL =
  struct
  local

    open FolParsing
    fun list ph  =      ph -- repeat ("," $-- ph)    >> (op::);

    fun pack ph =      "(" $-- list ph -- $")"      >> #1
                    || empty;

    fun makeQuant ((qnt,b),p) =
        Fol.Quant(qnt, b, Fol.abstract 0 (Fol.Fun(b,[])) p);

    fun makeConn a p q = Fol.Conn(a, [p,q]);
    fun makeNeg p      = Fol.Conn("~", [p]);

    fun term toks =
      (   id   -- pack term              >> Fol.Fun
      || "?" $-- id                      >> Fol.Var   ) toks;

    fun form toks =
      (   $"ALL" -- id -- "." $-- form    >> makeQuant
      || $"EX"  -- id -- "." $-- form    >> makeQuant
      || infixes (primary, Fol.precOf, makeConn)  ) toks
    and primary toks =
      (   "~" $-- primary                >> makeNeg
      || "(" $-- form -- $")"            >> #1
      || id -- pack term                 >> Fol.Pred   ) toks;
    in
        val read = reader form
    end
  end;
```

Instead, it relies on the precedences of the connectives. It invokes the parsing function *infixes* with three arguments:

- *primary* parses the operands of connectives.
- *precOf* defines the precedences of the connectives.
- *makeConn* applies a connective to two formulæ.

Most of the structure body is made private by a `local` declaration. At the bottom it defines the only visible identifiers, *form* and *read*. We could easily declare a reading function for terms if necessary.

Displaying. Signature *DISPLAY_FOL* specifies the pretty printing operators for formulæ and goals (which are sequents):

```
signature DISPLAY_FOL =
  sig
  val form: Fol.form -> unit
  val goal: int -> Fol.goal -> unit
  end;
```

The integer argument of function *goal* is displayed before the goal itself. It represents the subgoal number; a proof state typically has several subgoals. The sessions in Section 10.14 illustrate the output.

Structure *DisplayFol* implements this signature; see Figure 10.4. Our pretty printer must be supplied with symbolic expressions that describe the formatting. Function *enclose* wraps an expression in parentheses, while *list* inserts commas between the elements of a list of expressions. Together, they format argument lists as $(t_1, \ldots, t_n)$.

A parameter's name is printed, but not its list of forbidden variables. Another part of the program will display that information as a table.

The precedences of the connectives govern the inclusion of parentheses. Calling *form* $p \, k \, q$ formats the formula q — enclosing it in parentheses, if necessary, to protect it from an adjacent connective of precedence k. In producing the string `q & (p | r)`, it encloses `p | r` in parentheses because the adjacent connective (`&`) has precedence 3 while `|` has precedence 2.

Exercise 10.16   Explain the workings of each of the functions supplied to `>>` in *ParseFol*.

Exercise 10.17   Alter the parser to admit `q --> ALL x. p` as correct syntax for $q \to (\forall x . p)$, for example. It should no longer demand parentheses around quantified formulæ.

Figure 10.4 *Pretty printing for first-order logic*

```
structure DisplayFol : DISPLAY_FOL =
  struct
  fun enclose sexp = Pretty.blo(1, [Pretty.str"(", sexp, Pretty.str")"]);

  fun commas []          = []
    | commas (sexp::sexps) = Pretty.str"," :: Pretty.brk 1 ::
                                sexp :: commas sexps;

  fun list (sexp::sexps)     = Pretty.blo(0, sexp :: commas sexps);

  fun term (Fol.Param(a,_)) = Pretty.str a
    | term (Fol.Var a)      = Pretty.str ("?"^a)
    | term (Fol.Bound i)    = Pretty.str "??UNMATCHED INDEX??"
    | term (Fol.Fun (a,ts)) = Pretty.blo(0, [Pretty.str a, args ts])
  and args []               = Pretty.str""
    | args ts               = enclose (list (map term ts));

  fun formp k (Fol.Pred (a,ts))       = Pretty.blo(0, [Pretty.str a, args ts])
    | formp k (Fol.Conn("~", [p])) =
          Pretty.blo(0, [Pretty.str "~", formp (Fol.precOf "~") p])
    | formp k (Fol.Conn(C, [p,q])) =
          let val pf   = formp (Int.max(Fol.precOf C, k))
              val sexp = Pretty.blo(0, [pf p, Pretty.str(" "^C),
                                        Pretty.brk 1, pf q])
          in  if (Fol.precOf C <= k) then (enclose sexp) else sexp
          end
    | formp k (Fol.Quant(qnt,b,p))   =
          let val q    = Fol.subst 0 (Fol.Fun(b,[])) p
              val sexp = Pretty.blo(2, [Pretty.str(qnt ^ " " ^ b ^ "."),
                                        Pretty.brk 1, formp 0 q])
          in  if  k>0  then  (enclose sexp)  else sexp
          end
    | formp k _                         = Pretty.str"??UNKNOWN FORMULA??";

  fun formList [] = Pretty.str"empty"
    | formList ps = list (map (formp 0) ps);

  fun form p = Pretty.pr (TextIO.stdOut, formp 0 p, 50);

  fun goal (n:int) (ps,qs) =
    Pretty.pr (TextIO.stdOut,
               Pretty.blo (4, [Pretty.str(" " ^ Int.toString n ^ ". "),
                               formList ps, Pretty.brk 2, Pretty.str"|- ",
                               formList qs]),
               50);
  end;
```

Exercise 10.18   The inner parenthesis pair in q & (p1 --> (p2 | r)) is redundant because | has greater precedence than -->; our pretty printing often includes such needless parentheses. Suggest modifications to the function *form* that would prevent this.

Exercise 10.19   Explain how quantified formulæ are displayed.

10.7   *Unification*

Hal attempts to unify atomic formulæ in goals. Its basic unification algorithm takes terms containing no bound variables. Given a pair of terms, it computes a set of (variable, term) replacements to make them identical, or reports that the terms cannot be unified. Performing the replacements is called ***instantiation***. Unification involves three cases:

Function applications. Two function applications can be unified only if they apply the same function; clearly no instantiation can transform $f(?a)$ and $g(b, ?c)$ into identical terms. To unify $g(t_1, t_2)$ with $g(u_1, u_2)$ involves unifying t_1 with u_1 and t_2 with u_2 consistently — thus $g(?a, ?a)$ cannot be unified with $g(b, c)$ because a variable ($?a$) cannot be replaced by two different constants (b and c).

The unification of $f(t_1, \ldots, t_n)$ with $f(u_1, \ldots, u_n)$ begins by unifying t_1 with u_1, then applies the resulting replacements to the remaining terms. The next step is unifying t_2 with u_2 and applying the new replacements to the remaining terms, and so forth. If any unifications fail then the function applications are not unifiable. The corresponding arguments can be chosen for unification in any order without significantly affecting the outcome.

Parameters. Two parameters can be unified only if they have the same name. A parameter cannot be unified with a function application.

Variables. The remaining and most interesting case is unifying a variable $?a$ with a term t (distinct from $?a$). If $?a$ does not occur in t then unification succeeds, yielding the replacement ($?a, t$). If $?a$ does occur in t then unification fails — for possibly two different reasons:

- If $?a$ occurs in a parameter of t, then $?a$ is a 'forbidden variable' for that parameter and for the term. Replacing $?a$ by t would violate the proviso of some quantifier rule.
- If t properly contains $?a$ then the terms cannot be unified: no term can contain itself. For example, no replacement can transform $f(?a)$ and $?a$ into identical terms.

This is the notorious **occurs check**, which most Prolog interpreters omit because of its cost. For theorem proving, soundness must have priority over efficiency; the occurs check must be performed.

Examples. To unify $g(?a, f(?c))$ with $g(f(?b), ?a)$, first unify $?a$ with $f(?b)$, a trivial step. After replacing $?a$ by $f(?b)$ in the remaining arguments, unify $f(?c)$ with $f(?b)$. This replaces $?c$ by $?b$. The outcome can be given as the set $\{?a \mapsto f(?b)), ?c \mapsto ?b\}$. The unified formula is $g(f(?b), f(?b))$.

Here is another example. To unify $g(?a, f(?a))$ with $g(f(?b), ?b)$, the first step again replaces $?a$ by $f(?b)$. The next task is unifying $f(f(?b))$ with $?b$ — which is impossible because $f(f(?b))$ contains $?b$. Unification fails.

Instantiation of parameters. Recall that each parameter carries a list of forbidden variables; $b_{?a}$ must never be part of a term t substituted for $?a$. When a legal replacement is performed, the occurrence of $?a$ in $b_{?a}$ is replaced by the variables contained in t, not by t itself. For instance, replacing $?a$ by $g(?c, f(?d))$ transforms $b_{?a}$ into $b_{?c, ?d}$. Any substitution for $?c$ or $?d$ is effectively a substitution for $?a$, and therefore $?c$ and $?d$ are forbidden to the parameter.

For example, to unify $g(?a, f(b_{?a}))$ with $g(h(?c, ?d), ?c)$, the first step is to replace $?a$ by $h(?c, ?d)$. The second arguments of g become $f(b_{?c, ?d})$ and $?c$; these terms are not unifiable because $?c$ is forbidden to the parameter $b_{?c, ?d}$.

ℹ️ *Skolem functions.* Parameters are not widely used in theorem proving; more traditional are **Skolem functions**. The rules ∀:left and ∃:right, instead of creating the parameter $b_{?a_1, \ldots, ?a_k}$, could introduce the term $b(?a_1, \ldots, ?a_k)$. Here, b is a function symbol not appearing elsewhere in the proof. The term behaves like a parameter; the occurs check prevents unification from violating the rules' provisos. Skolem functions have advantages in automatic proof procedures, but they destroy the formula's readability; in higher-order logic they can even cause faulty reasoning.

The ML code. The signature specifies unification and instantiation functions, as well as an exception *Failed* for reporting non-unifiable terms:

```
signature UNIFY =
  sig
  exception Failed
  val atoms    : Fol.form * Fol.form -> Fol.term StringDict.t
  val instTerm : Fol.term StringDict.t -> Fol.term -> Fol.term
  val instForm : Fol.term StringDict.t -> Fol.form -> Fol.form
  val instGoal : Fol.term StringDict.t -> Fol.goal -> Fol.goal
  end;
```

The function *atoms* attempts to unify two atomic formulæ, while *instTerm*, *inst-Form* and *instGoal* apply replacements to terms, formulæ and goals, respectively.

We represent a set of replacements by a dictionary, using structure *StringDict* (Section 7.10); variable names are strings.

An atomic formula consists of a predicate applied to an argument list, such as $P(t_1, \ldots, t_n)$. Unifying two atomic formulæ is essentially the same as unifying two function applications; the predicates must be the same and the corresponding argument pairs must be simultaneously unifiable.

Structure *Unify* (Figure 10.5) implements unification. The key functions are declared within *unifyLists* in order to have access to *env*, the environment of replacements. Collecting the replacements in *env* is more efficient than applying each replacement as it is generated. Replacements are regarded as cumulative rather than simultaneous, just as in the λ-calculus interpreter's treatment of definitions (Section 9.7). Simultaneous substitution by

$$\{?b \mapsto g(z),\ ?a \mapsto f(?b)\}$$

would replace $?a$ by $f(?b)$, but our functions replace $?a$ by $f(g(z))$. This is the correct treatment for our unification algorithm.

Here are some remarks about the functions declared in *unifyLists*:

- *chase t* replaces the term t, if it is a variable, by its assignment in *env*. Nonvariable terms are returned without change; at each stage, unification is concerned only with a term's outer form.
- *occurs a t* tests whether the variable $?a$ occurs within term t; like *chase*, it looks up variables in the environment.
- *occsl a ts* tests whether the variable $?a$ occurs within the list of terms ts.
- *unify(t, u)* creates a new environment from *env* by unifying t with u, if possible, otherwise raising exception *Failed*. If t and u are variables then they must have no assignment in *env*; violating this condition could result in a variable having two assignments!
- *unifyl(ts, us)* simultaneously unifies the corresponding members of the lists ts and us, raising *Failed* if their lengths differ. (If two terms are not unifiable, the exception will arise in *unify*, not *unifyl*.)

The implementation is purely functional. Representing variables by references might be more efficient — updating a variable would perform a replacement, with no need for environments — but is incompatible with tactical theorem proving. Applying a tactic to a proof state should create a new state, leaving the original state unchanged so that other tactics can be tried. A unification algorithm could employ imperative techniques provided they were invisible outside.

Figure 10.5 *Unification*

```
structure Unify : UNIFY =
  struct
  exception Failed;

  fun unifyLists env =
    let fun chase (Fol.Var a) = (chase(StringDict.lookup(env,a))
                                  handle StringDict.E _ => Fol.Var a)
          | chase t            = t
        fun occurs a (Fol.Fun(_,ts))     = occsl a ts
          | occurs a (Fol.Param(_,bs))   = occsl a (map Fol.Var bs)
          | occurs a (Fol.Var b)         =
                    (a=b) orelse (occurs a (StringDict.lookup(env,b))
                                  handle StringDict.E _ => false)
          | occurs a _                   = false
        and occsl a = List.exists (occurs a)
        and unify (Fol.Var a, t)         =
                  if t = Fol.Var a then env
                  else if occurs a t then raise Failed
                                else StringDict.update(env,a,t)
          | unify (t, Fol.Var a) = unify (Fol.Var a, t)
          | unify (Fol.Param(a,_), Fol.Param(b,_)) = if a=b then env
                                                     else raise Failed
          | unify (Fol.Fun(a,ts), Fol.Fun(b,us))   = if a=b then unifyl(ts,us)
                                                     else raise Failed
          | unify _                       = raise Failed
        and unifyl ([],[])       = env
          | unifyl (t::ts, u::us) = unifyLists (unify (chase t, chase u)) (ts,us)
          | unifyl _             = raise Failed
    in unifyl end

  fun atoms (Fol.Pred(a,ts), Fol.Pred(b,us)) =
          if a=b then unifyLists StringDict.empty (ts,us) else raise Failed
    | atoms _                       = raise Failed;

  fun instTerm env (Fol.Fun(a,ts))   = Fol.Fun(a, map (instTerm env) ts)
    | instTerm env (Fol.Param(a,bs)) =
        Fol.Param(a, foldr Fol.termVars [] (map (instTerm env o Fol.Var) bs))
    | instTerm env (Fol.Var a)       = (instTerm env (StringDict.lookup(env,a))
                                         handle StringDict.E _ => Fol.Var a)
    | instTerm env t                 = t;

  fun instForm env (Fol.Pred(a,ts))   = Fol.Pred(a, map (instTerm env) ts)
    | instForm env (Fol.Conn(b,ps))   = Fol.Conn(b, map (instForm env) ps)
    | instForm env (Fol.Quant(qnt,b,p)) = Fol.Quant(qnt, b, instForm env p);

  fun instGoal env (ps,qs) = (map (instForm env) ps, map (instForm env) qs);
  end;
```

The unification function raises exception *Failed* when two terms cannot be unified. As in parsing, the failure may be detected in deeply nested recursive calls; the exception propagates upwards. This is a typical case where exceptions work well.

Function *instTerm* substitutes in parameters as described above. Each forbidden variable is replaced by the list of variables in the term resulting from the substitution. This could be done using *List . concat*, but the combination of *foldr* and *termVars* performs less copying.

ⓘ   *Efficient unification algorithms.* The algorithm presented here can take exponential time, in highly exceptional cases. In practice, it is quite usable. More efficient algorithms exist. The linear time algorithm of Paterson and Wegman (1978) is usually regarded as too complicated for practical use. The algorithm of Martelli and Montanari (1982) is almost linear and is intended to be usable. However, Corbin and Bidoit (1983) propose an algorithm based upon the naïve one, but representing terms by graphs (really, pointers) instead of trees. They claim it to be superior to the almost linear algorithms because of its simplicity, despite needing quadratic time. Ružička and Prívara (1988) have refined this approach to be almost linear too.

Exercise 10.20   What could happen if this line were omitted from *unify*?

```
if t = Fol.Var a then env else
```

Tactics and the proof state

Our proof procedure for the sequent calculus operates by successive refinements, working backwards from a goal. The proof tree grows up from the root. Coding the procedure in ML requires a data structure for **proof states**, which are partially constructed proofs. Inference rules will be implemented as functions, called **tactics**, on proof states.

10.8   *The proof state*

A formal proof is a tree whose every node carries a sequent and the name of a rule. Each node's branches lead to the premises of its rule. But the ML datatype corresponding to such trees is unsuitable for our purposes. Backward proof requires access to the leaves, not to the root. Extending the proof turns a leaf into a branch node, and would require copying part of the tree. The intermediate nodes would play no useful rôle in the search for a proof.

Hal omits the intermediate nodes altogether. A partial proof tree contains just two parts of the proof. The root, or **main goal**, is the formula we first set out to prove. The leaves, or **current subgoals**, are the sequents that remain to be proved.

A goal ϕ paired with the singleton subgoal list $[\vdash \phi\,]$ represents the initial state of a proof of ϕ; no rules have yet been applied. A goal ϕ paired with the empty subgoal list is a final state, and represents a finished proof.

If the full proof tree is not stored, how can we be certain that a Hal proof is correct? The answer is to hide the representation of proof states using an abstract type *state*, providing a limited set of operations — to create an initial state, to examine the contents of a state, to test for a final state, and to transform a state into a new state by some rule of inference.

If greater security is required, the proof could be saved and checked by a separate program. Bear in mind that proofs of real theorems can be extremely large, and that no amount of machine checking can provide absolute security. Our programs and proof systems are fallible — as are the theories we use to reduce 'real world' tasks to logic.

ⓘ *Approaches to formalizing an inference system.* While developing Edinburgh LCF, Robin Milner conceived the idea of defining an inference system as an abstract type. He designed ML's type system to support this application. LCF's type *thm* denotes the set of theorems of the logic. Functions with result type *thm* implement the axioms and inference rules.

Implementing the inference rules as functions from theorems to theorems supports forward proof, LCF's primitive style of reasoning. To support backward proof, LCF provides tactics. LCF tactics represent a partial proof by a function of type *thm list* → *thm*. This function proves the main goal, using inference rules, when supplied with theorems for each of the subgoals. A finished proof can be supplied with the empty list to prove the main goal. The classic description (Gordon *et al.*, 1979) is out of print, but my book on LCF also describes this work (Paulson, 1987).

Hal differs from LCF in implementing the inference rules as functions on proof states, not on theorems. These functions are themselves tactics and support backward proof as the primitive style. They do not support forward proof. The approach supports unification; tactics may update meta-variables in the proof state.

Isabelle (Paulson, 1994) uses yet another approach. Rules and proof states have a common representation in the typed λ-calculus. Combining these objects yields both forward and backward proof. This requires some form of higher-order unification (Huet, 1975).

10.9   *The ML signature*

Signature *RULE* specifies the abstract type of proof states, with its operations (Figure 10.6). Each value of type *state* contains a formula (the main goal) and a list of sequents (the subgoals). Although we cannot tell from the signature, each *state* contains additional information for internal use.

Figure 10.6 *The signature* RULE

```
signature RULE =
  sig
  type state
  type tactic   = state -> state ImpSeq.t
  val main      : state -> Fol.form
  val subgoals  : state -> Fol.goal list
  val initial   : Fol.form -> state
  val final     : state -> bool
  val basic     : int -> tactic
  val unify     : int -> tactic
  val conjL     : int -> tactic
  val conjR     : int -> tactic
  val disjL     : int -> tactic
  val disjR     : int -> tactic
  val impL      : int -> tactic
  val impR      : int -> tactic
  val negL      : int -> tactic
  val negR      : int -> tactic
  val iffL      : int -> tactic
  val iffR      : int -> tactic
  val allL      : int -> tactic
  val allR      : int -> tactic
  val exL       : int -> tactic
  val exR       : int -> tactic
  end;
```

Type *tactic* abbreviates the function type

$$state \rightarrow state\ ImpSeq.t,$$

where *ImpSeq* is the structure for lazy lists presented in Section 8.4. A tactic maps a state to a sequence of possible next states. The primitive tactics generate finite sequences, typically of length zero or one. A complex tactic, say for depth-first search, could generate an infinite sequence of states.

The function *initial* creates initial states containing a given formula as the main goal and the only subgoal. The predicate *final* tests whether a proof state is final, containing no subgoals.

The other functions in the signature are the primitive tactics, which define the inference rules of the sequent calculus. Later, we shall introduce **tacticals** for combining tactics.

The subgoals of a proof state are numbered starting from 1. Each primitive tactic, given an integer argument i and a state, applies some rule of the sequent calculus to subgoal i, creating a new state. For instance, calling

$$conjL\ 3\ st$$

applies $\wedge$:left to subgoal 3 of state *st*. If this subgoal has the form $\phi \wedge \psi, \Gamma \vdash \Delta$ then subgoal 3 of the next state will be $\phi, \psi, \Gamma \vdash \Delta$. Otherwise, $\wedge$:left is not applicable to the subgoal and there can be no next state; *conjL* will return the empty sequence.

If subgoal 5 of *st* is $\Gamma \vdash \Delta, \phi \wedge \psi$, then

$$conjR\ 5\ st$$

will make a new state whose subgoal 5 is $\Gamma \vdash \Delta, \phi$ and whose subgoal 6 is $\Gamma \vdash \Delta, \psi$. Subgoals numbered greater than 5 in *st* are shifted up.

Calling *basic i st* checks whether subgoal i of state *st* is a basic sequent. If subgoal i has a common formula on both sides then it is deleted in the next state. Otherwise, the tactic signals failure by returning the empty sequence. A more elaborate treatment of basic sequents is tactic *unify*.

Calling *unify i st* attempts to solve subgoal i of state *st* by converting it into a basic sequent. If it can unify a formula on the left with a formula on the right then it deletes subgoal i and applies the unifying substitution to the rest of the proof state. There may be several different pairs of unifiable formulæ; applying *unify* to the subgoal

$$P(?a), P(?b) \vdash P(f(c)), P(c)$$

generates a sequence of four next states. Only the first of these is computed, with the others available upon demand, since sequences are lazy.

10.10   *Tactics for basic sequents*

Structure *Rule* is presented in parts. The first part (Figure 10.7) defines the representation of type *state* and its primitive operations, and declares tactics for basic sequents.

Declaring type state. The `datatype` declaration introduces type *state* with its constructor *State*. The constructor is not exported, allowing access to the representation only inside the structure body. Type *tactic* is declared to abbreviate the type of functions from state to state sequences.

Functions *main* and *subgoals* return the corresponding parts of a proof state. The third component of a proof state is an integer, for generating unique names in quantifier rules. Its value is initially 0 and is increased as necessary when the next state is created. If this name counter were kept in a reference cell and updated by assignment, much of the code would be simpler — especially where the counter plays no rôle. However, applying a quantifier rule to a state would affect all states sharing that reference. Resetting the counter to 0, while producing shorter names, could also lead to re-use of names and faulty reasoning. It is safest to ensure that all tactics are purely functional.

Calling *initial p* creates a state containing the sequent $\vdash p$ as its only subgoal, with *p* as its main goal and 0 for its variable counter. Predicate *final* tests for an empty subgoal list.

The definitions of basic and unify. All tactics are expressed using *spliceGoals*, a function to replace subgoal *i* by a new list of subgoals in a state. The *List* functions *take* and *drop* extract the subgoals before and after *i*, so that the new subgoals can be spliced into the correct place.

The declaration of *propRule* illustrates how proof states are processed. This function makes a tactic from a function *goalF* of type *goal* → *goal list*. Applied to an integer *i* and a state, it supplies subgoal *i* to *goalF* and splices in the resulting subgoals; it returns the new state as a one-element sequence. It returns the empty sequence if any exception is raised. Exception *Subscript* results from the call *List*.*nth*(*gs*, *i*−1) if there is no *i*th subgoal; recall that *nth* numbers a list's elements starting from zero. Other exceptions, such as *Match*, can result from *goalF*.

The tactic *basic* is a simple application of *propRule*. It supplies as *goalF* a function that checks whether the goal (*ps*, *qs*) is a basic sequent. If so then it

Figure 10.7 *First part of* Rule — *tactics for basic sequents*

```
structure Rule :> RULE =
  struct
  datatype state = State of Fol.goal list * Fol.form * int

  type tactic = state -> state ImpSeq.t;

  fun main      (State(gs,p,_)) = p
  and subgoals  (State(gs,p,_)) = gs;

  fun initial p = State([ ([],[p]) ], p, 0);

  fun final (State(gs,_,_)) = null gs;

  fun spliceGoals gs newgs i = List.take(gs,i-1) @ newgs @ List.drop(gs,i);

  fun propRule goalF i (State(gs,p,n)) =
      let val gs2 = spliceGoals gs (goalF (List.nth(gs,i-1))) i
      in  ImpSeq.fromList [State(gs2, p, n)]   end
      handle _ => ImpSeq.empty;

  val basic = propRule
                (fn (ps,qs) =>
                   if List.exists (fn p => List.exists (fn q => p=q) qs) ps
                   then [] else raise Match);

  fun unifiable ([], _)     = ImpSeq.empty
    | unifiable (p::ps, qs) =
        let fun find []      = unifiable (ps,qs)
              | find (q::qs) = ImpSeq.cons(Unify.atoms(p,q), fn()=> find qs)
                               handle Unify.Failed => find qs
        in  find qs  end;

  fun inst env (gs,p,n) =
        State (map (Unify.instGoal env) gs,  Unify.instForm env p, n);

  fun unify i (State(gs,p,n)) =
    let val (ps,qs)  = List.nth(gs,i-1)
        fun next env = inst env (spliceGoals gs [] i, p, n)
    in  ImpSeq.map next (unifiable(ps,qs))   end
    handle Subscript => ImpSeq.empty;
```

returns the empty list of subgoals; the effect is to delete that subgoal from the next state. But if (*ps*, *qs*) is not a basic sequent then the function raises an exception.

The tactic *unify* is more complicated: it can return multiple next states. It calls *unifiable* to generate a sequence of unifying environments, and *inst* to apply them to the other subgoals. Function *next*, which performs the final processing, is applied via the functional *ImpSeq*. *map*.

The function *unifiable* takes lists *ps* and *qs* of formulæ. It returns the sequence of all environments obtained by unifying some *p* of *ps* with some *q* of *qs*. The function *find* handles the 'inner loop,' searching in *qs* for something to unify with *p*. It generates a sequence whose head is an environment and whose tail is generated by the recursive call *find qs*, but if *Unify*. *atoms* raises an exception then the result is simply *find qs*.

☠ *Look out for other goals.* When *unify* solves a subgoal, it may update the state so that some other subgoal becomes unprovable. Success of this tactic does not guarantee that it is the right way to find a proof; in some cases, a different tactic should be used instead. Any search procedure involving *unify* should use backtracking. On the other hand, solving a goal by *basic* is always safe.

Exercise 10.21   Give an example to justify the warning above.

10.11   *The propositional tactics*

The next part of *Rule* implements the rules for ∧, ∨, ¬, → and ↔. Since each connective has a 'left' rule and a 'right' rule, there are ten tactics altogether. See Figure 10.8.

The tactics employ the same basic mechanism. Search for a suitable formula on the given side, left or right; detach the connective; generate new subgoals from its operands. Each tactic returns a single next state if it succeeds. A tactic fails, returning an empty state sequence, if it cannot find a suitable formula. We can express them succinctly with the help of *propRule* and a new function, *splitConn*.

An example demonstrates the workings of *splitConn*. Given the string "&" and a formula list *qs*, it finds the first element that matches *Conn* ("&", *ps*), raising exception *Match* if none exists. It also copies *qs*, omitting the matching element. It returns *ps* paired with the shortened *qs*. Note that *ps* contains the operands of the selected formula.

The functional *propL* helps express sequent rules. Given a sequent, it searches for a connective on the left side. It supplies the result of the *splitConn* call to another function *leftF*, which creates new subgoals. The functional *propR* is similar, but searches on the right side.

Figure 10.8 *Part of* Rule — *the propositional tactics*

```
fun splitConn a qs =
  let fun get []                            = raise Match
        | get (Fol.Conn(b,ps) :: qs)        = if a=b then ps else get qs
        | get (q::qs)                       = get qs;
      fun del []                            = []
        | del ((q as Fol.Conn(b,_)) :: qs)  = if a=b then qs
                                              else q :: del qs
        | del (q::qs)                       = q :: del qs
  in (get qs, del qs)  end;

fun propL a leftF = propRule (fn (ps,qs) => leftF (splitConn a ps, qs));

fun propR a rightF = propRule (fn (ps,qs) => rightF (ps, splitConn a qs));

val conjL = propL "&" (fn (([p1,p2], ps), qs) => [(p1::p2::ps, qs)]);

val conjR = propR "&"
      (fn (ps, ([q1,q2], qs)) => [(ps, q1::qs),   (ps, q2::qs)]);

val disjL = propL "|"
      (fn (([p1,p2], ps), qs) => [(p1::ps, qs),   (p2::ps, qs)]);

val disjR = propR "|" (fn (ps, ([q1,q2], qs)) => [(ps, q1::q2::qs)]);

val impL = propL "-->"
      (fn (([p1,p2], ps), qs) => [(p2::ps, qs),   (ps, p1::qs)]);

val impR = propR "-->" (fn (ps, ([q1,q2], qs)) => [(q1::ps, q2::qs)]);

val negL = propL "~" (fn (([p], ps), qs)  => [(ps, p::qs)]);

val negR = propR "~" (fn (ps, ([q], qs))  => [(q::ps, qs)]);

val iffL = propL "<->"
      (fn (([p1,p2], ps), qs) => [(p1::p2::ps, qs),   (ps, p1::p2::qs)]);

val iffR = propR "<->"
      (fn (ps, ([q1,q2], qs)) => [(q1::ps, q2::qs),   (q2::ps, q1::qs)]);
```

The tactics are given by `val` declarations, since they have no explicit arguments. Each tactic consists of a call to *propL* or *propR*. Each passes in `fn` notation the argument *leftF* or *rightF*. Each function takes an analysed subgoal and
returns one or two subgoals. Thus *conjL* searches for a conjunction in the left
part and inserts the two conjuncts into the new subgoal, while *conjR* searches
for a conjunction in the right part and makes two subgoals.

10.12   *The quantifier tactics*

The mechanism presented above is easily modified to express the quantifier tactics. There are a few differences from the propositional case. The code
appears in Figure 10.9, which completes the presentation of structure *Rule*.

The function *splitQuant* closely resembles *splitConn*. It finds the first formula
having a particular quantifier, `"ALL"` or `"EX"`. It returns the entire formula
(rather than its operands) because certain quantifier tactics retain it in the subgoal.

Although our sequent calculus is defined using multisets, it is implemented
using lists. The formulæ in a sequent are ordered; if the list contains two suitable
formulæ, the leftmost one will be found. To respect the concept of multisets, Hal
provides no way of reordering the formulæ. The quantifier tactics ensure that no
formula is permanently excluded from consideration.

The tactics need a source of fresh names for variables and parameters. Calling *letter n*, for $0 \leq n \leq 25$, returns a one-character string from `"a"` to `"z"`.
The function *gensym* — whose name dates from Lisp antiquity — generates a
string from a natural number. Its result contains a base 26 numeral whose 'digits' are lower-case letters; the prefix `"_"` prevents clashes with names supplied
from outside.

The functional *quantRule* creates a tactic from a function *goalF*. It supplies
both a subgoal and a fresh name to *goalF*, which accordingly has type *goal* ×
string → *goal list*. When constructing the next state, it increments the variable
counter. Otherwise, *quantRule* is identical to *propRule*.

Each tactic is expressed by applying *quantRule* to a function in `fn` notation.
The function takes the subgoal (*ps*, *qs*) and the fresh name *b*; it returns one subgoal.

Tactics *allL* and *exR* expand a quantified formula. They substitute a variable
with the name *b* into its body. They include the quantified formula (bound to *qnt-
Form* using `as`) in the subgoal. The formula is placed last in the list; thus, other
quantified formulæ can be selected when the tactic is next applied.

Tactics *allR* and *exL* select a quantified formula and substitute a parameter into

Figure 10.9 *Final part of* Rule — *the quantifier tactics*

```
fun splitQuant qnt qs =
  let fun get []                                    = raise Match
        | get ((q as Fol.Quant(qnt2,_,p)) :: qs)    = if qnt=qnt2 then q
                                                      else get qs
        | get (q::qs)                               = get qs;
      fun del []                                    = []
        | del ((q as Fol.Quant(qnt2,_,p)) :: qs)    = if qnt=qnt2 then qs
                                                      else q :: del qs
        | del (q::qs)                               = q :: del qs
  in (get qs, del qs)  end;

fun letter n = String.substring("abcdefghijklmnopqrstuvwxyz", n, 1)

fun gensym n =
    if n<26 then "_" ^ letter n
    else gensym(n div 26) ^ letter(n mod 26);

fun quantRule goalF i (State(gs,p,n)) =
    let val gs2 = spliceGoals gs (goalF (List.nth(gs,i-1), gensym n)) i
    in  ImpSeq.fromList [State(gs2, p, n+1)]   end
    handle _ => ImpSeq.empty;

val allL = quantRule (fn ((ps,qs), b) =>
    let val (qntForm as Fol.Quant(_,_,p), ps') = splitQuant "ALL" ps
        val px = Fol.subst 0 (Fol.Var b) p
    in  [(px :: ps' @ [qntForm], qs)]  end);

val allR = quantRule (fn ((ps,qs), b) =>
    let val (Fol.Quant(_,_,q), qs') = splitQuant "ALL" qs
        val vars = Fol.goalVars ((ps,qs), [])
        val qx   = Fol.subst 0 (Fol.Param(b, vars)) q
    in  [(ps, qx::qs')]   end);

val exL = quantRule (fn ((ps,qs), b) =>
    let val (Fol.Quant(_,_,p), ps') = splitQuant "EX" ps
        val vars = Fol.goalVars ((ps,qs), [])
        val px   = Fol.subst 0 (Fol.Param(b, vars)) p
    in  [(px::ps', qs)]   end);

val exR = quantRule (fn ((ps,qs), b) =>
    let val (qntForm as Fol.Quant(_,_,q), qs') = splitQuant "EX" qs
        val qx = Fol.subst 0 (Fol.Var b) q
    in  [(ps, qx :: qs' @ [qntForm])]   end);
end;
```

---

its body. The parameter has the name *b* and carries, as forbidden variables, all the variables in the subgoal.

As we reach the end of *Rule*, we should remember that the tactics declared in it are the only means of creating values of type *state*. All proof procedures — even if they demonstrate validity using sophisticated data structures — must ultimately apply these tactics, constructing a formal proof. If the code given above is correct, and the ML system is correct, then Hal proofs are guaranteed to be sound. No coding errors after this point can yield faulty proofs. This security comes from defining *state* as an abstract type.

Exercise 10.22   Suggest a representation of type *state* that would store the entire proof tree. Best would be an encoding that uses little space while allowing the proof tree to be reconstructed. Sketch the modifications to *RULE* and *Rule*.

Exercise 10.23   Our set of tactics provides no way of using a previously proved theorem in a proof. A tactic based on the rule

$$\frac{\vdash \phi \quad \phi, \Gamma \vdash \Delta}{\Gamma \vdash \Delta}$$

could insert the theorem $\vdash \phi$ as a lemma into a goal.[3] Describe how such a tactic could be implemented.

Exercise 10.24   'Structure *Rule* does not involve *ParseFol* or *DisplayFol*, so faults in parsing and pretty printing cannot result in the construction of faulty proofs.' Comment on this statement.

Searching for proofs

Most of the programming is now behind us. We are nearly ready to attempt proofs on the machine. We shall implement a package of commands for applying tactics to a goal. This will demonstrate the treatment of proof states, but will also reveal the tedium of rule-by-rule proof checking. Tacticals, by providing control structures for tactics, will allow us to express automatic theorem provers in a few lines of code.

10.13   *Commands for transforming proof states*

The user interface does not read from the terminal, but consists of a set of commands to be invoked from the ML top level. This is typical of tactical

---

[3] This rule is a special case of 'cut'; its first premise could be $\Gamma \vdash \Delta, \phi$.

theorem provers. The most important command is 'apply a tactic,' and the tactic could be given by an arbitrary ML expression; therefore, the command language is ML itself. Remember that ML stands for Meta Language.

Hal's interface is crude. It merely provides commands for setting, updating and inspecting a stored proof state. Practical theorem proving requires additional facilities, such as an *undo* command for reverting to a previous state. Because a tactic can return several next states, applying tactics defines a search tree rooted in the initial state. A graphical user interface would provide means for exploring this tree. To keep the code simple, such facilities are left as exercises. Some ML systems can communicate with scripting languages such as Tcl/Tk, making it easy to put windows and menus on the screen. Good interface design requires, in addition, careful study of users' work habits.

Signature *COMMAND* specifies the user interface:

```
signature COMMAND =
  sig
  val goal    : string -> unit
  val by      : Rule.tactic -> unit
  val pr      : Rule.state -> unit
  val getState : unit -> Rule.state
  end;
```

The interface consists of the following items, which (except *pr*) act upon a stored proof state:

- The *goal* command accepts a formula ϕ, given as a string; it sets the stored proof state to the initial state for ϕ.
- The *by* command applies a tactic to the current state. If the resulting sequence of next states is non-empty, its head is taken to update the stored proof state. Otherwise, the tactic has failed; an error message is displayed.
- The *pr* command prints its argument, a proof state, on the terminal.
- The function *getState* returns the stored proof state.

Structure *Command* implements these items (Figure 10.10). The current state is stored in a reference cell, initialised with the fictitious goal `"No goal yet!"`.

Recall that a parameter, such as $b_{?c,?d}$, is displayed simply as b. The interface displays a table of each parameter, with its forbidden variables. Function *printpar* prints the line

```
b not in ?c ?d
```

for $b_{?c,?d}$; it prints nothing at all for a parameter that has no forbidden variables.

Figure 10.10 *User interface commands*

```
structure Command : COMMAND =
  struct

  val currState = ref (Rule.initial (Fol.Pred("No goal yet!",[])));

  fun question (s,z) = " ?" :: s :: z;

  fun printParam (a,[]) = ()        (*print a line of parameter table*)
    | printParam (a,ts) =
        print (String.concat (a :: " not in " ::
                              foldr question ["\n"] ts));

  fun printGoals (_, [])    = ()
    | printGoals (n, g::gs) = (DisplayFol.goal n g;   printGoals (n+1,gs));

  fun pr st =   (*print a proof state*)
      let val p  = Rule.main st
          and gs = Rule.subgoals st
      in  DisplayFol.form p;
          if Rule.final st then print "No subgoals left!\n"
          else (printGoals (1,gs);
                    app printParam (foldr Fol.goalParams [] gs))
      end;

  (*print new state, then set it*)
  fun setState state = (pr state;   currState := state);

  val goal = setState o Rule.initial o ParseFol.read;

  fun by tac = setState (ImpSeq.hd (tac (!currState)))
              handle ImpSeq.Empty => print "** Tactic FAILED! **\n"

  fun getState() = !currState;
  end;
```

Function *printgoals* prints a list of numbered subgoals. With the help of these functions, *pr* prints a state: its main goal, its subgoal list, and its table of parameters.

Exercise 10.25   Design and implement an *undo* command that cancels the effect of the most recent *by* command. Repeated *undo* commands should revert to earlier and earlier states.

Exercise 10.26   There are many ways of managing the search tree of states. The interface could explore a single path through the tree. Each node would store a sequence of possible next states, marking one as the active branch. Changing the active branch at any node would select a different path. Develop this idea.

10.14   *Two sample proofs using tactics*

To demonstrate the tactics and the user interface, let us do some proofs on the machine. For convenience in referring to commands, we open the corresponding module:

```
open Command;
```

Now we can perform proofs. The first example is brief, a proof of $\phi \wedge \psi \rightarrow \psi \wedge \phi$. The *goal* command gives this formula to Hal.

```
goal "P & Q  -->  Q & P";
> P & Q --> Q & P
> 1. empty  |-  P & Q --> Q & P
```

Now $\phi \wedge \psi \rightarrow \psi \wedge \phi$ is the main goal and the only subgoal. We must apply $\rightarrow$:right to subgoal 1; no other step is possible:

```
by (Rule.impR 1);
> P & Q --> Q & P
> 1.  P & Q  |-  Q & P
```

Subgoal 1 becomes $\phi \wedge \psi \vdash \psi \wedge \phi$, which we have proved on paper. Although $\wedge$:right could be applied to this goal, $\wedge$:left leads to a shorter proof because it makes only one subgoal.

```
by (Rule.conjL 1);
> P & Q --> Q & P
> 1.  P, Q  |-  Q & P
```

Again we have no choice. We must apply $\wedge$:right to subgoal 1. Here is what happens if we try a different tactic:

```
by (Rule.disjR 1);
> ** Tactic FAILED! **
```

This time, apply ∧:right. It makes two subgoals.

```
by (Rule.conjR 1);
> P & Q --> Q & P
> 1.  P, Q  |- Q
> 2.  P, Q  |- P
```

Tactics are usually applied to subgoal 1; let us tackle subgoal 2 for variety. It is a basic sequent, so it falls to *Rule.basic*.

```
by (Rule.basic 2);
> P & Q --> Q & P
> 1.  P, Q  |- Q
```

Subgoal 1 is also a basic sequent. Solving it terminates the proof.

```
by (Rule.basic 1);
> P & Q --> Q & P
> No subgoals left!
```

Most theorem provers provide some means of storing theorems once proved, but this is not possible in Hal. We go on to the next example, $\exists z . \phi(z) \to \forall x . \phi(x)$, which was discussed earlier.

```
goal "EX z.  P(z)  -->  (ALL x.  P(x))";
> EX z.  P(z)  -->  (ALL x.  P(x))
> 1. empty  |-  EX z.  P(z)  -->  (ALL x.  P(x))
```

The only possible step is to apply ∃:right to subgoal 1. The tactic generates a variable called ?_a.

```
by (Rule.exR 1);
> EX z.  P(z)  -->  (ALL x.  P(x))
> 1. empty
>      |-  P(?_a)  -->  (ALL x.  P(x)),
>          EX z.  P(z)  -->  (ALL x.  P(x))
```

We could apply ∃:right again, but it seems sensible to analyse the other formula in subgoal 1. So we apply →:right.

```
by (Rule.impR 1);
> EX z.  P(z)  -->  (ALL x.  P(x))
> 1.  P(?_a)
>      |-  ALL x.  P(x),
>          EX z.  P(z)  -->  (ALL x.  P(x))
```

Continuing to work on the first formula, we apply ∀:right. The tactic generates a parameter called _b, with ?_a as its forbidden variable. A table of parameters is now displayed.

```
by (Rule.allR 1);
> EX z.  P(z) --> (ALL x.  P(x))
> 1.  P(?_a) |- P(_b),
>                   EX z.  P(z) --> (ALL x.  P(x))
> _b not in  ?_a
```

Since the subgoal contains P(?_a) on the left and P(_b) on the right, we could try unifying these formulæ by calling *Rule.unify*. However, the forbidden variable of _b prevents this unification. Replacing ?_a by _b would violate the proviso of ∀:right.

```
by (Rule.unify 1);
> ** Tactic FAILED! **
```

The situation is like it was at the start of the proof, except that the subgoal contains two new atomic formulæ. Since they are not unifiable, we have no choice but to expand the quantifier again, using ∃:right. The variable ?_c is created.

```
by (Rule.exR 1);
> EX z.  P(z) --> (ALL x.  P(x))
> 1.  P(?_a)
>       |- P(?_c) --> (ALL x.  P(x)), P(_b),
>           EX z.  P(z) --> (ALL x.  P(x))
> _b not in  ?_a
```

The proof continues as it did before, with the two atomic formulæ carried along. We avoid applying ∃:right a third time and instead apply →:right.

```
by (Rule.impR 1);
> EX z.  P(z) --> (ALL x.  P(x))
> 1.  P(?_c), P(?_a)
>       |- ALL x.  P(x), P(_b),
>           EX z.  P(z) --> (ALL x.  P(x))
> _b not in  ?_a
```

The subgoal has a new formula on the left, namely P(?_c), and ?_c is not a forbidden variable of _b. Therefore P(?_c) and P(_b) are unifiable.

```
by (Rule.unify 1);
> EX z.  P(z) --> (ALL x.  P(x))
> No subgoals left!
```

Although the first attempt with *Rule.unify* failed, a successful proof was finally found. This demonstrates how parameters and variables behave in practice.

Figure 10.11 *The signature* TACTICAL

```
infix 6 $--;
infix 5 --;
infix 0 || |@|;
signature TACTICAL =
  sig
  type ('a,'b) multifun = 'a -> 'b ImpSeq.t
  val --          : ('a,'b) multifun * ('b,'c) multifun -> ('a,'c) multifun
  val ||          : ('a,'b) multifun * ('a,'b) multifun -> ('a,'b) multifun
  val |@|         : ('a,'b) multifun * ('a,'b) multifun -> ('a,'b) multifun
  val all         : ('a,'a) multifun
  val no          : ('a,'b) multifun
  val try         : ('a,'a) multifun -> ('a,'a) multifun
  val repeat      : ('a,'a) multifun -> ('a,'a) multifun
  val repeatDeterm : ('a,'a) multifun -> ('a,'a) multifun
  val depthFirst  : ('a->bool) -> ('a,'a) multifun -> ('a,'a) multifun
  val depthIter   : ('a->bool) * int -> ('a,'a) multifun -> ('a,'a) multifun
  val firstF      : ('a -> ('b,'c) multifun) list -> 'a -> ('b,'c) multifun
  end;
```

10.15   *Tacticals*

The sample proofs of the previous section are unusually short. The proof of even a simple formula can require many steps. To convince yourself of this, try proving

$$((\phi \leftrightarrow \psi) \leftrightarrow \chi) \leftrightarrow (\phi \leftrightarrow (\psi \leftrightarrow \chi)).$$

Although proofs are long, each step is usually obvious. Often, only one or two rules can be applied to a subgoal. Moreover, the subgoals can be tackled in any order because a successful proof must prove them all. We can always work on subgoal 1. A respectable proof procedure can be expressed using tactics, with the help of a few control structures.

The basic tacticals. Operations on tactics are called **tacticals** by analogy with functions and functionals. The simplest tacticals implement the control structures of sequencing, choice and repetition. They are analogous to the parsing operators --, || and *repeat* (see Section 9.2). So they share the same names, with the additional infix operator |@|.

Tacticals in Hal involve operations on sequences. Type *multifun* abbreviates types in the signature (Figure 10.11). The tacticals are not restricted to tactics.

They are all polymorphic; type *state* appears nowhere. Let us describe these tacticals by their effect on arbitrary functions of suitable type, not just tactics.

The tactical $--$ composes two functions sequentially. When the function $f--g$
is applied to x, it computes the sequence $f(x) = [y_1, y_2, \ldots]$ and returns the concatenation of the sequences $g(y_1), g(y_2), \ldots$. With tactics, $--$ applies one tactic
and then another to a proof state, returning all 'next next' states that result.

The tactical $||$ chooses between two functions. When the function $f||g$ is ap-
plied to x, it returns $f(x)$ if this sequence is non-empty, and otherwise returns $g(y)$.
With tactics, $||$ applies one tactic to a proof state, and if it fails, tries another.
The tactical $|@|$ provides a less committal form of choice; when $f|@|g$ is ap-
plied to x, it concatenates the sequences $f(x)$ and $g(x)$.

The tactics *all* and *no* can be used with tacticals to obtain effects such as repetition. For all x, $all(x)$ returns the singleton sequence $[x]$ while $no(x)$ returns the
empty sequence. Thus, *all* succeeds with all arguments while *no* succeeds with
none. Note that *all* is the identity element for $--$:

$$all--f = f--all = f$$

Similarly, *no* is the identity for $||$ and $|@|$.

Implementing the tacticals. Let us turn to the structure *Tactical* (Figure 10.12).
The rôle of sequence concatenation in $--$ is clear, but its rôle in $|@|$ may be
obscure. What is wrong with this obvious definition?

```
fun (tac1 |@| tac2) x = ImpSeq.append(tac1 x, tac2 x);
```

This version of $|@|$ may prematurely (or needlessly) call *tac2*. Defining $|@|$
using *ImpSeq.concat* ensures that *tac2* is not called until the elements produced
by *tac1* have been exhausted. In a lazy language, the obvious definition of $|@|$
would behave properly.

The tactical *try* attempts to apply its argument.

The tactical *repeat* applies a function repeatedly. The result of *repeat f x* is a
sequence of values obtained from x by repeatedly applying f, such that a further
application of f would fail. The tactical is defined recursively, like the analogous
parsing operator.

The tactical *repeatDeterm* also provides repetition. It is deterministic: it considers only the first outcome returned at each step. When the other outcomes are
not needed, *repeatDeterm* is much more efficient than *repeat*.

The tactical *depthFirst* explores the search tree generated by a function. Calling *depthFirst pred f x* returns a sequence of values, all satisfying the predicate *pred*, that were obtained from x by repeatedly applying f.

Figure 10.12 *Tacticals*

```
structure Tactical : TACTICAL =
  struct
  type ('a,'b) multifun = 'a -> 'b ImpSeq.t

  fun (tac1 -- tac2) x = ImpSeq.concat (ImpSeq.map tac2 (tac1 x));

  fun (tac1 || tac2) x =
      let val y = tac1 x
      in  if ImpSeq.null y  then  tac2 x  else y  end;

  fun (tac1 |@| tac2) x =
      ImpSeq.concat(ImpSeq.cons(tac1 x,   (*delay application of tac2!*)
                              fn()=> ImpSeq.cons(tac2 x,
                                              fn()=> ImpSeq.empty)));

  fun all x = ImpSeq.fromList [x];

  fun no x = ImpSeq.empty;

  fun try tac = tac || all;

  fun repeat tac x = (tac -- repeat tac || all) x;

  fun repeatDeterm tac x =
      let fun drep x = drep (ImpSeq.hd (tac x))
                      handle ImpSeq.Empty => x
      in  ImpSeq.fromList [drep x]  end;

  fun depthFirst pred tac x =
      (if pred x then all else tac -- depthFirst pred tac) x;

  fun depthIter (pred,d) tac x =
   let val next = ImpSeq.toList o tac
      fun dfs i (y, sf) () =
            if i<0 then sf()
            else if i<d andalso pred y
                then ImpSeq.cons(y, foldr (dfs (i-1)) sf (next y))
                else foldr (dfs (i-1)) sf (next y) ()
      fun deepen k = dfs k (x, fn()=> deepen (k+d)) ()
   in  deepen 0  end;

  fun orelseF (tac1, tac2) u = tac1 u || tac2 u;

  fun firstF ts = foldr orelseF (fn _ => no) ts;
  end;
```

The tactical *depthIter* explores the search tree using depth-first iterative deepening. It searches first to depth *d*, then depth 2*d*, then 3*d* and so forth; this ensures that no solutions are missed. Its other arguments are as in *depthFirst*. Its rather messy implementation is based upon the code discussed in Section 5.20.

Finally, *firstF* is a convenient means of combining primitive inference rules; see Figure 10.13 below.

Some examples. In order to demonstrate the tacticals, we first open their structure, making available the infixes.

```
open Tactical;
```

Now let us prove the following formula, which concerns the associative law for conjunction:

```
goal "(P & Q) & R  -->   P & (Q & R)";
> (P & Q) & R --> P & (Q & R)
>  1. empty  |-  (P & Q) & R --> P & (Q & R)
```

The only rule that can be applied is →:right. Looking ahead a bit, we can foresee two applications of ∧:left. With *repeat* we can apply both rules as often as necessary:

```
by (repeat (Rule.impR 1 || Rule.conjL 1));
> (P & Q) & R --> P & (Q & R)
>  1.  P, Q, R  |-  P & (Q & R)
```

Now ∧:right must be applied twice. We repeatedly apply the corresponding tactic along with *Rule*.*basic*, which detects basic sequents:

```
by (repeat (Rule.basic 1 || Rule.conjR 1));
> (P & Q) & R --> P & (Q & R)
> No subgoals left!
```

We have proved the theorem using only two *by* commands; a rule-by-rule proof would have needed eight commands. For another demonstration, let us prove a theorem using one fancy tactic. Take our old quantifier example:

```
goal "EX z.  P(z)  --> (ALL x.  P(x))";
> EX z.   P(z)  --> (ALL x.   P(x))
>  1. empty  |-  EX z.   P(z)  --> (ALL x.   P(x))
```

Let us *repeat* the tactics used in Section 10.14, choosing their order carefully. Certainly *Rule*.*unify* should be tried first, since it might solve the goal altogether. And *Rule*.*exR* must be last; otherwise it will apply every time and cause an infinite loop.

```
by (repeat (Rule.unify 1  ||  Rule.impR 1  ||
              Rule.allR 1  ||  Rule.exR 1));
> EX z.   P(z) --> (ALL x.   P(x))
> No subgoals left!
```

ⓘ   *A brief history of tacticals.* Tacticals originated with Edinburgh LCF (Gordon *et al.*, 1979). Similar control structures crop up in rewriting (Paulson, 1983), for expressing rewriting methods called *conversions.* The HOL system relies upon this approach to rewriting (Gordon and Melham, 1993, Chapter 23).

Tacticals in LCF and HOL resemble our parsing operators: they use exceptions instead of returning a sequence of outcomes. Isabelle tacticals return sequences in order to allow backtracking and other search strategies (Paulson, 1994). Hal's tacticals are closely based on Isabelle's.

Tacticals traditionally have names such as *THEN, ORELSE, REPEAT,* etc., but this violates the convention that only constructor names should start with a capital letter.

Exercise 10.27   What does the tactic *repeat*(*f* --*f*)(*x*) do?

Exercise 10.28   Does *depthFirst* really perform depth-first search? Explain in detail how it works.

Exercise 10.29   Describe situations where the sequence returned by -- or |@| omits some elements that intuitively should be present. Implement new tacticals that do not have this fault. Do -- and |@| have any compensating virtues?

Exercise 10.30   Tacticals *repeat* and *depthFirst* appear in their traditional form. Their efficiency is adequate for interactive proof but not for use in proof procedures. Code more efficient versions, not using --.

10.16 *Automatic tactics for first-order logic*

Using tacticals, we shall code two simple tactics for automatic proof. Given a subgoal, *depth* attempts to solve it by unification, or by breaking down some formula, or by expanding quantifiers. Quantifiers can be expanded repeatedly without limit; the tactic may run forever.

The components of *depth* are themselves useful for interactive proof, especially when *depth* fails. They are specified in signature *TAC*:

```
signature TAC =
  sig
  val safeSteps: int -> Rule.tactic
  val quant   : int -> Rule.tactic
  val step    : int -> Rule.tactic
  val depth   : Rule.tactic
  val depthIt : int -> Rule.tactic
  end;
```

The signature specifies five tactics:

- *safeSteps i* applies a nonempty series of 'safe' rules to subgoal *i*. These are any rules except ∃:right and ∀:left. Tactic *unify* is also excluded, because it can affect other goals.
- *quant i* expands quantifiers in subgoal *i*. It applies both ∃:right and ∀:left, if possible.
- *depth* solves all subgoals by depth-first search. It uses *safeSteps*, *unify* and *quant*.
- *step i* refines subgoal *i* by safe steps if possible, otherwise trying unification and quantifier expansion.
- *depthIt d* solves all subgoals by depth-first iterative deepening with increment *d*. It uses *step* 1, and is exhaustive but slow.

Structure *Tac* (Figure 10.13) shows how succinctly tactics can express proof procedures. The declaration of *safe* simply lists the necessary tactics, combined by *firstF*. Tactics that create one subgoal precede tactics that create two; apart from this, their order is arbitrary. Repeating *safe* via the tacticals ─ ─ and *repeatDeterm* yields *safeSteps*. We can see that *quant* expands at least one quantifier, perhaps two: if *allL* succeeds then it attempts *exR* too.

Of the two search tactics, *depth* is the faster, but is incomplete. It employs depth-first search, which can go down blind alleys. Also it applies *Rule . unify* whenever possible, regardless of its effect on other goals. Tactic *depthIt* remedies these points. Note that *step* uses not | | but | @ | to combine *Rule . unify* with the quantifier tactics; even if unification is successful, the search may investigate quantifier expansions too. Both search tactics test for final proof states using *Rule . final* (declared on page 425).

Let us try *Tac . depth* on some of the problems of Pelletier (1986). This is problem 39:

```
goal "~ (EX x.  ALL y.  J(x,y) <-> ~J(y,y))";
> ~(EX x.  ALL y.  J(x, y) <-> ~J(y, y))
> 1. empty |- ~(EX x.  ALL y.  J(x, y) <-> ~J(y, y))
```

Figure 10.13 *The structure* Tac

```
structure Tac : TAC =
  struct
  local open Tactical Rule
    in
    val safe =
          firstF [basic,
                  conjL, disjR, impR, negL, negR, exL, allR,  (*1 subgoal*)
                  conjR, disjL, impL, iffL, iffR                (*2 subgoals*)];
    fun safeSteps i = safe i -- repeatDeterm (safe i);
    fun quant i    = (allL i -- try (exR i)) || exR i;
    val depth      = depthFirst final (safeSteps 1 || unify 1 || quant 1);
    fun step i     = safeSteps i || (unify i |@| allL i |@| exR i);
    fun depthIt d  = depthIter (final, d) (step 1);
    end
  end;
```

Applying *Tac.depth* proves it:

```
by Tac.depth;
> ~(EX x.  ALL y.   J(x, y) <-> ~J(y, y))
> No subgoals left!
```

Problem 40 is more complicated.[4]

```
goal "(EX y.  ALL x.   J(y,x) <-> ~J(x,x))  -->            \
\           ~ (ALL x.  EX y.  ALL z.  J(z,y) <-> ~ J(z,x))";
> (EX y.  ALL x.   J(y, x) <-> ~J(x, x)) -->
> ~(ALL x.  EX y.  ALL z.  J(z, y) <-> ~J(z, x))
> 1. empty
>      |-  (EX y.  ALL x.   J(y, x) <-> ~J(x, x)) -->
>          ~(ALL x.  EX y.  ALL z.  J(z, y) <-> ~J(z, x))
```

This problem too is easily proved.

```
by Tac.depth;
> (EX y.  ALL x.   J(y, x) <-> ~J(x, x)) -->
> ~(ALL x.  EX y.  ALL z.  J(z, y) <-> ~J(z, x))
> No subgoals left!
```

---

[4] Since the goal formula does not fit on one line, the \ ... \ escape sequence divides the string over two lines.

Problem 42 is harder still: *Tac . depth* never returns.

```
goal "~(EX y. ALL x. p(x,y) <-> ~(EX z. p(x,z) & p(z,x)))";
> ~(EX y.  ALL x. p(x, y) <-> ~(EX z. p(x, z) & p(z, x)))
> 1. empty
>      |- ~(EX y.
>             ALL x.
>                p(x, y) <-> ~(EX z. p(x, z) & p(z, x)))
```

But our other search tactic succeeds:

```
by (Tac.depthIt 1);
> ~(EX y.  ALL x. p(x, y) <-> ~(EX z. p(x, z) & p(z, x)))
> No subgoals left!
```

It is worth reiterating that our tactics cannot compete with automatic theorem provers. They work by applying primitive inference rules, whose implementation was designed for interactive use. Their 'inner loop' (the tactic *safe*) searches for connectives in a profligate manner. No heuristics govern the expansion of quantifiers. This simple-looking example (problem 43) is not solved in a reasonable time:

```
goal "(ALL x. ALL y. q(x,y) <-> (ALL z.p(z,x) <->p(z,y))) \
\       --> (ALL x. (ALL y. q(x,y) <-> q(y,x)))";
```

Tactics work best when the logic has no known automatic proof procedure. Tacticals allow experimentation with different search procedures, while the abstract type *state* guards against faulty reasoning.

ⓘ *Other theorem provers.* Most automatic theorem provers are based on the resolution principle (Chang and Lee, 1973). They prove a formula *A* by converting ¬*A* to clause form (based upon conjunctive normal form) and deriving a contradiction. A popular resolution prover is W. McCune's Otter. For example, Quaife (1992) has used Otter for proofs in Peano arithmetic, geometry and set theory. Another impressive system is SETHEO (Letz *et al.*, 1992).

Tableau provers are less powerful, but more natural than resolution provers, since they do not require conversion to clause form. Examples include HARP (Oppacher and Suen, 1988) and the amazingly simple leanTAP (Beckert and Posegga, 1995), which consists of a few lines of Prolog. Tactic *depthIt* is loosely based upon leanTAP but is much slower.

The tactical approach combines modest automation with great flexibility. Systems apply it not for classical first-order logic, but for other logics of computational importance. LCF supports a logic of domain theory (Gordon *et al.*, 1979; Paulson, 1987). The HOL system supports Church's higher-order logic (Gordon and Melham, 1993). Nuprl supports a form of constructive type theory (Constable *et al.*, 1986). Isabelle is a generic theorem prover, supporting several different logics (Paulson, 1994).

Exercise 10.31   Draw a diagram showing the structures, signatures and functors of Hal and their relationships.

Exercise 10.32   Implement a tactic for the rule of mathematical induction, involving the constant 0 and the successor function *suc*:

$$\frac{\Gamma \vdash \Delta, \phi[0/x] \quad \phi, \Gamma \vdash \Delta, \phi[suc(x)/x]}{\Gamma \vdash \Delta, \forall x . \phi} \qquad \text{proviso: } x \text{ must not occur free in the conclusion}$$

Can you foresee any difficulties in adding the tactic to an automatic proof procedure?

Exercise 10.33   Declare a tactical *someGoal* such that, when applied to a state with n subgoals, *someGoal f* is equivalent to

$$f(n) \mathbin{||} f(n-1) \mathbin{||} \ldots \mathbin{||} f(1).$$

What does *repeat (someGoal Rule . conjR)* do to a proof state?

Exercise 10.34   Our proof procedure always works on subgoal 1. When might it be better to choose other subgoals?

Summary of main points
- The sequent calculus is a convenient proof system for first-order logic.
- Unification assists reasoning about quantifiers.
- The occurs check in unification is essential for soundness.
- Quantified variables can be treated like the bound variables of the λ-calculus.
- Inference rules can be provided as operations on an abstract type of theorems or proofs.
- The operations $--$, $||$ and *repeat* have analogues throughout functional programming.
- The tactical approach allows a mixture of automatic and interactive theorem proving.

PROJECT SUGGESTIONS

The exercises in this book are intended to deepen your understanding of ML and improve your programming skills. But such exercises cannot turn you into a programmer, let alone a software engineer. A project is more than a large programming exercise; it involves more than programming. It demands careful preparation: background study, analysis of requirements, design. The finished program should be evaluated fairly but thoroughly.

Each suggestion is little better than a hint, but with a little effort, can be developed into a proper proposal. Follow the attached references and prepare a project description including a statement of objectives, a provisional timetable and a list of required resources. The next stage is to write a detailed requirements analysis, listing all functions in sufficient detail to allow someone else to carry out eventual testing. Then specify the basic design; ML functors and signatures can describe the main components and their interfaces.

The preparatory phases outlined above might be done by the instructor, a student or a team of students. This depends upon the course aims, which might be concerned purely with ML, with project management, or with demonstrating some methodology of software engineering. The final evaluation might similarly be done by the instructor, the implementor or another team of students.

The evaluation should consider to what extent the program meets its objectives. Testing can be driven by the requirements analysis. Many projects are easy to do, but hard to do efficiently. Evaluation thus should consider performance as well as correctness; profiling tools can identify performance bottlenecks. Students might be expected to find and use the standard library modules — arrays, low-level word operations, etc. — that are appropriate for efficiency.

Some of the suggested projects have been done by Cambridge students, though not necessarily in ML. The others are there because they are interesting (at least to me) and are of suitable difficulty. They are intended to be particularly appropriate for ML — though practically anything can be done in ML unless it requires unsafe programming or is embedded in a system that mandates some other language. So, feel free to adopt project suggestions from other sources.

Unlimited precision integer arithmetic gives exact answers and never fails due to overflow. (Some ML systems provide this by default.) Knuth (1981) describes the algorithms, which apart from division are straightforward. He also suggests improved algorithms for operating on rational numbers.

Unlimited precision real arithmetic yields answers that are correct to any desired precision, automatically determining the precision required for intermediate calculations. Much effort has been devoted to finding the most efficient representation of a real number (Boehm and Cartwright, 1990). Ménissier-Morain (1995) recommends a convergent series of rationals of the form p/B^q. Computational stunts on this theme may be amusing, though definitely not easy (Gourdon and Salvy, 1993). You could also develop the numerical examples of Section 5.15.

The ***polynomial arithmetic*** example of Chapter 3 can be extended in several directions. You could provide additional operations, allow more than one variable or even implement a better GCD algorithm. See Davenport *et al.* (1993) or Knuth (1981). Unlimited precision integers are required.

Emulators can be fun: you bring an obsolete machine and its quaint software back to life. My personal favourite is the DEC PDP-8. The basic model can address 4096 12-bit words and has an instruction set with eight opcodes. The manuals are out of print, but information is available on the World Wide Web (Jones, 1995). Details such as the precise treatment of interrupts can be tricky. Emulated software must run fast enough to keep up with the user's typing!

Advanced tautology checkers include ordered binary decision diagrams and the Davis-Putnam proof procedure. OBDDs have applications in hardware and systems verification; Bryant (1992) is a classic description but Moore (1994) may be more appropriate for functional programming. Davis-Putnam is back in favour after many years; early books mention it (Chang and Lee, 1973), but the latest algorithms are described only in technical reports (Zhang and Stickel, 1994).

Theorem provers can be built in various ways upon the foundation provided in Chapter 10. The tableau method is easy to implement (Beckert and Posegga, 1995). Model elimination is also fairly straightforward (Stickel, 1988a). Andrews (1989) describes the matrix method in the context of higher-order logic; it is equally applicable to first-order logic. Only the ablest student should try implementing the resolution method (Stickel, 1988b); the refinements necessary for high performance demand complex data structures (Butler and Overbeek, 1994).

Consider writing a ***parser generator***: a simple LR(0) one, an SLR one, or perhaps an LALR(1) version with sophisticated error recovery. Good compiler texts, such as Aho *et al.* (1986), describe the necessary techniques.

Compiling projects are always popular. Select a small subset of ML and write an interpreter for it. The SECD machine yields call-by-value semantics, while graph reduction yields call-by-need. Field and Harrison (1988) describe such implementation methods, as well as type checking. Unless the syntax is trivial, use a parser generator such as ML-Yacc (Tarditi and Appel, 1994).

You should be familiar at least with Chapters 2–5, preferably also Chapters 7 and 8, before attempting any substantial project. Good luck!

BIBLIOGRAPHY

Aasa, A., Holmström, S., and Nilsson, C. (1988). An efficiency comparison of some representations of purely functional arrays. *BIT*, **28**, 490–503.

Abelson, H. and Sussman, G. J. (1985). *Structure and Interpretation of Computer Programs*. MIT Press.

Adams, S. (1993). Efficient sets – a balancing act. *Journal of Functional Programming*, **3**(4), 553–561.

Aho, A. V., Sethi, R., and Ullman, J. D. (1986). *Compilers: Principles, Techniques and Tools*. Addison-Wesley.

Andrews, P. B. (1989). On connections and higher-order logic. *Journal of Automated Reasoning*, **5**(3), 257–291.

Appel, A. W. (1992). *Compiling with Continuations*. Cambridge University Press.

Appel, A. W. (1993). A critique of standard ML. *Journal of Functional Programming*, **3**(4), 391–429.

Appel, A. W., Mattson, J. S., and Tarditi, D. R. (1994). *A Lexical Analyzer Generator for Standard ML*, version 1.5.0 edition. Distributed with Standard ML of New Jersey and through freeware archives.

Augustsson, L. and Johnsson, T. (1989). The Chalmers Lazy-ML compiler. *Computer Journal*, **32**, 127–141.

Backus, J. (1978). Can programming be liberated from the Von Neumann style? A functional style and its algebra of programs. *Communications of the ACM*, **21**, 613–641.

Bailey, R. (1990). *Functional Programming with Hope*. Ellis Horwood.

Barendregt, H. P. (1984). *The Lambda Calculus: Its Syntax and Semantics*. North-Holland.

Beckert, B. and Posegga, J. (1995). leanTAP: Lean tableau-based deduction. *Journal of Automated Reasoning*, **15**(3), 339–358.

Bevier, W. R., Hunt, Jr., W. A., Moore, J. S., and Young, W. D. (1989). An approach to systems verification. *Journal of Automated Reasoning*, **5**(4), 411–428.

Biagioni, E., Harper, R., Lee, P., and Milnes, B. G. (1994). Signatures for a network protocol stack: A systems application of Standard ML. In *LISP and Functional Programming*, pages 55–64.

Bird, R. and Wadler, P. (1988). *Introduction to Functional Programming*. Prentice-Hall.

Boehm, H. and Cartwright, R. (1990). Exact real arithmetic: Formulating real numbers as functions. In Turner (1990b), pages 43–64.

Boolos, G. S. and Jeffrey, R. C. (1980). *Computability and Logic*. Cambridge University Press, 2nd edition.

Boyer, R. S. and Moore, J. S. (1988). *A Computational Logic Handbook*. Academic Press.

Bryant, R. E. (1992). Symbolic boolean manipulation with ordered binary-decision diagrams. *Computing Surveys*, **24**(3), 293–318.

Burge, W. H. (1975). *Recursive Programming Techniques*. Addison-Wesley.

Burton, F. W. (1982). An efficient functional implementation of FIFO queues. *Information Processing Letters*, **14**, 205–206.

Butler, R. M. and Overbeek, R. A. (1994). Formula databases for high-performance resolution/paramodulation systems. *Journal of Automated Reasoning*, **12**(2), 139–156.

Cann, D. (1992). Retire Fortran? a debate rekindled. *Communications of the ACM*, **35**(8), 81–89.

Cardelli, L. and Wegner, P. (1985). On understanding types, data abstraction, and polymorphism. *ACM Computing Surveys*, **17**, 471–522.

Chang, C.-L. and Lee, R. C.-T. (1973). *Symbolic Logic and Mechanical Theorem Proving*. Academic Press.

Cohn, A. (1989a). Correctness properties of the Viper block model: The second level. In G. Birtwistle and P. A. Subrahmanyam, editors, *Current Trends in Hardware Verification and Automated Theorem Proving*, pages 1–91. Springer.

Cohn, A. (1989b). The notion of proof in hardware verification. *Journal of Automated Reasoning*, **5**(2), 127–139.

Constable, R. L. *et al.* (1986). *Implementing Mathematics with the Nuprl Proof Development System*. Prentice-Hall.

Corbin, J. and Bidoit, M. (1983). A rehabilitation of Robinson's unification algorithm. In R. E. A. Mason, editor, *Information Processing 83*. IFIP, Elsevier.

Cormen, T. H., Leiserson, C. E., and Rivest, R. L. (1990). *Introduction to Algorithms*. MIT Press.

Cousineau, G. and Huet, G. (1990). The CAML primer. Technical report, INRIA, Rocquencourt, France.

Damas, L. and Milner, R. (1982). Principal type-schemes for functional programs. In *9th Symposium on Principles of Programming Languages*, pages 207–212. ACM.

Davenport, H. (1952). *The Higher Arithmetic*. Cambridge University Press, 6th edition.

Davenport, J. H., Siret, Y., and Tournier, E. (1993). *Computer Algebra: Systems and Algorithms for Algebraic Computation*. Academic Press.

de Bruijn, N. G. (1972). Lambda calculus notation with nameless dummies, a tool for automatic formula manipulation, with application to the Church-Rosser Theorem. *Indagationes Mathematicae*, **34**, 381–392.

Dijkstra, E. W. (1976). *A Discipline of Programming*. Prentice-Hall.

Feynman, R. P., Leighton, R. B., and Sands, M. (1963). *The Feynman Lectures on Physics*, volume 1. Addison-Wesley.

Field, A. J. and Harrison, P. G. (1988). *Functional Programming*. Addison-Wesley.

Fitzgerald, J. S., Larsen, P. G., Brookes, T. M., and Green, M. A. (1995). Developing a security-critical system using formal and conventional methods. In Hinchey and Bowen (1995), pages 333–356.

FPCA (1995). *Functional Programming and Computer Architecture*. ACM Press.

Frost, R. and Launchbury, J. (1989). Constructing natural language interpreters in a lazy functional language. *Computer Journal*, **32**, 108–121.

Gallier, J. H. (1986). *Logic for Computer Science: Foundations of Automatic Theorem Proving*. Harper & Row.

Galton, A. (1990). *Logic for Information Technology*. Wiley.

Gansner, E. R. and Reppy, J. H., editors (1996). *The Standard ML Basis Library Reference Manual*. In preparation.

Gerhart, S., Craigen, D., and Ralston, T. (1994). Experience with formal methods in critical systems. *IEEE Software*, pages 21–28.

Gordon, M. J. C. (1988). *Programming Language Theory and its Implementation*. Prentice-Hall.

Gordon, M. J. C. and Melham, T. F. (1993). *Introduction to HOL: A Theorem Proving Environment for Higher Order Logic*. Cambridge University Press.

Gordon, M. J. C., Milner, R., and Wadsworth, C. P. (1979). *Edinburgh LCF: A Mechanised Logic of Computation*. Springer. LNCS 78.

Gourdon, X. and Salvy, B. (1993). Computing one million digits of $\sqrt{2}$. Technical Report 155, INRIA-Rocquencourt.

Graham, B. T. (1992). *The SECD Microprocessor: A Verification Case Study*. Kluwer Academic Publishers.

Grant, P. W., Sharp, J. A., Webster, M. F., and Zhang, X. (1995). Experiences of parallelising finite-element problems in a functional style. *Software—Practice and Experience*, **25**(9), 947–974.

Grant, P. W., Sharp, J. A., Webster, M. F., and Zhang, X. (1996). Sparse matrix representations in a functional language. *Journal of Functional Programming*, **6**(1), 143–170.

Greiner, J. (1996). Weak polymorphism can be sound. *Journal of Functional Programming*, **6**(1), 111–141.

Gunter, C. A. (1992). *Semantics of Programming Languages: Structures and Techniques*. MIT Press.

Halfant, M. and Sussman, G. J. (1988). Abstraction in numerical methods. In *LISP and Functional Programming*, pages 1–7. ACM Press.

Harper, R. (1994). A simplified account of polymorphic references. *Information Processing Letters*, **51**(4), 201–206.

Harper, R., MacQueen, D., and Milner, R. (1986). Standard ML. Technical Report ECS-LFCS-86-2, Department of Computer Science, University of Edinburgh.

Hartel, P. and Plasmeijer, R. (1996). State-of-the-art applications of pure functional programming. *Journal of Functional Programming*, **5**(3). Special issue.

Hennessy, M. (1990). *The Semantics of Programming Languages: An Elementary Introduction Using Structural Operational Semantics*. Wiley.

Hinchey, M. and Bowen, J. P., editors (1995). *Applications of Formal Methods*. Prentice-Hall.

Hoare, C. A. R. (1989a). Computer science. In Hoare and Jones (1989), pages 89–101. Inaugural lecture, Queen's University of Belfast, 1971.

Hoare, C. A. R. (1989b). Hints on programming-language design. In Hoare and Jones (1989), pages 193–216. First appeared in 1974.

Hoare, C. A. R. (1989c). An overview of some formal methods for program design. In Hoare and Jones (1989), pages 371–387. Reprinted from *Computer* **20** (1987), 85–91.

Hoare, C. A. R. and Jones, C. B., editors (1989). *Essays in Computing Science*. Prentice-Hall.

Hoogerwoord, R. (1992). A logarithmic implementation of flexible arrays. In R. S. Bird, C. C. Morgan, and J. C. P. Woodcock, editors, *Mathematics of Program Construction: Second International Conference*, LNCS 669, pages 191–207. Springer.

Hudak, P., Jones, S. P., and Wadler, P. (1992). Report on the programming language Haskell: A non-strict, purely functional language. *SIGPLAN Notices*, **27**(5). Version 1.2.

Huet, G. P. (1975). A unification algorithm for typed λ-calculus. *Theoretical Computer Science*, **1**, 27–57.

Hughes, J. (1989). Why functional programming matters. *Computer Journal*, **32**, 98–107.

Jones, D. W. (1995). The Digital Equipment Corporation PDP-8. On the World Wide Web at URL http://www.cs.uiowa.edu/~jones/pdp8/.

Kennedy, A. (1996). Functional pearls: Drawing trees. *Journal of Functional Programming*, **6**(3), 527–534.

Knuth, D. E. (1973). *The Art of Computer Programming*, volume 3: *Sorting and Searching*. Addison-Wesley.

Knuth, D. E. (1981). *The Art of Computer Programming*, volume 2: *Seminumerical Algorithms*. Addison-Wesley, 2nd edition.

Korf, R. E. (1985). Depth-first iterative-deepening: an optimal admissible tree search. *Artificial Intelligence*, **27**, 97–109.

Lakatos, I. (1976). *Proofs and Refutations: The Logic of Mathematical Discovery*. Cambridge University Press.

Landin, P. J. (1966). The next 700 programming languages. *Communications of the ACM*, **9**(3), 157–166.

Leroy, X. and Mauny, M. (1993). Dynamics in ML. *Journal of Functional Programming*, **3**(4), 431–463.

Letz, R., Schumann, J., Bayerl, S., and Bibel, W. (1992). SETHEO: A high-performance theorem prover. *Journal of Automated Reasoning*, **8**(2), 183–212.

Magnusson, L. and Nordström, B. (published 1994). The ALF proof editor and its proof engine. In H. Barendregt and T. Nipkow, editors, *Types for Proofs and Programs: International Workshop TYPES '93*, LNCS 806, pages 213–237. Springer.

Martelli, A. and Montanari, U. (1982). An efficient unification algorithm. *ACM Transactions on Programming Languages and Systems*, **4**, 258–282.

Mattson, Jr., H. F. (1993). *Discrete Mathematics with Applications*. Wiley.

McCarthy, J., Abrahams, P. W., Edwards, D. J., Hart, T. P., and Levin, M. I. (1962). *LISP 1.5 Programmer's Manual*. MIT Press.

Ménissier-Morain, V. (1995). Arbitrary precision real arithmetic: design and algorithms. Submitted to *Journal of Symbolic Computation*.

Mills, H. D. and Linger, R. C. (1986). Data structured programming: Program design without arrays and pointers. *IEEE Transactions on Software*

Engineering, **SE-12**, 192–197.

Milner, R. (1978). A theory of type polymorphism in programming. *Journal of Computer and System Sciences*, **17**, 348–375.

Milner, R. and Tofte, M. (1990). *Commentary on Standard ML*. MIT Press.

Milner, R., Tofte, M., and Harper, R. (1990). *The Definition of Standard ML*. MIT Press.

Moore, J. S. (1994). Introduction to the OBDD algorithm for the ATP community. *Journal of Automated Reasoning*, **12**(1), 33–46.

Nederpelt, R. P., Geuvers, J. H., and de Vrijer, R. C., editors (1994). *Selected Papers on Automath*. North-Holland.

Odersky, M., Wadler, P., and Wehr, M. (1995). A second look at overloading. In FPCA (1995), pages 135–146.

Ohori, A. (1995). A polymorphic record calculus and its compilation. *ACM Transactions on Programming Languages and Systems*, **17**(6), 844–895.

Okasaki, C. (1995). Purely functional random-access lists. In FPCA (1995), pages 86–95.

O'Keefe, R. A. (1982). A smooth applicative merge sort. Research paper 182, Department of AI, University of Edinburgh.

Oppacher, F. and Suen, E. (1988). HARP: A tableau-based theorem prover. *Journal of Automated Reasoning*, **4**(1), 69–100.

Oppen, D. C. (1980). Pretty printing. *ACM Transactions on Programming Languages and Systems*, **2**, 465–483.

Park, S. K. and Miller, K. W. (1988). Random number generators: Good ones are hard to find. *Communications of the ACM*, **31**, 1192–1201.

Paterson, M. S. and Wegman, M. N. (1978). Linear unification. *Journal of Computer and System Sciences*, **16**, 158–167.

Paulson, L. C. (1983). A higher-order implementation of rewriting. *Science of Computer Programming*, **3**, 119–149.

Paulson, L. C. (1987). *Logic and Computation: Interactive proof with Cambridge LCF*. Cambridge University Press.

Paulson, L. C. (1994). *Isabelle: A Generic Theorem Prover*. Springer. LNCS 828.

Paulson, L. C. (1995). Set theory for verification: II. Induction and recursion. *Journal of Automated Reasoning*, **15**(2), 167–215.

Pelletier, F. J. (1986). Seventy-five problems for testing automatic theorem provers. *Journal of Automated Reasoning*, **2**, 191–216. Errata, JAR 4 (1988), 235–236.

Penrose, R. (1989). *The Emperor's New Mind: Concerning Computers, Minds, and the Laws of Physics*. Oxford University Press.

Peyton Jones, S. L. (1992). Implementing lazy functional languages on stock hardware: The spineless tagless G-machine. *Journal of Functional Programming*, **2**(2), 127–202.

Peyton Jones, S. L. and Wadler, P. (1993). Imperative functional programming. In *20th Symposium on Principles of Programming Languages*, pages 71–84. ACM Press.

Quaife, A. (1992). Automated deduction in von Neumann-Bernays-Gödel set theory. *Journal of Automated Reasoning*, **8**(1), 91–147.

Reade, C. (1989). *Elements of Functional Programming*. Addison-Wesley.

Reade, C. (1992). Balanced trees with removals: an exercise in rewriting and proof. *Science of Computer Programming*, **18**, 181–204.

Reeves, S. and Clarke, M. (1990). *Logic for Computer Science*. Addison-Wesley.

Rich, E. and Knight, K. (1991). *Artificial Intelligence*. McGraw-Hill, 2nd edition.

Ružička, P. and Prívara, I. (1988). An almost linear Robinson unification algorithm. In M. P. Chytil, L. Janiga, and V. Koubeck, editors, *Mathematical Foundations of Computer Science*, pages 501–511. Springer. LNCS 324.

Sedgewick, R. (1988). *Algorithms*. Addison-Wesley, 2nd edition.

Sleator, D. D. and Tarjan, R. E. (1985). Self-adjusting binary search trees. *Journal of the ACM*, **32**(3), 652–686.

Smith, M. H., Garigliano, R., Morgan, R., Shiu, S., and Jarvis, S. (1994). LOLITA : A natural language engineered system. Technical report, Department of Computer Science, University of Durham.

Spafford, E. H. (1989). The Internet worm: Crisis and aftermath. *Communications of the ACM*, **32**(6), 678–687.

Srivas, M. K. and Miller, S. P. (1995). Formal verification of the AAMP5 microprocessor. In Hinchey and Bowen (1995), pages 125–180.

Stickel, M. E. (1988a). A Prolog technology theorem prover: Implementation by an extended Prolog compiler. *Journal of Automated Reasoning*, **4**(4), 353–380.

Stickel, M. E. (1988b). Resolution theorem proving. *Annual Review of Computer Science*, **3**, 285–316.

Tarditi, D. R. and Appel, A. W. (1994). *ML-Yacc User's Manual*, version 2.2 edition. Distributed with Standard ML of New Jersey and through freeware archives.

Thompson, S. (1991). *Type Theory and Functional Programming*. Addison-Wesley.

Tofte, M. (1990). Type inference for polymorphic references. *Information and Computation*, **89**, 1–34.

Turner, D. (1990a). An overview of Miranda. In Turner (1990b), pages 1–16.

Turner, D., editor (1990b). *Research Topics in Functional Programming*. Addison-Wesley.

Turner, D. A. (1979). A new implementation technique for applicative languages. *Software—Practice and Experience*, **9**, 31–49.

Turner, R. (1991). *Constructive Foundations for Functional Languages*. McGraw-Hill.

Uribe, T. E. and Stickel, M. E. (1994). Ordered binary decision diagrams and the Davis-Putnam procedure. In J. P. Jouannaud, editor, *Constraints in Computational Logics: First International Conference*, LNCS 845, pages 34–49. Springer.

Wadler, P. and Gill, A. (1995). Real world applications of functional programming. On the World Wide Web at URL `http://www.dcs.gla.ac.uk/fp/realworld/`.

Wiener, L. R. (1993). *Digital Woes: Why We Should Not Depend on Software*. Addison-Wesley.

Winskel, G. (1993). *The Formal Semantics of Programming Languages*. MIT Press.

Wirth, N. (1985). *Programming in Modula-2*. Springer, 3rd edition.

Wright, A. K. (1995). Simple imperative polymorphism. *Lisp and Symbolic Computation*, **8**(4), 343–356.

Zhang, H. and Stickel, M. E. (1994). An efficient algorithm for unit propagation. Technical Report 94-12, Computer Science Dept., University of Iowa.

STANDARD ML SYNTAX CHARTS

PROGRAMS AND MODULES

Program

Top level Declaration

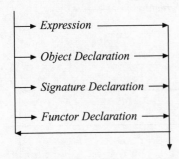

Object Declaration

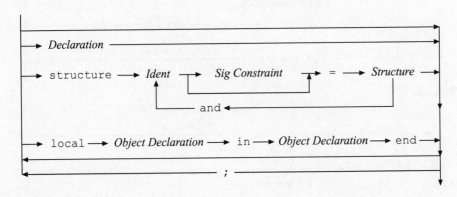

Signature Declaration

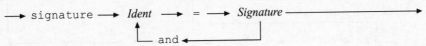

Sig Constraint

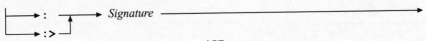

Functor Declaration

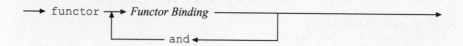

Functor Binding

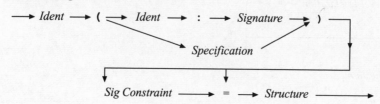

Structure

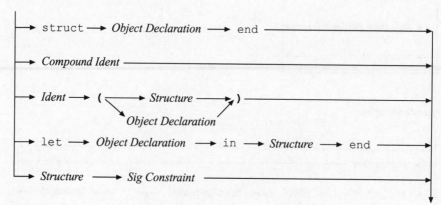

Signature

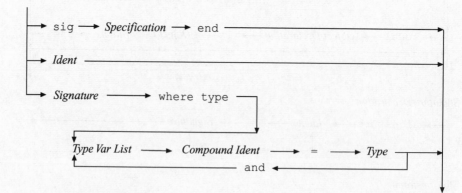

Specification

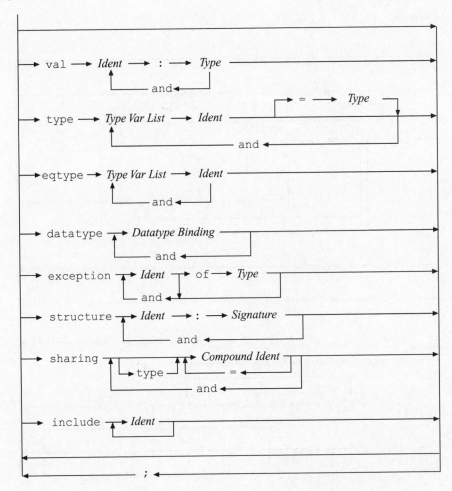

DECLARATIONS

Declaration

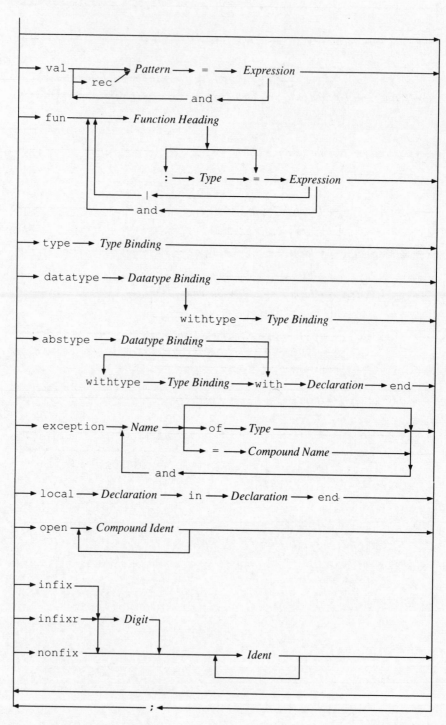

Function Heading

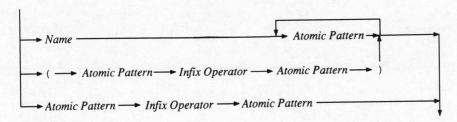

Type Binding

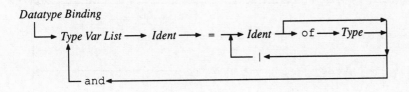

Datatype Binding

Type Var List

EXPRESSIONS

Expression

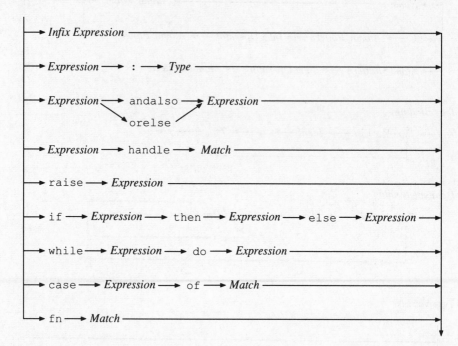

Infix Expression

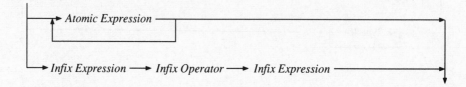

Atomic Expression

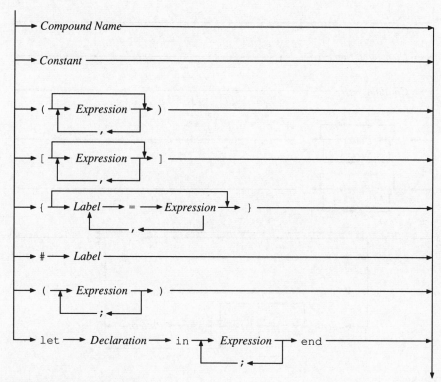

MATCHES AND PATTERNS

Match

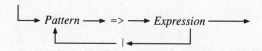

Pattern

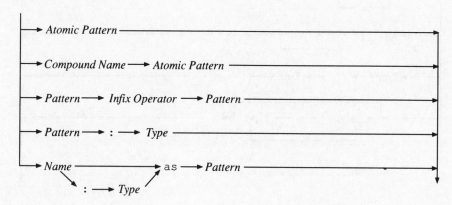

Atomic Pattern

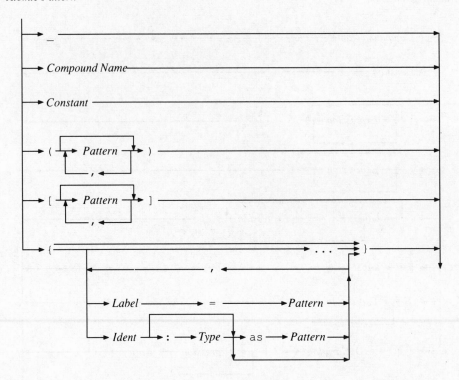

TYPES

Type

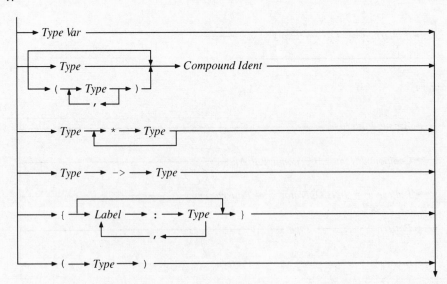

LEXICAL MATTERS: IDENTIFIERS, CONSTANTS, COMMENTS

Compound Ident

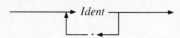

Compound Name

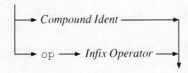

Name

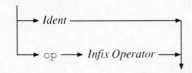

Infix Operator

any *Ident* that has been declared to be infix

Constant

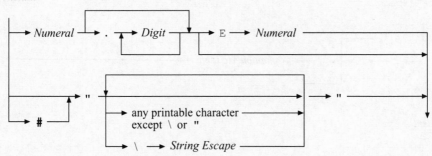

String Escape

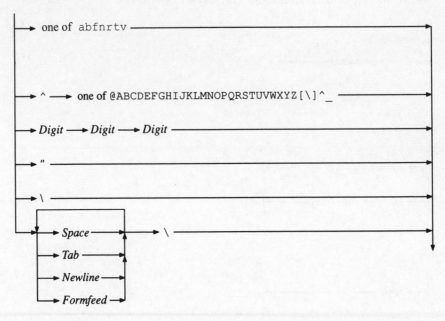

Numeral

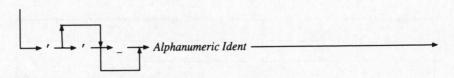

Type Var

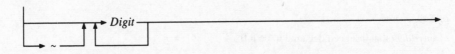

Ident

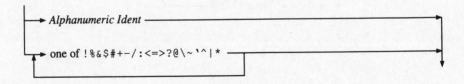

Label

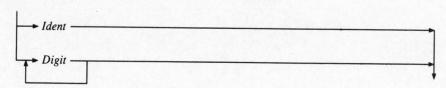

Alphanumeric Ident

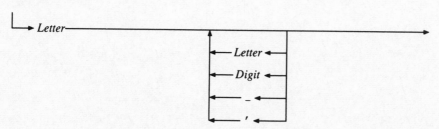

Digit ⟶ one of 0123456789 ⟶

Letter ⟶ one of ABCDEFGHIJKLMNOPQRSTUVWXYZ ⟶
abcdefghijklmnopqrstuvwxyz

Comment ⟶ (* ⟶ any text not containing ⟶ *) ⟶
(* or *) as a substring

⟵ *Comment* ⟵

INDEX